THE COPTS IN EGYPTIAN POLITICS

THE COPTS IN EGYPTIAN POLITICS

B. L. CARTER

CROOM HELM
London • Sydney • Dover, New Hampshire

Croom Helm Ltd, Provident House, Burrell Row,
Beckenham, Kent BR3 1AT

Croom Helm Australia Pty Ltd, Suite 4, 6th Floor,
64-76 Kippax Street, Surry Hills, NSW 2010, Australia

British Library Cataloguing in Publication Data

Carter, B.L.
The copts in Egyptian politics, 1918-1952.
1. Copts – Political activity.
2. Egypt – Politics and government –
1981 – .
I. Title
306'.2 JQ3881

ISBN 0-7099-3417-3

Croom Helm, 51 Washington Street, Dover,
New Hampshire 03820, USA.

Library of Congress Cataloging in Publication Data

Carter, B.L. (Barbara Lynn)
The copts in Egyptian politics.

Bibliography: p.
1. Copts–Egypt–Politics and government. 2. Egypt –Politics and government–1919–1952. I. Title.
DT72.C7C37 1986 323.1'1932'062 85-32005
ISBN 0-7099-3417-3

Printed and bound in Great Britain by Mackays of Chatham Ltd, Kent

CONTENTS

Acknowledgments

Note on Transliteration and Abbreviations

INTRODUCTION 1

- A. The Problem 1
- B. The Setting 3
  - 1. The Traditional Position of the Copts and Other Non-Muslims 3
  - 2. Population, Culture and Religious Divisions 5
    - a) Coptic Catholics 7
    - b) Coptic Protestants 8
  - 3. The Historical Background 9
- C. Overview of the Period 15

1. COMMUNAL ORGANISATION 26

- A. The Church 26
  - 1. The Majlis Milli's Struggle for Power 28
  - 2. Summary 38
- B. The Coptic Press 43
  - 1. <u>Misr</u> 43
  - 2. <u>Al-Watan</u> 46
  - 3. <u>Al-Manara al-Misriyya</u> 47
- C. Voluntary Associations 48

2. THE BRITISH, THE COPTS AND THE NATIONALIST MOVEMENT 58

- A. British-Copt Relations before the 1919 Revolution 58
- B. Zaghlul, the Formation of the Wafd and the 1919 Revolution 60
- C. Divide and Rule 65

D. Anglo-Egyptian Treaty Negotiations... 71
1. Independence and the Reserved Point for the Protection of Minorities 71
2. The Politics of Treaty Negotiations 76
E. Summary 79

3. THE LIMITS OF THE POLITICAL COMMUNITY AND EGYPT'S NATIONAL IDENTITY 89

A. Religion and the Political System.... 89
B. Theories of History and National Unity 95
1. Egyptianism.................... 95
2. Mediterraneanism................ 102
3. Arabism......................... 104
4. Marxism......................... 110
C. An Historiography of Copt-Muslim Relations......................... 113

4. REPRESENTATIVE INSTITUTIONS 128

A. The Legal Framework: The Egyptian Constitution..................... 128
1. Civil Rights.................. 128
2. Setting a Religion of State...................... 130
3. The Representation of Minorities in Parliament.............. 133
B. Coptic Political Representation, 1924-1952...................... 142
1. The Chamber of Deputies.......... 142
2. The Senate.................... 146
3. Local Councils................ 148
4. Limitations on Coptic Representation.............. 149
5. Coptic Expectations and Demands.. 152

5. THE COPTS AND PARTY POLITICS 161

A. The Wafd......................... 161
B. The Liberal Constitutional Party..... 181
C. The Palace....................... 184
D. The Sadist Party................. 187
E. The Wafdist Bloc................. 188
F. Summary.......................... 194

6. THE COPTS AND THE STATE 209

A. The Issue of Inequality.............. 209
1. Economic Behaviour............. 209
2. The Civil Service............. 212
a) Coptic Cabinet Ministers..... 220

3. Religious Instruction in State Schools................ 223
B. The Issue of State Control........... 230
1. Personal Status Jurisdiction..... 231
2. Government Limitations on the Freedom of Belief................ 239
C. One Response to Pressure: Conversion 240
D. Summary.............................. 241

7. ETHNICITY AND RELIGION IN THE STRUGGLE FOR POWER 256

A. The Religious Idiom and Party Politics 256
B. Religious Appeals and the Palace..... 260
C. Elections............................ 262
D. Communal Violence and the Role of the Muslim Brethren....................... 272
E. Another Coptic Response to Pressure.. 279
F. Summary.............................. 281

CONCLUSION 290

"Religion is for God alone and the Homeland is for ALL ITS PEOPLE"

BIBLIOGRAPHY 305

INTERVIEWS

NOTE ON TRANSLITERATION AND ABBREVIATIONS

Arabic words have been transliterated largely according to the system used in the *International Journal of Middle Eastern Studies*. However, at the recommendation of the publisher, diacritical marks and the symbols for the letters ^{c}ain and hamza were deleted. It is to be hoped that the reader who knows Arabic does not find these omissions confusing or, in some instances, amusing. A few Coptic names, which are not of Arabic origin have been transliterated into a more recognisable form. The main examples here are the names of three great churchmen: Sergius, Makarios and Cyril. In addition, some Egyptian place names, which have long been familiar to the English-speaking world, have been left in their standard form. These names include Cairo, Alexandria, Suez, Damietta and Luxor.

Various source abbreviations have been used in the footnotes, and these are explained below:

Egyptian Archives

CAS	Coptic Archaeological Society, Cairo. (The Society has a small library.)
CCEH	Centre for Contemporary Egyptian History and Documentation (Markaz Wathaiq wa Tarikh Misr al-Muasir), Dar al-Kutub, Cairo. F = File Cabinet. D = Drawer (From 1977-79, these cabinets rested against one wall, but may now have been moved. They contained a hand-written card index to some

	of the Abdin Palace archives.)
Chamber Debates	Madabit Majlis al-Nuwwab, Parliament Library, Cairo.
DM	Dar al-Mahfuzat, Citadel, Cairo.
DW	Dar al-Wathaiq, Citadel, Cairo.
PPF	Palace Press Files, CCEH, Dar al-Kutub, Cairo.
Senate Debates	Madabit Majlis al-Shuyukh, Parliament Library, Cairo.

Foreign Archives

CMS	Church Missionary Society, London.
LD	Lampson/Killearn Diaries, Middle East Centre, St. Antony's College, Oxford University.
PHS	Presbyterian Historical Society, Philadelphia, Pennsylvania, USA.

ACKNOWLEDGEMENTS

I wish to record here my gratitude for the help, kindness and hospitality offered by so many Egyptians during my two-year stay in their country and on subsequent visits. I want principally to thank Mirrit Boutros Ghali, Director of the Coptic Archeological Society, and his cousin, the late historian, Ibrahim Amin Ghali. Both gave freely of their time and knowledge. There were many others who also suffered my questions with patience and, among them, I would like to thank Louis Awad, Iris Habib al-Masri, Afaf Mahfuz and Sad Fakhri Abd al-Nur. I am also grateful to Nazek Farag Amin who shared her considerable knowledge of the Egyptian archives and helped greatly with introductions.

I am particularly indebted to two individuals who kept me company throughout much of this endeavour. To fellow-researcher Charles Tripp, I am grateful for a generous willingness to share and discuss ideas, information and sources and, on a more practical note, for many a cleared space on an Egyptian bus. My thanks also to Janet Marks who prepared the thesis for presentation, the manuscript for publication, and undertook many of the related administrative tasks which I, working in Yemen, could not have carried out.

I should also like to express my appreciation for the financial help of three institutions: the American Research Center in Egypt, the School of Oriental and African Studies, University of London, and the American Friends Service Committee in Philadelphia. Each funded a part of the research and writing. Without their generous support, this work would have been abandoned early.

My greatest thanks are reserved for my academic supervisor, Professor P.J. Vatikiotis, who has mastered the art of giving advice over great distances.

Acknowledgements

His cheerfulness in the face of a several years' barrage of complaining, confused, anxious and speculative letters has remained constant, as has his willingness to help. It is with some relief that I am finally able to lift from him the burden of further support.

I wish to note here that Barth's 'Introduction' in Frederik Barth (ed.), Ethnic Groups and Boundaries (Allen and Unwin, London, 1970), helped shape my thinking about the Coptic community.

Finally, let me enter the usual reminder here - there are many to whom credit is due for whatever is found praiseworthy in this thesis; the shortcomings, however, remain mine alone.

B.L. Carter
Sanaa,
Yeman Arab Republic, 1984

Introduction

A. THE PROBLEM

In a polity whose *raison d'être* was the perfection of a society in which Muslims could fulfil their religious obligations, the place of indigenous non-Muslims posed both theoretical and practical problems. How should such a polity deal with those who had been exposed to Islam and yet declined to accept its manifest truth? There were too many non-Muslims and they performed functions, particularly in Egypt, that were too critical to the well-being of the state to be either forcibly converted *en masse* or exterminated. Religion was already a political determinent. It became a social and economic determinent as well and set an individual's status, friendships, tax, entitlement to government benefits, code of law and sometimes even profession and living quarters. Non-Muslims were not citizens in the full sense because loyalty to the State and to the State's religion were inextricable.[1] They were not trustworthy, and therefore Muslims required some protection from them.

Although with time an extensive body of literature pertaining to religious minorities in the Islamic lands developed, the position of minorities was firmly fixed neither in theory nor in fact; it was time and place specific. Of course, there were similarities; the public did have an idea about the appropriate place for minorities, and this idea helped set regulations and perpetuate attitudes. Still, there was some flexibility in this system. A government could use Qur'anic verses and extracts from the Hadith, the two basic sources of Islam, to justify either a lenient and beneficent attitude towards a minority or a harsh and suppressive one. Sometimes it did not set an attitude but merely followed the lead of the mob. The choice depended to a large extent on other factors: general economic conditions, political turmoil, and the particular occupations and amount of wealth held by a minority among them.

The influx of Western ideas into Egypt in the nineteenth century began to change both the theory and practice of government and communal organisation. These ideas opened up new opportunities to the Copts to improve their community's status and to make an active contribution to the theory and practice of politics. The Copts had long been excluded from this arena; for the first time, new ways of thinking gave them a chance to play a serious role in determining their own destiny. Muslims, of course, as the majority, had the largest say in determining this future path; some helped the Copts seize these new opportunities and others advocated the retention of more traditional ways. This thesis, then, is concerned with the basic policy questions of how the Egyptians restructured the governing arrangements between the majority and minority in this changing system and what factors influenced that restructuring.

Related concerns are the effect of Islam on this process and the ways in which its precepts were applied to policy matters involving minorities; the influence of the British, as the slowly retiring colonial power on decisions affecting minorities; and the ways in which the Copts struggled to overcome an ethnic identity the display of which had involved considerable risk in the past and which had given them no right to act in the political sphere. How did various discriminatory practices alter? Finally, how useful are ethnic and religious loyalties in accounting for political conduct in this period?

The development of new arrangements was not fixed and sudden, as might be inferred from the establishment of a constitution and parliament in 1923, but was a process with both victories and setbacks. The question of whether a satisfactory accommodation was reached by the end of this period was one that would have drawn different answers from different people, and yet both Copts and the Muslim Brethren would have given a negative response.

B. THE SETTING

1. The Traditional Position of the Copts and Other non-Muslims

Prior to the nineteenth century, the particular place of non-Muslims in Muslim polities was determined largely by the fact that Islam granted the validity of and incorporated elements of Judaeo-Christian doctrine. Muslims were therefore willing, in a general sense, to let Christians and Jews practise their religion and be ruled by their own laws and religious leaders. This system, based on separation, minimised contacts between ethnic groups and was relatively successful in containing communal conflict; this does not, however, suggest that there was not pressure of various kinds on non-Muslims. Although semi-autonomous, these religious communities, or millets as they were called by the Ottomans who perfected the system, lived in close interdependence with the government. The ecclesiastical authorities were the government-sanctioned and supported heads of a community, and they dealt with the government on its behalf. For example, the Egyptian state relied on the Copts for taxes, the performance of certain kinds of jobs and sometimes the deflection of a mob's anger that might otherwise have been aimed towards the government. The Copts, in return, looked to the State for protection of their lives, property and right to worship; a protection which was reflected in their designation as Dhimmis or Protected Peoples and which was far more easily withheld by the State than were taxes by the Copts. The Copts also relied on the State to settle numerous intra-communal squabbles.[2] Despite the fact that the Copts disliked the Egyptian government's right to intervene in certain Coptic communal and religious matters, they often forfeited that independence and autonomy they had by inviting government mediation or partisan interference.

The Qur'an and Hadith are not entirely consistent in the behaviour towards non-Muslims that they enjoin upon Muslims. Some verses in the Qur'an react strongly to the hostility displayed towards Islam and the Prophet's divinely-ordained mission by Christians and Jews.[3] Others, notably in Suras II and V, advise that any man who believes in God and does good, be he Christian or Jew, will reap his just reward from the Lord and will have no cause for fear or sorrow. The Copts were in a particularly fortunate position, for the Prophet, who had a Coptic wife, preached especial kindness to them: "When you conquer Egypt, be kind to the Copts for they are your protegés and kith and kin".[4] Other sayings, however, abuse non-Muslims, emphasise their inferiority and warn Believers to be on their guard; for example, "deference to the unbeliever is unbelief".[5]

Non-Muslims suffered from specific disabilities, some of which were serious and interfered with their freedom of worship. For example, there were restrictions on repairing old churches and building new ones,[6] on bearing arms and testifying in court and on public behaviour and dress. The latter codes were meant to distinguish Copts from Muslims and protect the sensibilities of the latter.[7]

The disparate legacy allowed some governments, as noted, to show considerable generosity towards the Copts. The regulations were not always rigidly and routinely enforced, and the problems Copts suffered were sporadic. All citizens, of course, suffered from the exactions of oppressive government, but it may be true that the social and civil inferiority of the Copts made Muslim neighbours and the government especially inclined to take advantage of them.[8]

One perennial subject of controversy was the employment of non-Muslims in the state apparatus. There were two basic objections to this employment: (1) non-Muslims should not exercise power over Muslims, and (2) non-Muslims could not be trusted to pursue one of the goals of the state – the promotion of Islam.[9] Of necessity, these objections were generally overlooked, particularly in Egypt where the Copts dominated certain sectors of the civil service.

Necessity, however, was not a matter of great concern to some jurists; many argued that it was unlawful to appoint non-Muslims to positions of trust and influence, and others were willing to tolerate the employment of non-Muslims who served in an executive rather than legislative or ruling capacity. The weight of informed Muslim opinion, however, seems to have come down on the side of those opposed to hiring non-Muslims. Of course, non-Muslims were not only employed but sometimes reached positions of influence. These theories did have an effect, however, in that they left a lingering sense in Muslims of the impropriety of employing <u>dhimmis</u>. This meant that the position of such employees was precarious; they were subject to periodic and summary dismissal as well as to routine discrimination in promotions.

The position of non-Muslims was probably most precarious in times of political and/or financial stress. In a place where religion determined political loyalty, Copts were found to be regarded as a potential fifth column. Tensions also rose when Copts were indiscreet in their display of wealth or power. Muslims sometimes reacted sharply to any evidence that non-Muslims had forgotten their place.[10]

2. Population, Culture and Religious Divisions

Census statistics, which were compiled under British supervision in 1917 and 1927 and thereafter under Egyptian direction, can be accepted as reasonably accurate for the period but are not entirely without suspicion. The customary problems of collecting data were compounded by inept techniques for gathering information and a popular fear that correct and complete answers would increase one's vulnerability to government exactions. The figures relating to Egypt's minorities were perhaps the most suspect of all. The Copts complained repeatedly about the inaccuracy of the count, which usually numbered them at around seven per cent of the population, and they claimed to comprise fifteen to twenty per cent of the country's inhabitants. Given both that Copts and Muslims sometimes lied and that census-takers sometimes recorded the wrong religion due to a failure to ask about affiliation,[11] there was a certain margin for error. Most Christian estimates, both native and foreign, also erred, but on the side of generosity.

Egypt would not, of course, have been the first government to have undercounted its minorities in order to undercut the grounds on which communal desires rested. It is perhaps suggestive that the Orthodox Church has never been permitted to do a formal counting of its flock. However, in this period, there was little difference between census statistics compiled by the British and those compiled by the Egyptian government alone. Ultimately, it was and is impossible to determine the precise number of Copts. Even British officialdom showed signs of confusion in giving estimates that ranged between seven and twenty per cent of the population.

Copts lived in every province of Egypt and in no one were they in the majority. There were more Copts in Upper than in Lower Egypt, and a large number lived in Cairo and Alexandria.[12] The 1917 census recorded that seventy-six per cent of the Orthodox, ninety-one per cent of the Protestant and sixty-two per cent of the Catholic Copts lived in Upper Egypt. Slightly more than half of all Copts resided in four Upper Egyptian provinces: al-Minya, Asyut, al-Suhaj and Qina.[13] The 1937 census estimated the Copts at approximately five per cent of the rural population;[14] this suggests that they were marginally more urban than their Muslim compatriots. This lack of a geographic centre made it difficult for them to protect themselves from the occasional hostility of individuals or the State. It was also next to impossible to mount a separatist movement; they could not even hope to take their most populous province, Asyut, with a Coptic population of 22.4 per cent in 1917.[15]

One important element in preserving generally peaceful intercommunal relations was the high degree of cultural similarity. Egyptians were still fond of quoting Cromer's saying that a Copt was an Egyptian who worshipped in a church and a Muslim was one who prayed in a mosque.[16] The perceptions and values of Copts and Muslims were similar and both communities were at least partly aware of this. A Coptic peasant had more in common with a Muslim peasant than with wealthy co-religionists, although this did not imply that he had a firm consciousness of class and that class interests routinely prevailed over ethnic ones. Copts and Muslims probably did not generally share much of a feeling of community; they had fewer and more superficial contacts with one another than with members of their own group. These contacts, however, became more frequent and less superficial over the course of this century.

Even in the realm of religion, the division between Copts and Muslims was not as clear as Cromer's statement suggested. Both groups shared a number of superstitions.[17] For example, they visited the shrines of one another's saints,[18] and in some places in Upper Egypt it was not unusual for Muslims to attend the Good Friday church service.[19] Coptics priests were believed by many Muslims and Copts to possess the power of healing,[20] and their help was often sought by desperate Muslims.

There were three Coptic sects in Egypt; the only one that was both statistically and politically significant was the Orthodox sect, and its communal organisation will be dealt with in detail in Chapter One. The Protestant and Catholic communities were small, with a combined total of less than ten per cent of the entire Coptic population; and the Protestants were split into different groups. Neither

Protestants nor Catholics were without influence, in part because of their contacts with and dependency on foreigners. They were conduits for the transmission of Western ideas; and their missionary-run schools, which also educated Muslim children, were very influential. Protestants were more vocal and seemingly less traditional than Catholics and they played a significant role in promoting Anglo-American political ideas. They also adovated the reform of the Orthodox Church and and provided an example Orthodox reformers could envy. They, therefore, were more disliked by the Orthodox clerical establishment than were the quieter and less aggressive Catholics.[21] The latter were also brought closer to the Orthodox by their retention of the old liturgy and ritual. With rare exceptions, Coptic Catholics avoided politics. Protestants were far more active in this arena as is indicated by the careers of Akhnukh and Louis Fanus, Fahmi Wisa, George Khayyat, Makram Ubaid and Tawfiq Dus, although the latter two chose to advance their careers by returning to Orthodoxy.

Relations between these three communities were usually strained.[22] The Orthodox were understandably unhappy with attempts to lead astray the faithful, and they worried that the fragmentation of the community would hamper its ability to protect itself. The Orthodox were also troubled by the provocative acts of Christian missionaries, and they were fearful of being thought too close to sects whose connection to foreign interlopers could easily be damning in Muslim eyes. This was a real fear since Muslims could not be expected to make such fine distinctions between Copts and Copts.[23]

By the mid-1940s, the pressure of increased Muslim hostility obliged the Copts to overlook some of their differences in an attempt to counter the problem by collaboration. The three Coptics sects and other non-Muslim communities set up a Liaison Committee which met regularly and discussed co-ordination on matters of mutual concern. One particular interest was in government attempts to reform non-Muslim personal status jurisdiction, and another more general one was the worsening situation for non-Muslims.

a) <u>Coptic Catholics</u>. The first Copts were converted to Catholicism in Upper Egypt by Franciscan missionaries in the eighteenth century.[24] Their numbers grew slowly but steadily, and many may have converted during the brief period when the Catholic Muallim Ghali was chief secretary to the ruler,

Muhammad Ali. The community was protected by Austria-Hungary which claimed the right as an extension of its privilege, gained in 1699, to protect the Franciscan Mission. This right was not universally recognised and problems resulted when Austro-Hungarian consulates intervened in communal affairs.[25] An accord between the Egyptian and Austro-Hungarian governments finally granted the right of the latter to extend religious protection but with the understanding that this did not make Coptic Catholics foreign persons.

This right, of course, disappeared with the First World War. Coptic Catholics were also under the general and somewhat vague protection of France, although at least one agreement, no doubt signed at Austro-Hungarian insistence, specifically exempted Coptic Catholics from French protection. This protection, in any case, seems never to have amounted to very much; again Coptic Catholics remained under Egyptian jurisdiction.

Orthodox hostility was able to prevent the establishment of a Coptic Catholic clerical hierarchy until the nineteenth century.[26] The Vatican appointed the first Coptic Catholic Patriarch in 1895. Eventually, however, the community obtained independence from Rome; Patriarchs were thereafter appointed by the local synod of bishops, with the concurrence of both the Egyptian government and the Pope. In 1908 the community drew up an organic law and established personal status courts; both were formally recognised by the Egyptian government in 1910.[27] Despite links with Rome, Coptic Catholics turned out to be no more immune to the problems of factionalism and clerical corruption than the Orthodox.

b) Coptic Protestants. American Presbyterians were the largest and most active group of missionaries working in Egypt. They began the arduous task of spreading the Gospel in the mid-nineteenth century and, by 1878, had opened more than thirty-five schools. They soon found that it was easier to convert Copts than Muslims, and so they concentrated their efforts on Asyut.[28] Some wealthy Asyuti Copts became Protestant because they were disgusted with the backwardness and corruption of their own church. They may also have been attracted by a religion that seemed more modern, and that gave them close and perhaps useful links with Westerners.

The Protestants were recognised as a separate community in the middle of the last century and were granted limited jurisdiction in matters of personal status. Their leader was appointed, with the approval of the Egyptian government, by the community itself. In 1899, a communal council was established, and it included both laymen and clergy.[29] There were different Protestant groups, but the Council was dominated by the United Presbyterian Church of Egypt.[30] In 1926, this latter group became self-governing and independent from the American Presbyterian Church. Three years later, it had 20,200 communicants with an average Sunday church attendance of 27,000.[31] The total number of Egyptian Protestants was around 60,000, and the head of the Council was Alixan Abskharun Pasha, one of the wealthiest landowners in the country.[32]

3. The Historical Background

The Coptic community occupied an inferior position and lived in some expectation of Muslim hostility, which periodically flared into violence. Nevertheless, the Copts could and did take pride in portraying themselves as the original inhabitants and unchallenged holders of the title deed to Egypt. This was not a protrayal which Muslims accepted, but it was difficult for them to dispute Coptic ties to Egypt and the community's right to residence when the country had been a Christian and mainly Coptic country at the time of the Arab conquest in the seventh century, and could not be described as mainly Muslim in population until the tenth century.

The position of the Copts began to improve early in the nineteenth century under the stability and tolerance of the Muhammad Ali dynasty. Political assimilation dates from the middle of that century, when the Coptic community ceased to be regarded by the state as an administrative unit. In 1855, their main mark of inferiority, the jizya tax, was lifted. Shortly thereafter, the Copts, to their regret, lost their exemption from military service. They served on Egypt's appointed and elected representative bodies from the time the first Consultative Council was established in 1866, and they frequently reached high office.

Taking heart from this progress, the Copts became increasingly bold in voicing demands for equality; their audacity was either intentionally or unintentionally encouraged by the British presence. Accordingly, the first two decades of this century witnessed one of the not infrequent nadirs in intercommunal relations. There was much general unrest in this period, and tensions between Muslims and

Copts were only one aspect of the problem.[33] Good will between the two communities foundered on the rock of Coptic employment in the civil service, but there were other points of dissension as well. Both Coptic notables and the communal press were active in demanding equality in civil service appointments and promotions, the provision of Christian religious instruction in government schools, the institution of Sunday as a holiday for Christian schoolchildren and government employees, and the appointment of more Copts to Egypt's representative bodies. In 1908, the wealthy Coptic landowner Akhnukh Fanus, organised a Coptic Reform Society to promote these demands; and he tried briefly to establish a political party of similar ilk. Neither the British nor the Egyptian governments were receptive to Fanus' demands; he and his supporters were particularly disappointed by the reaction of the former.

The Copts had an uneasy relationship with the British: on the one hand, resentful of what they saw as inadequate support and, on the other, aware that the foreign presence guaranteed their safety. Some Copts believed that their community should not rely on the British for either the one or the other, but should put their efforts into achieving harmonious relations with their Muslim compatriots. Both branches of the early nationalist movement had Coptic adherents, although neither had large numbers of Christian supporters. Mustafa Kamil, the pre-eminent nationalist leader in this period, advocated equality between Copts and Muslims and spoke of their centuries-long harmonious relationship.[34] His party, al-Hizb al-Watani (the National Party), called on Copts to join Muslims in promoting the nationalist cause and in working for unity and harmony. Kamil's approach helped recommend his ideas to some Copts; but towards the end of his short life, he moved, to the alarm of the Copts, in an increasingly pro-Ottoman and pan-Islamic direction. These biases received additional emphasis after his death in 1908 by his followers, and those Copts like Murqus Hanna, Sinut Hanna and Wisa Wasif who had supported the movement abandoned it. The latter resigned from the party Executive Committee because of the anti-Coptic tone of its press. With these resignations, pressure within the party to maintain a conciliatory attitude towards the Copts was removed.[35]

The second branch of the nationalist movement, that which grew up around the newspaper al-Jarida, was more appealing to the Copts although generally less popular. Its audience was limited mainly to the well-educated. Its political thinking and nationalist goals were free of pan-Islamic and pro-Ottoman leanings and centred instead on Egypt as a unique cultural and political entity.[36] Among its Coptic supporters were Sinut Hanna and Fakhri Abd al-Nur, but this was a bad time for even modern nationalists to gain the general support of the Coptic community. In addition, the Umma group, abandoned by Gorst, grew increasingly anti-British and this perhaps made it less attractive to the Copts.

When Fanus' Coptic Reform Society decided in 1908 to push its claim for equality of employment, it sparked a lengthy and acrimonious press debate. At first, press reaction was mild; _al-Jarida_, _al-Liwa_ and _al-Muayyid_ all agreed that religion should not influence employment.[37] Then, _al-Liwa_ and _al-Muayyid_ abandoned their moderate approach and, along with _al-Dustur_, attacked Coptic demands.[38] _Misr_ and _al-Watan_, the two Coptic papers, responded in kind.

The one side characterised Islam and Muslim rule as oppressive, and the other criticised the temerity of the first and upheld the beneficence of Islam.[39] The Copts complained that they were inadequately represented in the bureaucracy, and the Muslims that the Copts monopolised the civil service.[40] Salama Musa and others believed that Shaikh al-Jawish, the editor of _al-Liwa_, was responsible for the poisonous exchange; but at least two later scholars charge the Copts with responsibility.[41] It is true that the Coptic press was more vigorous in expressing Coptic demands at this time than in previous decades, and no doubt this was seen by many Muslims as provocative. In June 1908, a concerned group of Copts met in Cairo to protest _al-Liwa_'s hostile tone, and many letters of complaint were sent to Gorst. A delegation was sent to the National Party, which was responsible for _al-Liwa_; however, while many members were reported to be unhappy with al-Jawish's articles, little was done by the party to moderate them.[42]

Out of the Coptic Reform Society grew in 1908 the Independent Egyptian Party in reaction to inter-communal hostilities and the Islamic colouring of the nationalist movement.[43] Akhnukh Fanus, the party's founder, first called it Ahrar al-Aqbat (Coptic Liberals), but changed the name under fire from other Copts.[44] Although seen by some as an attempt to create a religious party,[45] it had little in its programme that was of interest only to Copts. The party even appears to have attracted the support of a few conservative and wealthy Muslims,[46] and did not intend, after its initial blunder, to be a Coptic party. However, Fanus' reputation as an advocate of Coptic rights probably scared off both Muslim and Coptic support. Orthodox Copts would, in any case, have been suspicious of his Protestantism, and the Umma group, with its moderate political views, may have offered some competition. Whatever the reason, the party was a failure.

The appointment of the Copt Butrus Ghali, an experienced Cabinet Minister, as Prime Minister in November 1908, aggravated an already tense situation. He was not the first Christian to be appointed Prime Minister, but he may have been the first to be asked to serve at such an awkward time. He was, however, the first Coptic Prime Minister. He does not seem to have been imposed on the Khedive by the British. Gorst at first thought that Ghali's religion was an unsurmountable obstacle to the appointment.[47] Ghali was, however, very competent, and his relations with the Khedive were excellent.[48]

Muslims were disturbed by the appointment.[49] Sad Zaghlul wrote in his diary that he feared the press would make an issue of it and would thereby kindle accusations of religious fanaticism.[50] Curiously, al-Liwa was fairly restrained in its comments, but other newspapers, such as al-Dustur, more than made up for its moderation.[51]

Two years after the appointment, a Muslim nationalist with close connections to the National Party,[52] one Wardani by name, assassinated the Prime Minister. His reasons were mainly political. Butrus Ghali had by 1910 a number of black marks against him: he had sat on the bench at the Dinshawi trial, he had signed the Sudan condominium agreement, he had revived press censorship, and he was then known to favour an extension of the Suez Canal concession.[53] Still, Copt-Muslim tensions, as developed and exploited by the press, created an atmosphere conducive to murder. The Muslim and nationalist press naturally described the crime as a political act; the Copts, just as naturally, saw it as a religious one.[54] Wardani was, in fact, celebrated publicly not only as a nationalist but as a Muslim who had rid his people of an intolerably arrogant Christian.[55] Storrs, the Oriental Secretary, reported that groups of Muslims roamed the street singing about "Wardani who killed the Nazarene", and he noted that the assassin had become a national hero.[56] While the nationalists were stressing Wardani's political reasons to Europeans, they were, as K. Graham, the Adviser to the Ministry of the Interior, noted, using the religious aspects of the case to work up Muslim feeling in native circles. He added that sympathy for Wardani in the middle and lower classes had taken an anti-Christian and anti-Coptic turn. Graham clearly was concerned by the threat of Muslim-Copt violence, and he noted that there had been a few trivial attacks on Copts in Upper Egypt.[57] Gorst immediately added another Christian, Yusuf Saba, to the Cabinet to prove to Muslims, as he wrote in a letter to Cromer, that they had not gained a victory.[58] However, he chose a Christian of Syrian rather than Coptic extraction.

Coptic activists were appalled by the murder. They were perhaps equally upset by Gorst's contention that they had little support for their demands within the community, and so they called for a conference to discuss Coptic demands. The British reluctantly gave permission, and the conference convened in Asyut in March 1911. Qalini Fahmi Pasha, a Coptic notable with close ties to the Palace, thought that the Khedive had encouraged the conference out of a desire to embarrass Gorst.[59] Many Copts who later entered the political arena were in attendance: Murqus Hanna, Tawfiq Dus, Ilyas Awad, Fakhri Abd al-Nur, Sinut Hanna, Bushra Hanna and George Khayyat.[60] The conference, with strong backing from the Coptic press, presented a petition with its demands to the Khedive and the British. These demands were not new. The petition asked for better representation, equal access to civil service positions, the designation of Sunday as a holiday, equal access to state education and the provision of Christian religious instruction in state schools.[61]

Not all Copts favoured the idea of a conference although their numbers were not the majority that _al-Muayyid_ claimed for them.[62] The Patriarch, who was ninety-three and senile, was persuaded by the government to issue a statement disapproving of the conference before it convened.[63] However, his Bishop in Asyut, Makarios, a proponent of church reform, opened the conference. No leading Cairene family seems to have taken part in the conference;[64] mainly Upper Egyptians were in attendance. Both Wisa Wasif and Wasif Ghali opposed the conference, and the latter made his objections public.[65] Wisa felt that the British and not the Muslims were to blame for many Coptic grievances. It was the British, he believed, who determined hiring practices in the civil service.[66] Both men may also have objected to the conference because they had general political ambitions which the vigorous expression of communal complaints could easily upset.

Most elements of the press resented the conference and the demands that came out of it.[67] Al-Ahali, the organ of the Prime Minister, referred to the congress as a religious conspiracy;[68] and other newspapers accused the Copts of being the willing instruments of British policy.[69] One unpleasant repercussion was a riot in Asyut in April; there may have been other incidents of violence as well.[70]

With discreet government sponsorship,[71] a counter-congress was held to refute the sectarian bias of the Asyut conference. Moderate nationalists of the Umma group were involved in the conference which was held in Heliopolis. Curiously, the more extreme nationalists of al-Hizb al-Watani remained aloof; their leader, Muhammad Farid, saw the congress as an attempt by the British, who were hiding behind the Egyptian government, to divide the Egyptian people.[72] The congress was billed as an Egyptian and not a Muslim conference and, while some Copts did attend,[73] this did not prevent a complete rejection of Coptic demands.

Muslim delegates seem to have been very fearful of Coptic designs. The congress' Organising Committee reported their conclusion that the Copts were planning to form "a separate nation for themselves", and that they were relying on fabricated grievances to enable them, with British help, to gain precedence over the Muslim majority.[74] The body of this report, read by Lutfi al-Sayyid, deserves quotation:

> ...the principle is found that every country should have an established church and that such a religion will be that of the government or the majority...that a state should have more than one religion is perfectly unthinkable and it would be absurd to admit that religious minorities can exist animated by political ambitions towards the exercising of public rights other than those of an essentially religious nature that are guaranteed by freedom of worship. The religion of the Egyptian people is Islam. For Islam is both the religion of the government and that of the majority.[75]

The report went on to suggest that the reservation of seats for Copts in the Legislative Assembly was tantamount to admitting that the Copts could constitute a political minority whose interests differed from those of the majority. It added that the Copts had come to form "a separate section, whose pretensions will grow until they concentrate all power in Coptic hands. And the Copts will do this by relying on the fact that the occupying power is Christian".[76]

Delegates agreed that Islam must continue to be the official religion of Egypt. They concluded that religion should not be a factor in public employment, but at the same time insisted that certain administrative posts, like that of the governor of a province, should be held only by Muslims.[77] One motion put before the Congress called for an investigation into the excessive numbers of Copts in the civil service. Another insisted that the Copts enjoyed too large a share of government educational facilities, and a third condemned Egyptian treasury grants to Coptic institutions.[78] Despite such manifest concern about the Coptic role, the conference was relatively restrained, if only because of the co-operation of Gorst and the Egyptian government.[79] On a concluding note, the conference asked the Copts to return to their former attitude and also begged the Muslims to forget everything that had transpired. Both were asked to look to their common interests.[80]

In 1911, Gorst, who was hated by many Copts, was replaced by Kitchener. The latter had an awe-inspiring reputation; the Copts were ready to respect him and hoped that he would prove more amenable to their demands. They were far more welcoming of this appointment than the Muslim press. Kitchener, although unable to meet their requests, was able to calm the troubled sea of intercommunal relations, and the polemics diminished.[81] The declaration of a British Protectorate and the start of World War I put a final clamp on both sectarian and nationalist political activity until the end of the decade.

C. OVERVIEW OF THE PERIOD

A chronologically-arranged discussion of events in the first half of the century would illustrate that Copt-Muslim relations were bracketed by two periods of extreme hostility, the first occurring in the first decade of the century, and the last beginning in the 1940s or late 1930s. In between, came years of close partnership followed by something akin to indifference. The lines dividing these stages can be only roughly delineated. There was overlap, and traditional feelings of suspicion about the intentions and activities of the other group found expression in all the stages.

At the century's start, the Copts had at least come to tolerate the British Occupation, if not in all cases to support it. However great their disappointment with British behaviour was, their dissatisfaction with Muslim conduct was even greater. They began to register serious complaints about Muslim oppression in the mid-1890s. The relationship between the two communities reached a nadir which has already been described, between 1907 and 1911. In those years, acrimonious statements made by the press and by political activists and groups culminated in assassination and the holding of two opposing conferences. The British, who allowed this injurious situation to continue for some time, were ultimately, if somewhat inadvertently responsible for stopping it. The reimposition of press censorship in 1909 allowed them to stop the more irresponsible writings of communal activists. The murder of Butrus Ghali may have given the British further pause for thought because they were then careful to arrange that the Muslim response to the Coptic Asyut conference was moderate. They did this with the collaboration of the Egyptian government and Muslims whose greatest concern may have been that Egypt not appear barbaric in European eyes. The start of World War I and the imposition of a Protectorate on Egypt gave the Egyptians new and very different concerns. They also provided the British with a greater ability to prevent some of the more damaging manifestations of sectarian sentiment.

After the war, nationalist ferment bubbled up again but in different fashion. The new movement, which was based on liberal and egalitarian beliefs, and the revolution it sponsored in 1919 not only welcomed Coptic participation, but actively sought it. Past grievances were forgotten by both communities in this attempt to acquire independence and build a new and just society. Coptic support for this work was generous and enthusiastic: even the clergy took part in demonstrations and gave patriotic speeches.

The Coptic reward for providing both leaders and followers to the movement was substantive incorporation into the post-independence political system. Copts were accorded equality in the constitution and were given at least a theoretically equal opportunity to be elected to Egypt's representative bodies. They played an influential role in the most popular and powerful party of the period, the Wafd. Their association with this party helped to legitimise their new political role in Muslim eyes. Copts were represented in other political parties as well and frequently changed party affiliation in an attempt to find the party which would be most hospitable to Christians in general and themselves in particular. There perhaps was also some anxiety, which must be considered as natural in any minority, not to be found on the losing side.

In the 1920s, there was almost no aspect of political activity from which the Copts were barred. Throughout this decade, which was replete with friendly feelings betwen Christians and Muslims, the struggle to establish a secular and democratic polity received a number of setbacks. One such setback was the introduction of Islamic religious principles and sentiments into political discourse. All parties fell prey to the temptation to use this handy weapon against opponents since it was one which was readily understood and responded to by the masses. A natural accompaniment to the use of Islam was sectarian propaganda which was aimed at the new role the Copts were attempting to play in the society and polity. This auxiliary weapon was potentially extremely damaging to both opponents and the political system because it, too, relied on ancient and tighly-held prejudice for its firepower. Sectarian propaganda was used in the first parliamentary election in 1923 and was re-employed sporadically, if with increasing frequency, thereafter. It seemed to have little effect in that first election but it was, by the 1930s, reaching a much more receptive audience.

As already noted, a certain low level of ethnic propaganda, consisting primarily of occasional unflattering statements appearing in the press or made by individual politicians with or without party sanction, as well as sporadic violence, was and is a constant in this society, owing to the residue of 1,200 years' tradition. What began to appear in Egypt even as early as the late 1920s but more commonly in the 1930s, however, was different. It was a more concerted and organised attempt to gain and keep power by relying partly on traditional prejudices, and it therefore threatened to upset the new and fragile political system. Even in the late 1920s, one can begin to note a new Coptic anxiety about the ability of Muslims to co-exist with Christians on an egalitarian basis. This anxiety was most clearly demonstrated in the reappearance of customary Coptic grievances, such as the one about discrimination in the civil service.

Still, the situation did not begin to go seriously wrong until the 1930s. Islam became an increasing factor in politics, not only because of its usefulness as a tactic but because the economic dislocations of the Depression and the inability of the parliamentary system to function as it was meant to convinced some Egyptians to seek alternate solutions to pressing problems. The democratic system also encouraged the participation of those who had had little voice in the past and who were inclined, in considerable numbers, to be very traditional in outlook.[82] Organisations relying more seriously on Islamic precepts and with a few pretensions of interest in secularism, democracy or any of the pillars of the new polity began to flourish and play an active role. These groups included Misr al-Fatat, the Young Men's Muslim Association and the Muslim Brethren. Students at al-Azhar were also increasingly involved in political work. Copts began to be excluded from an increasingly large area of political activity. They were less and less able to voice their legitimate concerns and became increasingly estranged from the polity.

The removal of the British as a factor in the Muslim-Copt equation after 1936-7 left the community unprotected at a time when it felt increasingly threatened. However, the coming of World War II and the imposition of martial law did bring a temporary respite, if only because a stop was put to all kinds of political activity.

In the late 1940s and 1950s, inter-communal relations again showed a serious deterioration and were perhaps worse than they had been in 1907-11 because there was less economic and social stability. Hostility between Muslims and Copts was merely one aspect of a deteriorating political situation and a bad economic one. To the Copts, it had come to appear that there was no role for them in politics, not even at the level of the blandest statements made by politicians. Many Muslims, on the other hand, believed that the Copts had taken full advantage of the democratic system to usurp the place that rightfully belonged to Muslims. The communal situation became so polarised that Copts and Muslims felt that they had no common interests which would allow them to co-operate in even the most basis endeavours, such as expelling the British. As a result,

Coptic participation and power in the political arena declined. There were fewer and fewer Copts willing to undertake the perils of political leadership. Many Copts also withdrew their support from the nationalist movement and hoped vainly that the British would come to the rescue.

In the end, it was not the British who halted the deterioration in inter-communal relations but Jamal Abd al-Nasir and his co-conspirators. In seizing power and stopping a wide variety of threatening and destabilising political activity, they also halted the expression, both verbal and physical, of communal hostilities. They scorned the use of sectarian propaganda. This did not mean that the Copts became reconciled to the new regime. Many Christians felt that the regime had a clear bias against them. It did, however, mean that ethnic hostilities ceased their destructive downward spiral. By the time of the accession of Sadat in 1971, the groundwork was laid for a period of amiable co-operation.

NOTES

1. See Albert Hourani, _A Vision of History: Near Eastern and Other Essays_ (Khayats, Beirut, 1961), p.74.

2. Otto Meinardus, _Christian Egypt: Faith and Life_ (American University in Cairo Press, Cairo, 1970), p.356.

3. There are several such verses in _Suras_ II and V. For example, one verse in _Sura_ V instructs Believers not to take Jews and Christians as friends because they were the friends only of each other: 'Whoso of you makes them his friends is one of them. God guides not the people of the evil doers'. See _The Koran Interpreted_, trans. by A.J. Arberry, Part II (New York, 1973), p.136.

4. Quoted in _Shaykh Damanhuri on the Churches of Cairo_, edited and translated by Moshe Perlman (University of California Press, Berkeley, 1975), p.4. Another Hadith reads that 'Whoso revileth a _dhimmi_ will be flogged on judgment day with lashes of fire'. When Amr ibn al-Ass was Viceroy in Egypt, the Caliph Umar reminded him that the Prophet had said, 'Whoso unfairly treateth a covenantor or imposeth too heavy a burden on him, will I be his adversary on judgment day...' Al-Sayyid Muhammad al-Khidr Husain, Tolerance in Islam , _Nur al-Islam_ 3 (part 6) (1932), 16.

5. From al-Ashbah w-al-Nazair; quoted in Shaykh Damanhuri, p.56.

6. Two sayings on this subject are attributed to the Prophet. The first insists that no church be erected in Islamic territory, and once a church has been destroyed it should not be rebuilt. The second is that there should be 'no celibacy in Islam nor church construction'. Shaykh Damanhuri, p.52.

7. See those listed in M. Belin, "Fetoua Relatif à la condition des Zimmis", Journal Asiatique, 4eme série, tom.19 (1852), pp.97-110. One list of apparel specified that dhimmis could not wear shoelaces and, if they wore shoes without laces, the shoes were to be coarse material and unpleasant colour. Shaykh Damanhuri, p.56.

8. As Avedis Sanjian points out in his discussion of Armenians in The Armenian Communities in Syria under Ottoman Dominion (Harvard University Press, Cambridge, Mass., 1965), pp.274-5.

9. Richard Gottheil, 'An Answer to the Dhimmis: Translation of a Manuscript by Ghazi Ibn al-Wasiti', Journal of the American Oriental Society XLI (1921), 418. E.I.J. Rosenthal, Political Thought in Medieval Islam (Cambridge University Press, Cambridge, 1958), p.83. I. Belin, 'Fetoua Relatif a la Condition des Zimmis', Journal Asiatique 18 (1851), 417-516.

10. A.S. Tritton, The Caliphs and Their Non-Muslim Subjects (London, 1930), p.232.

11. J.D. Pennington, 'The Copts in modern Egypt', Middle Eastern Affairs 18 (1982), 159.

12. In 1917, seventy-five per cent of all Copts lived in Upper Egypt, fifteen per cent in Lower Egypt, and ten per cent in the Governorates of Cairo, Alexandria, the Canal, Damietta and Suez. All the 1917 data are from The Census of Egypt (1917), vol.2 (Cairo 1921).

13. R. Betts, Christians in the Arab East (Lycabettus Press, Athens, 1964), p.61. This is from the 1940 census.

14. G. Baer, Population and Society (Oxford University Press, London, 1964), p.97.

15. In 1917, the Coptic population of Jirja was 15.6 per cent; of al-Minya, 17.4 per cent, and of Qina, 7.8 per cent. The other provinces had smaller percentages of Copts.

16. Lord Cromer, Modern Egypt, vol.2 (Macmillan, London, 1908), p.206.

17. Sir John Bowring observed that Christian 'females are equally secluded and have their harems like other Orientals. In the remote part of Egypt, [the Copts] practise polygamy and circumcise their children...In the rural districts, the habits of the Copts are scarcely distinguishable from those of the Arabs...They adopt with the Musulman all the superstitions of the country, whether superstitions be of Mahometan or Christian origin...The Musulmans are less prompt to credit Christian superstitions than are the Copts to adopt those of the Musulmans...' Report on Egypt and Candia (W. Clowes and Sons, London, 1840), p.8.

18. Winifred Blackman, The Fellahin of Upper Egypt (George Harrap, London, 1927), pp.248-58.

19. FO.407/187 No.237 (Enclosure): Memorandum on the Coptic Church, 11 September 1920.

20. Blackman, The Fellahin of Upper Egypt, pp.213-14.

21. Père Anawati noted that in Alexandria the Coptic Catholics were viewed by the Syrian Catholics as a backward and uninfluential lot. Interview, 23 April 1979.

22. Interview Mirrit Ghali, 4 December 1978, and Père Anawati, 23 April 1979.

23. However, Misr did report in 1947 on a Catholic Copt who failed to obtain an Egyptian passport. Egyptian officials suggested that he apply for an Italian passport when he told them, at their insistence, that he owed allegiance to the Pope. Misr, 25 December 1947, 1.

24. See the list of converts in P. Gabriele Giameradini, I Primi Copti Cattolici (Edizione del Centro Francescana di Studi Orientali Christiani, Cairo, 1958).

25. There was no Capitulations agreement recognising Austro-Hungarian protection of Coptic Catholics. FO.371/3204, J209031/209031/16. DW Majlis al-Wuzara, Raqm Muhafaza 4, al-Majmua 155, Tawaif Qibtiyya. File 16 which is inside File 14.

26. H.A.R. Gibb and Harold Bowen, Islamic Society and the West, vol.1 (Oxford University Press, London, 1957), p.248.

27. DW Majlis al-Wuzara, Raqm Muhafaza 4, al-Majmua 155, awaif Qibtiyya. File 16 which is inside File 14.

28. The missionaries still wanted to convert Muslims, but they thought that this task would be facilitated if they could train enough Copts to work as evangelists.

29. DW Majlis al-Wuzara, Raqm al-Muhafaza 4, al-Majmua 141, Tawaif Qibtiyya. Files 18, 21 (inside File 14).

30. In the 1960s, fourteen members of the twenty-man council were Presbyterian. Otto Meinardus, Christian Egypt: Ancient and Modern (American University in Cairo Press, Cairo, 1977), p.574

31. In thirty years' time, the number of communicants had increased by 322.75 per cent. Rev. J.R. Alexander, A Sketch of the Story of the Evangelical Church (Whitehead Morris, Alexandria, 1930), pp.43-7.

32. FO.141/752, 353/80A/33.

33. Peter Mellini, Sir Eldon Gorst: the Overshadowed ProConsul (Hoover Institution Press, Stanford, 1977), p.118.

34. Pierre Condor, 'L'évolution Historique des Coptes d'Egypte', Cahiers de l'Orient Contemporaine 22 (1950), 138. Albert Hourani, Arabic Thought in the Liberal Age, 1798-1939 (Oxford University Press, London, 1962), p.207.

35. Both Wisa Wasif and Murqus Hanna continued to work for an improvement in communal relations. Before and after his resignation from the party, Wasif opposed the Coptic demands then being made, perhaps from a fear that Coptic activists would provoke Muslims and eventually divide the communities. Wasif had opposed Fanus' reform society and his political party as well; accordingly, the Coptic press referred to him as traitor to his people. See Muhammad Sayyid Kailani, al-Adab al-Qibti: Qadiman wa Hadithan (Dar al-Qawmiyya al-Arabiyya, Cairo, 1962), p.86; Samira Bahr, 'Al-Aqbat fi al-Hayat al-Siyasiyya fi Misr', unpublished PhD thesis, University of Cairo 1977, pp.397-8.

36. Salama Musa remarked on the fact that the Copts were attracted by the group's idea of Egypt for the Egyptians in The Education of Salama Musa, trans. L.O. Schuman (Leiden, 1961), p.43.

37. Egyptian Gazette, 12 June 1908, 5.

38. Al-Liwa was the newspaper of the National Party and al-Muayyid of the Constitutional Reform Party. The latter party had one Copt on its executive committee, Ilyas Awad. Al-Muayyid, which was edited by Shaikh Ali Yusuf, was the old paper of Riyad Pasha. Some of the anti-Coptic articles appearing in al-Dustur were written by Abbas al-Aqqad.

39. For a translation of one of these articles, see Alfred Cunningham, Today in Egypt (Hurst and Blackett, London, 1912), pp.345-9.

40. Kailani, al-Adab al-Qibti, p.89.

41. Salama Musa, The Education of Salama Musa, p.49; Kailani, al-Adab al-Qibti, p.70; Abd al-Latif Hamza, Qissat al-Sihafa al-Arabiyya fi Misr (Matbaat al-Maarif, Baghdad, 1967), p.101.

42. Egyptian Gazette, 19 June 1908, 3, and 22 June 1908, 5.

43. L.Y. Yunan, Al-Hayat al-Hizbiyya fi Misr, 1881-1914 (Al-Ahram, Cairo, 1970), p.46.

44. Bahr, 'Al-Aqbat fi al-Hayat al-Siyasiyya fi Misr', p.409.

45. Ibid., p.409.

46. Ibid., p.236.

47. Samir Seikaly, 'Prime Minister and Assassin: Butrus Ghali and Wardani', Middle Eastern Studies 13 (1977), 115-7.

48. Seikaly thinks that Ghali was chosen because both the Khedive and the British thought he was submissive and would be easy to manipulate. Ibid., 115-7.

49. Ronald Storrs, Orientations (Nicholson and Watson, London, 1945), p.83.

50. Bahr, 'Al-Aqbat fi al-Hayat', p.418.

51. Samir Seikaly, 'The Copts under British Rule, 1882-1914', unpublished PhD thesis, University of London 1967, p.147.

52. FO.141/802, 81/pol./1910.

53. FO.371/890, 20791/5946/16.

54. Including al-Watan. Seikaly, 'The Copts under British Rule, 1882-1914' p.147.

55. FO.371/890, 20791/5946/16. The British, however, thought that Ghali had been able to keep some of the more troublesome spirits in the Coptic community in check, and that Wardani had done a disservice in removing this restraint. FO.371/111, 10869/5672/16.

56. Storrs, Orientations, p.84; FO.141/802, 81/pol./10.

57. He felt that these attacks were greatly exaggerated by the Coptic press. FO.141/802, 81/pol./10.

58. Quoted by Mellini, Gorst, p.204.

59. Seikaly, 'The Copts under British Rule, 1882-1914', p.232.

60. Bushra Hanna was Chairman, Tawfiq Dus Secretary, and Sinut Hanna Treasurer. Ramzi Tadrus, al-Aqbat fi al-Qarn al-Ishrin, vol.3, (Jaridat Misr, Cairo, 1911), p.88.

61. <u>The Coptic Conference Held at Assiout on March 6, 7 and 8, 1911</u>: <u>the Speeches</u> (no place, no date). American missionaries in Asyut were generally supportive of Coptic demands. They were invited to attend the conference, but to the great relief of the Residency, were told by the American Agent in Cairo not to attend. FO.371/113, 19118/19118/16.

62. Tariq al-Bishri, 'Misr al-Haditha Bain Ahmad w-al-Masih', <u>al-Katib</u> 109 (1970), 115.

63. FO.371/1111, 18689/5672/16.

64. Seikaly, 'The Copts under British Rule, 1882-1914', p.232.

65. Bishri, <u>al-Katib</u> 109, 115.

66. Bishri, <u>al-Katib</u> 111 (1970), 127-8, quoting an article by Wisa Wasif in <u>La Bourse Egyptienne</u>, 12 May 1922.

67. Cunningham, <u>Today in Egypt</u>, pp.92-7, translates and prints articles from the press.

68. See <u>al-Ahali</u>, 7 and 8 March 1911: quoted in FO.371/111, 10869/5672/16.

69. FO.371/1111, 13807/5672/16. Press attacks against the Copts grew worse after the conference. The press law does not appear to have been used by the government in any attempt to moderate the violence of the attacks. Ironically, the Coptic press had, shortly before this, been severely penalised under the press law for writing slightingly of Arab civilisation and literature. FO.371/1111, 13525/5672/16.

70. FO.371/1111, 10869/5672/16.

71. Riyad Pasha, the president of the conference, kept in close touch with the Minister of the Interior. Almost the entire conference consisted of set speeches which were approved beforehand. FO.371/1113, 18097/16024/16.

72. Abd al-Rahman al-Rafii, <u>Muhammad Farid</u> (Maktabat al-Nahda al-Misriyya, Cairo, 1948), p.244.

73. The only Copt to give a speech was Gabriel Khalil, and he spoke on the protection and encouragement of Egyptian industry. FO.371/1113, 18097/16024/16.

74. <u>Minutes of the Proceedings of the First Egyptian Conference Assembled at Heliopolis, 29 April to 4 May 1911</u> (Alexandria 1911), pp.5-6.

75. Ibid., p.6.

76. Ibid., p.6.

77. Ibid., pp.10-13.

78. FO.371/1113, 18097/16024/16.

79. Mellini, <u>Gorst</u>, p.227.

80. FO.371/1113, 16024/16024/16.

81. Severianus, 'Les Coptes de l'Egypt Musulmane', *Etudes Mediterraneenes* 6 (1959), 80.

82. Albert Hourani makes this point about the contemporary Middle East, but it also applies to Egypt in the earlier period. See Hourani's 'Conclusion' in *Islam in the Political Process*, ed. James P. Piscatori (Cambridge University Press, Cambridge, 1983), pp.226-7.

Chapter One

COMMUNAL ORGANISATION

A. THE CHURCH

By this century, the church was a crumbling fortress, less and less able to protect those who sheltered within its walls. It had lost many of its administrative functions, and both corruption and incompetence had opened it to the depredations of laymen and outside predators. The church, however, remained an important element in the lives of many Copts; for centuries it had been the one institution which had represented the community and served as its refuge. Even those who had lost some or all of their faith were slow to cut their communal bonds. This lingering sense of ethnic identity, as much imposed by Muslims as deliberately retained by Copts, helped the church preserve some independence of action, a remarkable feat given how little agreement there was as to who should hold the balance of power within the community.

The unity of the orthodox church was broken first by missionaries. Some Copts left the fold for these newer Christian sects, while others were stirred, from the mid-nineteenth century, to demand reform in their own church. The latter had two goals: the correction of abuses such as simony, and the acquisition of a voice in church affairs. Both, the reformers felt, had an important bearing on the community's well-being and future. They saw the church as backward, corrupt and lazy; an ancient and malfunctioning organisation in need of a push into the twentieth century. They wanted to limit clerical responsibility in those affairs of the community which were not strictly religious or theological. This was not simply because they had come to accept a European division between spiritual and temporal matters, but because the clergy, in their view, had failed to attend to the practical side. For example, the Muslim chairman of the Chamber's Judiciary Committee noted in 1927 that the ecclesiastical committee charged with establishing Coptic schools had failed in its appointed task.[1] The reformers wished to build not only schools but also hospitals, orphanages and seminaries. They hoped to educate better the clergy and the community and to improve the organisation of charity.

Most of those supporting reform were drawn from the educated middle class and the landed gentry. They had been exposed to Western thinking and a few had even abandoned Egyptian in favour of European culture. Their aim seemed to be to redesign the church as some kind of Western parliamentary system with all decisions and offices subject to the will of the people.[2] This is an odd model to choose for a church whose very survival says something about the aptness of its ways, and it may partly demonstrate the influence of American Presbyterian missionaries whose own church functioned along reasonably democratic lines.

The clergy, of course, had once controlled practically all areas of life in the community: religion, justice, charity and education among them. Their role was not only being increasingly questioned but had also been substantially diminished. They understandably felt threatened by the better-educated and often more articulate laymen.[3] They were not, whatever the reformers liked to believe, all corrupt, unthinking and reactionary. The clergy were, of course, interested in protecting their personal power, but many also hoped, by maintaining the church's ancient arrangements to preserve the community's cohesion and religious character, for therein lay safety. They had powerful friends both in the Palace,[4] and among the lay élite. The latter, drawn in past times from high officialdom, probably had traditionally allied itself with the higher clergy to the benefit of both, and sometimes, no doubt almost incidentally, to that of the community as well. Both were helped by the fact that the great mass of Copts, although often the victims of clerical waste and corruption, had a tendency, born of long habit, to follow the lead of their clergy rather than the latter's new rival. Not all the clergy, however, opposed the reform movement. Those who supported it were admittedly few, but their influence was disproportionately great because they fragmented the clerical monolith.[5]

The rigidity of both the clergy and the reformers embittered the conflict and made a solution all but impossible; ultimately it harmed a system which both were trying to preserve, however different their means. In this fight for power, no one was accountable for the community's well-being. Various outsiders were sometimes drawn into the conflict to help settle it. The government, the Palace and the British all had important roles to play, only the last were consistently in favour of reform.[6] They were also the most reluctant to intervene.

1. The Majlis al-Milli's Struggle for Power

In 1874, the government bowed to popular pressure and established a popularly-elected Coptic Lay Council (Majlis al-Milli) with the right to participate in church affairs. Clerical opposition, however, was constant, and the Council functioned only sporadically. A new Majlis was elected in 1883, and a new law gave it significant power, the exercise of which was still successfully blocked by the clergy. Two later laws, dated 1908 and 1912, emasculated the Council,[7] but by doing so enabled it to meet regularly.

Reformers always played an important role in the Council and came to dominate its deliberations. The Majlis was the chief mechanism by which they sought to gain control of the community. Because Council elections were held only in Cairo and the Council sat in that city, Cairenes played a disproportionate role in the Council's life. That body would probably have been more conservative and more genuinely representative had voting been by diocese. Some Council members were in fact bound by the horizon of the community, but many had wider interests and were involved, for example, in national politics as well. An advantage was seen in electing politicians and high officials to the Majlis; they could then represent the Council to their party and the government.[8] The additional public exposure brought by Council membership was probably useful to many Coptic politicians, particularly those representing Cairene constituencies with many Coptic inhabitants.

At the heart of the dispute between the clergy and key members of the Council was the control of monastic endowment (*waqf*) revenues. Five thousand feddans had been endowed for the particular use of the seven surviving monasteries, which were charged with the responsibility for only about one hundred monks and an income in 1926 of £E300,000.[9] The

Abbots disposed of huge sums as they saw fit, while rumours of waste and wrong-doing abounded. For example, in 1919-20 Dair al-Muharraq earned £E1.5 million in cotton sales, a sum which seemingly disappeared.[10] Monastic incomes were only rarely spent on the welfare of their intended beneficiaries, the monks, let alone on the entire Coptic community. The monks lived in dire poverty and received little, if any, education; only the poorest of the poor and those avoiding conscription saw monastic life as a refuge of any sort.

These large revenues, then, were the key to the success of lay reform plans. The Council, with the backing of many Copts, wished to establish a system of accountability by supervising incomes and expenditures. Some Copts despaired of this solution and advocated more extreme solutions such as the dissolution of all monasteries or supervision of monastic endowments by the Ministry of (Muslim) Endowments.[11]

By 1926, the reform movement had gathered such speed that its opponents could only interrupt and no longer break its momentum. The two Coptic newspapers, various Coptic societies, the national and local diocesan lay councils, the latter of which functioned primarily as personal status courts, were all demanding reform. Understandably, they focused on changing the Majlis charter to give the Council control of the endowments and the reformers more power in its deliberations.

Suryal Jirjis Suryal opened the campaign in the Senate in June 1926 by pointing to the many petitions of complaint against clerical mismanagement that the Senate had received. He then moved for a return to the Majlis law of 1883 and the abolution of the 1908 and 1912 laws.[12] He asked for a Council membership of twenty-four, who would be chosen by an electorate of all adult male Copts. Bishop Lukas, a Senator appointed to represent the church, argued that the Council already had enough authority; the ecclesiastics, by virtue of their position, wer entitled to exercise the greater share of power. His argument was not persuasive, and the draft law was passed to the Committee for Suggestions and Petitions in July. Suryal had, however, failed in his attempt to skip this particular step in the process. He had requested that the bill be submitted directly to the Judiciary Committee, which would have hastened the passage of the bill through the Senate. The Bishop and his supporters argued successfully against this and were able to persuade their colleagues that the circumstances were not so extraordinary as to demand the circumvention of normal Senate procedures. Theirs was obviously a delaying tactic.[13]

Only two members of the high clergy supported the reform, the Metropolitan of Asyut, and the Bishop of Manafalut and Abu Tij.[14] The rest opposed any reduction in clerical privilege, and none more so than Yuannis, the Metropolitan of Alexandria. In August the Patriarch submitted a petition, apparently written by Yuannis, to the Senate objecting to Suryal's plans and presenting the case for ecclesiastical supervision of monastic endowments.

The Coptic press printed pages and pages of letters and telegrams supporting Suryal and was unrestrained in its criticism of the clergy. One article in Misr, a daily Coptic paper, accused the clergy of being so busy selling feddans that they served Mammon and not God.[15] Other newspapers, including al-Muqattam, Wadi al-Nil and the Liberal Constitutionalist al-Siyasa, praised Suryal's plan.

The Judiciary Committee eventually received the draft law and approved it in 1927. Bishop Lukas had tried to postpone consideration of the Committee's report until yet the following session, while Suryal, in some trepidation lest the government fall, continued to urge the Senate to act quickly. The merits and demerits of the draft law, which gave the Majlis the right to supervise endowments, schools, churches, societies, monasteries, personal status and the Coptic press, were not debated in either Chamber. Some Senators tried to send the bill back to committee on a technical point, but failed.[16] The coalition government forced the bill through Parliament and a large majority in each house voted in its favour before the end of the session. It became law in July 1927.[13] All Copts, except the absent Bishop Lukas, voted for the law; curiously, Wafdist Copts played only a small part in the debate. If Patriarch Cyril had not been senile and ill,[17] the reformers might not have been so successful. No one was firmly in control of the community, and this gave both free rein to clerical abuse and an opportunity to remedy the problem. The British, although they approved of this project, did not intervene on its behalf.[18]

One sign of the church's weakness was that there was no accepted method of choosing a Patriarch. This was not a new problem; in past centuries, a preference was voiced but not always followed for monastic candidates who were usually, but not always, elected by an electorate whose composition varied.[19] There were three Patriarchal elections in the first half of this century; all were controversial, and each time the problem was different. The variety in custom gave each side in an election dispute a number of precedents on which to draw. Essentially, these three elections provided additional opportunities for the reformers to attempt to take control of the community.

In 1926, the age and senility of Patriarch Cyril drove the reformers to argue with the Synod over whose right it was to appoint a deputy to act for the Patriarch. By tradition, it was the right of the latter two; the reformers, fearing the appointment of the tough and reactionary Metropolitan Yuannis, argued for the people.[20] Nothing happened due to the fact that the government, whose responsibility it was to confirm such an appointment refused to take sides. In August 1927, the quarrel became heated when Cyril died. The Synod asked Yuannis to serve as Acting Patriarch while the reform party, hoping to prevent him from using the office to his advantage, pushed for an immediate election.[21] However, the reformers first wanted to change the election regulations, set in 1908, which gave the government the right to choose the electors. After long argument, the reformers failed, and in 1928 the government did exactly as they feared, packing the assembly with men who were not necessarily even Orthodox Copts.[22]

The reformers' candidate for Patriarch was Yuhanna Salama, deputy (wakil) of the Khartoum diocese, who had quarrelled with his Bishop and also been married in his youth.[23] He was therefore not a favourite with the Synod, but he was popular with Copts in the Sudan and the British, who liked his progressive ideas. British approval may have led the reformers to expect British help; it may equally have harmed Yuhanna in the King's eyes, and may help to explain the latter's preference to Yuannis.[24] King Fuad was eager to settle the election so that a new Metropolitan could be named to Ethiopia,[25] and so he called on two Coptic politicians, Qalini Fahmi and Tawfiq Dus, to help secure the speedy election of Yuannis. In fact, almost all Coptic politicians became involved in various ad hoc attempts to resolve differences.

Many Copts detested Yuannis, and the Coptic press was full of articles attacking him. In December 1927, an illegally constituted assembly of 260 people representing Lay Councils and notables, elected Yuhanna Salama Patriarch, and asked the government to confirm their choice.[26] The legitimate Nominations Committee condemned the meeting while the Majlis al-Milli applauded it and requested the British to block any government decision against Salama.[27] The British were aware of the strong clerical opposition to Salama and, while sympathetic, decided against intervention. They did act to secure the reform party a royal audience, but this did not bear fruit.[28]

The lack of agreement on a draft election law continued to delay the election. The government was reluctant to decide the matter and so continued to prolong Yuannis' appointment as Acting Patriarch, thereby inevitably strengthening his hand. Finally, the government set up an assembly of ninety-six clerics and laymen, who were individually informed of the King's wishes by the energetic Tawfiq Dus. Acting in deference to those wishes, the assembly elected Yuannis Patriarch in December 1928 by a vote of ninety-one to five. Both the manner of his election and his subsequent behaviour created doubts about his willingness and ability to protect the community.

It is not surprising, given Yuannis' support from the government, that the 1927 Majlis al-Milli law was ignored by the clergy and did not, therefore, solve the problem of monastic endowments. In 1928, the Coptic Minister of Agriculture, Nakhla al-Mutii, suggested to the bemused Prime Minister the creation of a joint lay-clerical committee responsible for the endowments and to the Lay Council as one possible solution.[29] The Prime Minister, so desperate that he overlooked his fear that the Wafd would choose to profit from the expected opposition of both reformers and clergy, approved the plan. Palace pressure may have been behind his decision.[30] The joint committee, designed to have a pro-clerical majority, was announced by Royal Decree in December 1928, but was still not functioning by the following spring due to the seeming inability of the two sides to co-operate at any level.

Other problems, which had nothing to do with the major one of endowments, presented themselves with monotonous regularity. The imposition of a Bishop of unsavoury reputation[31] on al-Minya without first taking the customary poll of local opinion, brought two thousand Minyans to a protest meeting in May 1930,[32] and a flood of telegrams opposing the Bishop's investiture to the Palace.[33] The Lay Council threw its weight behind the protestors and declared the investiture null and void. A second problem arose in the staffing of the Patriarchate; both the Patriarch and the Council wished to dismiss an individual of the other's appointing. One was accused by the Council of encroaching on its prerogatives, and the other by the Patriarch of financial incompetence.[34]

The Patriarch believed that the solution to his problem lay in a return to the Council law of 1912. It is possible that, through his old ally the Palace, he pressed the government to act because rumours circulated that the Council would be reconstituted to make it more amenable to the wishes of the Patriarch and the Prime Minister.[35] The Residency, asked to intervene by both the reformers and the Anglican Bishop in Egypt, did not do so until 1931. Sir Percy Loraine, the High Commissioner, believed that his scope for action was limited,[36] but he finally asked his Oriental Secretary, Walter Smart, to impress upon Prime Minister Sidqi the desirability of avoiding retrograde measures. With British approval, Sidqi asked Nakhla al-Mutii to mediate.[37] The latter accepted this thankless task and, after informing the Majlis that the government had no intention of altering its charter,[38] worked out a compromise on some issues in June.

The Council of Ministers accepted the compromise solution which (1) left the Bishop of al-Minya in place and thereby confirmed the Patriarch's right to invest Bishops; (2) dismissed the official accused of incompetence by the Patriarch but suggested a Lay Council member to replace him; and (3) ordered the Patriarch's appointee to restrict his duties to those of a private secretary. Smart construed this as a significant victory for the Majlis al-Milli.[39] The Majlis apparently disagreed for its suddenly withdrew its consent.[40] In retaliation, Patriarch Yuannis first threatened to retire to a monastery, leaving the community to wallow in its confusion, and then in February he changed all the locks at the Patriarchate to prevent entry.

Loraine emphatically wished that the Patriarch would carry out his threat. He was equally tired of the reformers who were always "trying to get their battles fought by someone else...,"[41] and he believed that it was undesirable to espouse their cause too openly. The Foreign Office, however, wanted him to intervene and even suggested that he press the King.[42] Loraine resisted this proposal, explaining that British representations had been frequent and adequate.[43] The Prime Minister, he reported, had dropped any idea of dissolving the present Majlis. British intervention as well as communal resistance had another effect: the Egyptian government finally instructed the Patriarch to withdraw the new Bishop from al-Minya. This would have been a significant victory for the Lay Council had not the Patriarch refused to co-operate.[44]

Twice in 1932, the Holy Synod petitioned Sidqi to weaken the Majlis,[45] and once in 1933 the Patriarch, through Tawfiq Dus,[46] presented a similar plan. Sidqi liked the latter proposal but, upon consideration, suggested a solution that was less drastic but would still leave the Patriarch in control.[47] Loraine asserted his belief that the laity and not the clergy required protection, and informed Sidqi that he saw no justification for a change in the Council composition. The Prime Minister replied that the chaos caused by the perennial quarrel about the spending of church income was reason enough.[48] Sidqi's scheme was not to be gifted with success; the Foreign Office, like Loraine, found it unacceptable and had its disapproval voiced to the King.[49]

In another attempt to solve the problem of endowments, yet another joint lay-clerical committee was formed in 1937. It made as little progress as the old committee,[50] and in June the Holy Synod gave up and announced that it would retain control of the endowments. At the same time, the Lay Council reaffirmed that it regarded the 1928 decree setting up the first joint committee as invalid.[51]

The luck of the reformers changed when in 1944 they were able to replace the late Patriarch Yuannis with the reform-minded Makarios. Although initial developments were encouraging, the course of this Patriarchal election ran no more smoothly than that of the preceding one. When Yuannis died in 1942, Yusab, Metropolitan of Jirja, was elected Acting Patriarch with little opposition. Even more surprising was the rapidity with which the Majlis and Synod agreed on new election regulations. These latter established an electorate of the clergy, the educated and the well-to-do. If not widely representative of the community, it was at least a body with which there could be no tampering.[52] _Misr_ happily described the new regulations as giving the community the right to elect its highest religious official, _vox populi vox Dei_.[53]

The problem this time occurred over the question of electing a monk. The new law required it; however, an explanatory memorandum issued with the law seemed to allow exceptions. Since rival sides could quote the article or the memorandum, the debate grew lively. Both the reformers and the clergy favoured monastic candidates initially; each group later split internally on the issue.

Unfortunately, the only monastic candidate put forward was a former government official named Wadi Said. Having taken orders only recently, his timing scandalised many; but he did have the support of certain reform elements, including members of the Majlis.[54] Metropolitan Yusab was the main contender on the other side, and he had the support of several important Coptic politicians. Misr had published articles on all the candidates and at least simulated neutrality; the British felt that the paper actually favoured the election of a Bishop.[55] All Bishops, of course, had once been monks. Yusab also had the support of al-Muqattam.

Letters advocating the election of Makarios, dredged up from the forgotten depths of the last election, began to appear in Misr. Makarios also had the support of the Wafdist al-Misri.[56] His great age perhaps discouraged some, but others apparently saw him as a good man who could pave the way for a genuine monastic candidate at some not too distant date.[57] It is also possible that the supporters of both Wadi and Yusab saw Makarios as a compromise candidate who would allow them more time to marshal their respective forces for the next Patriarchal election.

The election was delayed bec se the Synod refused to recognise Wadi as a monk.[58] In deference to this, the Nominations Committee withdrew him from the list of candidates in July 1943. Throughout the autumn, the Lay Council insisted that Wadi was a legitimate nominee, whereas Bishops were not. Eventually, the Council was forced to give way on both points; without Wadi, it was silly to insist on a monk.

The disappointed Council swung its weight behind Makarios. One clear sign of the times was that all the nominees promised reform and, in the final weeks before the election, contention rested on which candidate was the most progressive. Makarios' commitment to reform went back to at least the early 1920s, and he, perhaps accordingly, was elected in January 1944.

Makarios soon proposed that endowments be handed to a committee which would be elected by the Majlis and approved by the Patriarch. The income would be devoted first to improving monastic conditions and then to whatever other projects the Patriarch thought worthwhile.[59] The reformers, seemingly, had no objection to this. They were more interested in overseeing the accounts and determining that the money was spent wisely than in choosing how the money would be spent, particularly when the Patriarch who would allocate revenues was a known reformer and one to whom they had access.

Makarios' proposal aroused a storm of protest among the clergy who sent a delegation in May to the Minister of the Interior to enlist his support. The delegation failed, and the Wafd government confirmed Lay Council control of monastic endowments. The Wafd had no reason to contradict the expressed wish of the head of the community and was perhaps concerned to placate, at least partially, those Copts inclined to follow the Coptic politician Makram Ubaid out of the party.

Meeting in the wake of this decision, the Holy Synod determined that the Patriarch had violated church law.[60] A delegation was sent to the British Embassy to plead their cause and to express the fear that the government might attempt to overcome their resistance by force. They apparently conquered this fear; a Lay Council committee, sent to take a preliminary look at the _waqf_ accounts, found the Abbots very unco-operative.

The clergy only needed patience, for by July the honeymoon was over. The Majlis thought it could dictate and, once the Patriarch tired of this, quarrelling began.[61] Makarios soon came under the influence of his fellow ecclesiastics.[62] Annoyed with the Lay Council, he withdrew to a monastery in August and did not return for two months.[63] Away from lay influence, he lost any remaining reformist tendencies. Inevitably, his return did not improve the situation; the Council, with much of the community behind it, clung tenaciously to its right to control monastic endowments.[64] Makarios asked the government for a decree proclaiming his jurisdiction over secular and financial church affairs, but he died before it could be issued.[65]

It was less than two years after his election that Makarios died. The community, after arguing for some months over the advantage of monastic candidates, finally agreed in March 1946 to strike the clause demanding the election of a monk from the regulations. Another problem raised by the last election, occurred over the question of whose right it was to validate a nominee.[65]

Yusab, Wadi and one other candidate were approved by the Nominations Committee in April; and the election was set for May. The influential Coptic writer, Salama Musa, came out in support of Yusab in *Misr*. As Musa pointed out, a Bishop might be expected to have more administrative and worldly knowledge than a monk,[67] given prevailing monastic educational standards. Of course, Wadi was exceptional for a monk, but he may have lost supporters due to a suspicion that he would encounter problems with the Synod if elected. Yusab also had the support of over half the Lay Council, and he was finally elected Patriarch in the least controversial of the three elections. He was helped by a strike which kept many of his opponents among the electors housebound, while his supporters were taken to the polls in army lorries sent by General Basili Sidqi.[68]

Yusab, who was elected with the support of reform elements, also agreed to Majlis supervision of endowments and then changed his mind after the election. As always, the problem was partly due to the Council's persistent lack of tact in trying to dictate to the Patriarch.[69] In 1947, the community split over the appointment of a foreign Anglican as instructor at the seminary. Half the Lay Council opposed the appointment and resigned.[70] This, in turn, generated a new problem: the Patriarch wanted elections for an entirely new Majlis scheduled, while the Vice-President and effective head of the Council, al-Minyawi, held that the law only allowed for by-elections to fill the vacant seats.[71] Several months later, the issue had still not been decided; the Council could not function and there was a backlog of personal status appellate cases. In disgust, the Patriarch left Cairo and refused to return. It was rumoured that he had left it up to the Council of Ministers to settle the affair.[72]

Patriarch Yusab appears to have been a weak individual who was prey to the arguments of anyone more forceful than he. Al-Minyawi and his supporters merely compounded the problem by splitting the Council over a matter as unimportant as an instructor at the seminary. Even loyal backers like *Misr* began to suggest the need for a change in the Council's ways,[73] and some even proposed a more drastic reallocation of duties.[74]

In 1948, the government issued the *fatwa* that Makarios had requested in 1945. It confirmed the Patriarch's position as head of the Majlis al-Milli and stipulated that the Council-elected Deputy or *Wakil* (still al-Minyawi) could act only at the Patriarch's designation.[75] It is not clear that this *fatwa* was of much use to Yusab, although it may have helped him disburse funds more freely.

Again in 1949, Council elections were delayed due to an attempt by the Patriarch to restrict the electorate. Hoping to force the issue, he first declared in November that the Council was no longer legally constituted and its decisions therefore void, and then in February that he would retire to a monastery if the government did not act on his request. The government, hoping to solve at least this kind of problem permanently, made Parliament amend the Council charter to give the Minister of the Interior the power to appoint a commission to replace the Council until elections could be held. In addition, all Council decisions from the end of its term in October were validated.[76] The Commission appointed by the Ministry had a clerical bias, and this drove al-Minyawi and some other Copts on the Commission to withhold their participation.[77] However, the Commission held elections that summer (1950) and the reformers won a majority.

Yusab's pontificate was perhaps even more troubled than that of his predecessors. Again in 1951, some Council members resigned when the Patriarch fired the Director of the Patriarchate and appointed someone else. This was the prerogative of the Council, not the Patriarch. Accusations of clerical corruption and incompetence grew more and more frequent as the Patriarch came under the influence of his valet who was reportedly selling bishoprics for £E5,000, and was perhaps collecting this fee at some later date from endowment revenues.[78] As many as sixteen of the nineteen episcopal appointments made by Yusab may have been sold in this fashion.[79] Finally, in 1955, the clergy and the government agreed to the Patriarch's deposition.

2. Summary

Events in the Coptic community mirrored a similar ferment in the Muslim community, and periodic attempts were made to reform various Muslim religious institutions.[80] The government had always had more control over the Muslim religious establishment than it had over the Copt, but its power over the latter grew. Partly this was due to the fact that the government was increasingly treating the Copts as individual citizens rather than members of a corporate body with rights and duties of its own.[81] In addition, the government benefited, although sometimes reluctantly from the stalemate between laymen and clergy.

It was, of course, not unusual for the government to intervene in the internal affairs of the community, nor for the various factions in a communal dispute to ask for government support.[82] What was new was the number of both Copts involved and outsiders whose help could be sought; the British, the Cabinet and the Palace were at times the object of appeal.

The Patriarch was a public official, subject at a minimum to government confirmation. In addition, the Majlis al-Milli was under the jurisdiction of the Ministry of the Interior. The state had the authority to determine how power would be divided in the community and which group would supervise endowments. It was not only slow to make such decisions, but it was often unwilling or unable to enforce them once made. At different times, the government scolded or cajoled both the Majlis al-Milli and the Patriarch, but it seemed unable to take stronger action. It never tried to force the monasteries to deliver *waqf* accounts to the Majlis, and the clergy obviously felt relatively free to ignore the government.

The government was, to an extent, caught between Palace support of the Patriarch and British sympathy for the reformers. Palace-tied governments, like that of Sidqi in the 1930s, were especially pushed to strengthen clerical power, but were usually prevented from doing so by the British. Some notable successes, however, were achieved: the imposition of Patriarch Yuannis on the community, the creation of a committee in 1928 to remove control of the endowments from the Law Council, and the 1948 *fatwa* confirming the Patriarch as head of the Council.

Of course, it was easier to contemplate interfering with the Majlis al-Milli than dictating to the Holy Synod. With the whole of the Western world as an audience, the government was understandably cautious about openly opposing the Patriarch who was the symbolic, if not always accepted, leader of the Copts.

The British played an important role in encouraging reform, but intervened only when some action of the Egyptian government threatened the reform party of the Majlis.[83] They avoided squabbles in which the Egyptian government was not involved. They were interested only in protecting the community from the government and not from itself; after the Anglo-Egyptian treaty was signed, intervention in this area ceased. It is, however, interesting to note that the British intervened most often during their 1929-34 period of self-effacement when Loraine was High Commissioner. Government threats to reform or alter communal government were probably greatest at this time.

The community no longer had an accepted hierarchy of authority. Its fragmentation could have incidentally served the purpose of the state because it prevented the Copts from presenting a united front. Some Copts even invited the government to assume greater responsibility for the community. Government power did, in fact, grow in certain areas; witness the 1950 law amending the Lay Council charter because the community could not agree on election regulations. The rivalry between clergy and laymen did then hamper whatever protection the millet system was able to offer the Copts, and perhaps hastened its ultimate ruin. However, the main government reaction when faced with Coptic affairs was not one of delight at an opportunity, but of sheer annoyance owing to the intractability of the problem. As one Foreign Office official noted in 1935, the government no sooner tried to remedy Coptic grievances than the various factions began quarrelling violently over what form the remedies would take; and, before the government secured agreement, it would fall and a new one would come into office.[84]

Although many members of the Majlis thought the traditional ordering of the community was archaic, most fought hard against government encroachments in areas such as education and personal status jurisdiction. They were interested in weakening the clergy only to their own advantage and not that of the government. They were, however, proponents of equality, and they complained about government and private discrimination against Copts.

The institution of parliamentary government broadened the arena of struggle. Traditionally, the government sought the advice of its own Coptic officials or the clergy on communal affairs. Now Coptic politicians also sought to persuade the government of the validity of their views in the dispute; and the government used them to help mediate whenever endemic quarrels reached epidemic proportions. The Majlis wanted to see advocates of communal reform elected to Parliament so that its views could be represented. The clergy also recognised the usefulness of this, and in 1925 the monastery Dair al-Muharraq spent £E2,000 on an election party for Tawfiq Dus.[85] There is some question, however, as to the extent to which politicians and even high officials used these channels. Some, like Dus, relied on them as a power base. Others may have been more hesitant to represent any one side in a communal dispute for fear it might damage their career. Still others, although relatively few in number, were not interested in communal affairs at all. Many politicians may have been more interested in communal affairs before 1919; after that date, the chance to participate in national politics gave them an alternative. To the extent that the Wafd and its Coptic politicians were interested in the problem, they generally sympathised with reform. It was the coalition government of 1927 and the Wafd government of 1944 which made changes favourable to the Majlis.[86] Other parties proved more lukewarm toward reform, although the movement had important supporters among non-Wafdists. Non-Wafdist governments, however, created the 1928 endowments committee with strong clerical representation and considered changing the Lay Council charter in the early 1930s. It was also a non-Wafdist government that issued the 1948 _fatwa_ confirming the Patriarch as head of the Lay Council.

The lay reformers, although bitterly deploring government intervention when it benefited the clergy, were happy to countenance it when it was in their favour. They were able to weaken the tie between the state and the Patriarch, and this in turn weakened the Patriarch's ability to represent his flock to the government. Now that the government was relying less on the church for other things, it may have looked less to the church to present communal views.

The church was, in any case, cautious about appealing publicly to the government and Palace on behalf of the Copts. It had to take care that its very visible actions did not jeopardise the community. This care was perhaps particularly exercised by the Patriarch, who rarely made direct pleas to the government or Palace. Because of his position as head of the community, his opposition to or advocacy of any given proposal could have had more symbolic meaning than practical value. In addition, none of the three Patriarchs in this period had so much support among Copts that they could afford to antagonise potential or existing allies. Makarios and Yusab were, in any case, too weak to be able to protect Coptic interests effectively. It is interesting, however, that they chose the two most radical and activist priests in the church, Murqus Sergius and Ibrahim Luqa, to serve as their deputies (Wakil). As will become clear later, these man, and particularly Sergius, were active and outspoken in the community's defence. It is not clear, however, that they always acted with the foreknowledge of the Patriarch. Both Makarios and Yusab showed signs of being unable to manage church affairs, let alone more complicated issues involving the government and Muslim populace.

The Majlis' success in gaining control of the community was limited. It spent most of its energy in trying to gain what it saw as all its rights, rather than exercising the ones it had, and foolishly made almost every issue a point of contention. It was not always a responsible body and absenteeism was chronic. Murqus Simaika, founder of the Coptic Museum, argued that the Council was financially incompetent; those estates it did manage showed an annual deficit, which was met by selling property.[87] Iris al-Masri thinks that from the early 1940s the Majlis was of limited value and lost much prestige in the eyes of Copts.[88] This may be true, particularly from 1947. With periodic resignations from the Council and the protracted election dispute which took place in 1949-50, the Council could not have met very often or have accomplished much when it did meet. At a time when the Copts were at increasing risk in the larger society, the Majlis, along with the clergy, was expending its energies on intra-communal problems.

Given that endowments were such a hotly contested prize, and that there probably was some truth to allegations of clerical ineptitude and corruption, it would be surprising if they were not mismanaged. Unfortunately, the church was secretive about the amount of property it owned; there are no statistics reliable enough to permit firm conclusions about the fate of the endowments and their revenue over time.

Clerical and lay estimates of monastic holdings ranged between five thousand and nine thousand feddans.[89] Expenses were low and profits from land and property were, at least in some years, quite high. Dair al-Muharraq had thirty-five monks and an annual income of £E100,000 in 1927.[90] Twenty-one years earlier, when the monastery's income had totalled only £E9,633, its expenses had reached £E1,233, leaving an eighty-seven per cent profit.[91] No doubt some of this profit was invested to produce still larger incomes; certainly, little of it was spent on improving monastic conditions.

B. THE COPTIC PRESS

The number of periodicals published in Egypt in the past century and the range of views they expressed are surprising given the small size of the literate public. Few could support themselves from subscription rates; as one Copt in the business said, there was no quicker way to financial ruin than to start a newspaper.[92] Most periodicals relied on special subsidies from those whose opinions they expressed. The uncertainty in funding, however, meant that periodicals frequently changed hands and, on occasion, showed startling reversals in political allegiance. The relative freedom accorded the press made it a useful political and social tool, and sometimes newspapers were suspended because of the violence of their attacks on the government.

Coptic periodicals follow this general pattern and provide evidence of a lively, if disunited, communal life. Copts published religious, intellectual and political periodicals, some of which were meant to appeal to Muslims as well as Christians. Internal communal matters were a natural concern: articles covered such assorted topics as Coptic history, Coptic cultural and religious mores and, of course, the various quarrels over church organisation.

Although Coptic periodicals did not speak with one voice, they did unite on some issues. They helped to promote, some more consciously than others, communal solidarity; and they sometimes defended Coptic interests. Their freedom in voicing complaints about discrimination suggests considerable Muslim tolerance. From the mid-1940s especially, Coptic periodicals encouraged the idea there there was a Coptic political perspective rather than as many political views as there were Copts. They even encouraged co-operation between the normally hostile Coptic Christian sects. Three of the most important Coptic periodicals will be reviewed here. Two, _Misr_ (Egypt) and _al-Watan_ (The Homeland), were daily papers, and one, _al-Manara al-Misriyya_ (The Egyptian Lighthouse) was sometimes published weekly, and sometimes monthly.

1. _Misr_

Misr was the chief Coptic organ in the period under study. It sometimes served as a regular party paper with a Muslim as well as Coptic readership; and, at other times, it addressed itself mainly to communal concerns. It was founded in 1895 by a wealthy Asyuti who wished to counteract the relatively pro-clerical views of al-Watan. The paper consistently advocated an increase in lay participation in church affairs. Its self-conscious role was as a watchdog of the Copts,[93] and after 1930, it was the only daily organ reporting on clerical activities. It was a leader in the communal reform movement, and its support for the Coptic Lay Council offered that body some protection from government, if not clerical, interference.

Misr probably had a largely middle-class and educated audience. It received financial support from printing the announcements of the Lay Council, the Patriarchate, Coptic societies and the government. Particularly after 1930, it had a virtual monopoly on the announcements of communal organisations. It may have received covert subsidies from reformers. There is some evidence that it at times received a direct subsidy from the Patriarchate[94] and at times from the Wafd.[95]

Misr purported to guide the Copts in national as well as communal affairs. The paper supported the British Occupation and defended the Copts from the attacks of the Muslim press in the troubled first decade of this century. It was then a stronger champion of Coptic rights than at any other time until the mid-1940s.

In 1918, Misr experienced a change of heart and became both vehemently anti-British and pro-Wafdist. Financial difficulties were partly responsible for the conversion, after which circulation soared.[96] Misr became a major Zaghlulist organ with both Copts and Muslims on staff. For example, one series of articles written by the Coptic nationalist Sinut Hanna in 1919 played an influential role in bringing down the Muhammad Said ministry.[97]

When Adli became Prime Minister in 1921, and quarrelled with Zaghlul, Misr moved into the moderate Adlist camp and Mahmud Azmi, a noted secularist, was named editor. During the Tharwat ministry, which followed that of Adli, the paper vacillated between Adli and Zaghlul,[98] but eventually chose to support the latter. By November 1922, Misr was attacking the new Liberal Constitutionalist party with which Adli had ties. The paper remained Wafdist, albeit with varying degrees of enthusiasm, for most of the next three decades.

Until 1925 Misr was an important Wafdist organ publishing mainly articles of national concern. Then again, during the 1928 Mahmud cabinet, when many Wafdist periodicals were suspended, the party leaned heavily on *Misr*. Staff from the suspended *Kawkab al-Sharq* joined *Misr*, and Abbas al-Aqqad continued to write for the paper even after *Kawkab* resumed publication. The depredations of the Sidqi regime increased the Wafd's reliance on *Misr*; by May 1931, it was the only Wafdist paper in circulation, and al-Aqqad was again editor. Its attacks on Sidqi persuaded the latter to have the paper suspended; it soon reappeared with al-Aqqad at the helm again.

Misr's ties with the Wafd would never again be so close. After the owner's death in 1932, his sons kept some distance from politics until the Wafd returned to power in 1936. The paper was enthusiastically Wafdist until the shock of the disastrous 1938 election defeat inspired caution. The paper was perhaps obliged to support the Wafd in 1937-8 because it was the only party defending national unity. There was, however, little criticism of the 1938-9 Mahmud government. *Misr*, purportedly pleased with the Wafd's return to power in 1942, avoided comment on the argument between al-Nahhas and his Coptic ally, Makram Ubaid. It neither rushed to support Ubaid after his split from the party, nor continued to back the Wafd. *Misr* was soon complaining that the Wafd refused to allocate it enough newsprint; it had to suspend publication twice in 1944. The paper was relieved to see Ahmad Mahir made Prime Minister in 1944, but none the less newsprint remained scarce.

From 1946, *Misr* assumed a markedly communal character and largely withdrew from the national political arena. Under Salama Musa, who became Editor in 1942, *Misr* was so zealous in its defence of Coptic rights that the Sidqi government accused the paper of fanaticism and refused to publish any more announcements in its pages.[99] In the increasingly charged atmosphere of communal tension, *Misr* sought to protect the minority by attacking the majority. It assailed the bigotry of the Muslim Brethren, doubted the wisdom of British withdrawal, and criticised the 1950 Wafd cabinet.

For much of this period then, *Misr* was attached in some measure to the Wafd. To an extent, it was responsible for creating and maintaining Coptic support for that party; it later both mirrored and encouraged Coptic dissatisfaction with the party. If at times *Misr* overlooked parochial interests in its enthusiasm for national ones, its links with the Wafd were an advantage and afforded more protection to the community than a strongly sectarian stand. Its disaffection from the political system dates from the 1938 election and with the Wafd from 1942-3. The Wafd did not need *Misr*'s support after 1938 because it had several periodicals expressing party views. *Misr*'s backing may even have entailed some risk given the accusation made during the 1938 campaign that the Wafd was a Coptic clique.

2. *Al-Watan*

The first of the Coptic dailies was founded in 1878, and it backed the ecclesiastics in their struggle to limit the say of laymen in church affairs. Although willing for a brief period before World War I to countenance reform, its more consistently pro-clerical stance guaranteed it a Patriarchal subsidy.[100] With its sale in 1923 to a lawyer, the paper became an advocate of communal reform.

Al-Watan opposed the British occupation until the 1890s, when it became a staunch defender of both the British presence in Egypt and Coptic rights.[101] Lacking its rival's talent for prediction, *al-Watan* continued to favour the British well into the 1920s. It condemned both the revolution and Zaghlul, urged co-operation with the British and begged the Egyptians to present their views to the Milner Mission.[102] Unlike the nationalists, it celebrated the 1922 granting of independence.[103] *Al-Watan*'s attitude towards the nationalist ferment was not as clear as these arguments might suggest, either because the newspaper genuinely had mixed feelings or because it had come to realise how little support there was for the retention of British control. *Al-Watan* did, in some articles, try to promote Copt-Muslim equality, but at the same time was dubious about the chances for quality's long-range success. In 1919, it proposed that the Coptic Ramses Club be open to Muslim membership, and in September 1920 suggested that it was unnecessary to include in a treaty clauses stipulating Coptic equality because Copts and Muslims had become one.[104]

Al-Watan was, at this time, primarily concerned with national and not communal affairs. Like *Misr*, it had Muslims on staff and backed Adli when he became Prime Minister. The fact that Muslims could even temporarily write for Coptic papers meant that Copt-Muslim differences had blurred, their place taken by a more critical issue. Muslim writers probably helped attract Muslim readers without losing any of the paper's traditional Coptic audience.

With *al-Watan*'s sale in late 1923, the paper

began to support the Wafd ministry. Unfortunately, it was too late. The Wafd did not need two Coptic papers. *Misr* had both a stronger claim on the party's affection and a larger circulation. In fact, *al-Watan*'s mistake may have been to look too much like its rival, with similar views on church and national affairs. It began to appear sporadically in 1927, and finally disappeared in 1930.

Al-Watan was most influential in the period before the First World War. It appealed, until 1924, to older, more traditional Copts who were comfortable with the *status quo* and who exhibited some degree of Anglophilia.[105] The radical change in viewpoint in 1924 occurred not only because of a change in ownership, but because there were fewer readers who opposed communal reform and supported the British. *Al-Watan*'s defection left the Patriarch without a mouthpiece, and it left the British with only *al-Muqattam* of the Arabic press to express their views.

3. *Al-Manara al-Misriyya*

This journal in 1928 succeeded one published by its owner, Murqus Sergius, in the Sudan. Sergius, a radical priest with a parish in Cairo, was a popular if notorious figure. Known for his advocacy of church reform, he also acquired a reputation as a fiery orator during the 1919 revolution. For all but two brief periods which occurred between 1944 and 1952, he and his journals were the bane of the Patriarchate because of their strong advocacy of reform. He served as Patriarchal Deputy (*wakil*) for both Makarios and Yusab and, while doing so, was as enthusiastic a supporter of clerical privilege as he had been previously of lay rights.

Although *al-Manara* was primarily interested in religious affairs, it also dealt with Copt-Muslim relations.[106] Its owner broke with the Wafd in the 1920s; consequently, his journal had no party affiliation and tended to evaluate issues in terms of their affect on the Coptic community. It defended Coptic rights even when other Coptic journals were slow to do so, and it routinely reported incidents of communal violence. *Al-Manara* frequently protested against discrimination and government interference in communal affairs;[107] it also attacked the Muslim Brethren, called for the dissolution of all Islamic societies, and deplored Muslim oppression of Copts.

C. VOLUNTARY ASSOCIATIONS

In the past century, many Coptic societies were founded and flourished. They had different aims, but most combined religious sentiments with social objectives. Their ultimate purpose was to serve the community and, while some chose to do this by circulating devotional pamphlets, others helped by building schools and hospitals. At least one society was formed for the sole purpose of encouraging church reform, but many became involved in lay-clerical quarrels and most seemed to back the reform party. These societies tried to compensate for the weakness of the community; one task they assumed was the church's traditional responsibility for charity. At the same time, they reinforced communal bonds by encouraging religious faith and communal schooling. They helped keep the Coptic poor from looking elsewhere for help, and they provided a social outlet for their members. They limited the attraction of Islam by providing for the same needs and satisfactions as did parallel Muslim organisations. They also helped keep a dispersed community in touch, and they provided an innocuous forum in which the Coptic élite could discuss communal problems.

Coptic voluntary associations provided services that the state either was unable to provide due to limited resources, or was unwilling to provide for non-Muslims. In trying to lighten the burden of being a Copt in a Muslim society, these organisations were doing as much of a service for the government as they were for individual Copts. Copts generally felt that the government should help any society acting for the public good, regardless of religious affiliation.[108] This was something the government was reluctant to do because grants to Coptic societies or the church often drew fire from the opposition press.[109] Grants generally were made to Coptic institutions on special occasions, like Christian holidays, and gifts sometimes came from the Palace, but money was not budgeted routinely. These societies could not plan on the basis of an annual allocation in the government budget. Coptic charities that helped Muslims and Copts were more likely to benefit from government largesse. For instance, the Coptic Hospital, which provided free treatment for more Muslims than Copts in 1922-3, received aid from the Ministry of the Interior.[110]

Most members of the Lay Council, which nominally supervised these societies, were active in association life. The societies had considerable independence and there was little formal co-ordination of their activities or views.[111] From time to time, appeals were made for unity and talks were held, but they were unproductive.[112] In 1947, Salama Musa unsuccessfully called upon Coptic societies to form an agency to find employment for young Copts and investigate charges of discrimination.[113] Coptic societies generally were not outspoken in their defence of Coptic rights, at least not until the late 1940s.

Most association members were at least middle class; they came from the landed gentry, the civil service, commerce and the professions. Coptic politicians often joined communal societies; no doubt some were active with the hope of strengthening their electoral support in the community. Since many members had some role in government, they may have used their influence on behalf of the community, and particularly in encouraging government support for church reform.

The government had always, of course, given more money to Muslim societies and had had correspondingly more control over them than over Coptic societies. From the 1940s, the government showed an inclination to increase its control over both kinds of societies, but without a concomitant desire to increase its funding for Coptic associations. Partly the government had a legitimate interest in protecting both the contributors to and beneficiaries of private charity, but it may also have been suspicious of voluntary activities that duplicated, at least in theory, those social services the government was now trying to provide to both Copts and Muslims. Perhaps the government feared that some of these associations could come to challenge its authority and undermine its legitimacy.

The Copts naturally saw government interference as an infringement on their autonomy and objected bitterly. A 1945 law regulating donations gave the Ministry of Social Affairs considerable power over Coptic societies, including the implicit right to inspect church accounts.[114] Three years later the Ministry ruled that churches must obtain its permission to collect donations and put out poor boxes.[115] In addition, the Ministry ordered certain Christian associations to keep a register of speakers with summaries of their sermons. As the French Embassy noted, this allowed the government to take steps against those associations showing too great a concern with the inequities of Egyptian society.[116]

What was more disturbing was the announcement that the Ministry hoped to keep a proportion of Coptic to Muslim societies similar to the Coptic percentage of the population. Misr argued that this was blatantly discriminatory and noted glumly that Coptic societies were so busy fighting the government for the right to exist that they had little time for good works.[117] By the early 1950s, the Ministry was refusing to give funds to Coptic organisations serving only Copts.[118] In 1951, when the government actually planned to supervise collections in churches, the Patriarch was moved to protest; the government, at least in this one instance, retreated.[119]

NOTES

1. This was Sabri Abu Alam. Chamber Debates, twenty-third session, 25 June 1927.

2. One reformer insisted in 1920 that the Coptic people had the right to elect all the clergy, including the Patriarch. Jirjis Awad, Biwaraq al-Islah: Tariq al-Islah al-Manshud, parts 6 and 7 (al-Matbaat al-Misriyya, Cairo, 1920), p.67.

3. The rivalry was fuelled partly by the fact that the clergy came from poorer families than did the reformers and resented the opportunities and advantages of their opponents. Samir Seikaly, 'The Copts under British Rule, 1882-1914', p.73-4.

4. Patriarch Cyril, who died in 1927, may have feared that progressive opinions would earn him the enmity of the Palace which was rumoured to have been responsible for the suspicious death of his reforming predecessor. Ibid., p.71.

5. Among its ecclesiastical supporters, whose reform activities sometimes won them excommunication or banishment, were Metropolitan Makarios of Asyut, the Bishop of Manfalut and Abu Tij, and the priests, Murqus Sergius and Ibrahim Luqa.

6. The enthusiasm particularly of British churchmen and missionaries for Coptic church reform led the Coptic clergy to suspect that all British interference was ultimately designed to win converts to Anglicanism.

7. The 1883 law gave the Council control of monastic endowments. The Council was never able to gain de facto control from the Patriarch and in 1908 lost de jure control as well. The 1912 law reduced the number of elected members. It gave the Council control of those non-monastic endowments in Cairo, but turned over the supervision of other endowments,

schools, monasteries and convents to the Patriarch.

8. The Wafdist politician, Ibrahim Faraj, recalls that he was asked to run for election to the Council in 1939 by the organisation's Vice-President al-Minyawi and other Coptic notables. Interview, 13 June 1979.

9. Suryal Jirjis Suryal, in a petition to the Senate, noted that there were less than two hundred monks in 1906, a figure which had decreased to about a hundred by 1926. Misr, 18 March 1944, 3; 20 March 1944, 3; 21 March 1944, 3.

10. Misr, 23 March 1944, 3. The Abbot of Dair al-Muharraq was noted for his investments in land. His lack of concern for the welfare of his monks caused repeated revolts in the monastery from the 1920s.

11. Among those who proposed this were Murqus Fahmi, a speaker at the 1911 Asyut conference; Nashid Hanna, a member of the Asyut Lay Council; and the newspaper al-Siyasa. See The Coptic Conference Held at Assiout on March 6, 7 and 8, 1911, 57; Misr, 10 July 1926, 1,3.

12. Curiously, Suryal was a member of the royalist al-Ittihad party and yet here, as well as in the election of Yuannis as Patriarch two years later, opposed the wishes of the King. FO.141/819, 17612/6/25.

13. Senate Debates, twenty-eighth session, 28 June 1926.

14. Misr, 3 July 1926, 2.

15. Misr, 14 August 1926, 1. Another article accused the Bishops of killing the Copts as the Jews had killed Christ. Misr, 16 November 1926, 1.

16. New legislation, such as the 1925 Majlis al-Hasbi law (see Chapter Six), made some provisions of the 1883 law obsolete.

17. For the pertinent debates, see Senate Debates, 28 June 1926 and 30 May 1927, and Chamber Debates, 25 June 1927.

18. He was said to have fallen under the influence of a relative who was embezzling church funds. FO.141/686, 8609/7/26.

19. Ibid.

20. Knowing that they were in the wrong, they asked Parliament to grant the Lay Council the right to appoint the Deputy. Parliament declined.

21. FO.141/685, 8424/51/27.

22. FO.141/758, 92/5/31.

23. FO.371/20129, J166/166/16.

24. Interview with Iris al-Masri, 14 August 1979.

25. Only the Patriarch could consecrate a Metropolitan, but the King feared that the Ethiopians would take advantage of the stalemate and name an Ethiopian Metropolitan. Qalini Fahmi, *Mudhakkirat*, vol.2 (Matbaat Misr, Cairo, 1944), p.111.

26. There is some confusion as to whether this was an election or a nomination. The Residency described it as the former. *Misr*, however, used both 'tarshih' (nomination) and 'intikhab' (election) to describe the same act. Judging from the fuss the meeting created, the British interpretation was correct. FO.141/685, 8424/59/28 and 8424/78/28; *Misr*, 16, 17, 19 and 20 December 1927, 1. The government, due to countervailing pressures, delayed confirmation of Yuannis' appointment as Acting Patriarch until just after this meeting.

27. FO.141/685, 8424/51/27.

28. FO.141/685, 8424/70/27.

29. FO.141/685, 8424/59/28 and 8424/78/28.

30. In a Cabinet meeting on 27 October, the King announced that he would leave the room until the Cabinet agreed to changes in the administration of Coptic endowments. The King had pressed for this for some time, but the Prime Minister had insisted that they would only reap criticism by doing so. After the meeting Mahmud threatened to resign partly over the endowment issue, and partly over the matter of appointing Sidqi as Auditor-General. FO.407/207 No.45, Mr. Hoare to Lord Cushendun, 28 October 1928.

31. FO.141/758, 92/32/31.

32. *Misr*, 16 May 1930, 5.

33. DW, Abdin Palace Archives, Tawaif Diniyya 1.

34. As the Residency pointed out, the latter's only crime was acting in the interests of the Council and 'thus embarrassing the Patriarch in his disposal of Coptic Church funds'. FO.141/758, 92/9/31.

35. FO.371/758, 92/9/31. As Sidqi himself noted, the Coptic reform party was full of his political opponents. FO.407/217, No.17, Sir Percy Loraine to Sir John Simon, 16 January 1933.

36. FO.371/15409, J47/47/16.

37. FO.141/758, 92/9/31.

38. *Egyptian Gazette*, 7 January 1931, 5.

39. FO.141/758, 92/9/31. Points 2 and 3 confirmed provisions of the 1927 law.

40. It was primarily upset over government confirmation of the troublesome Bishop. The Council claimed that it did not want to set a precedent for government intervention, despite that fact that some

of its members had been eager for British intervention. FO.141/758, 92/14/31.

41. FO.141/758, 92/9/31.

42. Murray in the Foreign Office minuted in March that the British could intervene under the third Reserved Point, but should do so only if they could be inconspicuous. Henderson was the one suggesting pressure on the Palace. FO.371/15409, J663/47/16.

43. For example, he persuaded Sidqi to prevent the excommunication of the Patriarch's *bête noire*, Ibrahim Luqa. See also, FO.371/15409, J1293/47/16.

44. FO.141/758, 92/30/31.

45. *Misr*, 10 November 1932, 3.

46. By this time, Dus had replaced Qalini Fahmi as the chief intermediary between the Patriarch and the Palace. Qalini was making his rounds spitefully referring to the Patriarch as 'that animal'. FO.141/686, 8609/57/29.

47. FO.141/749, 20/1/33.

48. Sidqi was particularly annoyed because the clergy were no longer being paid and the government had had to grant money for their support. FO.407/217, No.7, Sir Percy Loraine to Sir John Simon, 16 January 1933.

49. FO.141/749, 20/8/33.

50. *Misr*, 9 August 1937, 1. This committee had ceased meeting in 1930.

51. It did so on the grounds that the decree had not been submitted to a parliament and contradicted the 1927 law which had. *Al-Ahram*, 18 June 1937, PPF.

52. Ultimately, 3,580 electors qualified. *Egyptian Gazette*, 4 February 1944, 3.

53. *Misr*, 17 August 1942, 1.

54. He had led an exemplary and celibate life before becoming a monk. Interview with Iris al-Masri, 24 August 1979.

55. FO.371/35530, J1217/2/16.

56. The Wafd may have supported Makarios because its opponents were backing Yusab. See FO.371/35530, J1217/2/16.

57. Interview with Iris al-Masri, 24 August 1979.

58. *Misr*, 1 November 1943, p.3.

59. FO.371/41316, J906/14/16.

60. By sparking *fitna*. *Misr*, 30 May 1944, 2.

61. Interview with Iris Habib al-Masri, church historian and daughter of an influential Coptic official of the time, 24 August 1979.

62. FO.371/45931, J2266/10/16.

63. This was in part owing to his dismay at yet another government attempt to reform non-Muslim status jurisdiction.

64. A meeting of one thousand people held by the Tawfiq Society, a Coptic benevolent association, voted in June to back the Lay Council. The latter also had the support of the local Lay Councils. _Misr_, 16 March 1946, 1.

65. Sergius, in the name of the Acting Patriarch, was still trying to obtain this decree in March 1946. _Misr_, 18 June 1945, 2.

66. The Lay Council was claiming this right. _Misr_, 5 March 1946, 1.

67. _Misr_, 16 April 1946, 1.

68. Interview with Iris al-Masri, 24 August 1979.

69. Interview with Iris al-Masri, 24 August 1979.

70. Including Habib al-Masri, Raghib Iskander, Tawfiq Dus and Murad Wahbah.

71. By law, the Patriarch was President of the Council. _Misr_, 5 June 1947, 1.

72. _Misr_, 28 November 1947, 1.

73. _Misr_, 2 July 1948, 1.

74. i.e., the Coptic Unity Society. _Misr_, 5 November 1947, 3.

75. _Misr_, 29 June 1949, 3.

76. _Chamber Debates_, ninth session, 6 March 1950.

77. _Misr_ was also unhappy with the Committee's composition. _Misr_, 2 and 10 May 1950, 1.

78. French Embassy Archives, Box 144, File 31/2, the Ambassador to the Minister of Foreign Affairs, 7 March 1953.

79. Meinardus, _Christian Egypt: Faith and Life_, p.42.

80. The passage of the 1927 Majlis al-Milli law coincided with Parliament's assumption of control over the affairs of al-Azhar and its satellite schools. In addition, the Qadi school was reorganised and suggestions to reform Islamic personal status law and abolish private endowments were put forward. FO.141/566, 17008/108/27.

81. See E. Kedourie's parallel comment about Iraq in _The Chatham House Version and Other Middle Eastern Studies_ (London, Frank Cass, 1970), p.306.

82. See Meinardus, _Christian Egypt: Faith and Life_, pp.355-0, for examples.

83. The British either considered playing or played a greater role in Coptic church affairs in

the Sudan and Ethiopia. In the late 1920s, they refused to let the Metropolitan of Khartoum return to the Sudan because his behaviour had been scandalous, and they wanted his wakil, the reformist Hanna Salama, left in charge. In 1926-7, they were as opposed as the Egyptians to the investiture of an Ethiopian as Metropolitan to Ethiopia. Qalini Fahmi consulted frequently with the Residency on this subject. The Foreign Office even wondered if the appointment of an Anglophile Metropolitan could not somehow be discreetly engineered. FO.141/686, 8609/4/26.

84. FO.371/19082, J515/153/16.

85. Senate Debates, twenty-eighth session, 28 June 1926.

86. Wafdists, as part of the 1927 coalition government, may have remembered the approach for help that the reformers had made to Zaghlul and the party in the mid-1920s. It was, however, a Wafd government which appointed in 1950 a majority of supporters of the clergy to the temporary commission which held new Lay Council elections. This decision by the Wafd perhaps reflects a decline in Coptic support for the party.

87. FO.141/755, 124/6/33.

88. Interview with Iris al-Masri, 24 August 1979.

89. See the following for various estimates: Misr, 7 August 1926, 1; 16 March 1944, 3; 20 March 1944, 3. Ramzi Tadrus, al-Aqbat fi al-Qarn al-Ishrin, vol.1 (Cairo, 1911), pp.136-7. Gabriel Baer, A History of Land Ownership in Modern Egypt, 1800-1950 (London, Oxford University Press, 1962), p.179.

90. Misr, 16 March 1944, 3, quoting Suryal's memorandum to the Senate, 14 April 1927.

91. Misr, 20 March 1944, 3.

92. Misr, 27 April 1935, 7.

93. Misr, 5 August 1931, 5.

94. This is curious given Misr's views. However, in 1946, the Patriarchate gave Misr £E1,400, a subvention it then threatened to cancel if Salama Musa continued as Editor. Yusab may have arranged the subsidy because Musa supported him in his campaign to become Patriarch. He now wanted Musa fired because the latter had upset the government. DW, Abdin Palace Archives, Tawaif Diniyya, Memorandum 15, 8 December 1946.

95. Interview with Ibrahim Faraj Masiha, 13 June 1979.

96. Anwar al-Jundi thinks that circulation was

around 4,000 early in the century. Another source claims that it climbed to 10,000 in 1919, but this sounds wildly inflated. Anwar al-Jundi, al-Sihafa al-Siyasiyya (Cairo, 1962), p.150; Severianus, 'Les Coptes de l'Egypte Musulmane', Etudes Mediterranéennes 6 (1969), 80.

97. Misr was suspended because of these articles. Tariq al-Bishri, 'Misr al-Haditha Bain Ahmad w-al-Mashi', al-Katib 115 (1970), 130.

98. One Palace observer recorded that it lacked a precise political colour. CCEH, Abdin Palace Archives, Note on the Political Press in Egypt, undated but probably written between June and November of 1922.

99. This entailed considerable loss for the paper. Misr, 13 May 1956, 1.

100. FO.407/186, No.237 (enclosure), Memorandum on the Coptic Church, 1920.

101. Seikaly, 'The Copts under British Rule, 1882-1914', p.122; al-Jundi, al-Sihafa, p.150; FO.371/895, 47092/47092/16.

102. One Residency official applauded its 'sensible articles', FO.407/184, No.182, Sir M. Cheetham to Earl Curzon, 15 March 1919. See also al-Watan, 8 November 1919, 2; 20 November 1919, 2; 8 December 1919, 2; 15 May 1920, 2; 3 August 1920, 1; 22 September 1920, 2; Egyptian Mail, 29 March 1919, 2.

103. Al-Watan, 29 March 1922, 2.

104. Al-Watan's opinion on the Ramses Club was quoted in the Egyptian Gazette on 11 July 1919, 4. Its view on the treaty appeared in al-Watan, 23 September 1920, 2.

105. FO.407/186, No.203 (enclosure), Note on the Egyptian Press, 1920.

106. The radical priest Ibrahim Luqa, published a similar journal (al-Yaqza) which, unlike its owner, seems to have restricted its scope to church affairs. Luqa, like Sergius, was for some time Yusab's wakil.

107. See March and April 1948. The journal did assume a somewhat more temperate tone during Sergius' two terms as Patriarchal Deputy (wakil) under Makarios and Yusab.

108. See M. Fahmi's speech, The Coptic Congress Held at Assiout, p.48.

109. For example, al-Thaghr objected in 1937 to the Ministry of Finance's modest contribution of £E1,000 to Coptic schools in Qina, pointing out that the secondary school of a Muslim charitable institution in Aswan had had to close because of a lack of funds. Al-Thaghr, 1 April 1937, 1.

110. DW Abdin Palace Archives, Tawaif wa Jamiyat Diniyya 2. Letter from President Jirjis Antun to Hassan Nashat Pasha, 31 March 1925.

111. One association, the Union of Coptic Societies, was able to bring some societies together, but it still spoke as one voice among many.

112. A number of societies met in March 1936 to discuss unity, but their talks bore no fruit.

113. Misr, 25 June 1947, 1.

114. Law No.49 (1945) was designed to protect the public by supervising the collection and use of donations. See Misr, 14 December 1946, 1.

115. French Embassy Archives, Box 144, File 31/2, M. Gilbert Arvengas to M. Georges Bidault, 15 March 1948; Misr, 20 April 1948, 3.

116. French Embassy Archives, ibid., 29 April 1948.

117. Misr, 20 April 1948, 3.

118. Zaghib Mikhail, Farriq...Tasud! al-Wahda al-Wataniyya (no place, no publisher, no date), p.171.

119. Misr, 17 February 1951, translated in The Cry of Egypt's Copts (Phoenica Press, New York, 1951), pp.10-11.

Chapter Two

THE BRITISH, THE COPTS AND THE NATIONALIST MOVEMENT

A. BRITISH-COPTS RELATIONS BEFORE THE 1919 REVOLUTION

The British attitude towards the Egyptians was marked by a belief in the superiority of Western culture so strong that not even the fact that some Egyptians shared that culture's religion inclined the British to make exceptions. In their eyes, Coptic Orthodoxy lacked 'the true and spiritual part of Christianity',[1] and therefore bore no resemblance to European Christianity. Missionaries, frustrated in their attempts to convert Muslims, were particular proponents of this view. One Anglican association working in nineteenth-century Egypt declared its refusal to tolerate the 'soul-destroying heresy of the Copts'.[2] Many missionaries were eager to persuade Copts to adopt their brand of Christianity. As a religion replete with strange rituals and superstitions, Coptic Christianity had failed, as Cromer so nicely put it, to provide its adherents with any moral benefit.[3] Copts were sometimes portrayed as compulsive liars[4] who were servile and addicted to alcohol.[5] Perhaps behind these harsh judgments lay a dismay that the Copts, by failing to distinguish themselves from their Muslim compatriots, succeeded in questioning Western notions about Christianity's superiority to Islam.

The British in Egypt, unlike those in India, did not seem to prefer one ethnic group to another, perhaps because Egyptian communal differences were less distinctive.[6] There were, in any case, few benefits to be derived from favouring Copts in this overwhelmingly Muslim society; and the British were usually careful lest their actions be interpreted by Muslims in this light. British preferences, however, matter less than Coptic and Muslim perceptions of those preferences. Each community was convinced that the British favoured the other. Muslims believed that the British had set aside their fellow Christians for special treatment.[7] Copts, who expected this treatment, were disappointed and viewed the neglect of their complaints as indicative of a preference for Muslims.[8]

However, the Coptic attitude towards the Occupation did depend partly on the state of intercommunal relations which were in turn influenced by Muslim perceptions of the relationship between the British and the Copts. It was easier for the Copts, as Christians and an already subject people, to adjust to foreign non-Muslim rule. Whatever their differences with the British, and they had many, the Copts were accepting of a British presence whenever communal relations were strained. When relations with Muslims were good, the British presence naturally seemed less vital and desirable.

The Copts felt British injustice most keenly in the matter of the Egyptian civil service. From the time of Khedive Ismail's deposition, they saw Coptic positions sacrificed to a policy of retrenchment and then lost to Syrians and Armenians and finally the British.[9] One missionary reported in 1884 that a majority of Copts opposed the British Occupation because so many Coptic officials had been dismissed.[10] Gorst, responding to what he thought was a legitimate _Egyptian_ grievance, tried to increase Egyptian employment in the civil service. However, the Copts believed that only Muslims benefited from his plan. Copts were particularly disturbed by what they saw as the loss of senior jobs. It is unlikely that they held such jobs in great numbers before the Occupation, but it is possible that the British were reluctant to award too many top positions to Copts for fear of seeming biased. The British certainly did believe that the Copts, as non-Muslims, were ill-fitted to hold positions like those in the upper echelons of the provincial administration.[11] The Copts became increasingly dissatisfied with the British attitude towards them; and the hardships that they, along with Muslims, suffered during World War I reinforced their discontent and helped set the stage for Coptic participation in the nationalist movement.

B. ZAGHLUL, THE FORMATION OF THE WAFD AND THE 1919 REVOLUTION

Egyptian notables began meeting informally to discuss Egypt's future at the end of 1917. Other than one such visit paid by Akhnukh Fanus to Zaghlul in the spring of 1918,[12] no Copt seems to have participated in the discussions. That can be attributed partly to Zaghlul's eagerness to include elected members, among whom there were no Copts, of the old Legislative Assembly. In addition, there was a certain amount of social segregation, and both Muslims and Copts had yet to reconsider the Coptic attitude towards independence.

By the time of the Wafd's visit to Wingate in November 1918, two groups had coalesced; one around Zaghlul and the other around Prince Umar Tusun. One Copt, Sinut Hanna, had joined the Prince's circle, but he was soon lured into the Wafdist camp.[13] He was a desirable candidate owing to his influential and wealthy Bani Suwaif family and his membership, although only appointed, in the Legislative Assembly. A second Copt, George Khayyat, was recommended for membership by his fellow Asyuti, Muhammad Mahmud, and was accepted after Sinut.[14] Khayyat, a wealthy Protestant, was the American Consul in Asyut, and the Wafd had probably hoped to use him to influence American opinion.[15] The Wafd now consisted of twelve Muslims and two Copts. Wasif Ghali, son of the late Prime Minister, Butrus, was the next Copt to join the Wafd.[16] He was an obvious choice given the importance of his family and the fame that he had gained by publishing nationalist articles in the French press. The readiness of the Zaghlulists to accept Coptic supporters and allow them a productive role owed much to the political ideas of the pre-war Umma party. These post-war nationalists had no interest in pan-Islam and believed that the interests of their own country superseded all other considerations.

Little public attention was paid to the Zaghlulists until the arrest and exile of four senior members.[17] Although Misr began publishing articles lauding Copt-Muslim unity in January, neither it nor al-Watan followed the Wafd's activities until the March 1919 uprising. Other newspapers also printed articles promoting fraternity, and this helped make Coptic participation in the nationalist movement possible. Al-Watan was cautious about this idea of unity and warned of the difficculty of achieving it; without equality, noted the paper, it was a house built on sand.[18] Seeing itself as the special representative of Coptic interests, a role it did not think Misr was fulfilling, al-Watan aimed a barrage of criticism at Coptic leaders in the Wafd and claimed that they did not represent the community.[19] Not all Copts, then, supported the nationalists. Murqus Simaika insisted in January 1919 that he had no faith in Muslim justice and believed that a British yoke was lighter than a Muslim one.[20] Many, many Copts, however, supported Misr's views and were eager to play a role in the struggle for independence.

The British were incensed by this 'opportunistic' betrayal. One Englishman called it yet 'another instance of the desertion of a natural ally in our time of need'.[21] The British believed that they had been fair to the Copts but, knowing that the Copts thought otherwise, they should not have taken umbrage at the Coptic defection. One popular British explanation was that the Copts had joined the nationalists from a fear of what would happen to them if they did not.[22] It was true, as one British official later noted, that Muslim tolerance was more vital to the Copts than 'remote and not always effective alien Christian support',[23] but there was little sign of fear. The Copts had never been reluctant to voice their objections to nationalist ideas in the past. Not surprisingly, the British chose to ignore the positive reasons the Copts had for joining the movement; and some officials, despite strong evidence to the contrary, continued to believe that the Copts secretly wished the British to remain paramount in Egypt.

Salama Musa later recalled that some Muslims also suspected the new Coptic attitude; it took the 1919 revolution to remove any lingering doubts about Coptic loyalty.[24] This two-month revolution was a heady lesson in the delights of Muslim-Copt collaboration. It established an ideal unity to which Egyptians often referred because fraternal feelings were stronger at this time than at any time thereafter. Two images of the 1919 revolution dominate the Egyptian mind and Egyptian historiography: one is of a demonstration bearing aloft a banner inscribed with a crescent and cross and the other is of priests and shaikhs sharing the pulpit in mosques and churches. Memory is always selective, but in this case it is not inaccurate. Both images symbolise unity, and it is interesting that it is these symbols that prevailed rather than some gesture indicating a more active and violent resistance to the colonial regime. Perhaps the explanation for this lies in the fact that unity was such an unprecedented and therefore memorable phenomenon.

Muslim ulama and Coptic clergy did have an important role in the revolution, both in fomenting opposition to the British and in cementing unity. Shortly after news of Zaghlul's deportation spread, Murqus Sergius led a huge demonstration to al-Azhar and was the first Coptic priest to speak from its pulpit.[25] A similar invitation was extended in following days to other priests. Ahmad Amin, an Azhari alim, later recalled his fondness for demonstrations in which he in his turban shared a carriage with a priest in a cassock, the two of them a living symbol of Egyptian unity. He recollected too that he always carried with him the cross and crescent flag.[26] Sometimes nationalist demonstrations even carried pictures of the Patriarch.

Priests and shaikhs visited one another and attended each other's religious services; even the Mufti of Egypt called on the Patriarch and the latter reciprocated.[27] Until the mid-1920s, churches, like mosques, were the scene of many a meeting held in the nationalist interest. Secular politicians realised that the involvement of religion in their cause worked to their advantage; the time would come, however, when they would realise the harm it could do. The participation of the clergy had a symbolic use in illustrating Muslim tolerance and a practical one in drawing Coptic support to the nationalists. It also defeated attempts to label the nationalist movement a religious one.

The Coptic role in the revolution was highly visible and substantial, and Copts were involved in all its facets: demonstrations, strikes,[28] propaganda, terrorism,[29] organisation and policy-making. There were, for example, three Copts on a committee which organised an important and effective strike of government offficals. Nationalist committees in many provinces included Copts, and the one in Asyut contained a majority of Copts.[30]

Fraternisation between Copts and Muslims was frequent, open and somewhat ostentatious. Meetings celebrating unity were held all over Egypt, and religious holidays became special times for exhibiting brotherhood. Muslims, for example, took part in the Easter festivities of 1919,[31] and Copts helped Muslims celebrate the Id al-Fitr at the end of June.[32] More than a little bad poetry was written on the theme of unity, and Misr continued writing articles in praise of brotherhood.

After Zaghlul's release in April, Sinut, Khayyat and Wisa Wasif travelled with the Wafd to Paris for the Peace Conference. Wisa and Wasif Ghali, who was already in Paris, were put in charge of propaganda, an activity which required good French. Khayyat joined a committee charged with organising meetings. The Wafdists, with their live Copts and their written endorsements from Egyptian Jews, made it clear to those they met that they had the support of Egypt's minorities.[33]

Back at home, the Wafdist Central Committee soon had several wealthy and mainly landowning Coptic members: Murqus Hanna, leader of the Egyptian Bar since 1914; Tawfiq Dus, a clever lawyer of doubtful reputation; Kamil Butrus; Dr. Habib Khayyat, George's brother; Fahmi Wisa, another Protestant; and Sarufim Mina Ubaid.[34] In September, Sinut returned to help the Central Committee; for a time, there was some thought of sending him to the United States, but his talents as a publicist were needed in Egypt.[35] The British were soon so concerned with his denunciation of the Milner Mission that they ordered him to his country estate for a number of weeks.

Several Wafdists, recognising the need for English speakers, wanted the able Oxford-educated Copt, Makram Ubaid, to work with them. Like Sinut, Ubaid was considered for an American assignment, but he appears to have wanted too much money.[36] He also wanted to be made a member of the Wafd. However bright he appeared on paper, no one in Paris knew him personally;[37] Zaghlul wrote to one of Ubaid's advocates, Abd al-Rahman Fahmi, that he preferred to see something of Ubaid's work before adding him to the Wafd. The Central Committee in Cairo was not happy with this answer and more letters were exchanged until Ubaid was invited to join the inner circle in the spring of 1920. The party then acquired a superb orator whose skills enriched the party for many years and beggared it when he left.

Disagreements among the nationalists were more common than co-operation. There were arguments over tactics and everyone seemed to be jockeying for position. Two of Zaghlul's strongest backers in this internal wrangling were Wisa Wasif and Sinut.[38] The break came in the spring of 1921 over whether Prime Minister Adli Pasha or the more popular Zaghlul would lead negotiations with the

British. A majority of Wafdists thought Zaghlul's insistence on heading the delegation was unreasonable, and they deserted to Adli's faction.

The only three members of the original Wafd who remained with Zaghlul were Sinut, Wasif Ghali and Wisa Wasif.[39] A few months later the Wafd was even more visibly Coptic.[40] In this year and the next the Wafd lost the support of many large landowners. It is curious that Coptic landowners, by and large, did not desert the party.

Some Copts feared that this visibility would poison unity and excite popular feeling against the community.[41] Wafdists too may have feared that the conspicuousness of their Coptic members would damage the party and so they paid great attention to promoting unity in the next months. In April a Wafd publication claimed that the Egyptians were a unique and homogeneous race, sharing physical and mental characteristics.[42] Ubaid, still backing Zaghlul, claimed in another pamphlet that Egypt presented a striking example of religious toleration and unity. He praised Egyptian Muslims for rejoicing in the universal brotherhood that was the true spirit of Islam and added that the Egyptians did not make distinctions on the basis of religion.[43]

In November, Adli's negotiations with the British collapsed and he resigned from office. The following month, the British threatened Zaghlul and several supporters with banishment unless they retired to their villages. Zaghlul, Sinut, Ubaid and some others rejected the ultimatum and were exiled. The rest moved to the countryside but eventually resumed active political work. The exile, which the British hoped would strengthen the moderates, seems to have had the opposite effect. Eight of the schismatics, including George Khayyat, returned to the Wafd at this time. They probably hoped to take over the name and organisation, because most again left when they found that this would be impossible. Khayyat was one of two who stayed. Other new members were admitted to the Wafd, including Murqus Hanna, who was personally recommended by Zaghlul.[44] Wisa Wasif and Wasif Ghali published announcements stating the Wafd's determination to continue the fight.[45] Several Wafdists, including Fakhri Abd al-Nur, a wealthy Coptic landowner, published a manifesto calling for a boycott of the British. Murqus Hanna was one of the more active members and was responsible for issuing several circulars and proclamations.[46] Wafdist activities made it difficult for any Ministry to function and, in July 1922, Murqus Hanna, George Khayyat, Wasif Ghali and others were arrested and imprisoned. Arrests continued and every time Wafdist ranks were decimated, a new committee was formed. In late autumn, Raghib Iskandar, ex-member of the secularist Democratic Party,[47] and the priest Butrus Ghabryal were among those actively campaigning for the Wafd in the Delta. Fakhri, who became a member of the Wafd's inner circle in July 1922, was an active speaker. In December, another Copt, Sadiq Hinain, returned from a propaganda tour in Europe. Most of these activists were arrested at one time or another. In 1923 those under arrest and in exile were released. The Wafd then set about reorganising itself and preparing for elections. Until the 1940s, when a new generation of politicians began to come forward, most important Wafdists had something to do with the party in this period.

On more than one occasion, Zaghlul himself spoke of the brotherhood of Copts and Muslims. His tolerance and lack of any connection with pre-war communal tensions inspired both Copts to trust him and Muslims to welcome Coptic participation. It is possible that he originally sought Coptic representation in the Wafd to prove that his organisation was not fanatical or even religious;[48] but Copts who joined the party later were added because of the skills they possessed and the devotion to the cause they displayed.[49] Had these men been seen as representatives of their community, the Wafd would quickly have foundered in the aftermath of Zaghlul's break with Adli. Of course, talent was not the sole requirement for membership. The first Copts who joined the Wafd were members of prominent families which could be relied upon to contribute funds and rally support in their home province.

C. DIVIDE AND RULE

Contemporary Egyptian historiography generally attributes communal problems in the period 1882-1952 to a British policy of divide and rule.[50] This is what many people of the time believed. The Wafdist newspaper al-Balagh wrote in 1925 that the British had successfully relied on a policy of encouraging inter-communal hatred until Zaghlul succeeded in uniting the Egyptians.[51] Even before the well-being engendered by the 1919 revolution, some Muslims and Copts claimed that the Egyptians, despite religious differences, had always lived in harmony; both dated discriminatory policies from the time of the British Occupation. This trend continued into the troubled 1950s; one compendium of Coptic grievances, which was published around 1951 and immediately banned, placed British policy at the root of the communal problem.[52] This testimony became a kind of article of faith, and it certainly was wise, if not fair, to blame internal problems on outsiders.

Although British rule eventually gave Muslims and Copts the pretext on which to unite, it was also an irritant to communal relations. The comments of Lord Cromer and Edward Lane on the degree of assimilation notwithstanding, the British regarded Copts and Muslims as two distinct communities. They did, after all, expect the Copts to understand that British rule was in their interest. There is little doubt that the British found the Copts useful. Both Cromer and those missionaries working in Egypt either believed or liked to pretend that the Occupation had saved the Copts from a massacre. While it is not untrue that Ahmad Urabi, in the closing days of the 1881 revolt, tried to use religious feeling to rally supporters, it seems distinctly unlikely that the Copts were threatened with any kind of genocide. Cromer, anxious about the fate of the supposedly temporary Occupation, used alleged threats against the Copts to reinforce his superiors' determination to stay in Egypt. He never, for example, reported that some Copts opposed the Occupation;[53] and when he sent troops to Upper Egypt to extend British hegemony, his ostensible reason was to protect the Copts from the fanaticism of the Mahdi.[54] While the extent to which he personally believed that Muslim fanaticism presented a danger is unclear, it is certain that others believed it and that is was therefore a convenient instrument. Particularly in his last years as Agent, Cromer may have used religious tensions to advance both British interests and his own.[55]

Gorst, who felt that minorities were too frail a reed upon which to lean, disapproved of Cromer's tactic. Upon succeeding the latter, he hoped to make British rule 'more sympathetic to Egyptians in general and to Muslims in particular'.[56] The appointment of Butrus Ghali as Prime Minister seemed to many to be an odd way of fulfilling this ambition, and they interpreted the appointment as an attempt to detach the Coptic community from the nationalist movement.[57] This explanation seems unlikely; there was little Coptic support for the nationalists at that time and few prospects that that support would grow. Communal tensions must have made Copts reluctant to participate in a political movement that could have had an unpredictable and perhaps unfavourable effect on the community in the future. Gorst had already earned Coptic enmity by opposing communal demands, and his own inclinations suggest that he had little interest in attracting Coptic backing if it meant the further sacrifice of Muslim support. It is possible, of course, that Gorst hoped to mute Coptic opposition to him and to secure, at the same time, the good will of influential missionaries. A more plausible explanation, given the Khedive's role in the appointment and Gorst's initial objection to Ghali, can be found in the fact that Ghali was an able man who had obtained the respect of both the Khedive and the British. Gorst had a strong interest in improving British relations with the Khedive, with whom, as he well knew, Ghali had some influence.[58] Perhaps the Khedive hoped that this appointment would attract to him that Coptic support which was lost to the nationalists. It should also, however, be noted that Christian Prime Ministers could be more amenable to Khedival control than their Muslim colleagues, both because they had very little meaningful support outside the Palace and because Muslim opposition to the appointment would keep them more dependent on the good will of the Khedive.

The most frequently given example of divide and rule between 1918 and 1952 is the appointment of Yusuf Wahbah as Prime Minister in 1919.[59] This is portrayed as a British attempt to drive a wedge between Coptic and Muslim nationalists. It is not an implausible picture; the British resented Coptic adherence to the nationalist movement, and the appointment at least potentially, risked raising inter-communal suspicions with violence an all-too-likely consequence. However, Coptic opposition to the nationalists would not have been a substantial help to the British because Coptic support was not essential to the success of the nationalist movement. Their opposition would, of course, have provided a fillip to the British, who could once again use their concern for Coptic safety to justify the Occupation. If the British did have an ulterior motive in appointing a Coptic Prime Minister, there is no mention of it in the correspondence between the Agency and London. Abd al-Rahman Fahmi feared that the intention of the British was only to distract the nationalists from more pressing matters, and certainly the nationalist did feel called upon to react to the appointment.[60]

However, most suspicions about British motives fall prey to the realisation that there were almost no candidates for the office of Prime Minister. The nationalists hoped to keep the position vacant in order to deprive the Milner Mission of a government with which to negotiate. The Foreign Office feared that the Sultan would either abdicate or be assassinated if they could not find someone willing to accept the post.[61] Wahbah, who was not first choice,[62] was the best the British could do in a very difficult situation. Given British eagerness to win acceptance of the Milner Mission, they would no doubt have preferred a Muslim Prime Minister with more political credibility. Although Wahbah had served in many cabinets, including his predecessor's, he was a colourless political figure and not one around whom even the Copts would rally.[63] He answered well the dictum of one wit for those forming cabinets: 'Parmi les Coptes, cherchez la nullité'.[64] There was curiously little consultation within the British government before the appointment was made. Allenby does not seem to have discussed the matter with the Foreign Office, perhaps a sign of few options and strong backing. London was worried by Wahbah's lack of influence and character, but feared mainly that his Christianity would draw more fire than that to be expected by a Prime Minister co-operating with the British.

It is likely that Muhammad Said, Wahbah's predecessor, bears part of the responsibility for the appointment. The two men were close[65] and this was one way Said could maintain his influence. Said did not want to be blamed for talking with the Milner Mission, and the British had known that in sending the Mission they courted his resignation.[66] It was much safer for Said to resign and let Wahbah suffer the opprobrium attached to collaborating with the British.

The Coptic response to the appointment was swift and sharp; perhaps the Copts feared, as Abd al-Rahman Fahmi suggested, that their new-found unity with Muslims would founder on the rock of Yusuf Wahbah.[67] _Misr_ roundly condemned Wahbah, and Sinut, in particular attacked him in the newspaper's pages.[68] Wisa Wasif and other Copts insisted that Wahbah did not represent the community. At one November meeting, called and chaired by a representative of the Patriarcnate, two thousand Copts came to protest.[69] The speakers, including Murqus Sergius, praised national unity and swore to disavow anyone who accepted cabinet office. The meeting telegraphed to Wahbah a demand for his resignation.[70] Similar meetings were held in churches all over Egypt, and fraternisation between Copts and Muslims was particularly marked at this time.

Copts sent several delegations to remonstrate with Wahbah, and many Egyptians wrote him threatening letters.[71] Several hundred Copts signed a document repudiating him and any man who co-operated with the Protectorate. They also condemned the British for trying to make it appear that the Copts approved of the cabinet and its policy.[72] At no point did those Muslims who disapproved of Wahbah attack him on sectarian grounds. Many newspapers insisted that the cabinet was not a Coptic cabinet, and they recalled their strong attacks on the Muhammad Said Ministry.[73]

There was some support for Wahbah. The conservative al-Watan commented that unity was perhaps not as strong as the Copts like to think if they felt compelled to go to such great lengths to repudiate a Coptic Prime Minister.[74] The paper wondered why Wahbah should bear the brunt of the attack when his Muslim colleagues were just as responsible, but clearly there could be no government without a Prime Minister. Al-Watan had supported the Said ministry, so its attitude towards Wahbah was not a departure occasioned by his religion. At no point did the paper suggest that the Copts should support the cabinet because Wahbah was a Copt. Whatever the ulterior motive of the British, if there was one, Wahbah's appointment may actually have strengthened Coptic-Muslim unity, at least in the short term.

In December 1919, an unsuccessful attempt was made on Wahbah's life by Iryan Yusuf Sad, a Coptic student. Iryan had joined a secret society called the Black Hand, but his immediate superiors appear to have been working at the behest of Abd al-Rahman Fahmi's secret apparatus.[75] He volunteered for the assassination knowing that if a Muslim killed the Prime Minister, inter-communal problems could result. Wahbah was a target solely because he formed a government at a time when the nationalists hoped to prevent the formation of a government. However, his would-be assassin may have feared that Wahbah endangered the standing of the Copts.

After doing his best to avoid taking any stand on Egypt's future, Wahbah resigned in May 1920. It is not clear why he chose to accept an obviously dangerous position. Perhaps he felt that British gratitude would secure his political future; intead, it effectively ruined it. Not even the British were happy when they learnt that Wahbah would be a member of a negotiating delegation the Sultan was trying to form in 1921. They knew that he was a British creature who could not even claim to represent the Copts.[76]

The British may have practised divide and rule without having a conscious and malicious policy to that effect. Akhnukh Fanus complained in a letter to the Agency in 1906 that the British were making a 'religious consideration the basis of a civil distinction in Egypt'.[77] There is evidence that the British perpetuated and extended divisions which already existed in some form to administer India; did they also do this in Egypt? India is a useful point of comparison because the Egyptians themselves often compared their country to India. In the latter case, the British saw ethnic and religious divisions as natural ones and made use of them to govern a large and politically fragmented area; as Kenneth Jones has pointed out, sometimes the British in India were most influential when they only hoped to administer and not influence. He noted one example, that of the census, which listed people by ethnic category and therefore helped to institutionalise social divisions and create a mentality in which numbers were equated with strength.[78] For a time, the British in India organised army units by ethnic group. They also instituted communal electorates which gave rise to communal organisations making communal demands. Not all such measures were taken for administrative ease. Some clearly were designed to check Indian nationalism.[79] The Indians no doubt were conscious of religious differences, but whether these would become as politically viable as they did without British encouragement is not clear.

The Indian and Egyptian situations were not identical. The Muslims were thirty per cent of India's population; their numbers gave them a greater claim on British attention than the Copts had. In addition, there were areas in which Muslims were in a majority. The Asian subcontinent was less easy to rule than Egypt which had strong central government and accessible geography. Despite Fanus' claim, religion had been used to make civil and administrative distinctions in Egypt. The British cannot wholly be blamed if they accepted the fact that religious divisions had political importance; some Egyptians, in fact, continued to argue that religious divisions should be used as political determinants.[80] The Copts were a conscious community, feeling more in common with one another than a Bengali Muslim may have felt with a Punjabi Muslim. Because of the nature of their history and that of their country, they may also have felt more loyalty to an entity called Egypt than a Bengali Muslim to an entity called India.

The British occupied Egypt to end chaos, improve an inefficient and debt-ridden administration, forestall foreign intervention and protect communications with India. It was in their interest, therefore, to maintain a stable and peaceful government. A policy of encouraging ethnic conflict, with its potential for escalation into violence which could spark outside intervention, could well have been counter-productive to British aims. Any Muslim backlash against Coptic Christians could eventually have included foreign Christians whose home governments might have been eager to become involved. The 1919 solidarity between Muslims and Copts may even be construed, as Wingate pointed out, as a tribute to British even-handedness and the absence of any attempt to sow discord.[81] The British, in fact, were not nearly as receptive to Coptic demands in Egypt as they were to Muslim ones in India. Nor, at ten per cent of the population, were the Copts very useful as an administrative division.

If the British government did not practise a deliberate policy of divide and rule, it sometimes let the Egyptian government or the latter's opponents make unhindered use of the ethnic weapon. It seems only to have intervened when it feared that foreign Christian lives or orderly administration were threatened. Examples of political appeals made on ethnic grounds and the British reaction to them are discussed in Chapter Seven.

D. ANGLO-EGYPTIAN TREATY NEGOTIATIONS

1. Independence and the Reserved Point for the Protection of Minorities

Britain's decision to extend formal protection to Egypt's minorities was, as nationalists argued, potentially the most divisive action the British had taken. The latter, however, saw it as a partial cure for divisions already inherent in Egyptian society. They were genuinely concerned, in the wake of the Armenian massacres, for the safety of Middle Eastern minorities. In addition, missionaries in Egypt pressed the British government to protect their new converts and other Egyptian Christians. The Curzon draft treaty, presented to Sultan Fuad in December 1921, detailed civil rights for Egypt's minorities.[82] Although these negotiations were unsuccessful, the Egyptian negotiating team did accept the draft's list of civil liberties.

In February 1922, when Britain unilaterally granted Egyptian independence, it reserved certain prerogatives for itself. The third Reserved Point gave Britain the right to intervene in Egyptian affairs to protect minorities and foreigners. Although the clause may have been left deliberately vague to allow Britain a wide latitude for interference, the government does not appear to have clearly defined the protection it was offering. One confused official in the Residency noted that the guarantees in the Curzon draft had been included in haste and at the last minute; that they had had 'nothing definite in mind when they inserted it'.[83] Eventually, agreement did emerge that the protection provided in the draft treaty should guide British intervention on behalf of minorities.[84] At no time between 1922 and the conclusion of the 1936 treaty, did the British construe the reservation as merely affording the Copts the protection of life and limb. The Residency often interfered to protect the community's autonomy and integrity.[85]

Coptic opposition to the reserved point was vehement; even al-Watan condemned it.[86] The Copts insisted that they were not a minority and that any division made between Copts and Muslims was artificial.[87] They feared that this reservation would destroy national unity and serve as a ready excuse for British interference in Egyptian affairs.[88] Salama Mikhail wrote a pamphlet condemning this reservation, and Copts protested in many parts of Egypt. In one important meeting in St. Peter's church in Cairo in May, leading Coptic and Muslim Wafdists attacked all the reserved points and demanded the return of their exiled leaders.

Given the frequent declarations of unity, the British could not have been surprised by the Coptic reaction. In 1921, British negotiators had heard the Coptic ex-Minister Yusuf Suliman Pasha argue that there were no minorities and no majorities in Egypt.[89] In the 1924 negotiations, the British showed some willingness to drop their claim to protection. In April a memorandum prepared for the cabinet noted that the Copts had joined the nationalists and had secured generous representation in both parliament and the cabinet and had also obtained adequate protection in the Constitution.[90] Allenby, sharing this view, suggested that the claim of protection was an embarrassment rather than an advantage. He noted that it had acquired a false importance in Egyptian minds and suggested the British drop it.[91] A draft agreement drawn up by the Foreign Office in September did not mention minorities; Zaghlul, however, did. In the second of three conversations he had with Ramsay MacDonald, he asked the British to abandon their protection of minorities.[92] MacDonald did not reply; it was the issue of the Sudan, however, that brought the negotiations to an end.

Neither Prime Minister Tharwat's 1927 draft treaty nor the Foreign Office's amended version mentioned minorities. It would seem that the British government felt that the Egyptian Constitution adequately protected the civil rights of all Egyptians. During the 1929 Mahmud-Henderson negotiations, the British government submitted a draft Note recognising that the protection of minorities was the exclusive concern of the Egyptian government.[93] The subject was revived within British circles during the 1930 negotiations,[94] but it was not formally discussed by the negotiators.[95] Both Makram Ubaid and Wasif Ghali opposed any mention of minorities in the treaty.[96] However, Paragraph 14 of a Note attached to the Egyptian counter-draft gave the Egyptian government responsibility for its own minorities.[97]

Even after the 1930 negotiations ended in failure, missionaries continued to argue that Egyptian responsibility was contingent on the assumption that the Egyptian government adequately protected religious liberty. Because it had never done so, the missionaries wanted the issue raised at future negotiations.[98] During the 1936 negotiations, the Egypt Inter-Mission Council insisted that the treaty recognise the protection of minorities as a legitimate British concern. The Council claimed, possibly with some accuracy, that Egyptian Christians who had been satisfied with the Egyptian Note in 1930, now had some concern.[99] The Foreign Office was reluctant to raise the issue after it had already dropped it, and so tried to placate the missionaries by suggesting an Egyptian guarantee to the League of Nations.[100] After the treaty, which made no mention of minorities, was signed in 1936 and Egypt applied for League membership, missionaries began lobbying for an Egyptian promise to the League.[101] The British government pressed the Egyptian government to make a voluntary statement concerning minority rights to the League, but al-Nahhas declined to make any statement which he saw as admitting the right of other bodies to intervene in Egypt's domestic affairs.[102] Ubaid was said to be adamantly opposed to any statement because he feared the Copts would be accused of seeking foreign protection.

The Copts were not unanimous in rejecting a need for protection. In 1935, Murqus Sergius suggested that the Copts would be better off if the British remained in Egypt. He claimed that the British had filled a necessary function in protecting minorities, and he remarked on the hypocrisy of Egyptian Muslims supporting those Indian Muslims who objected to rule by the Hindu majority.[103] Increasingly, Copts came to share his view. In the period after World War II, they were alarmed by growing hostility in the Muslim community. _Misr_ demanded that the new treaty being contemplated in 1946 include a clause protecting equal rights for minorities.[104] _Misr_ also proposed that a new constitution separating religion and state be drafted in tandem with a new treaty. The paper added that the Copts had to be certain that British evacuation would not be at their expense before they could support it.[105] The Embassy noted that it had received a number of petitions from Copts expressing anxiety about the consequences of British withdrawal; many Copts appear to have held the unspoken hope that the 1946 negotiations would break down.[106] In 1947, _Misr_ criticised Ubaid for trying to arrange independence for Egypt. The paper said that it was wrong to discuss the deliverance of Egyptians from British until they had secured the deliverance of Egyptians from Egyptians.[107]

Coptic fears raise the question of how much protection the British actually afforded the community. The Copts, as previously noted, frequently called on British help to resolve internal communal problems and also problems _vis-à-vis_ the government. The British, although annoyed by Coptic importuning, acted when the government planned to strengthen the hand of the clerical party or increase its own power over the Copts. British actions were often decisive in persuading the government to abandon such plans. In 1933, the British government even discussed whether their obligation to protect minorities compelled them to intervene to secure religious instruction for Christian student in government schools.[108]

There was little the British could do to prevent sporadic violence against the Copts, although they sometimes tried.[109] They could, however, have done more to blunt some of the sectarian propaganda that helped lead to violence. They did little to stop the anti-Coptic statements of the Egyptian government or its opposition, and such statements became a general feature of election campaigns.[110] The British showed concern in only three election campaigns and, curiously, all of these occurred after the 1936 treaty was signed. Lampson intervened in 1938 and 1943. Campbell expressed official concern about the use of the Copts as a campaign tactic in 1949. He perhaps did so because the Embassy was looking forward to a Wafdist victory and did not want an already tense communal situation aggravated.

The Residency (or later the Embassy) was more likely to attempt to halt anti-Christian propaganda when that propaganda appeared to threaten foreign Christians in Egypt. In 1932-3, the Residency was very worried when Prime Minister Sidqi's opponents mounted a violent campaign against the often tactless and provocative acts of Christian missionaries. British officials raised this concern frequently with the government and Palace,[111] but were not unsympathetic with the government's plight.[112] They understood that if Sidqi's government failed to equal or outbid the opposition's demonstrated religious feeling, it risked appearing indifferent or hostile to Islam. If, on the other hand, the government took part in the campaign and attempted to take strong measures against missionaries, it risked British intervention and censure. Either way, the cabinet's longevity was threatened.

As a rule, the Embassy showed less interest in defending the Copts after signing the 1936 treaty. In 1947, one Foreign Office official minuted that, as far as they were concerned, Egypt's responsibility to the Copts was set only 'by her duties as a member of the UN, by the freedom accorded under her own constitution and by the conscience of her Ministers'.[113] Some Britons felt that the Copts were better off without foreign guarantees and that it was unwise of the Copts to lean too heavily on British support in arguments with the government. The Embassy continued to report on intercommunal relations, a sign of at least nominal concern. In 1950, there was some Anglican church pressure on the Foreign Office to safeguard religious liberties in a new Anglo-Egyptian treaty.[114] However, the Foreign Office could hardly demand new powers when the purpose of a new treaty was to reduce the old ones. Ironically, British inaction came at a time when the Copts were increasingly eager for British action. As early as 1938, one Embassy official on a visit to Upper Egypt, recorded Coptic anger at the British for failing to represent their interests. He reported a year later that the Copts were still anxious about the future;[115] it was an anxiety that grew throughout the following decade.

2. The Politics of Treaty Negotiations

No better marker of the assumptions Muslims made about the attitude of the Copts to the British exists than the public discussion of treaty negotiations. Because of this, all Egyptian negotiating teams were careful to balance Muslim and Copt members.[116] Popular beliefs had either receded or simply were not played upon until the 1929 negotiations. Then the Liberal Constitutionalists, fearing that the Wafd would sabotage their treaty, made the supposed reliance of the Copts on the British an issue. They tried to pin opposition to the treaty on the Copts and specifically on the Copts in the Wafd. This new charge was simply an extension of one made frequently in the past by al-Siyasa, as the paper itself admitted.[117] Muslims, in al-Siyasa's view, had no influence in the party and al-Nahhas was 'nothing but a zero on the left side or an instrument in Ubaid's hand'.[118]

Al-Siyasa suggested that the Copts were as concerned as were foreign communities in Egypt with what special promises would be made to them in the treaty.[119] The Copts, concluded the paper, did not want a treaty because a British evacuation would leave them at the mercy of Muslims.[120] Such statements apparently played on British fears as much as public ones. Every time the Wafd negotiated with the British, the Residency suspected that the Copts in the party would sabotage the talks.

Al-Siyasa, charging the Copts with monopolising power in the administration, reminded its readers that the Copts had recently held two portfolios and the presidency of the Senate.[121] It also complained of other prominent jobs in Coptic hands,[122] and contended that some high positions should be reserved for Muslims. To forestall doubts, al-Siyasa assured its readers that it was not prejudiced against the Copts, and incorrectly claimed that the Liberal Constitutionalist party had more Coptic members than the Wafd.[123]

Al-Siyasa's attacks soon grew ugly. The paper invented a story about Upper Egyptian tax collectors, almost all Copts, making propaganda against the treaty. It reported that these collectors were terrifying the peasantry with talk that a treaty would spark first widespread Egyptian military conscription and then war in Ethiopia on behalf of the British.[124] The peasants, remembering their treatment at the hands of the British during World War I, were not eager to repeat the experience. The collectors were also accused of claiming that the British planned to deprive Egypt of much of her water by irrigating the Sudan. Water was a delicate issue and one which easily aroused peasant fears.[125] Apparently the government, to maximise its political gains, ordered al-Siyasa's articles against the Copts to be printed in brochure form and distributed.[126]

The fact that the Liberals could think of no other weapon against Wafdist opposition to the treaty indicates a bankruptcy of policy, if not a lack of support. No doubt Wafdist agents were working against the treaty, but it is unlikely that the Wafd would have relied on men who were bitterly hated by the peasantry. Even if a majority of Coptic tax-collectors were Wafdists, and they may well have been, it is just as unlikely that they would have risked their precious jobs by spreading anti-government propaganda. The British, surprisingly, gave some credence to the Liberals' tales, although they had no more proof than al-Siyasa. Sir Percy Loraine thought the Copts in the Wafd might wreck the treaty because the British had relinquished their insistence on protecting minorities.[127]

Makram Ubaid was blamed for the Wafd's refusal to announce its opinion on the draft treaty.[128] He was singled out by al-Siyasa, not only because he was a Copt and Secretary-General of the Wafd, but because he had just returned from an anti-treaty propaganda mission to London.[129] Upon his return, a leaflet was distributed in Alexandria claiming that the Copts, wishing to destroy the treaty, had contributed £E10,000 to his mission.[130] Every issue of al-Siyasa in mid-September criticised Ubaid, and the latter felt compelled to deny publicly the newspaper's charges.[131]

Al-Siyasa accused the Copts of secretly plotting to use the nationalist movement to gain power over Muslims.[132] The newspaper al-Thaghr, in repeating such stories, warned that the majority would not submit to Coptic domination.[133] Other papers, including al-Akhbar and Avenir, joined the anti-Coptic outburst. Curiously, al-Siyasa was at the same time claiming that the Wafd, no doubt meaning the Muslim Wafd as distinct from the Coptic Wafd, was actually pleased with the treaty.[134]

Misr, al-Muqattam and al-Balagh responded with particular sharpness to these charges. The latter commented that the great nationalist, Zaghlul, had united Muslims and Copts and that al-Siyasa, in trying to divide the two, was serving British ends.[135] Al-Muqattam also harked back to the glorious days of solidarity and warned those who dragged religion into the treaty debate that it could lead to civil strife (fitna).[136] Misr, as befitted a Coptic and Wafdist newspaper, made the most vigorous defence of the Copts and the strongest attack on the Ministry for fostering a communal policy. The paper condemned al-Siyasa's attempt to destroy national unity. Like al-Balagh, Misr suggested that the Liberals were not so much protecting Islam and Muslims, as they were advancing their own political interests.[137]

In 1930, the Wafd came to power and Wisa Wasif, the new President of the Chamber, portrayed his election as a repudiation of the Liberals' anti-Coptic campaign.[138] However, al-Siyasa continued this campaign and in March was pointlessly accusing Coptic tax-collectors of working against the Wafd's treaty negotiations.[139] Understandably, the charge was subdued. It made little sense to accuse Copts of blocking a treaty which the Wafd, supposedly dominated by Copts, was doing its best to secure. Al-Siyasa even charged that Copts had too great a role in trying to secure the treaty that Copts at home opposed.[140] Religion did not colour all of al-Siyasa's remarks about the negotiations; most of them were, in fact, directed at Wafdist recalcitrance.

The Residency was even more suspicious than al-Siyasa. Sir Samuel Hoare in the Foreign Office minuted that nobody believed that the Copts wanted a change: 'Makram will simply hold out for an unobtainable maximum in order that he and his brethren may continue to be patriots and heroes...'[141] It is possible that Ubaid did feel obliged to maintain a more extreme position than his fellow Muslim delegates because his loyalty could more easily be questioned. For example, in November 1929, he was said to be trying to convince al-Nahhas of the necessity of scrapping the Mahmud-Henderson draft treaty and beginning negotiations again from scratch. Other Wafdists wished to start negotiations with Mahmud's draft. However, Makram had a point; as even the Residency grudgingly admitted, the Wafd could not condemn Mahmud and accept Mahmud's treaty.[142] Makram proved particularly obstreporous during the 1945-46 treaty revision negotiations, but this pose was conconant with his increasing use of anti-British zeal as a political tactic. Despite these instances, Makram played a significant role in obtaining agreement on a treaty in 1936. His helpful attitude was remarked on more than once by the British.[143] Later, when negotiations broke down, Makram and David Kelly drafted a formula that allowed the negotiators successfully to conclude the treaty.[144] There seems to be no evidence that Makram or any other Copts on negotiating missions sabotaged any treaty because they desired the British to remain in Egypt.

E. SUMMARY

Paradoxically, then, the British presence in Egypt was both a restraint on and an encouragement of Muslim hostility to Copts. It was inevitable that some Muslims would identify the Copts with their British overlords because of the shared religion of the two. The British expectation that Copts and Muslims would have different interests and would respond differently to the Occupation did not help the Copts secure good relations with their compatriots. The presence of British troops in the country peobably was reassuring to many Copts; but the British disinclination to act after 1936, at a time when the community was increasingly threatened, left the British presence only as a provocation and aggravation of Muslim feeling without doing anything to secure Coptic safety and equality.

NOTES

1. M.L. Whately, Among the Huts in Egypt (Seeley, Jackson and Halliday, London, 1873), pp.149-50.
2. S.H. Leeder, Modern Sons of the Pharaohs (Arno Press, New York, 1973), p.310. (First published 1918.)
3. Lord Cromer, Modern Egypt, II (Macmillan, London, 1908), p.205.
4. Leeder, Modern Sons, p.328.
5. Ibid., p.327, quoting Blackwood's Magazine, August 1911.

6. Cromer wrote that bigotry, ignorance and vice were traits shared by both Muslims and Copts. Cromer, Modern Egypt, II, p.207.

7. Copts seeking jobs from British employers sometimes made their appeal in the name of the Saviour. Leeder, Modern Sons, p.326.

8. See Kiriakus Mikhail's letter of complaint to The Times, 20 September 1910, quoted in FO.371/894, 38033/38033/16.

9. Murqus Simaika listed the grievance about the civil service as one reason why the Copts joined the nationalists in 1919. FO.371/3711, J12835/1180/16. Hourani also thinks that fewer Coptic officials were employed in this period than previously. Albert Hourani, Minorities in the Arab World (no publisher, London, 1947), p.229.

10. CMS Archives, Klein to the Secretary of CMS, 7 July 1884, E/133.

11. FO.141/742, 4902/2/17.

12. Lashin Abd al-Khaliq Lashin, Sad Zaghlul wa Dawrah fi al-Siyasa al-Misriyya, II (Maktabat Madbuli, Cairo, 1975), p.121.

13. Perhaps Sinut felt that the Prince, in the long run, would be less hospitable to the Copts than the Zaghlulists. Al-Aqqad suggests that he was offered Wafd membership only when it was learnt that he was about to join a delegation that Muhammad Said was trying to form. Abbas al-Aqqad, Sad Zaghlul: Sira wa Tahiya (al-Matbaat al-Hijaziyya, Cairo, 1936), p.256.

14. Zaghlul mentioned this fact in his diary. It is quoted in Lashin, Sad Zaghlul, II, p.163.

15. The Zaghlulists were aware of the influence that missionaries had on their home governments. The British saw Khayyat as a nonentity and it is true that his political career was undistinguished. He was, however, very active in the early years and was arrested twice in 1922. He was perhaps chosen to represent the well-educated and well-off Protestant community. FO.371/3204, J195347/186090/16.

16. There are several versions of how the Copts joined the Wafd. Fakhri Abd al-Nur recalls that he took the initiative, talking first to Ali Sharawi about the possibility of Coptic representation and then to Copts in the Ramses Club. The latter appointed a delegation of three, including Fakhri and Sinut to visit Zaghlul. When the four men met, Wasif Ghali was the first person they chose, then Sinut and Khayyat. Ghali only joined later than these two because the cable inviting him

went astray. Abbas al-Aqqad, on the other hand, suggests that the Copts sent Wisa Wasif to talk to Sad and that Wisa, himself declining to be the first Coptic member, suggested Ghali. There seems to be no confirmation of either tale in Zaghlul's diary. Fakhri Abd al-Nur, 'Mudhakkirati', al-Musawwar, 21 March 1969, p.34; Abbas al-Aqqad, Sad Zaghlul, pp.225-6.

17. As Muhammad Mahmud pointed out to Grafftey-Smith. Lawrence Grafftey-Smith, Bright Levant (John Murray, London, 1970), p.65.

18. Al-Watan, 7 March 1919, 1; 7 February 1919, 1; and 16 April 1919, 2.

19. Tariq al-Bishri, 'Misr al-Haditha bain Ahmad w-al-Masih', al-Katib 115 (1970), 137-8.

20. FO.371/3711, J12835/1180/16.

21. Murray Harris, Egypt Under the Egyptians (Chapman and Hall, London, 1925), p.162.

22. Ibid., p.162; FO.371/3717, 8291/24930/15.

23. FO.141/685, 8424/51/27.

24. Musa, The Education of Salama Musa, p.108.

25. Sergius was nick-named 'the silver-tongued'. He was arrested that spring after an incendiary four-hour speech at a mosque in Cairo. Ahmad Abukif, 'Sergius Khatib Thawrat 1919', al-Musawwar, 7 March 1969, 34. FO.371/3720, 152737/24930/16.

26. Ahmad Amin, My Life, translated by Issa Boullata (E.J. Brill, Leiden, 1978), p.133.

27. Egyptian Mail, 21 March 1919, 2. Azhari ulama and students also visited the Patriarch. Fakhri Abd al-Nur, 'Mudhakkirati' (unpublished typescript, 1924), p.2.

28.For example, Raghib Iskandar was a leading agitator among railway workers in 1919. FO.371/4983, J1495/93/16.

29. Both Raghib and Najib Iskandar belonged to secret societies. The famous Vengeance Society had six Coptic members and yet another society, the Torch, was headed by Murqus Hanna and Najib Ghali.

30. FO.371/3715, 59542/24930/16.

31. FO.371/3717, 87540/24930/16.

32. DW Mahfuzat Raqm 1, Makhtut Raqm 4, Abd al-Rahman Fahmi's Memoirs (unpublished), 29 June 1919, p.424.

33. Mahmud Abu al-Fatah, Maa al-Wafd al-Misri (no publisher, no place, no date), pp.68-9.

34. DW Mahfuzat Raqm 1, Makhtut Raqm 3, Abd al-Rahman Fahmi's M moirs, 11 April 1919, pp.272-4.

35. FO.371/3720, J152737/24930/16. See his influential series of articles in Misr: 15 October 1919, 2; 3 November 1919, 1; and 10 November 1919, 1.

Al-Watan attacked Sinut for his articles critical of the Ministry on 13 November 1919, 3, 24 November 1919, 2, and 25 November 1919, 1.

36. Muhammad Anis, D rasat fi Wathaiq Thawrat 1919, Vol.I (Cairo, no date), pp.54-5.

37. Muhammad Mahmud probably saw Ubaid as a threat to his position. He had already quarrelled with Sidqi, and Zaghlul may have been reluctant to upset him further by admitting Ubaid to membership. Thawrat 1919 (Muassasat al-Ahram, Markaz al-Wathaiq w-al-Buhuth al-Taarikhiyya li-Misr al-Muasira, Cairo, n.d.), pp.444-5.

38. When Abd al-Rahman Fahmi was arrested that summer, Sinut Hanna wanted to break off negotiations with the British, and quarrelled bitterly with Adli over the issue. Even Zaghlul thought that Sinut had been overly zealous in the matter. Sinut may have been one of the few in Paris to know about the secret terrorist organisation run by Fahmi. See al-Akhbar, 21 August 1963, 4; Bah , al-Aqbat, p.545; Dr. H. Munis, 'Dawr al-Aqbat fi Thawrat 1919', Akhir Saa, 16 May, part 2, 1973, 21.

39. George Khayyat did not leave at this point, but drifted away a few months later.

40. The Residency reported that the Wafd had six Coptic and two or three Muslim members. The Copts were Sinut, Ubaid, Wisa Wasif, Sadiq Hinain and Salama Mikhail. The last two were actually added in 1922 and not in 1921 as the report suggests. FO.407/190, No.55, Report on the General Situation in Egypt, 4-10 August 1921.

41. Al-Watan, 25 June 1921, 3.

42. DW Mahfuzat Majlis al-Wuzara, Mawduat Majlis al-Nizar, 13J, Sad Zaghlul w-al-Dustur, Mufawadat al-Wafd al-Misri, 22 April 1921.

43. W. Makram Ebeid, Complete Independence v. the Milner Scheme (The Caledonian Press, London, 1921), p.9.

44. FO.407/213, J395/395/16.

45. Al-Bishri, al-Katib 115 (1970), 128.

46. He was doing this in conjunction with Salama Mikhail. FO.407/193, E4241/61/16.

47. The Democratic Party was founded in 1919 to advocate secularism and democratic government. The Copt, Aziz Mirhum, was Secretary-General of the party until its collapse in 1922. The party split over the issue of negotiations in 1921. A majority of the Executive sided with Adli and, in a somewhat questionable manner, added several new members to thwart those members backing Zaghlul. Raghib Iskandar, then a member of the Executive, resigned

and became a Wafdist. FO.407/186, No.35, Field-Marshal Viscount Allenby to Lord Curzon, 12 January 1920; Charles Smith Muhammad Husayn Haykal, pp.177-81.

48. Al-Bishri, al-Katib 115 (1970), 126. Some nationalists were eager to prove that their movement was not a religious one. At one April 1919 strike meeting, Azhari students demanded public recognition of this fact. FO.371/3717, 75215/24930/16.

49. One exception to this was the appointment of Murqus Hanna as Vice-President of the Central Committee, a move meant to counter the appointment of Yusuf Wahbah as Prime Minister.

50. However, Egyptian historians vary in their willingness to recognise the existence of communal problems. Some cling tenaciously to the myth of undisturbed unity.

51. Ahmad Shafiq, Hawliyat Misr al-Siyasiyya, Vol.2 (1925) (Matbaat Shafiq Basha, Cairo, 1929), pp.449-50.

52. Zaghib Mikhail, Farriq Tasud! Al-Wahda al-Wataniyya w-al-Akhlaq al-Qawmiyya (no publisher, Cairo, no date), p.10.

53. Seikaly, 'The Copts', p.124.

54. Ibid., p.98.

55. Mellini, Sir Eldon Gorst, pp.125-8.

56. The London and Egyptian English-language press were unhappy with Gorst and wrote sympathetically about Coptic demands in the hope of embarrassing him. Ibid., pp.128, 144, 152, 208-13.

57. Wilfred Blunt was one such individual. Peter Mellini, Gorst's biographer, appears to be another. Ronald Storrs also thought that Gorst had advised the Khedive to appoint Ghali, but he did not attempt to explain Gorst's motives. Mellini, Sir Eldon Gorst, pp.166-7; Storrs, Orientations, p.71.

58. Mellini, Sir Eldon Gorst, p.166.

59. Anis, Darasat Wathaiq, I, p.50. Mahfuzat Raqm 1, Makhtut Raqm 5, Abd al-Rahman Fahmi's Memoirs, 3 December 1919, p.625. It was Fahmi who arranged for Murqus Hanna's appointment as Vice-President of the Central Committee.

60. Anis, Darasat Wathaiq, I, pp.50-1.

61. FO.371/3720, 145201/24930/16.

62. Sirri Pasha, who was offered the post first, declined.

63. In the opinion of Murqus Simaika, Wahbah had shown no interest in the concerns of his community since the early 1890s and was of no use to the Copts as a Cabinet Minister. FO.371/3711, 12835/1180/16.

64. FO.371/3717, 75210/24930/16.

65. Qalini Fahmi, whose comments on colleagues must be viewed with caution, suggested in January 1919 that Yusuf Wahbah had risen to high office by bribing Muhammad Said. FO.371/3711, 12835/1180/16.

66. FO.371/3720, J153490/24930/16.

67. Anis, Darasat Wathaiq, I, .51.

68. See Misr, 22 November 1919, 1.

69. Egyptian Mail, 25 November 1919, 1.

70. Abd al-Rahman al-Rafii, Thawrat Sanat 1919, Vol.2 (Maktabat al-Nahda al-Misriyya, Cairo, 1946), p.82.

71. The Times, 2 December 1919.

72. Egyptian Mail, 25 November 1919, 1.

73. See al-Ahali, quoted in the Egyptian Mail, 28 November 1919, 2.

74. Al-Watan, 24 November 1919, 2.

75. When Zaghlul formed a cabinet, Iryan was pardoned and put on salary. Al-Bishri, al-Katib 115 (1970), 135; Mustafa Amin, al-Kitab al-Mamnu: Asrar Thawrat 1919, Vol.1 (Dar al-Maarif, Cairo, 1976), pp. 133-4.

76. FO.371/6293, E2839/260/16.

77. CAS Box C1: Coptic Question 1, Letter from A. Fanus to Harry Boyle, November 1906.

78. Kenneth Jones, Arya Dharm: Hindu Consciousness in the Nineteenth-century Punjab (University of California Press, Berkeley, 1976), p.317. The Egyptian census also broke the population down into religious groups.

79. One example is Lord Curzon's 1904 creation, over the objections of many Muslims and all Hindus, of Muslim and Hindu provinces in the previously united Bengal. Some scholars see this as an attempt to foster Muslim at the expense of Hindu power. Asoka Mehta and Achyut Patwardhard, The Communal Triangle in India (Kitabistan, Allahabad, 1942), pp.54, 75.

80. See Kyriakus Mikhail's letter to The Times, 20 September 1910, reprinted in FO.371/894, 38033/38033/16. Another one who felt that Muslims and non-Muslims should be separated administratively was an interpreter in the Mixed Court of Appeals in Alexandria. FO.371/3717, 82216/24930/16.

81. FO.371/3711, J1235/1180/16.

82. The rights in the Curzon draft, the relevant portions of which are included below, were modelled on those in the Treaty of Sèvres and were more explicit than those included in the Egyptian Constitution:

24. Egypt undertakes to assure full and complete protection of life and liberty to all inhabitants of Egypt, without distinction of birth, nationality, language, race or religion. All inhabitants of Egypt shall be entitled to the free exercise, whether public or private, of any creed, religion or belief, whose practices are not inconsistent with public order or public morals.
25. All Egyptian nationals shall be equal before the law, and shall enjoy the same civil and political rights without distinction as to race, language or religion.
Differences of religion, creed or confession shall not prejudice any Egyptian national in matters relating to the enjoyment of civil or political rights, as, for instance, admission to public employments, functions and honours or the exercise of professions and industries.
26. Egyptian nationals who belong to racial, religious or linguistic minorities shall enjoy the same treatment and security in law and in fact as the other Egyptian nationals. In particular, they shall have an equal right to establish, manage and control, at their own expense, charitable, religious and social institutions, schools and other educational establishments, with the right to use their own language and to exercise their religion freely therein.

83. FO.371/452, 14544/5/22.

84. FO.141/452, 14544/1/22.

85. For example, in 1934 the Foreign Office instructed the Residency to raise, with the King if necessary, the Egyptian government's unsatisfactory attitude on the subjects of religious instruction for Coptic students in government elementary schools and the reform of non-Muslim personal status jurisdiction. See Chapter Six for more details. FO.371/17976, J2067/7/16.

86. _Al-Watan_, 11 March 1922, 1.

87. _Misr_, 5 March 1922, 1.

88. _Al-Watan_, 6 March 1922, 2.

89. _Misr_, 15 February 1939, 1, 10.

90. FO.371/10040, E3242/368/16.

91. FO.371/10042, E6661/368/16.

92. This meeting was held on 29 September. FO.371/10042, E8440/368/16.

93. For the text see FO.371/13850, J3287/5/16.

94. The Egypt Inter-Mission Council suggested that the Egyptian government send a Note saying that

Egyptians would respect the liberties guaranteed by their constitution. Booth, the Judicial Adviser, thought it unwise to press Egyptian delegates on this issue. FO.141/626, 223/7/30, 223/9/30, 223/13/30; FO.141/771, 405/6/31, 405/7/31. American missionaries seemed even more concerned than British missionaries. Owing at least in part to this pressure, the State Department instructed the American Ambassador to Great Britain to raise the subject with the Foreign Office and to state that the view of the Egypt Inter-Mission Council was considered reasonable by the US government. US Department of State Archives, No.883.404/18 and 20 (1930, file 59).

95. FO.141/771, 405/6/31.

96. FO.141/6262, 223/40/30.

97. FO.371/14612, J1432/4/16.

98. FO.141/626, 223/42/30.

99. FO.141/613, 376/1/36.

100. FO.141/613, 376/4/36. The idea of a guarantee to the League was discussed as early as 1931. FO.141/771, 405/6, 7/31.

101. The missionaries, who had the support of the Archbishop of Canterbury, were thinking along the lines of a similar Iraqi promise made to the League.

102. FO.371/23365, J2896/1342/16.

103. Al-Manara al-Misriyya, 18 February 1935, 3-5. Prior to this, in 1933 during an anti-missionary campaign, Sergius said he feared that the Copts who had supported British withdrawal had done so only to find that the Muslims wished to rule Egypt alone. Al-Siyasa condemned Sergius for this comment which it said suggested that the Copts ought to prefer a continuing British presence in Egypt. See al-Siyasa, 10 July 1933, 4.

104. Misr's reason was that the constitution named Islam the religion of state. Misr, 29 November 1946, 1.

105. Misr, 15 April 1946, 1.

106. FO.371/53331, J2368/57/16. FO.371/53304, J2076/39/16.

107. Misr, 15 April 1947, 3.

108. FO.371/17032, J1647/1647/16. See Chapter Six for further discussion of this topic.

109. In one early example, the British pressed the Egyptian government in 1853 to stop the Cairene ulama from fanning fanaticism. Seikaly, 'The Copts', p.20.

110. See Chapter Seven for more details.

111. See, for example, FO.141/752, 353/42/33; 353/96/33.

112. FO.141/752, 353/42/33.

113. FO.371/63029, J802/152/16.

114. Misr, 9 October 1950, 1.

115. FO.407/224, Enclosure in No.2, A Report on a Visit to Upper Egypt by Mr. Hamilton, December 1939.

116. The British could explain the presence of Uthman Muharram on the 1930 negotiating team only by saying that he was needed to prevent the Coptic members from being in the majority. The delegation was later expanded. FO.371/14607, J635/4/16.

117. Al-Siyasa, 8 September 1929, Palace Press Files.

118. Al-Siyasa, quoted in Mustafa al-Feki, 'Makram Ubayd: A Coptic Leader in the Egyptian National Movement', unpublished PhD thesis, University of London, 1977, p.111.

119. Al-Siyasa, 8 September 1929, Palace Press Files.

120. Al-Siyasa, 29 and 30 May 1929, Palace Press Files.

121. Al-Siyasa, 11 September 1929, Palace Press Files.

122. Al-Siyasa, 17 September 1929, Palace Press Files.

123. Al-Feki, 'Makram Ubayd', p.111.

124. The fighting was supposed to take place because of an argument over the headwaters of the Nile. Misr, 8 September 1929, 2.

125. Al-Siyasa, 6 September 1929, Palace Press Files.

126. Journal de Caire, 18 September 1929, Palace Press Files.

127. FO.371/13847, J2615/5/16.

128. Al-Siyasa, 11 September 1929, Palace Press Files.

129. Al-Siyasa, 6 September 1929, Palace Press Files.

130. Al-Feki, 'Makram Ubayd', p.110.

131. Misr, 17 September 1929, 3.

132. In the newspaper's view, only fanatical Copts joined the Wafd. Al-Siyasa, 17 September 1929, Palace Press Files.

133. Egyptian Gazette, 14 September 1929, 2; FO.407/209, Enclosure in No.33, Memorandum respecting the Egyptian Press, 7-13 September 1929.

134. Misr, 17 September 1929, 3.

135. Al-Balagh, 30 May 1929, Palace Press Files.

136. Al-Muqattam, 11 September 1929, Palace Press Files.

137. Misr, 13 September 1929, 1.

138. Misr, 15 January 1930, 1. Al-Siyasa complained that only Coptic societies had been given notice of the celebrations scheduled for the opening of Parliament.

139. Misr, 7 March 1930, 1.

140. Al-Siyasa, 6 April 1930, 1. See also 9 February.

141. FO.371/14611, J1308/4/16.

142. FO.371/13849, J3132/5/16.

143. See British praise for Makram's 'superhuman efforts' in FO.371/20115, J6712/2/16. See also, FO.371/20115, J6711/2/16. By contrast, Mahmud's obstructionism is condemned in more than one passage; nor surprisingly, non-Wafdists on the negotiating team were less than eager to help the Wafd obtain a treaty. See FO.371/20115, J6712/2/16 and J6528/2/16.

144. Sir David Kelly, The Ruling Few (Hollis and Carter, London, 1952).

Chapter Three

THE LIMITS OF THE POLITICAL COMMUNITY AND EGYPT'S NATIONAL IDENTITY

A. RELIGION AND THE POLITICAL SYSTEM

Perhaps the most fundamental effect of Western influence was to call into question the very foundation of Egyptian society and politics. Egyptian intellectuals were confronted with the problem of why their society and also others ruled by Muslims had failed to keep pace with those technological advances which had allowed the West to establish hegemony over the East. If Muslim society were innately inferior, as Europeans liked to think, what then did this say about Islam, at the heart of Egyptian and Arab civilisation?

Europeans often blamed Islam for the backwardness of the Muslim world. Some Egyptians accepted this interpretation and were ready to condemn the religion in its entirety; others preferred to cast their stone at the role Islam had ideally and historically played in politics. Religious opinion, of whatever shade, was naturally concerned to prevent both this denigration and any corresponding praise, however implicit, of Christianity as responsible for European success.[1]

To identify the causes of the weakness was at the same time to suggest remedies. There was no consensus on either, except perhaps that some change was necessary. Remedies centred around what should be adopted from the West and what indigenous traditions could be profitably retained. Secularists, for example, constructed an entirely new foundation, based on reason and common interests, for politics and society. In their ideal society, religion was removed from the public sphere and restricted to the private. Traditional Muslims, on the other hand, upheld the older belief that Islam was inseparable from politics. The fact that the two were not then inseparable was blamed for the Islamic world's loss of independence;[2] Muslims had failed to follow the principles of their religion and were suffering the consequences. The ideal was a society organised around Islam and for the fundamental purpose of practising Islam. The boundaries of the political community were set by adherence to Islam and therefore could include only Muslims.

Those on the Islamic side of the fence differed among themselves on the amount of borrowing permissible.[3] However, there was some consensus that the kind of borrowing advocated by the secularists would create a poor Egyptian copy of Europe and would give the West a greater hold over the East. They would not abandon religious feeling as society's main bond,[4] and many saw only a purified and revitalised Islam as capable of defeating Western control and protecting the territorial and cultural integrity of the Muslim peoples. Some Muslims saw this purified Islam and the society it would spawn as the goal; others, like al-Afghani, took a more instrumental view of religion.

This debate began in the nineteenth century. One religious thinker who had some influence in the first part of this century was Rashid Rida. His journal, _al-Manar_, consistently called for a return to the simplicity of an earlier Islam, and a society in which the connection between religion and government was closer than it was in twentieth-century Egypt.[5] Rida tried to prove that the Muslim world's backwardness was due to problems that could be solved and not to innate inferiority. One article in _al-Manar_ saw an explanation in moral depravity and the ignorance of science.[6] For Rida, religion was the root of political and social cohesion. As a Syrian and devout Muslim, he wanted to rid the Middle East of non-Muslim rule, but not by means of nationalism. For example, _al-Manar_ criticised the Liberal Constitutionalist _al-Siyasa_ for calling 'a Muslim and an Arab...a foreigner if he does not belong to the same country as themselves'.[7] Although Rida's journal failed to survive his death in 1935, some of his views found new champions, most notably in the Muslim Brethren.

The more conservative Egyptian religious establishment also argued for Islam to be given more power over people's lives.[8] For them, this was a 'bread and butter' issue; and they tended, like Rida, to see 'nationality' as determined by religion. Such thinking was interpreted, not without justice, by the Copts and even by the British, as saying that there was no real and meaningful place for non-Muslims in a Muslim country.

A number of organisations, whose political strength was based partly on their religious commitment, advocated a greater say for religion in politics and criticised the more secular political parties for a lack of devotion to Islam. Misr al-Fatat (Young Egypt), renamed the National Islamic Party in 1940, was one group that was vocal in its support of Islamic principles. It demanded, like the Shabab Muhammad (Young Men of Muhammad) who were a splinter group of the Muslim Brethren, that Islamic religious law serve as the basis for legislative life. From the very beginning Young Egypt mixed its political propaganda, which was nationalist and zenophobic, with religion.[9] As early as 1934, the Residency defined the group's 'ultimate goal' as Egyptian leadership of Islam in alliance with other Arab powers.[10] While Young Egypt did have Coptic members, these Copts were not of any statistical or real importance. Most of the group's Cairo branches were in Muslim areas and there were several around al-Azhar. In 1934, Azharis were reported to be joining the organisation in substantial numbers.[11] The Young Men of Muhammad also advocated the replacement of parliament by Islam's Majlis al-Shura (Consultative Council), the boycott of anything made or delivered by non-Muslims and the restitution of the jizya tax.[12]

The Shabab were a fringe group, but the Muslim Brethren were not; and this latter organisation, with its large following became the most powerful exponent of an Islamic order. In their eyes, any division between religious and political life was artificial,[13] and they blamed the West for denying Islam its right to rule.[14] Because the state existed only to serve religion,[15] the Brethren were critical of the political élite for failing to protect Islam.[16] Much of their activity was directed against Western hegemony, and they made a strong claim at a time when the Wafd was losing credibility, to be considered the only genuine nationalists. It was a nationalism, however, that rested more on religious feeling than any sense of territorial identity.

The ideal of Islamic unity exerted a strong pull on some Muslims, for whom the wholly imaginary simplicity of an earlier time when the Muslim world was united was a compelling vision. One symbol of that unity was the Caliphate, the supreme Islamic religious office, abolished by the Turks in 1924.

Many Muslims seemed eager to re-establish the position, and potential political gains as well as religious duty figured in their attempts. In Egypt, public feeling was strong mainly in the few years following Turkey's unilateral action, although there was some renewal of sentiment when the young and seemingly pious Faruq ascended the throne in 1936. The Caliph had, after all, sat far away in Istanbul and had only marginally affected Egyptian lives. Many *ulama* were sincere in their desire for a Caliph,[17] even if their activity was conveniently tied to King Fuad's and later Faruq's ambition to be named Caliph.[18]

Neither the Wafd nor the Liberal party wanted an Egyptian Caliph.[19] Both understood that no political party could compete with a Caliph-King whose political authority derived from religious rather than constitutional sources. It was not easy, however, to oppose the Caliphate and maintain a reputation for religiosity, particularly when each party was trying to denigrate the other's commitment to Islam.

The Copts were wary of the Caliphate and indeed all Islamic unity schemes. They understood that Egypt could not survive as a semi-secular democratic system were its monarch named Supreme Commander of all Muslims, even if the domain of his Caliphate coincided with Egypt's borders. The Coptic press was justifiably cautious in its comments in the 1920s, when enthusiasm and hope for a revival were strongest.[20] Later, the Coptic press, if not frank, was at least more open in its concern; this mirrored the freedom the Wafd then felt to voice its convictions.[21]

All elements of the press wrote about Islamic issues such as this, and many devoted increasing space to them from the 1930s. The party press could not afford to be left behind some of the more vigorous Islamic groups. Even the Wafdist press fell prey to this need; witness the name chosen for one of the later Wafdist newspapers, *al-Jihad* (The Holy War). In 1947, another Wafdist paper, *al-Misri*, termed India's declaration of war against Pakistan a war against Islam. At the same moment, the Wafdist *al-Balagh*, whose editor Abd al-Qadir Hamza, was for some years involved in Islamic-Arab affairs, was listing the advantages of Islamic unity. Salama Musa was perhaps understandably moved to comment that it was no longer easy to distinguish between the Wafdist and Muslim Brethren press.[22] Several of the literati mirrored this press interest and took up writing about traditional Islamic themes and heroes: some of these, like Muhammad Husain Haikal and Taha Husain, had promoted secular ideas in the past. It seems clear that this heightened interest in Islamic themes both responded to and encouraged the renewal of religious sentiment in Egypt.

The Copts did have a say in this debate about the nature of Egyptian society and politics, although their right to speak up was not universally accepted in Egypt and their comments were increasingly discredited and ignored as time passed. Many Copts with an interest in national affairs promoted secular ideas. The traditional tie between Islam and government had precluded an identifiable non-Muslim role in determining the course of society and politics, and had made the Copts marginal. Only by excluding religion from government or by the more personal act of conversion to Islam, could the Copts escape their marginality. Secularism promised to broaden the political community and reduce the political and social importance of the division between Muslims and Christians. Copts, who had new ambitions raised by the spread of Western ideas, could opt for nothing else, and they understandably saw the confusion of Islam and politics[23] as something directly harmful to their interests; it threatened both liberty and tolerance. Misr insisted that theocracy was anachronistic and that only secular democratic government was akin to the spirit of the age.[24] Salama Musa, one of the most important Coptic secularists,[25] promoted a Western conception of religion: both Islam and Christianity were designed to be religions of private faith and not government supervision. Both Misr and al-Watan consistently promoted the separation of religion and politics:

> The world knows...that the source of grief and war to humanity throughout history has been the appeal of religion to politics and the refuge politics has found in religion. Peace and prosperity were established in a country only when politics and religion were kept apart.[26]

Of course, Christian advocacy of a Western orientation drew suspicion because the Copts, after all, shared a religion with the hated British. One contemporary scholar insists that the Copts should have recognised that Islam was 'the chief safeguard of man's identity in that part of the world, the champion par excellence in the long conflict between East and West...,' but they could not share his conclusion that doing so would lead to a common victory.[27] Unlike many Egyptian Muslims, the Copts did not feel compelled to defend a whole civilisation against Europe. While they might have felt a strong tie to eastern Christianity, they had no similar tie to Islamo-Arab culture and were not inclined to dispute Western claims about that culture's inferiority. Some might even have advanced such claims in order to lay the groundwork for a new secular society.

There were, of course, many Muslims who rejected the idea that Islam was a suitable basis for political life. They hoped that a Western democratic government would do for Egypt what others believed Islam could do: free Egypt and establish a more just and egalitarian society. Lutfi al-Sayyid was one of the first to help lay a foundation for a polity in which Muslims and Copts could participate on an equal basis.[28] He rejected pan-Islamic unity as far-fetched, and believed that only common interests, which were determined largely by shared geographic space, could unite men. As the 1911 Heliopolis Conference's Organising Committee's report, which was read by Lutfi, declared, there could be 'no doubt that political strife between individuals and parties should be based on their respective interests and not their religious beliefs'.[29] Among those intellectuals who shared his bent were Haikal, Taha Husain, Tawfiq al-Hakim, Mahmud Azmi and Khalid Muhammad Khalid. Their society was one in which reason would guide action and religion fill spiritual needs.[30]

It was the secularists who dominated politics in the 1920s. The two major political groups of this decade and perhaps the era, the Wafd and Liberal Constitutionalist parties, were founded as secular organisations aimed at obtaining power within the framework of a democratic system. Neither, however, was able to resist the occasional temptation to make improper political use of religious issues; they were not so unlike the royalist parties in this.[31] As one Residency official put it in 1934, 'Heresy-hunting is...a popular activity of the Opposition press in Egypt under any regime...'[32] Two later political groups, the Sadist party and the Wafdist Bloc, were both splinter groups of the Wafd and adhered to its secular ideas. Almost all parties, however, capitulated to the strong religious feelings evident in the 1940s. It is interesting to speculate whether the Coptic politician Makram Ubaid became at this time a peculiarly rabid anti-British nationalist precisely because he could not use Islam[33] and needed something to equal its intensity. It was the manifest strength of these feelings that forced the Copts out of the political arena and left few Muslims secularists with the courage both to defend and encourage Coptic participation. It was not that the religious thinkers had finally defeated the secularists, but the balance seemed definitely to have shifted.

B. THEORIES OF HISTORY AND NATIONAL UNITY

History, except as practised in some academic circles, is rarely the simple rendering of a factual past but usually serves current needs and is moulded by them. Many Egyptian intellectuals of this era were absorbed by the question of who the Egyptians were and how they defined their heritage. Egyptian history was long and splendid, but not all parts of it were equally appealing to all readers. Some rejected segments of that history for political or religious reasons,[34] others neglected parts through sheer ignorance. Some described the inhabitants of the Nile Valley as Arabs and others as Egyptians, Muslims or Europeans. As Mirrit Ghali has suggested, this inability to agree on an identity is partly due to a tendency to see Egypt's historical periods as self-contained and mutually exclusive.[35]

This problem of competing definitions was not a negligible one. Membership in the Egyptian nation could be made exclusive, and the excluded could eventually lose their right to participate in politics. Egypt had been defined, and still was by many, as a Muslim country. The Copts could not belong to a culture or polity defined by Islam. Coptic and Muslim secularists tried, partly through their use of history, to base the Egyptian identity on something other than religion. Coptics efforts contributed towards the development of a theory of Egyptian character which included Muslims and Copts and ignored the one source of division between the two, religion.

1. Egyptianism

There are several important Egyptian nationalists, Lutfi al-Sayyid and Zaghlul among them, who sought to build a nationalism based on Egypt as a territorial entity and to impose this modern allegiance on the older one. In pursuit of this objective, they proposed that the Egyptian character was unique; sharing some traits with other peoples, but still possessing a particular identity based on a particular historical experience. Some nationalist thinkers began with Pharaonic Egypt and tried to reconcile this civilisation with subsequent periods. Others concentrated solely on the Pharaonic heritage and neglected 1,300 years of Egypt's Arab and Islamic history. Whatever the emphasis and however great the recognition of historical continuity, ancient Egypt was an age in which most Egyptians could take pride. A polity which was sovereign and powerful and a civilisation which was advanced gave some promise of the heights to which Egypt could legitimately aspire.[36]

Sparked by excavations beginning in the last century and fuelled by the discovery of Tut Ankh Amun's tomb in 1922, interest in the Pharaonic past became an intellectual infatuation of the 1920s. Many Muslims were ready to praise Pharaonic civilisation and its attainments. With the exception of Salama Musa, Muslims were, in fact, the chief exponents of Pharaonism or the idea that the Egyptian character was inextricably bound to the Pharaonic spirit. Lutfi al-Sayyid was perhaps the first to suggest that the Egyptian character was built around a Pharaonic core. The Copts, however, were among the first to show an interest in and an identification with Egypt's ancient heritage; and the Coptic press was an important vehicle for conveying information about the Pharaonic period. Certain European Egyptologists like Gaston Maspero, seem partly, if not wholly, responsible for persuading the Copts that they were direct descendants of this impressive civilisation.[38] Maspero suggested that Egyptian Muslims were largely Christians who had converted to Islam, but who also lacked the racial purity of the Copts.[39] Egyptian Muslims, then, were a kind of substandard Copt, a notion which would not have pleased the country's majority. The Assyriologist A.H. Sayce went even further with his extravagant insistence, apparently shared by Flinders Petrie, that the Copts, because of their glorious past, held Egypt's future in their hands.[40]

These ideas were discussed with great excitement by the Copts. A heritage of power and high culture was naturally more exciting than one of bondage and subservience, and was to be preferred. It was difficult for many Muslims to accept that this weak community had once been great, and some liked to comment that the Copts were not the sons of the Pharaohs, but rather the descendants of captive slaves of the Pharaohs.[41] Perhaps the Copts also had trouble accepting this past: some of their self-congratulatory writing may have been as much designed to convince themselves as Muslims and foreigners of their true worth.

The discovery of the ancient past sparked a parallel Coptic interest in the Christian period. A Coptic Museum was founded and societies were formed to encourage the study of Coptic history and the Coptic language.[42] The latter had been used only for liturgical purposes for centuries; few priests, let alone laymen, could claim fluency. In 1916, al-Watan suggested that the Copts reject Arabic as a foreign tongue and return to their native one.[43] A later Coptic proposal was that all Egyptians study Coptic because of its connection to hieroglyphics. Echoing Maspero, some Copts deduced from the notion that all Egyptians had a Pharaonic core, the theory that all Egyptians had a Coptic one as well. As Murqus Simaika commented, all Egyptians were Copts; some Copts just happened to be Muslim while others were Christian.[44] Here he reduced the importance of religious belief to the merest historical accident, but it was not a reduction that was likely to win Muslim acceptance. Attempts to revive Coptic were unsuccessful: communal history, however, proved more accessible. In the early 1950s, the Society of the Coptic Nation, al-Umma al-Qibtiyya, sparked a new interest, particularly among the young, in the community's past. This came at a time when the Copts felt their identity as Egyptians threatened and when Pharaonism's appeal was largely dead.

The point Pharaonism's formulators were trying to make was that Egyptians had a remarkable history and were a distinct nationality. They were most successful as well as most numerous and active in the 1920s and early 1930s; after that Pharaonism's popularity faded. The Copts did retain a strong interest in the movement, although it was primarily the preoccupation of the well-educated. It can have had little meaning or attraction for the masses.

Two of its more intelligent proponents were Haikal and Taha Husain, although the latter was more interested in the notion of a regional Mediterranean culture. Husain argued that most Egyptians were descended in a direct line from the Pharaonic Egyptians and were untainted by Arab blood. He insisted that Arab civilisation, when compared with the older one, had had a meagre impact on Egypt. Accordingly, he maintained both that Egypt had little in common with her Arab neighbours,[45] and that neither language nor religion could provide an adequate foundation for unity.[46]

Haikal shared these sentiments and publicised them in al-Siyasa, the Liberal paper under his editorship. He too saw a strong link to the Pharaonic past;[47] throughout the 1920s he wrote articles extolling this ancient civilisation and calling for a revival of its literature and art.[48] He hoped that Pharaonism would inspire the creation of a national literature;[49] but, by the 1930s, he was, at least publicly, showing more interest in Islam. In 1933, he admitted in Thawrat al-Adab that Egyptian culture was the product of her entire history and that the Islamic period was also worthy of study.[50] His interest in the latter period later increased.

Another important writer, Tawfiq al-Hakim, believed, like Husain, that environment determined national character. In noting the obvious differences in the geography of the Arabian peninsula and that of the Nile Valley, he proposed that the Egyptians reject Arab culture in favour of their indigenous one. He too described the chain between the Egyptian peasant and his Pharaonic forbears as unbroken and strong.[51] Foreign conquerors might have introduced, in his eye, an element of moral corruption into Egypt; but they had not succeeded in compromising the ancient spirit of her people.[52]

To Salama Musa, the Pharaonic era was not only relevant to Egypt, but was to be regarded with awe, as something almost sacred.[53] He too believed that the Egyptians were superior to the Arabs because of their Pharaonic blood.[54] Musa tried to encourage the erection of Pharaonic statues and memorials, believing that such solid evidence would reinforce the Egyptians' sense of continuity.[55] Musa's ambition, evident in so much of his writing, was to gain recognition for the existence of a specific Egyptian culture.

The Coptic press maintained a steady enthusiasm for the Pharaonic period; and portrayed ancient Egypt, in sometimes vivid stretches of the imagination, as the source of science, civilisation and even constitutional government.[56] Misr repeatedly chided those who concentrated on Egypt's Islamic period and ignored the older heritage.[57] The paper encouraged the study of Pharaonic history and may have devoted more space to the discovery of antiquities than any other newspaper.[58] It was disturbed that the Egyptian government declined to support excavations and that the majority of Egyptologists were foreigners writing in foreign languages.[59]

To establish an inheritance in which Islam and Arab culture played no part was to establish a common ground on which Muslims and Christians could stand. The Copts did not wish to be reminded of a time during which they had existed on the extreme fringes of society. It was more satisfactory to focus on an earlier period in which they could claim to have been full participating members and which had also received a Western stamp of approval. The Copts, therefore, made this collective possession of a national history the chief element in national feeling.[60] They had little choice since they could not turn to language or religion.

Arabic was often emphasised as a critical factor in establishing an Arab identity. The importance of the language was, however, not entirely overlooked by some wishing to establish an Egyptian national identity. The Egyptians had a distinctive colloquial dialect, and some Copts and Muslims were interested in using it to Egyptianise literary Arabic. Copts, having less of an attachment to the literary language, were perhaps the most ardent proponents of this. There was a considerable gap between those who desired 'to realise our national character by using our tongue',[61] and those who, for reasons either of artistry or increasing literacy, hoped to write the living language of the Egyptian people. Among those in the latter category were Lutfi al-Sayyid, Haikal, Qasim Amin, and Yusuf Idris. Louis Awad and Salama Musa had reasons that were primarily political.[62] The former, who went to the trouble of elaborating a theory for the literary use of the colloquial, later wished that he had used the colloquial quietly and without any fuss in his writings owing to the fire his theory drew.[63] Musa described Arabic as fossilised and felt that language must develop if progress was to be made in other spheres.[64] He believed that classical Arabic had suppressed Egyptian nationalism,[65] and he and others argued for an Egyptian literary language that would help isolate Egypt from the Arab world.[66]

There was a curious parallel between the phil-Pharaonics, both Muslim and Copt, and those Muslim proponents of what Abdullah LaRoui calls 'cultural nationalism'.[67] Instead of choosing early Islamic civilisation to defend and glorify, as did the latter, the phil-Pharaonics focused on a more remote time and a culture whose antiquity and enlightenment could be compared to advantage with the parvenue civilisation and more recent progress of Europe. While men like Rashid Rida pointed to the glories of Arab science and European borrowings from it, the phil-Pharaonics stressed ancient Egyptian science and its heirs, the sciences of ancient Greece and medieval Europe. Egypt was not only a civilisation which could stand up to that of Europe, but it was one which required no defence in European eyes. Westerners were ready to praise ancient Egypt, but not perhaps to see any strong link between the Egyptians under Britain's thumb and those of a long-passed era. Of course, the phil-Pharaonics were not attempting to establish a neo-Pharaonic state, as Rida and the Ikhwan were attempting to establish an Islamic one, nor did they have a very strong desire to emulate such remote ancestors except in general categories such as sovereignty and art. Ancient Egypt was the culture which had established their greatness as a people, but it was not their model.

The Pharaonic strain of thought was not without it critics, who were proud of their Islamic heritage and saw its influence as paramount in contemporary Egypt. There were, of course, Muslims who accepted the merit of Pharaonic civilisation, but who declined to credit any theory which reduced thirteen hundred years of Arabo-Islamic history to triviality. A further problem was that the closer blood connection of the Copts to the Pharaonic Egyptians made the Copts, in an Egypt of primarily Pharaonic character, a kind of natural aristocracy, and this was a distasteful idea.[68]

The Syrian Rashid Rida's al-Manar criticised the Pharaonic movement and attacked its Coptic advocates as tools of British policy.[69] The journal al-Risala expressed similar views and insisted that Egypt's only past of note was her Islamic one; all traces of the spirit and culture of Pharaonic Egypt had disappeared.[70] Both the Muslim Brethren and the Syrian-Christian-owned al-Hilal rejected the Pharaonic movement, albeit for different reasons. Hassan al-Banna wrote that the Brethren welcomed 'ancient Egypt as a history in which there is glory, pride, science and knowledge', but emphatically rejected any suggestion that Egypt return to the ways prevale before 'God granted her the teaching of Islam'. Several proponents were lost to the Pharaonic cause in the 1930s, including al-Aqqad,

Haikal and Ahmad Husain; Taha Husain, with his long religious training, had never entirely ignored the importance of Islamic culture. Except among the Copts, the movement seemed to be dead by 1940; and those like Abd al-Rahman Azzam and Sati al-Husri, who continued to criticise it through the 1950s and 1960s, were only shadow boxing. Of course, their real target was not Pharaonism specifically, but rather the concept that the Egyptians constituted a distinct nationality with a unique history, spirit and culture. It must have seemed to many that the phil-Pharaonics had surrendered to Europe by implicitly accepting Europe's judgement that Arab civilisation could not be defended while the older one could be.

Wafdists and Liberal Constitutionalists were among those who were sympathetic to the Pharaonic movement,[72] but neither were so committed to secularism or Pharaonism that they avoided using religious feeling for political gain. The Liberals, for example, created an issue out of Zaghlul's final resting place in 1930. Zaghlul's family and the Wafd government wanted to bury him in a Pharaonic-style tomb. _Al-Siyasa_ seized the opportunity this presented and ran a series of articles criticising the design as heretical.[73] In words more suitable to the Muslim Brethren press, the paper proclaimed the Pharaohs infidels and, in another statement bordering on the criminal, called on pious Muslims to wipe out all traces of this civilisation.[74] _Misr_ attacked this as an attempt to replace patriotic sentiments with religious ones,[75] and added drily that expressions of religious fervour from _al-Siyasa_ could only be regarded as suspect in the light of the Ali Abd al-Raziq affair.[76] _Al-Balagh_ also criticised the Liberals for this hypocritical demonstration of piety. The newspaper defended Pharaonic art as worthy of imitation because it was Egyptian art and, in addition, gave the usual and increasingly obligatory illustrations of Wafdist sensitivity to Islam.[77]

The Liberals, of course, hoped to weaken the Wafd by proving that Wafdists had a shallow commitment to religion. _Al-Siyasa_ recommended that a religious opinion (_fatwa_) on the acceptability of a Pharaonic tomb be solicited.[78] For good measure, this campaign was coupled with anti-Coptic remarks. Ubaid was blamed for the tomb design and was accused of having overridden the inclination of Mme. Zaghlul and al-Nahhas for an Islamic-style tomb.[79] The Copts were again accused of having excessive influence in both Wafdist councils and the diplomatic corps.[80]

An unattractice pseudo-Pharaonic mausoleum was finally built. The Liberals were clever to see the symbolic importance of the tomb, but their efforts to rouse public ire over the idolatrous resting place of their beloved leader failed. The Sidqi government solved any lingering difficulties by making the tomb a national pantheon. It had a few distinguished Pharaonic mummies moved into the tomb to co-habit with Zaghlul. Predictably, the Wafd was unhappy with this desecration,[81] but perhaps conservative Muslims found it even more distasteful.

2. Mediterraneanism

Those who formulated and publicised the notion that Egypt was a part of a general Mediterranean civilisation were not necessarily opposed to Pharaonism; two of the most active publicists, Taha Husain and Salama Musa, were, in fact, enthusiastic Pharaonists. Pharaonism was, of course, designed to give Egypt a cultural 'edge' by pointing to a glorious and unequalled heritage. Mediterraneanism, on the other hand, was meant to fix that 'edge' by establishing an identity with at least a part of Europe. This theory tying Egypt to European civilisation through the Mediterranean created less public interest than Pharaonism, and was even more distinctly the plaything of the intelligentsia. As Edward Said has noted, any suggestion that Egypt was European marked only the cultural identity of the suggester and not that of the vast majority of Egyptians.[82] At heart here, as another scholar has suggested, was not only a desire to prove that Egypt was unique, but that her culture and mind were rational and intrinsically modern.[83] The proponents of the existence of a distinct Mediterranean culture tried to establish that the Egyptians, as the cultural and intellectual equals of Europeans, deserved a democratic and sovereign government. While it was not necessarily wrong to suggest that Egypt shared elements of her culture with Greece, Spain and Italy, the tendency to overlook cultural and historical differences was as mistaken as failing to note any similarities would have been.

Taha Husain, who remarked on Egyptian admiration for European civilisation, progress and education, wrote that the Egyptians thought and felt as Europeans and strove to emulate a European political system.[84] This was yet another kind of cultural surrender to Europe. In claiming that Egypt was fundamentally like Europe, it suggested that much of what Europe offered was worth emulating. It was an idea which appealed to many Muslims and Copts of a liberal democratic persuasion because it provided an appropriate political context for parliamentary democracy. However, it probably had greater general appeal to Copts. As fellow Christians, the Copts already felt some link with Christian Europe. Many wealthy Copts had, as noted earlier, adopted European culture in place of their own, which had made them marginal. Wasif Ghali, who was perhaps most comfortable expressing himself in French, was one such Copt.[85] Unfortunately, this new allegiance estranged them from the majority of their compatriots and brought suspicion on the whole Coptic community.

Salama Musa, seeing Pharaonic Egypt as the source of the ancient world's civilisation,[86] believed that Egypt's links, through the Greeks and Romans, to the West were stronger than those, through the Arabs, to the East.[87] Egypt's ties to the East were religious and therefore, by definition, anachronistic. Musa wanted Egypt to emulate the 'advanced' West; the East constituted a drag on Egypt and could keep her from the progress of which she was capable.[88] To prove Egypt's ability to emulate the West, he confused what to many was a clear division of East and West by positing a middle ground, Mediterranean civilisation. Christianity, Judaism and Islam had all originated in the Middle East, therefore Egyptians and Europeans shared elements of a culture.[89] Musa, at one point, extravagantly suggested that there was no difference between the Arab and the ancient Egyptian cultures.[90] He was still discussing these ideas and finding considerable support for them at the Young Men's Christian Association in the late 1940s.[91]

Taha Husain also liked to suggest that Egypt and Europe were culturally one, and he tried to demonstrate the influence of ancient Egypt on Greece and later of Greek thought on Egypt.[92] He, too, pointed to Christianity's Eastern origin; and he argued that Islam, born in the same region, could not make Egypt Eastern if Christianity had not had the same effect on Europe. He added that Islam had not only benefited from Greek thought, but had at one time made this thought available to Europe.[93] Taha's East is the Far East,[94] and few would disagree with him by arguing that Egypt had more in common with China than with Europe. Like Musa, he tried to establish a foundation for emulating Western ways: he insisted that the Egyptians had long realised that a religion and a political system were two separate things and that a constitution and state must rest on a practical foundation.[95]

Mirrit Ghali promoted a vision of an Egypt which included Western and Eastern influences. He described Egypt as the meeting ground of two civilisations.[96] Few saw as clearly as he that Egyptian culture was the product of her entire history and that no era could be excluded without robbing that culture of some of its wealth.[97]

3. Arabism

Those who defined Egypt as an Arab country had a blind spot as well, but their interpretation at least had chronological merit. They concentrated on the years following the Arab conquest and ignored those that preceded it. Egypt's obvious cultural and religious affinities to her Arab neighbours were in their favour, but to assume that Arab civilisation had obliterated all traces of Egypt's pre-Islamic culture was as perverse as crediting that civilisation with no influence.

There were two sorts of theorists here: those who saw Egypt as Arab because she was Muslim and for whom, therefore, religion and national identity were inextricably entwined, and those who wished to build a foundation for including Egypt in a secular pan-Arab union. The first were not necessarily opposed to the goal of the second, but rather tended to see Arab unity as a step towards the ultimate aim of Islamic unity. The latter were secularists and some, like Sati al-Husri, went to great lengths to keep religion out of their theory.[98] Religion was incidental, a fact which was witnessed by the important contributions Syrian Christians made to pan-Arab thinking.

Shared history and common language were often described as the parents of the Arab nation. Al-Husri distinguished between Arab and Islamic history and promoted the existence of a highly civilised pre-Islamic Arab nation in the peninsula. Language was a more important ingredient than history; and he argued, in a similar vein, that Arabic had flowered before the divine revelation of the Quran.[99] By the importance he gave linguistic unity in his writings, he made Islamic unity impossible; the Muslim countries spoke many different languages. Language was problematic enough for Arab unity. The various colloquial dialects of Arabic made cross-national or intra-regional communication diffcult, and al-Husri condemned them as divisive.

The work of al-Husri and other secular pan-Arabs not withstanding, the common man did not find it easy to disentangle pan-Arabism from Islam. The Arabs, after all, only had a common history because of Islam; and the connection between the language and the religion could only be ignored by the most obtuse. It was precisely because of this latter connection that the Copts were barred from study at the Dar al-Ulum, which trained language instructors, and from teaching Arabic in schools.[100] In 1951, the Ministry of Education, noting this connection between language and the Quran and Hadith, and voicing its dismay, ordered an investigation into rumours that private schools were employing non-Muslims to teach Arabic.[101] To insist, as the Copts did, that Arabic was their native tongue and that there were Christians who had spoken it before the advent of Islam, served them nought; this helps explain the desire of some Copts to Egyptianise literary Arabic.

For years, the most enthusiastic proponents of Egypt's Arab character were non-Egyptians like Sati.[102] They saw Egypt's wealth and large population as critical to establishing a successful Arab nation.[103] Their initial efforts were frustrated by an official and popular lack of interest in pan-Arabism. Many politicians and intellectuals were promoting the idea of a particular Egyptian identity.

They clearly had some success; their compatriots had some sense of being Egyptian rather than Arab. This did not mean that the Egyptians lacked sympathy with their co-linguists and especially with those who were also trying to throw off the colonial yoke. There was, for example, considerable support for the Syrians in their 1925 revolt against the French. As Makram Ubaid noted in 1931, however, Egypt could not give much attention to other Arabs until she had settled her own national question.[104] Only when the states in the region gained or were approaching independence and became active in inter-Arab affairs, did Egypt come to see an Arab role as in her interest.[105] Palestine was an important catalyst, and the situation there made increasing claims on Egyptian attention from the late 1930s.

Like many other Egyptians, Wafdists were until this time preoccupied with Egyptian concerns and did not take any real notice of the pan-Arabists. In a remark characteristic of this preoccupation, Zaghlul in 1921 answered a proposal that the Egyptians and Arabs join forces to secure their mutual independence negatively, noting that zero plus zero was still zero.[106] The Wafd did, on occasion, voice brotherly feelings and, while such sentiments were no doubt genuine to a degree, they could also be used to get at one's opponents. In a speech to the Senate in 1937, al-Nahhas made the first official party statement supporting the Arabs in Palestine.[107] That same year, Wasif Ghali opposed the Palestine partition plan in the League of Nations. From this time, statements backing Palestinian Arab demands and condemning British policy became frequent. Palestine did not then appear to be a high-risk issue, and parties other than the Wafd were also vocal on the subject.[108] By 1944, Wafdist concern with pan-Arab issues prompted Leon Castro, a Jewish lawyer and early supporter of the Wafd, to accuse al-Nahhas of abandoning the policy of Zaghlul who had feared that Arab unity would lead to religious fanaticism. It seemed a clear sign of the times that _al-Balagh_ hotly defended Zaghlul from this imagined attack by insisting that the man had never said that Egypt was _not_ an Arab country. The newspaper construed Castro's comment as an attack on both Islam and Egypt.[109]

Only a short time after this, al-Nahhas signed the Arab League protocol. King Faruq, having finally abandoned his caliphal ambitions in favour of pan-Arab ones, helped set a pan-Arab course for Egypt, without necessarily bothering to inform or obtain the consent of his government.[110] A political role in Arab affairs was, however, one thing and unity another. When the Syrian prime minister proposed immediate unification in 1951, the reaction of some Egyptians was still chilly. The influential journalist Mustafa Amin likened the prime minister's idea to the situation of a farmer who, having failed to cultivate one half a _feddan_ (Palestine), was proposing to take on the cultivation of one thousand _feddans_.[111]

In the 1920s and 1930s, the Liberals sometimes advocated co-operation with Arab countries, but they always stopped short of political unity.[112] _Al-Siyasa_, its judgement obscured by enthusiasm for the struggle against the British, even suggested in 1931 that Muslims and Jews in Palestine unite to gain their independence.[113] Pushed by the same considerations as the Wafd, the Liberals began to show greater interest in pa-Arabism at roughly the same time as their political opponents. Increasingly, for all parties, the supposed lack of proper brotherly feelings for Arab neighbours became yet one more stick with which to beat an incumbent government.[114]

The Copts, without a great leap of the imagination, could not see themselves as Arabs and in this they differed from Syrian Christians. One of the better-known Egyptian pan-Arabists, Abd al-Rahman Azzam, made just such a leap in an effort to persuade the Copts. He promoted the odd idea that Egypt had been an Arab country before the birth of Jesus. This, of course, made the Copts Arab; not only did it make them Arab, argued Azzam with a flourish, but it made some of them more Arab than the inhabitants of Mecca and Mdeina.[115] The Copts, however, were not convinced; they saw Arabism as a doctrine which even in its secular guise could be used to exclude them from national life.[116] Being a minority in Egypt was uncomfortable enough; the prospect of being an even smaller minority in a greater Arab state did not bear contemplation. One scholar thinks that there is some evidence to suggest that Wafdists, at least until the tide became too sweeping in the late 1930s, worried that plans for Arab co-operation and unity could increase sectarian feeling in Egypt. Al-Nuqrashi was one Wafdist who claimed to feel such a concern in 1931.[117] This concern, if actually felt, would support Leon Castro's contention that Zaghlul believed that an Arab unity movement could foster religious fanaticism.

Salama Musa, echoing Lutfi al-Sayyid, pointed to the differences between the various Middle Eastern peoples and sceptically asked what the Westernised Lebanese had in common with the more backward Saudis and Sudanese.[118] As the 1940s progressed, the Copts became increasingly worried about pan-Arab sentiment. They saw themselves as potential if not actual victims of this dangerous idea. Some tried to discredit it by calling it a plot to distract Egypt from her real interests:[119] the British were responsible for both the mess in Palestine[120] and the creation of the Arab League, an organisation which the Copts found at best suspect. Salama Musa was one who tried to use British support for the League against it.[121] He called it an Islamic league and insisted that it would finally accomplish, by increasing religious fanaticism, what the British had been trying to do for years: the division of Muslims and Copts.[122] Louis Awad also objected to the League;[123] and others, writing in

Misr, described the League as a religions organisation. Their emphasis was always on the fact that the people of the Nile Valley were Egyptian and not Arab.[124]

One rather unlikely supporter of pan-Arabism was the Copt Makram Ubaid. Never much interested in the traditions of his community, he may well have been the only Copt to deride Pharaonism publicly,[125] and to insist that the Egyptians were Arabs.[126] He went even further and applauded Arab unity because it had the capacity to make Muslims and Copts indistinguishable.[127] This, of course, was exactly what his co-religionists feared. They were well aware of whose distinguishing characteristics would be obliterated. Of course, public pronouncements, particularly those of politicians, do not signify personal commitment; and Makram's support for pan-Arabism, especially in the latter part of the constitutional monarchy, may have been a tactic to overcome the handicap of his Christian background.[128] He was never an important theorist of pan-Arabism, and his early statements on the subject have probably had too much attention paid to them. In fact, in one article, he called for an Arab unity which was only a kind of solidarity to help fight imperialism and develop economic resources; he did not suggest that the Arabs give up their separate nationalisms.[129] One of the planks in his party's platform called for the encouragement of pan-Arab co-operation as a step towards unity.[130] While his definition of unity may, by this time, have lacked clarity, his zeal for the concept did not. His support for the pan-Arab cause increased as the fortunes of his party declined and as other parties made greater use of religious propaganda. Pan-Arabism and anti-British zeal were Makram's secular replacements.

Those organisations which did the most to promote the Palestinian cause, until the late 1940s, like the Muslim Brethren, Misr al-Fatat, Shabab Muhammad and the Young Men's Muslim Association, were moved more by religious than pan-Arab sentiment.[131] At a Brethren meeting in 1936, the Supreme Guide invited both Copts and Muslims to defend Palestine. When the audience voiced its objections to Coptic participation, he pointed out that fairness demanded this since Muslims had helped defend Abyssinia against the Italians: 'If the Copts respond to the call, good; if they do not, we will see that they suffer for it'.[132]

No doubt many Copts hoped to avoid a Palestinian entanglement.[133] Events in Palestine had so aggravated Egyptian Muslim sentiment that attacks on Egyptian Jews and foreign Christians were becoming common, and these did not inspire confidence. The Copts feared, with some cause, that Muslims would suspect them of having more in common with Palestinian Jews than Muslim compatriots. For example, the 1938 election campaign saw a group of Azhari demonstrators rather wildly demand that the Copts be expelled and sent to Palestine.[134] As a conservative Christian community, the Copts had little sympathy for the Jews in any case.

When Murqus Sergius, then the Patriarch's Deputy, was invited to a major anti-partition rally in 1947, he declined to attend. He told a visiting delegation that he would not fight the Jews, a fellow minority, at a time when the Copts were facing increasing discrimination at home. He added that those Copts who had supported his appearances at al-Azhar in 1919 would not countenance them now.[135] Cooler or more cowardly heads prevailed because the Patriarch attended the meeting in Sergius' place.[135] Coptic religious dignitaries appear to have attended other partition rallies as well.[137]

Few Copts in 1947 were as vocal as Sergius, and only a fool would have opposed Egyptian policy once the war began. The church, of course, never differed publicly with the government in foreign policy matters; and it had, in any case, a real concern about the fate of its wealthy Jerusalem endowments. The church preferred that the endowments not be under the jurisdiction of a country with whom Egypt was at war.[138]

It is not altogether surprising that the war sparked some enthusiasm among Copts. Christian Palestinians were, after all, fighting alongside Muslim Palestinians. Misr praised the Egyptian war effort and condemned Zionist plans. Article after article hammered away at the need for Copt-Muslim unity and reminded readers that, although al-Banna called the war a '*jihad*', Copts too were fighting.[139] Even Salama Musa, in a burst of patriotic fervour, called on all Egyptians to do their duty.[140] Despite these efforts, the Copts remained suspect and by 1951 were being regularly likened to the Jews. Some Copts wondered whether Israel would welcome them if they were banished from Egypt, and Sergius glumly remarked that they might eventually be forced to seek such a refuge.[141] He complained that the Copts had become foreigners in their own country at a time when every foreign Muslim was considered a citizen.[142] This, to the Copts, was the manifest danger of Arabism.

4. Marxism

The Marxist movement in Egypt, formed by several disparate and schismatic groups rather than one disciplined party with strong Comintern links, provided an alternate focus of loyalty and placed the political community in an international context. It was a context which dissolved religious, ethnic and national distinctions.

Until the Second World War, the communist movement in Egypt was small, uninfluential and dominated, perhaps even monopolised, by foreigners. Jews, Armenians, Syrians, Lebanese, Russians and other Europeans were involved, but few Egyptian Muslims and Copts.[143] The various nationalities tended to stick together and their audience was very limited, given the miniscule size of the proletariat.[144] In 1925, the Residency noted that there were two main Marxist groups: one run by a Syrian with members from several ethnic and national groups, and a second composed of Russians and Europeans.[145] These men were outsiders. If they were not themselves European, they were European-educated and -influenced. They had few ties to Egypt and no roots in the country. They could not and generally did not wish to be Egyptian. Accordingly, a movement which held out the hope of political participation and the promise of membership in a larger society was bound to have a certain attraction for them.

One Copt who did show an early interest in socialism was Salama Musa, but he usually was considerably in advance of even the intellectual vanguard of his own community. In 1920, in the wake of the Russian revolution, he was associated in the founding of an Egyptian socialist party, the first organisation of its kind in the country.[146] Musa, however, was much taken up with Fabian ideas; Marxist-Leninist doctrine seems not to have appealed to him. The party soon collapsed, and while Musa continued to promote theories of economic and social reform, evolution (a subject on which he wrote with almost religious fervour), and progress, he remained apart from later and more orthodox manifestations of Marxism in Egypt. He was perhaps too much of an Egyptian nationalist to be attracted by an international perspective.

Other than Musa, the Copts were not greatly interested in the early movement but were content to explore their community's destiny within the framework of the political order they had helped to establish. This behaviour, perhaps atypical of a minority, shows the extent to which they felt themselves to be citizens of Egypt. As an indigenous minority, they did not have to look beyond the borders of their own country. Religious ties were strong, and many Copts were reluctant to involve themselves in a movement known to be Godless. There was little incentive, at this time at any rate, for them to work for the overthrow of the new and largely untried political system; a system which not only promised equality but gave them an opportunity to wield such power as their talents fitted them to exercise. The chief political desideratum of Copts and Muslims in that period was the acquisition of genuine independence. While Salama Musa's Socialist Party had shared this desire, its successors were preoccupied primarily with class conflict.[147] This was not a concern of many Egyptians at that time, and it can only be counted as a tactical error if the Marxists were interested in increasing their support among the Egyptian population. Some of them may not have been very interested in this; even as late as the early 1940s, the organisation Iskra resisted suggestions that it Egyptianise its membership from a fear that this would erode its political sophistication.[148]

From the Second World War, there was a marked increase in Marxist activity,[149] due in part to increased Marxist interest in national liberation. Study circles developed into more formal groups, which split and formed themselves into new groups; journals were published, many of them short-lived; and the movement began to grow in influence. It began to acquire support among Egyptians, Muslims and Copts, and was particularly influential among students, labour and the left wing of the Wafd. In the early 1940s, membership was still dominated by foreigners and Jews. Even as late as 1948, the British Embassy noted that Jews were still among the leading communists in Egypt.[150] One scholar has suggested that Coptic support for the movement was also strong,[151] but this is difficult to substantiate. There does not seem to have been a disproportionate degree of Coptic participation in the Marxist movement at any time, not even when the movement was stronger and had, to an extent, Egyptianised.[152] By 1952, Walter Laqueur noted that the leadership of the communist movement was almost entirely Muslim.[153]

Still, there were Copts connected with various Marxist groups, and some occupied positions of importance in them. Perhaps Coptic participation can be linked with the increasing hostility shown to the Copts by the Muslim population of this period. These groups, no doubt, showed a firmer commitment to secularism than did the legitimate political parties. They were uninterested in religious affiliation. Of course, many politicians claimed a similar lack of interest, but few showed it. The Marxist periodical al-Tatawwur, begun in 1940, published a number of articles in its short life insisting on a separation between religion and state.[154] It promoted secularism, defended freedom of religion and criticised those who confused politics with religion.[155] These are not positions from which many in the Coptic community would have dissented. Still, it may be more fruitful to explore general reasons for Muslim and Copt participation in the movement. The legitimate political system had bankrupted itself; parties were interested only in power and not in the welfare of the Egyptian people. They had neither succeeded in getting rid of the British nor in creating an honest and just government. The standard of living of ordinary Egyptians had declined, and many who joined the Marxist movement had a fierce concern for economic justice and equality. It should be said that these groups were not concerned only with class struggle, but that they also seemed to draw individuals possessing a variety of advanced or radical views; for example, some were very concerned with the liberation of women.

George Hinain, the son of the early Wafdist Sadiq Hinain, may have been the most important Marxist Copt in this later period.[156] He came from a wealthier background than most Egyptian Marxists and, after flirting with several groups, seems to have ended up a Trotskyite.[157] The orthodoxy of his attachment to this Marxist heresy is not known. In 1939 he belonged to the Society for Art and Freedom (Jamaat al-Fann wa al-Hurriyya) which had, as its name suggests, primarily literary and artistic interests. The group started a magazine, the first three issues of which Hinain financed. He withdrew his support when his friend Anwar Kamil broke away to form Bread and Freedom (al-Khubz wa al-Hurriyya). Hinain became responsible for the financial side of Kamil's periodical Development (al-Tatawwur),[158] and he was later connected with the founding of the journal The New Dawn (al-Fajr al-Jadid). He wrote occasional articles for these journals and, of course, provided money and financial advice.[159]

Two other Copts connected with al-Tatawwur were Tawfiq Hanna Allah and Ramses Yunan.[160] Yunan, an artist, seems to have been one of the more radical members of al-Khubz. He was, at any rate, an ardent feminist.[161] Anwar Abd al-Malik, the well-known critic and historian;[162] Lutfi Allah Suliman,[163] and Assad Halim, a Coptic convert to Islam, also had connections with the Marxist movement.[164]

None of these groups was interested in Egypt's sectarian problems, although Jewish members must have had some concern about their increasingly delicate position in Egyptian society. Al-Tatawwur did show some concern with religious fanaticism; and it criticised those political parties which resorted to religious tactics.[165] Many Marxists seemed caught up in the struggle to Egyptianise the movement and in anti-British or anti-government activities.

The Marxist movement's vision of a secular and just society had much to recommend it. One factor which may have militated against Coptic support was that some groups, like the New Dawn, supported Arab unity.[166] In addition, the composition of the movement encouraged the public, egged on at times by the government, to make a connection between minorities and communism. Sidqi in 1946 claimed that the communists were in collusion with the Zionists, and in 1948 Parliament voted to declare war on Israel 'in defence of Arab rights and against communist atheism'.[164] The Copts were already being likened to the Jews; to court Marxism must have been seen by many in the community as courting disaster. A further consideration was that some Marxist groups were collaborating with and had even won some members from the Muslim Brethren and Ahmad Husain's Socialist Party. These new Marxists were likely to have retained their old attitude towards the Copts.

C. AN HISTORIOGRAPHY OF COPT-MUSLIM RELATIONS

Many Egyptian writers, summing up the long centuries of Copt-Muslim co-habitation, interpreted history in the light of their reaction to communal relations in their own time and their goals for the future. Muslims naturally stressed Muslim tolerance; many nationalists, eager to establish an independent and democratic state, suggested an historical background of communal solidarity and brotherhood. For example, Mustafa Kamil declared in an 1895 speech that Copts and Muslims had co-existed peacefully for thirteen centuries, and that their religious differences had never had any political import.[168]

Despite this, Egyptian writers in the period before World War One, when communal relations were tense, often seemed to suppress examples of peaceful inter-ethnic co-operation and concentrated on episodes of conflict in Egyptian history. The Copts tended to portray the Arabs as usurpers; in a happier period, they would praise the latter for lifting the Byzantine yoke. Some Copts, echoing Maspero, tried to establish a clear separation from Muslims by arguing that their descent from the Pharaonic Egyptians made them racially different.[169] Much later, this claim was repeated by Muslims who were prejudiced against the Coptic community. In 1937, Shaikh al-Maraghi, to drive home his denunciation of Coptic influence, stated that the Copts were a racial as well as a religious minority.[170]

The 1919 revolution, which deserves most of the credit for persuading Muslims to regard Copts as genuine Egyptians, gave birth to an article of faith which was frequently repeated. According to this conviction, Copts and Muslims have lived in harmony since the Arab conquest and are one and not two peoples.[171] Murqus Simaika's belief that the Copts were a race with both Muslim and Christian members, is only one of many attempts to posit such a unity. Once, when Copts were accused of presenting special demands as the price of their participation in the revolution, _Misr_ indignantly denied the charge and said that the Coptic experience of Muslim rule had not led the Copts to fear that they would be excluded from a share in government.[172] A month later, _Misr_ wrote of the love and ties which had bound Muslims and Copts from the time of the Arab conquest.[173] Peaceful co-existence in past and present were stressed and the former was used to buttress the latter. It became almost treasonous to suggest that there were any disagreements between the two communities.

Some Copts, accepting that the British presence contributed to their security, described the period immediately after the 1882 Occupation as a golden age in Coptic history.[174] However, even with all the intercommunal problems in the period before the First World War, the Copts were willing to blame some of their problems on the British. The need for an outside scapegoat increased after the 1919 revolution, although some writers preferred to pretend that no inter-communal tensions which demanded the presence of an agent provocateur in fact existed. Even in the trouble 1950s, some Copts continued to maintain that Christians and Muslims had been equal until the time of the Occupation.[175] The pre-Occupation Egyptian government was said to have treated all of its subjects equally:

> ...the different Islamic governments which successfully ruled over Egypt, and which you [the British] count as despotic and tyrannic, did not treat their members in such a way as you have treated them. History is before you and it tells you that when the Muslims occupied Egypt in the early part of the seventh century they contented themselves with supervising the principal affairs of the country and left the administration of all its affairs in the hands of its owners, the Copts, who continued to conduct all administrative and financial affairs, century after century...It is true that the Copts were responsible for many events in those dark ages which harmed them, but it was the rabble and the ignorant which caused problems while the princes and the governors denied them...When the English occupied Egypt in 1882 the Copts filled all the principal offices in the government... (and the English deprive them of them).[176]

As the Egyptians moved away from the revolution in time, they felt less compelled to see the whole past as rosy. Copt-Muslim relations before 1919 were portrayed accurately as black. This was done not in the interest of historical truth but to glorify the revolution and Zaghlul, the man who brought Copts and Muslims together.[177] From the late 1930s, there is little concern with a mythology of Copt-Muslim brotherhood, beyond some rather feeble assertions that they were one people, because ethnic problems were again on the rise. Present disunity made past unity seem unlikely. The Copts longed for the golden days of the revolution and were disappointed with the failure of the polity to live up to its theoretical underpinnings.[178] This perhaps is mainly indicative of a human tendency to see past eras as untroubled and placid. One Copt proposed in 1951 the formation of a Committee of

Historical Studies which could remind people of the good old days and the role the Copts had played in the national movement.[179]

Certainly the Copts became more sceptical of any Muslim insistence on the historical tolerance of Islam in theory and practice.[180] The Society of the Coptic Nation helped disillusion any remaining romantics by exploring all eras of Coptic history, including the more sorry ones. The Sunday-school movement also helped focus the Copts on their history in Egypt. By highlighting their separation from Muslim compatriots in the past, it strengthened feelings of division in the present.

Copts in the late 1970s described the 1918-52 period as a golden age in communal relations, and often reacted sharply to suggestions that problems existed.[181] The Nasir era was remembered, at least by well-off Copts, most unpleasantly;[182] these people had good reasons for preferring the constitutional monarchy. At least until late 1979, Sadat's rule was portrayed favourably and was described by by one Copt as a silver period.[183] After this, increasing communal tensions altered the Copts' perceptions of Sadat, and even the Nasir era came to assume a more favourable aspect in the eyes of some Copts.

NOTES

1. Al-Urwa al-Wuthqa 4 (3 April 1884); reprinted in a volume of the same title (Cairo, 1957), 23-6. The Strongest Bond was the short-lived journal of Shaikhs al-Afghani and Abduh.

2. To Shaikh al-Afghani, one significant failure was that Muslims had not maintained unity, which he termed a religious obligation. Ibid., 9 (22 May 1884); reprinted on p.70 and ibid., 5 (10 April 1884); reprinted on pp.30-2.

3. Al-Urwa al-Wuthqa in noting that Western nations frequently borrowed from one another to their mutual benefit, criticised Eastern rulers for hindering that process. Ibid., 9 (22 May 1884); reprinted on p.71.

4. Al-Afghani scorned nationalism, which he saw as divisive, and he promoted religious solidarity as the only way to bring together the strength of the East and pit it successfully against the might of the West. Ibid., 2 (20 March 1884); reprinted on pp.9-11; ibid., 9 (22 May 1884); reprinted on pp.67-72.

5. E.I.J. Rosenthal, Islam in the Modern

Nation State (Cambridge University Press, Cambridge, 1965), p.82. Al-Manar contained more articles on current affairs than the more strictly religious periodicals like Majallat al-Azhar.

6. Al-Manar 31 (22 October 1930: 1349 AH): 449-65.

7. Quoted by Charles Adams in Islam and Modernism in Egypt (Oxford University Press, London, 1933), p.194.

8. They believed that there could be no struggle between religious and civil authorities as there had been in Europe because in Islam there was no division between the two. Muhammad Farid Wajdi, 'The Office of Caliph and Democracy', Majallat al-Azhar 10 (1939: 1358 AH), 36-8.

9. FO.141/498, 220/1/34.

10. FO.141/498, 220/6/34.

11. FO.141/498, 220/2/34.

12. Misr, 26 April 1946, 1. When Salama Musa complained about the Shabab the following year, they accused him of trying to spark rebellion (fitna), Misr, 3 May 1947, 1.

13. Five Tracts of Hassan al-Banna, trans. Charles Wendell (University of California Press, Berkeley, 1978), p.6. The Brethren objected to mixing an alien system of government with Islam because it would ruin the natural ability of Islam to operate to the best advantage of mankind. See Sayed Kotb, Social Justice in Islam, trans. John Hardie (Octagon Books. New York, 1970) (first Arabic edition, 1945), p.91. Another Brethren ideologue was moved by Islam's modernity to call its system of government 'a free democracy' and 'a tempered socialism'. Muhammad al-Ghazzali, Our Beginning in Wisdom, trans. Ismail al-Faruqi (American Council of Learned Societies, Washington, DC, 1953), pp.6, 13.

14. Al-Banna argued, as did Rashid Rida, that a contributing factor was the transfer of power to non-Arabs who did not understand Islam. This is an argument several pan-Arabists made to account for the decline of the Arab world. Five Tracts of Hassan al-Banna, p.19.

15. Richard Mitchell, The Society of Muslim Brothers (Oxford University Press, London, 1969), p.247.

16. Al-Nadhir 1 (No.12: 1938: 1357 AH), 2-3. In 1941, Prime Minister Husain Sirri was so annoyed by al-Banna's criticism of his government that he banished the latter to Qina. FO.141/838, 305/37/42.

17. Not even they, however, agreed on the need for a Caliph. In 1925, Shaikh Ali Abd al-Raziq

claimed in a book that neither the Quran nor the Hadith made the office incumbent upon Muslims. Religious circles reacted so vehemently to this that public and government attention was focused on the unfortunate Shaikh. Al-Manar and many others particularly objected to his claim that the establishment of a state was not a part of the Prophet's divine mission; this, of course, implied that a division between religion and politics was not only acceptable but ordained. Al-Manar noted indignantly that Muslims would have to give up one-half of their religion if they were to adopt al-Raziq's understanding of Islam. Feeling was so strong that few of those who approved of al-Raziq's words dared to defend them; most rather weakly argued for the right of free expression. Wisely, this is all the Coptic press attempted to do. See al-Watan, 20 August 1925, 1, and 5 September 1925, 1. See also Ali Abd al-Raziq, al-Islam wa Usul al-Hukm (Cairo, 1925), pp.119-29. Adams, Islam and Modernism in Egypt, p.267.

18. See the description of Azhari activity in Fakhr al-Din al-Zawahiri, al-Siyasa w-al-Azhar (Cairo, 1945), pp.209-17.

19. This did not prevent either party from using the issue for political gain. In 1931, the Wafd gave some support to the General Islamic Conference in Jerusalem in the hope of discomfiting Sidqi and the Palace. The latter was concerned that the Conference would upset its goal of an Egyptian Caliphate. Then in 1938, the Liberals advocated an Egyptian Caliphate as a campaign tactic. See al-Siyasa, 26 January and 27 January 1938, PPF.

20. Both al-Watan and Misr restricted themselves to bland reporting on revival activities. See al-Watan, 5 March 1925, 1, and 13 March 1925, 1.

21. Misr, 2 February 1938, 1; al-Jihad, 23 January 1938, PPF.

22. He was no doubt worried about Brethren-Wafd contacts. Misr, 26 November 1947, 1.

23. See Mikhail Fanus' speech at The Coptic Conference Held at Assiout, 6, 7 and 8 March 1911, (no place, no date), pp.6-12.

24. Misr, 22 January 1938, 1.

25. Syrian Christians, because of their disproportionate press influence, played a perhaps larger role than the Copts in promoting secular ideas in Egypt.

26. Al-Watan, 21 September 1922, 1.

27. Jacques Berque, Egypt: Imperialism and

Revolution, trans. Jean Stewart (Faber and Faber, London, 1972), p.261.

28. Salama Musa commented that it was Lutfi's work which allowed him to be a nationalist in Egypt, The Education of Salama Musa, p.44.

29. Minutes of the Proceedings of the First Egyptian Congress Assembled at Heliopolis, 29 April to 4 May 1911 (Alexandria, 1911), p.6.

30. Al-Siyasa, 24 July 1926, 5; Ibrahim Ibrahim, 'The Egyptian Intellectuals between Tradition and Modernity' (unpublished PhD thesis, University of Oxford, 1967), pp.95, 104-5.

31. This subject will be discussed in greater detail in Chapters Five, Six and Seven.

32. FO.371/17976, J2067/7/16.

33. He did, however, attempt to maintain demonstrably friendly relations with the Muslim Brethren. His success in doing so was limited, and the endeavour was probably viewed as hypocritical by just as many Muslims as Copts.

34. Lecture by Mirrit Ghali at l'Institut d'Egypte, 7 November 1977.

35. Mirrit Ghali, 'Essay: The Egyptian National Consciousness', Middle East Journal 32 (1978), 56-60

36. Charles Wendell, The Evolution of Egypt's National Image (University of California Press, Los Angeles, 1972), p.123.

37. See Misr, 20 and 27 February 1927, 1.

38. An interview with Maspero in a Coptic periodical and a lecture he gave at the Ramses Club in 1908 were both seminal in conveying to the Copts the idea that the blood line had remained pure from the time of the Pharaohs. Samir Seikaly, 'Coptic Communal Reform 1860-1914', Middle Eastern Studies 6 (1970), 269. Before this time, the Copts, like the Muslims, were not interested in ancient Egypt. See Storrs, Orientations, p.94.

39. Seikaly, 'Coptic Communal Reform 1860-1914' 269.

40. Ibid., 269; Seikaly, 'The Copts under British Rule, 1882-1914', p.94.

41. Misr, 13 March 1939, 1.

42. The Committee of Coptic History was one such society. It was formed in 1919 to promote the teaching of Coptic history in Coptic schools.

43. Al-Watan, 13 January 1916, quoted in Muhammad Sayyid Kailani, al-Adab al-Qibti Qadiman wa Hadithan (Dar al-Qawmiyya al-Arabiyya, Cairo, 1962), p.51.

44. Al-Ahram, 3 February 1926, 1.

45. Interview in al-Makhshuf, quoted in al-Majalla al-Jadida, December 1938, 75-6.
46. Taha Husain, Mustaqbil al-Thaqafa fi Misr (Dar al-Maarif, Cairo, 1938), pp.21-3.
47. Muhammad Husain Haikal, Thawrat al-Adab (Maktabat al-Nahda al-Misriyya, Cairo, 1965), p.138.
48. Muhammad Darwazah, al-Wahda al-Arabiyya (Beirut, 1957), p.344. Haikal even believed that early Islamic literature had been influenced by Pharaonic culture. Al-Siyasa al-Usbuiyya, 20 October 1928, quoted in Samira Bahr 'Al-Aqbat fi al-Hayat al-Siyasiyya fi Misr' (unpublished PhD thesis, Cairo University, 1977), pp.291-2.
49. Haikal, Thawrat al-Adab, p.138.
50. Smith feels that at this point the Islamic past was still subordinate to the ancient one. Charles Smith, 'Muhammad Husayn Haykal: An Intellectual and Political Biography' (unpublished PhD thesis, University of Michigan, 1968), pp.291-6.
51. Hilary Kilpatrick, The Modern Egyptian Novel (Ithaca Press, London, 1974), pp.42-3.
52. Tawfiq al-Hakim, Awdat al-Ruh (Maktabat al-Adab wa Matbaatuha, Cairo, 1973, first edition, 1933), pp.53-64.
53. Ibrahim, 'Egyptian Intellectuals', p.177.
54. Salama Musa, al-Yawm w-al-Ghad (al-Matbaat al-Asriyya, Cairo, 1927), p.235
55. Ibrahim, 'Egyptian Intellectuals', p.223. One of the less happy results of this enthusiasm for ancient Egypt was the spawning of a neo-Pharaonic school of architecture and sculpture: witness that memorial to Egyptian independence, the 'Egypt Awakes' statue of a sphinx and a woman throwing off her veil.
56. Misr, 12 April 1919, 1.
57. Misr, 18 September 1933, 1.
58. Anis Sayigh believes that the Coptic press paid more attention to discoveries than what he calls 'the Islamic press'. Anis Sayigh, al-Fikra al-Arabiyya fi Misr (Matbaat Haikal al-Gharib, Beirut, 1959), p.211.
59. Misr, 3 November 1947, 1.
60. Donald Reid, The Odyssey of Farah Antun (Bibliotheca Islamica, Minneapolis, 1975), p.101.
61. Al-Majalla al-Jadida, May 1931, 789.
62. See Awad's discussion of his use of the colloquial in his poetry in the introduction to Plutoland. He argues that the precedence local European languages gained over Latin weakened the power of the religious hierarchy, but not the essence of Christianity, and he implied that it would be no bad thing were this to happen in Egypt. See

his Blutuland (Matbaat al-Karnak, Cairo, 1947), pp.11-13. Awad now admits that he advocated the use of the colloquial to undermine religion and help establish a secular society. Interview on 29 February 1980.

63. Ibid.

64. Salama Musa, al-Balagha al-Asriyya w-al-Lugha al-Arabiyya (al-Matbaat al-Asriyya, Cairo, 1945), pp.53, 71.

65 Ibrahim, 'The Egyptian Intellectuals', p.220.

66. Darwazah, al-Wadha al-Arabiyya, p.349.

67. Adbullah La Roui, The Crisis of the Arab Intellectual: Traditionalism or Historicism (University of California Press, Berkeley, 1976), pp. 114-6.

68. Wendell, The Evolution, p.163.

69. Al-Manar 31 (20 December 1930: 1349 AH), 45.

70. Al-Risala, 11 October 1933, 3-4. According to Sylvia Haim, the journal's editor, Ahmad Hassan al-Zayat, saw Arab unity as a prelude to Islamic unity. See her Arab Nationalism: An Anthology (University of California Press, Berkeley, 1962), p.53.

71. Mitchell, The Society of Muslim Brothers, p.266. Some opponents labelled the Pharaonic movement as yet another attempt by the British to divide and rule. See Sayigh, al-Fikra al-Arabiyya, p.101; Ahmad Tarabain, al-Wahda al-Arabiyya Bain 1916 wa 1945 (Mahad al-Darasat al-Arabiyya al-aliyy, Cairo, 1957), p.189.

72. Ibrahim Faraj Masiha, a retired Wafdist politician, insists that the Egyptians have Pharaonic blood running through their veins and that their blood absorbed and predominated over the blood of their Arab counterparts. Interview 13 June 1979.

73. Al-Siyasa, 23 January, 6 February and 20 April 1930, quoted in Smith, Muhammad Husain Haikal, p.238. Al-Siyasa, 13 February 1930, quoted in the Egyptian Gazette, 14 February 1930, p.4. Unfortunately, this volume of al-Siyasa is missing from Dar al-Kutub, so these sources could not be confirmed.

74. Misr, 10 January 1930, 4.

75. Misr, 13 February 1930, 3.

76. Misr, 15 February 1930, 4.

77. The paper noted that all mosques built by the Wafd government were in the Arab style, but that in any case, this style had nothing to do with Islam. Al-Balagh, 6 February 1930, 2.

78. The article continued, '...the present

Cabinet must understand that it is the first...to look with contempt on the religious feelings of Muslims'. Al-Siyasa, 13 February 1930, quoted in the Egyptian Gazette, 14 February 1930, 4.

79. Al-Siyasa, 22 April 1930, 5.

80. Misr, 13 February 1930, 1.

81. See Abbas al-Aqqad's article in Misr, 1 December 1931, 1. In 1937, the mummies were moved out of the tomb, and Zaghlul was left in peaceful solitude.

82. Edward Said, Orientalism (Pantheon Books, New York, 1978), p.323.

83. Ernest Dawn, From Ottomanism to Arabism (University of Illinois, Urbana, 1973), p.188.

84. Taha Husain, Mirat al-Islam, quoted in Ibrahim, 'Egyptian Intellectuals', p.44.

85. He was often criticised for this by the opposition press. See al-Siyasa al-Usbuiyya, 11 June 1927, 3-4.

86. Musa, al-Yawm w-al-Ghad, p.236.

87. Ibid., p.248.

88. Ibid., p.241.

89. Salama Musa wrote several articles in al-Hilal on this theme. See al-Hilal, July 1927, 1072-4, and 1 December 1928, 177-81, for examples.

90. Musa, al-Yawm w-al-Ghad, p.236.

91. Milad Hanna, Nam Aqbat Lakin Misriyyun (Maktabat Madbuli, Cairo, 1980), pp.90-3.

92. Taha Husain, Mustaqbil al-Thaqafa fi Misr (Dar al-Maarif, Cairo, 1938), pp.12-14.

93. Ibid., pp.21-3.

94. Taha Husain, The Future of Culture in Egypt, trans. Sidney Glazer (American Council of Learned Societies, Washington, DC, 1954), pp.4-5.

95. Ibid., p.6.

96. Mirrit Ghali, The Policy of Tomorrow, trans. Ismail al-Faruqi (American Council of Learned Societies, Washington, DC, 1953, first Arabic edition, 1933), pp.108-9.

97. At times, Salama Musa also suggested that Egypt look to both her Arab and Pharaonic eras for inspiration. See al-Majalla al-Jadida, May 1932, 791; Musa, al-Yawm w-al-Ghad, pp.235-6.

98. Sati al-Husri, 'Muslim Unity and Arab Unity', in Haim, Arab Nationalism: An Anthology, pp.147-53.

99. William Cleveland, The Making of an Arab Nationalist (Princeton Studies on the Far East, Princeton, 1971), pp.121-3.

100. This ban was only made official by Ministerial decree in 1940. Misr, 12 April 1946, 1.

101. Misr, 12 February 1951, 1.

102. It is interesting, however, that very early proponents of the idea of the existence of an Arab nation excluded Egypt from membership.

103. Sati al-Husri was one such. See Cleveland, The Making of an Arab Nationalist, pp.134-5.

104. Ralph Coury, 'Who "invented" Egyptian Arab nationalism?', Part I, International Journal of Middle Eastern Studies 14 (1982), 253.

105. Leonard Binder, 'Ideological foundations of Egyptian-Arab nationalism', in Ideology and Discontent, ed. David Apter (Free Press of Glencoe, New York, 1964), p.136.

106. The Wafd in 1921 was hoping for the support of the French against the British so they dared not back the Syrians against the French.

107. Sayigh, al-Fikra al-Arabiyya, p.241.

108. Ibid., p.194; FO.371/23364, J1973/774/11.

109. Egyptian Gazette, 14 September 1944, 3.

110. Kedourie, The Chatham House Version, pp.215-6.

111. Akhbar al-Yawm, 24 January 1951, quoted in Anwar Chejne, 'Egyptian Attitudes to pan-Arabism', in Middle East Journal XI (1857), 261-2.

112. Al-Siyasa, 14 June 1933, 1.

113. Egyptian Gazette, 19 November 1931, 4.

114. For example, in 1932 al-Siyasa accused the Minister of Foreign Affairs of trying to isolate Egypt from her Arab neighbours. In another article the paper criticised the Ministry of Education because it had invited foreign scholars to speak on subjects other than 'Eastern, Islamic and Arab' topics. Al-Siyasa, 5 August 1932, p.4; al-Ittihad, 3 April 1933, 1.

115. Al-Hilal, September-October 1943, 462-3, quoted in Haim, Arab Nationalism: An Anthology, p.51. Azzam, in a letter to Hamilton at the Sudan Agency, blamed Arabism's lack of success in Egypt in the 1920s on 'the movement of Egyptian nationalism with Zaghlul at its head and a very strong Coptic element...', FO.141/744, 834/1/33.

116. They did not oppose a degree of co-operation, al-Watan, 18 August 1926, 1.

117. Coury, 'Who "invented" Egyptian Arab nationalism?', Part I, 256.

118. Misr, 6 August 1937, 1.

119. The Cry of Egypt's Copts, p.3.

120. Misr, 25 May 1948, 1.

121. Misr, 17 April 1946, 1.

122. Misr, 6 July 1946, 1.

123. Interview with Louis Awad, 29 February 1980.

124. Misr, 30 November 1946, 1, and 4 December 1946, 1.

125. He did so on a visit to Syria, and he promised to use his influence to bring about closer ties with Egypt. Egyptian Gazette, 19 September 1931, 4, 8.

126. Makram Ubaid, 'al-Misriyyun Arab', al-Hilal (April 1939), 33. See Sylvia Haim's Arab Nationalism for easy access to this article.

127. Sayigh, al-Fikra al-Arabiyya, p.173.

128. Azzam suggests that if was Makram's enthusiastic reception in Syria in 1931 that made him into a friend of Arab unity. FO.141/744, 834/1/33.

129. Ubaid, 'al-Misriyyun Arab', 32-3.

130. Bahr, 'Al-Aqbat fi al-Hayat', p.173. In October 1944, Makram claimed that all true Egyptians, Muslim and Copt, believed in the pan-Arab plan, and he condemned al-Nahhas for his past opposition to unity. Egyptian Gazette, 11 October 1944, 3.

131. J.W.D. Gray, 'Arab Nationalism: Abdin against the Wafd', The Middle East Forum 38 (1962), 18. Sayigh concedes that there is some truth in this in al-Fikra al-Arabiyya, pp.240-1. As Misr noted, all Brethren and Shabab propaganda on Palestine had a religious colour. It charged that they had made religion into a 'call for blood, killing, hostility and hatred'. Misr, 17 May 1947, 1. See also Misr, 6 September 1951, 2 for a similar complaint about Misr al-Fatat. Kedourie believes that it was the Brethren's championship that alerted the Egyptian masses to the problem, and this could help to explain Coptic wariness. Elie Kedourie, 'Religion and secular nationalism in the Arab world', in The Middle East: Oil, Conflict and Hope, ed. A.L. Udovitch (Lexington Books, Lexington, 1976), p.185.

132. FO.141/536, 403/12/36.

133. Al-Manara al-Misriyya, 2 April 1951, quoted in The Cry of Egypt's Copts, pp.18-19.

134. Kedourie, The Chatham House Version, p.200.

135. French Embassy Archives, Box 144, File 31/2, Revue des Periodiques Arabes, 31 December 1947. This is from al-Manara al-Misriyya, 13 December 1947.

136. Ibid., Situation de la Communaute Copte en Egypt, 24 January 1948.

137. FO.371/62993, J6319/13/16.

138. The Greek Orthodox Patriarch shared this view and declared that, in the absence of an international mandatory or Arab state as guardian of the

Holy Places, he preferred that custody remain in Muslim hands. FO.371/63021, J5123/79/16.

139. Misr, 21 May 1948, 1.

140. Misr, 27 May 1948, 1.

141. Al-Manara al-Misriyya, 19 February 1951, reprinted in The Cry of Egypt's Copts, pp.20-1.

142. Al-Manara al-Misriyya, 5 March 1951, 1.

143. In those days it was much safer to be a communist if you held a foreign passport. Mohammed Heikal, Sphinx and Commissar: The Rise and Fall of Soviet Influence in the Arab World (Collins, London, 1978), p.39.

144. Ibid., p.39.

145. FO.371/10909, J1932/1153/16.

146. Musa, The Education of Salama Musa, p.137.

147. Walter Laqueur, Communism and Nationalism in the Middle East (Frederick Praeger, New York, 1956), p.37. See also, M.S. Agwami, Communism in the Arab East (Asia Publishing House, London, 1969), p.5.

148. Laqueur, Communism and Nationalism, p.42.

149. Russia's entry into the war meant that British vigilance against the communists relaxed. Heikal, Sphinx and Commissar, p.47.

150. FO.371/69259, J3914/2410/16.

151. Ibrahim, 'Egyptian Intellectuals', p.285.

152. One Coptic author notes that whenever Coptic opponents of the regime were arrested in the late 1940s, they were accused of being communists, just as Muslim opponents were charged with belonging to the Muslim Brethren. If this is true, it could make the number of Coptic Marxists appear artificially high. Hanna, Nam Awbat Lakin Misriyyun, p.92.

153. Laqueur, Communism and Nationalism, p.51.

154. Rifat al-Said, al-Sihafa al-Yasariyya fi Misr, 1925-1948 (Maktabat Madbuli, Cairo, 1977), p.106.

155. Ibid., pp.105, 107.

156. Ahmad Sadiq Sad, Safahat min al-Yasar al-Misri 1945-6 (Maktabat Madbuli, Cairo, 1976), pp.39-45.

157. Mohammed Heikal notes that Coptic support for the Trotskyite movement was strong, but offers no supporting evidence. Heikal, Sphinx and Commissar, p.142.

158. Said, al-Sihafa, p.83.

159. Hinain was a Francophile. He wrote in French by preference and had a keen interest in Impressionism. He was eventually ejected from the movement, perhaps for bourgeois tastes, and retired to Paris. Interview with Ibrahim Amin Ghali,

19 March 1979.

160. Said, al-Sihafa, pp.96, 102.

161. Ibid., p.85.

162. FO.141/1158, 66/109/47.

163. Suliman presented himself as a Copt, but may have been of Syrian extraction. His masquerade may have been the result of attempts to Egyptianise the movement. Interview with Ibrahim Amin Ghali, 19 March 1979.

164. From the early 1940s, he was connected with various Marxist groups and in 1950 was a member of the Central Committee of the Egyptian Communist Party. FO.371/80354, E1011/6/16.

165. Said, al-Sihafa, p.107.

166. Ibid., pp.136-7.

167. Heikal, Sphinx and Commissar, p.52.

168. Seikaly, 'The Copts under British Rule, 1882-1914', 138.

169. Some Copts before the war did countenance a common descent, but Muslims were not at that time interested in claiming Pharaonic ancestors. See the speeches of Mikhail Fanus, Akhnukh Fanus and Murqus Hanna at Coptic Conference Held in Assiout, pp.6-18, 33-9.

170. FO.407/221, No.27, D.V. Kelly to Mr. Eden, 2 September 1937.

171. See, for example, Misr, 23 April 1919, quoted in FO.371/3717, 78459/24930/16.

172. Misr, 25 April 1919, quoted in FO.371/3717, 78459/24930/16.

173. Misr, 21 May 1919, 1.

174. Ramzi Tadrus, the Coptic biographer, is one who did. Seikaly, 'The Copts under British Rule, 1882-1914', 172.

175. Zaghib Mikhail, Farriq asud, p.10. One contemporary writer, Muhammad Kailani, suggests that problems were due partly to the British and partly to some misguided Copts. See his al-Adab al-Qibti, p.70.

176. Misr, 11 November 1921, 1.

177. Misr, 25 July 1931, 1.

178. Misr, 27 and 28 August 1951, 1.

179. Misr, 13 August 1951, 1.

180. Two books on the subject of Muslim-Copt relations, Mikhail's Farriq Tasud, and Jak Tajir's al-Aqbat w-al-Muslimun (no publisher, Cairo, 1951), were banned by the government when they were published in the early 1950s. The government was not eager to have these relations scrutinised. DW, Abdin Palace Archives, Tawaif Diniyya 1.

181. Interview with Kamal al-Malakh, the Cop-

tic Assistant Chief Editor of al-Ahram, 9 November 1978.

182. Nasser's pronounced pan-Arab policy led some Copts to recall Maspero's 1908 lecture and to regard Egypt's Pharaonic heritage as once again their unique possession. See the speech by a Ministry of Education official, Kamil Mikhail al-Said on 27 January 1955, at a church in Shubra, Al-Aqbat Ibna al-Faraina (Cairo, 1956), p.37.

183. Interview with Kamal al-Malakh, 9 November 1978.

Chapter Four

REPRESENTATIVE INSTITUTIONS

A. THE LEGAL FRAMEWORK: THE EGYPTIAN CONSTITUTION

At the Asyut conference in 1911, Mikhail Fanus spoke for many Copts when he asked his compatriots to set aside the idea that the Copts constituted a group apart from the rest of the nation.[1] The law had long recognised and even reinforced religious differences and when there was talk of drafting a constitution in 1908, at the height of communal hostilities, many Copts feared that a constitution would perpetuate their inferior status. Their concern was premature because a constitution was not, in fact, drawn up until 1922.

The constitution is important not only because it set the framework for political activity in this period, but because the debate surrounding it illuminates different attitudes towards minorities and their place in the political system. Was the constitution, once in effect, able to fulfil Fanus' hope and establish the ascendancy of one view of minorities over all others?

1. Civil Rights

Copts had long argued that although they shouldered an equal burden of the responsibilities of a citizen, they did not enjoy equality in the exercise of rights. Their freedom of worship was circumscribed by various regulations and was often hampered by the illegal interference of Muslims with religious processions. They suffered from discrimination in many areas of Egyptian life and hoped to cure it with a political system that granted them adequate representation. They wanted Egypt's constitution to enshrine the civil and political equality which was so lavishly praised during the 1919 revolution.

The Constitutional Commission began meeting in

April 1922 and was as representative as an appointed body opposed by the Wafd could then be. Wafdists had demanded the election of a constituent assembly which would have brought younger men of more radical views and diverse backgrounds into the deliberations. The Palace instead chose a small commission of notables, including four Copts.[2] The Wafd's boycott left both the political composition of the Commission and the deliberations of that body conservative. The Wafd, which maintained a position of blanket opposition to the proceedings, did, however, take an influential stand on the subject of minority representation.

When Husain Rushdi, Chairman of the Commission, raised the issue of constitutional protection for minorities, he did so partly to banish the incubus of British intervention. He suggested several safeguards including freedom of worship and equality in political and civil rights.[3] His proposal was neither irregular nor unexpected. The Commission had studied several European constitutions, most of which made provisions of this kind, and had chosen the Belgian constitution as a model. Belgium had sectarian problems, and its constitution took communal fears and desires into account.

Rushdi told a subcommittee charged with the actual drafting that he wanted Egypt's minorities so well protected by the constitution that the British would have no grounds for maintaining the third Resserved Point. There was substantial agreement on both this and his suggested guarantees, with the possible exception of Shaikh Bakhit who, as Mufti of Egypt, represented a more conservative cast of mind.[4] Three articles were drafted and the subcommittee's report to the whole committee made clear that these were not a new departure but a recognition of historical fact. As the report stated, the Egyptians had always been equal under the law.[5] Despite a fair degree of religious tolerance, this claim was not precisely true; it was simply another example of making modernity acceptable by proving its coincidence with tradition. The Commission, meeting in August, approved these three articles and they appeared in the Constitution as Articles 3, 12 and 13. The first guaranteed that the Egyptians were equal before the law and in right and duties; no distinction was to be made on the basis of origin, language or religion. Article 12 promised freedom of belief, and Article 13 freedom of worship as long as it did not infringe upon public order or morals.

None of these clauses officially recognised

minorities; in a political sense, they did not exist. The principle of freedom of conscience could perhaps fairly be regarded as the modern equivalent of the old communal autonomy, although the Copts expected the new provision to be more far-reaching than the old. The guarantee of equal rights and duties was a radical departure and went well beyond what the old system had afforded non-Muslims. The question that occurred to few Copts in 1922 but to many in later years, was the ability of this particular legal document, which reflected the opinions of a portion of the élite, and it would seem, to a lesser extent, the expectations of Europe, to change popular Egyptian attitudes. The government often found that it was unable to enforce those very guarantees of equality which the constitution provided.

The Commission's anticipation of British expectations was an important element in the acceptance of the idea of equality. Not only British but European expectations were a concern; such protections were an integral part of any modern, democratic constitution. These were simply safeguards which were, in this era, considered constitutional good form. Coptic participation in the revolution was fresh in the public mind; such guarantees could be portrayed, and sometimes were, as the legitimate 'price' of this participation. There seems to have been no objection to the three articles, not even by those <u>ulama</u> on the Commission. Shaikh Muhammad Shakir, former Vice-Rector of al-Azhar and a member of the 1913-14 Legislative Assembly, wrote to Rushdi that it was reasonable to guarantee every man the right to practise his faith.[6] Indeed, it was reasonable, but in the final reckoning Articles 3, 12 and 13 were overshadowed, and to an extent even negated, by the provision making Islam the religion of state.

2. Setting a Religion of State

As noted, many Egyptians argued for a separation between religion and politics. The incorporation of an article naming Islam the religion of state made this impossible from the outset. The Commission, without demur from its non-Muslim members and with no discussion, agreed to its inclusion.[7] This article, as Subhi points out, did not create a new situation, but rather confirmed an old one.[8] Of course, a number of European constitutions named a religion of state, but the dynamic between religion and government in these countries was not what it was in the Islamic world. The Commission's members either failed to see or felt unable to correct the contradiction inherent in the special obligations this article imposed on the government and the promise of equality to all Egyptians, regardless of their religion.[9]

The 1911 Heliopolis Conference had insisted, despite its billing as a non-sectarian meeting, that Islam must be the official religion of Egypt. Not many Muslims would have dissented publicly in 1922; only the Wafd had the popular support to do so but it is unlikely that they would have been willing to run the risk. Zaghlul knew, in 1924, that it taxed his popularity just to keep two Copts in his cabinet, a much less drastic step. Few, if any, members of the Constitutional Commission were radical in their political ideas. Nor did the Palace subscribe to the time's most modern views, except those contributing to royal power; and it was conscious of its strong ties to the Islamic religious establishment. The ruler traditionally had a duty to protect and promote the worship of Islam; this became a task of the constitutional monarchy as well.

The Commission's Coptic members did not object to this clause, nor was there much opposition from Copts outside the Commission. Al-Watan, however, clearly preferred that a state religion not be established because it would lead to discrimination and the division of the Egyptian people.[10] Many Copts seemed to feel that the constitution adequately protected their interests, and they counted on the continuance of Muslim good will. After all, religious qualifications were given no formal political significance in the constitution; that document might even initially have been a spur to equality and unity. Copts frequently expressed a desire for a separation of Islam and politics; this general sentiment is not, however, equivalent to a clear statement that there should be no state religion. In fact, in 1930 Salama Musa rather curiously declared that he, as an Egyptian, was obliged to defend Islam because it was the religion of his country.[11] Makram Ubaid, in a similar but typically more glib statement, announced on several occasions that he was 'a Muslim in country and a Christian in religion'.

Copts only clearly began to voice their concern about being 'Muslim in country' in later years when the protections and promised equality of the constitution were demonstrably inadequate. As Misr observed in 1951, the article naming a state religion had turned out to be the most important of all.[12]

By then it was less likely than ever that a formal separation between Islam and politics could be made. From the mid-1940s, Salama Musa and others writing in the pages of Misr called for a constitutional amendment disestablishing Islam as the state religion.[13] In 1948, Murqus Sergius circulated a petition for signature among Copts calling for the separation of religion and state and for complete equality.[14] Misr criticised those Egyptians who called Israel a religious state when their own country was not exempt from the charge,[15] and Salama Musa commented that religion ought not to be used to serve the interests of the state.[16]

Byt this time, the Copts had lived for several years with Article 149. It did not make Egypt a theocracy, but it did oblige the government to build mosques, teach religion, train Imams, celebrate Muslim holidays and adhere, at least in part, to religious law.[17] In addition, the King was charged in the constitution with various religious responsibilities; he was, for example, the head of religious institutions. Public funds collected from Muslims and Copts, were distributed inequitably, and certain benefits accrued to one sector of the population alone.[18] Walter Smart, the Oriental Secretary, noted that enormous sums were spent on Islamic institutions while no similar or even proportional sum was allocated for Coptic institutions.[19] The income from Muslim endowments grew increasingly inadequate for funding Muslim institutions, and the government was obliged to fill the gap out of tax revenues. By 1946, almost ninety per cent of al-Azhar's budget came directly from the government.[20] When that institution's budget was discussed in the Senate in 1939, Dr. Ibrahim Bayumi Madkur pleaded with his colleagues not to argue over sums: Islam was the religion of state; it must be protected and religious education provided to coming generations.[21] Generally, neither the Senate nor the Chamber quibbled over al-Azhar's budget, which between 1923 and 1937, increased by more than six times.[22] The government spent more per student on Islamic theological training than it did on secular education.[23]

Copts seem never to have asked for an end to all religious allocations; they simply desired that the principle of equality or proportionality be recognised.[24] For example, it turned out to be impossible, despite Coptic importuning, for the Egyptian government to fund a proportional amount of Christian education for its Christian students. The government could not participate in training teachers of Christianity; nor could it pay their salaries and allocate both time and space in a public institution. In a general sense, then, Article 149 meant that Coptic aims were not identical to those of the state. It was clear to many Copts that their well-being as a community could easily be set aside at those times when it conflicted with other, higher priority aims of the state.[25]

The more serious problem was not the naming of a religion of state, but the fact that the much vaunted guarantees of freedom of worship and equality were not inviolable and were not taken seriously. When a Coptic convert to Islam wished to return to Christianity, the court denied him permission on the grounds that the state's religion did not recognise the right of apostacy. Ramses Jabrawi very properly noted that this contradicted the constitution's promise of freedom of belief.[26]

Ultimately, Article 149's reinforcement of the traditional relationship between Islam and government prevented the full political integration of the Copts and made a secular polity legally impossible. How could the Copts be part of a national community which undertook as one of its tenets the necessity of defending and promoting Islam?

3. The Representation of Minorities in Parliament

Even before the Constitutional Commission met, the question of granting minorities porportional representation in parliament was raised and sparked heated public discussion.[27] The idea was not unprecedented. Akhnukh Fanus' short-lived political party had hinted at the desirability of guaranteed representation in its 1908 platform. At the 1911 Asyut conference, Murqus Hanna pointed to the Belgian system of proportional representation and implied that Egypt would do well to emulate this arrangement.[28] When no Copts were elected to the 1913-14 Legislative Assembly, four were appointed, recognising at least informally the need to make some arrangement for a minority voice.[29]

When the subject came up in 1922, it divided partly along Wafd-non-Wafd lines.[30] Those Muslims supporting minority representation tended to be hostile to the Wafd and included the followers of Adli and Tharwat. The same generalisation cannot comfortably be made about the Copts. Some who advocated proportional representation were bound by the horizon of the community. The Wafd and the National Party opposed minority representation; they kept the debate on this subject within the framework of the nationalist struggle against the Occupation.[31]

There were two main arguments. The first was one of necessity. As Tawfiq Dus pointed out, few Copts had won seats on Egypt's representative bodies; what guarantee, he asked, had they that now they would be elected? Their guarantee, answered his opponents, was to be found in the events of the revolution and its aftermath. A new pattern had been set: Copts would be elected because of the interests they represented and the skills they possessed or defeated because of the lack thereof, and not because they were Copts. It was never clearly stated by Dus that the Copts, as a community, might occasionally have interests that differed from their Muslim compatriots and therefore needed to be guaranteed a place to present them. The tone of his argument was more that Copts, as loyal Egyptians, wished to help in governing Egypt.

The second point of discussion was whether minority representation would encourage or discourage British intervention to protect minorities. Those who took the latter view predicted that, because there would be no arrangement which would permit minorities to vent complaints, the British would be called upon to interfere on their behalf. Opponents claimed that guaranteed representation would encourage intervention because the scheme was a British plot to divide the Egyptian people. Both were wrong, since the British were content merely to record this debate.

In a subcommittee meeting in May, Tawfiq Dus recommended fixed minority representation.[32] He pointed to the 1914 Legislative Assembly and suggested that minorities must have a voice in any body deciding on laws which would affect them as well as Muslim Egyptians. He proposed the following plan: elections would be held and, if an inadequate number of minorities were elected, either a second general election, with Muslims and Copts voting, could be held to make up the Coptic quota, or the Chamber could elect the number needed from among those minority candidates who had lost. This was a ludicrous, costly and time-consuming scheme, but Dus' opponents chose to focus on the value and need for a minority voice and not Dus' specific proposal, which would not have guaranteed the expression of non-Muslim views. His plan meant first that there would be no fixed number of seats in parliament and so the number of Copts to be elected would have to be determined anew after every election. With Muslims voting, it was unlikely that partisans of communal interest would be elected. Had Dus' scheme been enacted, the Coptic voice in parliament would not have been any louder than it was, although there could have been a few more quiet Coptic politicians sitting in parliament in 1950. Proportional representation also raised the sticky issue of how many Copts there actually were.

It is not clear why Dus fixed on this kind of arrangement. Perhaps he was merely testing the waters and, if hospitably warm, hoped to develop his plan into one that provided for more genuine minority representation. If, however, he was working at the behest of the Patriarch, who took care not to offend the Palace, the weakness of his scheme is perhaps understandable. Perhaps, too, Dus and other Copts merely made a mistaken link between the quantity of representatives and the quality of representation. Certainly, the entire debate was conducted as though the two were connected. Of course, other supporting minority representation did advocate that only the minority itself vote for its representatives.

Abd al-Hamid Badawi, chief legal adviser to the subcommittee, objected to the idea and pointed out that the British were not insisting on special representation for minorities. He presented as evidence those post-World War I treaties which only promised Eastern European minorities the protection of their civil rights. Dus, like earlier Copts, had quoted from the Belgian constitution, but Badawi insisted that the Flemish and Walloon communities were political and not religious groups. He added that the Egyptian Chamber was designed as a political body with deputies representing the whole country, and not merely a religious sect. Badawi believed that minority representation would fix the importance of a religious division which otherwise would diminish.

In a later meeting, Badawi suggested that it was political heresy (<u>bida</u>) to incorporate religious or racial minorities in Western representative institutions. He added that if the Copts were granted a fixed number of seats, it would be difficult to deny seats to the other minorities, including foreign ones, in Egypt. Cromer's plan would then be realised and Egypt would be a "stage for religious and racial discord".[33] Badawi insisted that they did not have the competence to draw up this kind of a constitution.

Dus commented that however equal all Egyptians

were made in the constitution, differences would continue to exist; the monarch, for example, would always be a Muslim.[34] The subcommittee's discussion made no progress and, after rejecting a suggestion that Coptic notables be invited to express their views, members decided to hold the matter for the full committee.

It is interesting to speculate on Dus' motives. He was not known for his interest in the welfare of his community, but it is possible that he thought that minority representation would fix his own star in the political firmament. He was, as noted, reasonably close to the Patriarch and may have been acting at his behest. Dus spent part of May on a propaganda tour of Asyut[35] and, ignoring a subcommittee ban, published his views in _al-Ahram_.[36] He felt compelled to disagree publicly with the many newspapers calling minority representation a British plot to divide Egypt; he insisted he was concerned not with the welfare of the Copts but with the danger Egypt faced without minority representation. Dus was criticised by the press and was accused of representing himself and not the Copts; otherwise, wrote one paper, he would not have joined the Adli government when all his co-religionists were opposing it.[37] Salama Mikhail wrote in the pages of _al-Akhbar_:

> Let Tawfiq Dus know that the Copts prefer to sustain all the sufferings he fears to come from their compatriots rather than record in the constitution...that which makes them look like foreigners...and impute to their compatriots the charge of fanaticism and ungratefulness. It is far better for them to lose everything than to see the constitution...contain a clause on which the foreigner can rely in accusing the Egyptians of backwardness and mistrust of each other and of still clinging to old religious differences...thereby finding a way of intervention in the...internal affairs of their country.[38]

Perhaps the most sophisticated debate to appear in the press was the one which occurred betweem Mahmud Azmi and Aziz Mirhum.[39] The first was a Muslim and the second a Copt, and both were committed secularists and charter members of the short-lived Democratic Party. Mirhum opposed minority representation while Azmi supported it. The latter, chief editor of al-Istiqlal, published a series of articles which one Egyptian scholar claims were inspired by the British in an attempt to divide Muslims and Copts.[40] Azmi, claiming that national solidarity demanded minority representation, backed proportional representation, but stipulated that only Copts participate in electing Coptic representatives. The Egyptians, he wrote, were still motivated by religion and, it was only fair, when a state religion had been fixed, to regard religious groups as political groups and to have those groups represented in parliament.[41] His paper claimed that most Copts were afraid to express their approval of fixed representation, and therefore was pleased when Ilyas Awad announced that the Patriarch supported the idea.[42]

Very early in the debate Mirhum warned of the danger of dividing the country into a majority and minorities. He said that if the Christian members of the Commission presented themselves as representatives of Coptic opinion, they lied.[43] Mirhum insisted that such divisions were anachronisms; political and economic groups would grow out of them, and the constitution should aid this process and not hinder it.[44] In his eyes, Azmi was denying those secular and democratic ideas in which he claimed to believe, and he attacked Azmi for mingling religious, social and political questions. He believed that granting the minorities special seats meant that they would never be absorbed into the body politic; religion would always be tied to government.

Azmi also wished to eliminate the importance religious expressions had in social and political life. Until this could be done across the board, there would still be a majority and a minority; nationalism was not enough to unite the two as long as family, education, the court system and other factors prevented a full blending of the different ethnic groups. He insisted that as long as the constitution did not abolish outmoded special principles and institutions, the minorities needed special representation.[45]

Salama Musa felt that minority representation was pointless since the Muslim majority would have enough votes to pass any law it wanted and could also defeat any minority bill it opposed.[46] If, he wrote, communal representatives were able to reach their goals through alliances and agreements with other parties, then they would have exceeded their specific minority role.

In May, Taha Husain was moved to pick up his

pen. He too blamed the British for this disagreement; once again, they were trying to foment discord between moderates and extremists and between Muslims and non-Muslims. He wrote that Egypt had begun to follow European ways and accordingly the differences between Muslims and non-Muslims were disappearing little by little:

> Every equality exists between Muslims and non-Muslims, but some want to keep the minority separate and give it a special existence it has not got now. They want Christians equal before the law but separate from Muslims with special representation. They wrong both the majority and the minority.[47]

Our new government, he continued inaptly, would have no tie to religion. The King would receive his power, through the constitution, from all the Egyptian people and not from Islam.

The Coptic community had mixed reactions to proportional representation. The Orthodox were split, whereas the Council of the Evangelical Church supported it.[48] Monseigneur Sidfawi, Head of the Coptic Catholic community, commented in an interview that those Coptic Catholics to whom he had talked feared that minority representation would harm national unity; the Monseigneur cautiously refrained from offering his own opinion.

The Orthodox Lay Council sent a message supporting minority representation to the Constitutional Commission.[49] Misr invited the Lay Council to a meeting in an attempt to persuade them to reverse their decision but failed. The Orthodox Bishops of Isna, Dair al-Muharraq, al-Minya and Sanbu also made known their support. The Patriarch initially kept a low profile; this equivocation, which al-Bishri suggests was intentional,[50] led each side to claim his support. Al-Anba Yuannis, as his representative on the Constitutional Commission, took no stand on this issue in the subcommittee discussion. However, it appears that the Patriarch supported minority representation; the church, as the most well-organised and articulate of the community's institutions, could only gain by it. The church had no serious communal rival at that time, and it would easily have influenced or dominated the communal members of parliament. Finally, in June, the Patriarch came out in an interview in favour of the idea. Wafdist Copts formed a deputation to plead their case before the Patriarch, but he refused to see them. Curiously, he gave two interviews after this and managed in both to obscure his position.[51]

The conservative Coptic newspaper, al-Watan, may have been the first to advocate proportional representation. In an article published in March, the paper, after going to lyrical lengths to demonstrate Coptic loyalty to Egypt, reminded its audience that the Copts were still a minority. They wanted to serve their country and share in the work of the legislature, yet they feared that they might not be represented in that body.[52] The following day, al-Watan suggested that it was in Egypt's interest to protect her minorities in order to deprive Britain of the right to meddle.[53] The denial of parliamentary representation would lead the minorities to complain, and their complaints would result in foreign intervention.[54] Al-Watan claimed that, expect for Badawi, the only ones opposed to communal representation were Wafdists; even the Beduin wanted special rights written into the constitution.[55]

There were many Coptic critics of proportional representation,[56] but the most vehement ones were Wafdists, many of whom resisted the idea on the grounds of nationalism or secularism.[57] Zaghlul was an old opponent, believing that parliament should divide on issue or party lines and not ethnic ones.[58] Characteristically, both the Wafd and Misr denied that there were minorities in Egypt; all Egyptians were of one race and no Egyptian Copt had an identity separate from his Muslim brother.[59] Misr was very concerned that minority representation would constitute a legal separation between Muslims and non-Muslims.[60] The paper argued that, although Egypt was still officially a religious state, religion would not be relied upon for political ideology. Misr published letters and telegrams from many Copts who were opposed to guaranteed representation.

On 12 May, the Wafd announced its official belief that minority representation would be a prop for the British; division had been the policy of Milner, Curzon and all of Egypt's enemies, and it was incompatible with the welfare of the nation.[61] Most important Coptic Wafdists wrote in the press on this issue, including, as already noted, Salama Mikhail. Wisa Wasif published an article in La Bourse Egyptienne insisting that only political parties be represented in parliament; Copts who won seats would be present as deputies and not Copts.[62] Raghib Iskandar warned of rebellion (fitna) if parliament were divided along ethnic lines. Parliament, he added, was not meant to act as a religious council.[63] To supplement this writing, Fakhri Abd al-Nur propagandised in Jirja, and Najib Iskandar at the Ramses Club and in Cairo.[64]

Coptic Wafdists called for a community meeting to be held on 19 May 1922 at St. Peter's Church in Cairo.[65] Between one hundred and five hundred Copts turned up,[66] and they applauded Zaghlul, his exiled comrades and Salama Mikhail. Salama gave two speeches in which he attacked minority representation as heretical (bida). He gave the crowd examples of the important role Copts played in the Wafd, and said that it would be unfortunate to exchange a representation based on feelings for a representation based on law. Wisa Wasif, Antun Jirjis, Shaikh Mustafa al-Qayati and others also spoke. A final report was issued attacking minority representation as heretical and dangerous to national unity.[67]

In July al-Azhar made known its views. In a letter to the Head of the Royal Diwan, the ulama complained about an article written by Mahmud Azmi.[68] This article had advocated both secularism and minority representation, and the ulama asked for an injunction to prevent Azmi from publishing articles against Islam. They probably were more upset by his advocacy of secularism than by his support for minority representation. Their letter only pointed to the danger of raising the latter subject when the country had achieved unity.

It does seem that the opponents of minority representation were in the majority. The King, showing as much discretion as the Patriarch, was probably an opponent, a position which was perhaps made clear to the members of the Constitutional Commission when they took up the matter in August.[69] Dus began by noting that the press debate had been acrimonious, and he pointed in particular to an article in al-Ahram by the Watanist, Ibrahim Desuqi Abaza, who claimed that the Copts desired minority representation because they had no faith in Muslims or in the new political arrangements. The Copts, claimed Dus, were intimidated by such statements, and felt unable to present their real views. Dus, after repeating his personal opinion, asserted that the Patriarch favoured minority representation. Presumably, he had some authority to make this claim.

Ibrahim al-Hilbawi and Abd al-Aziz Fahmi countered Dus' views, and the latter suggested that Dus proposed making elections a struggle between religions rather than between political parties and ideas. Dus here suggested a weighting of the electorate which would give twenty per cent of the seats to minorities. A proportional scheme, based on the 1917 census, would have given the minorities a much smaller number. Yusuf Qattawi, representing the Jewish community, and Metropolitan Yuannis agreed with Dus' views. The Metropolitan claimed that minority representation would help preserve unity. Badawi, the most articulate member of the opposition on the Commission, unaccountably was absent, but Ali Mahir upheld his views. Qalini Fahmi, here serving his master the King rather than the Patriarch, joined the opposition. A vote was taken and Dus' proposal was defeated by a vote of fifteen to seven.

Tariq al-Bishri calls the defeat of proportional representation a victory for those supporting nationalism and secularism.70 The victors did not wish to deprive the Copts of parliamentary seats. They genuinely believed that the voters would not choose candidates according to an ethnic criterion but because they represented an important interest or had effective campaigning skills. They did not see the Copts as a minority in the Eastern European or even Belgian sense, and believed that Dus' reminder of the failure of any Copts to be elected to the 1914 Legislative Assembly was irrelevant. Coptic Wafdists perhaps feared to lose their influence in party councils if they suddenly became the representatives of a small and insignificant community. If Copts were awarded seats because they were Copts, they could not claim to represent the nation; any political role they wished to play would be circumscribed by their ethnic origin.

The quarrel was not cast in ethnic or religious terms, if only because so many Copts vigorously opposed the idea. Muslim intimidation does not seem to have been a factor in this Coptic position. Since most people then seemed to be backing the Wafd, most people supported the Wafd's objection to the scheme. Although the issue perhaps would not have arisen in a Wafdist-dominated constituent assembly, the Wafd probably was less annoyed with the idea of proportional representation than it was with the appointment of a commission by its opponents. It was the latter who were developing the political framework within which the Wafd would have to operate. The party was then in an awkward position with most of its important leaders in exile or under arrest, and minority representation was a good issue for rallying the faithful. Political "moderates" were at least willing to consider the question, and those on the Commission might have backed Dus, had there been more Coptic and British pressure for the institutionalisation of minority representation and less Wafdist and Royal opposition. Had the Commission conceded a specified number of seats in parliament to minorities, it would still not have been the equivalent of putting substantial power into minority hands.

B. COPTIC POLITICAL REPRESENTATION, 1924-1952

1. The Chamber of Deputies

Elections for the lower house, which were sometimes direct and sometimes indirect, were held more frequently than those for the Senate. Eligibility, with no property or status restrictions, were relatively open. Competition between candidates, however, was rarely unfettered. Election boycotts by one party or another were not uncommon, nor was the gentlemanly division of constituencies by a coalition of parties. Only the Wafd seemed to have both the broad appeal and financial ability necessary to field candidates in almost every constituency. Weaker parties were unable to do this and sometimes declined to nominate candidates in districts which they suspected would be won by politicians standing for other parties. These factors held to explain the surprising number of candidates returned unopposed. The voters in approximately one-half of the constituencies which elected Copts in this period had no choice. It might be most correct to extrapolate from this not so much a willingness among the general population to elect Christians, as an inclination on the part of the parties to nominate Copts to stand for election.

Copts were adequately represented in the Chamber. In 1924, the opponents of minority representation rejoiced when the first election vindicated their view and Copts won more seats than would have been allocated to them in a proportional scheme based on the 1917 census.[71] The percentage of seats occupied by Copts often topped their official proportion of the population; however, if the Coptic complaint that their numbers were undercounted was true, then they were underrepresented. In some Chambers, Coptic representation was suprisingly low, as will be seen in the following breakdown of seats. Copts were less well represented from the 1940s than they were in the 1920s.

Year[72]	Number of Copts	Number of Seats	Percentage of Coptic Seats
1924	16	214	7.5
1925	13	214	6.1
1926	16	214	7.5
1929	20	235	8.5
1931	4	150	2.6
1936	20	232	8.8
1938	6	264	2.3
1942	23	264	8.7
1945	12	264	4.5
1950	8	320	2.5

What is immediately apparent to someone familiar with this period is that the Copts won more seats whenever the Wafd won an election; that is, in 1924, 1929, 1936 and 1942. Coptic representation was adequate in two Chambers with strong Wafdist representation: the short-lived Chamber[73] which was less than half Wafdist, and the coalition assembly of 1926. Most of the Copts who won seats in these last two elections were Wafdist. The 1931 elections, overseen by the Sidqi government, were not an accurate expression of popular feeling; and few Copts were nominated or returned.[74] The 1938 elections were exceptionally corrupt and its victors made heavy use of religious and anti-Coptic propaganda. It is not surprising to find that the winning parties nominated few Copts and that few of those who did run were elected. Although the 1945 Chamber was dominated by a non-Wafdist coalition, more Copts were elected to seats because of the participation of the al-Kutla party. The latter, organised by Makram Ubaid, nominated two-thirds of the successful Coptic candidates in this election.

Given this pattern which suggests both that the Wafd had more Coptic support and that the Copts were more influential in this party than in other parties, the 1950 election constitutes an anomaly. The 1950 election was a dramatic victory for the Wafd, at last come in from six years in the political wilderness. The party presented only seven Copts to the electorate[75] and the Copts consequently won fewer seats than they had in the 1931 elections. This low figure indicates that Coptic support for the Wafd had declined and/or that the Wafd was unwilling or unable to replace those Copts who had walked out with Makram Ubaid in 1942. Most of al-Kutla's Coptic candidates were ex-Wafdists, and the party failed to secure any seats in the 1950 election. With the decimations of both al-Kutla and the Grim Reaper, the Wafd had lost most of its important Coptic members, including men who had been in the party since 1919 and had impeccable revolutionary credentials. These were politicians who commanded considerable popular support, at least in association with the Wafd, and it was hard for the party to find adequate substitutes. This task was made even more difficult by the increase in communal tensions in the late 1940s. At one time, the mass of Muslim Egyptians, who were mainly Wafdist in sympathy, were probably more willing to countenance the election of a Coptic Wafdist than a Coptic Liberal Constitutionalist or Ittihadist. By 1950, the Muslim population may have been less willing to vote for any Copt, whatever his party affiliation. The low number of Copts nominated in 1950 perhaps also supports the contention that the Copts had largely withdrawn from the political arena in response to what they saw as their deteriorating position. They believed that the Wafd had forsaken them. *Misr* complained about the small numbers of Copts nominated by the party;[76] that *Misr* had never registered the same complaint about the other parties indicates that it did not have the same expectations of them.

Few Copts were elected officers of the Chamber. The Wafd attempted to have Wisa Wasif elected one of the two Vice-Presidents in 1924 and failed.[77] It had better luck two years later, and in 1928 was able to secure his election to the Presidency of the Chamber.[78] Wisa's role in leading Parliament in passing a vote of no confidence in the government which had just illegally dissolved it in 1928 helped ensure his re-election in the Wafd-dominated Chamber of 1930. In 1936, Kamil Sidqi, another Wafdist, was elected Chamber Vice-President.

Copts were returned from a wide range of constituencies, with Coptic populations which varied in size. Setting aside urban constituencies in Cairo and Alexandria, about two-thirds of the districts which returned Copts were in Upper Egypt and one-third in the Delta. The only Delta province never to elect any Copts was al-Sharqiyya. Copts were returned from every Upper Egyptian province except from al-Faiyum and the predominantly Nubian Aswan. Both had fewer Copts than any other Upper Egyptian province, and one of the Aswan seats was usually reserved for a member of the Jewish community. That Copts often were elected from constituencies with a very small percentage of Coptic inhabitants indicates a certain acceptance of their political role by Muslims, although election often had less to do with the number of Copts in a district than the number of *feddans* owned by Copts or the party affiliation of the Coptic candidates. It does, however, indicate something about the strength of the Wafd to say that it was the only party which could get a Coptic candidate elected in a Delta constituency.[79] Copts were returned from several Cairene constituencies, including the heavily Coptic Shubra and Ezbekia, and from two Alexandrian districts where many Copts lived, al-Labban and al-Attarin.

No district seems to have been automatically allocated to Coptic candidates. Even Christian Ezbekia, which included the Patriarchate, was sometimes consigned to and won by a Muslim candidate. There were constituencies, however, in which it is difficult to imagine a Copt running and, while they were theoretically open to Christian candidates, no Copts were ever nominated to stand in them. Examples of such districts are the exclusively Muslim Darb al-Ahmar in Cairo and Tanta, a city of some religious significance in the Delta.

Wafdists occasionally ran in two constituencies in the same elections, although Makram Ubaid seems to have been the only Wafdist Copts to have done so. In 1926 he ran in his home constituency of Qina town and in Matubis, al-Gharbiyya, a district with few Copts. He won both seats and relinquished the latter to a Muslim replacement. In 1929 he ran again in Qina and also in al-Muski, Cairo, an almost exclusively Muslim constituency. Again, he won both seats. This perhaps was meant to prove that one of the Wafd's important Copts had as much Muslim support as Christian. It may also have been done to preserve the seat for a Wafdist or to indicate that Wafdists could be elected outside those constituencies where their families had land and influence. Unfortunately, these conclusions seem a little forced given that Makram was the only candidate running in Matubis and al-Muski in these elections. In 1938 he ran in Shubra and Qina but he, along with most other Wafdists, failed to win a seat.

Coptic representatives in the Chamber did not differ in background from their Muslim colleagues. Many were wealthy landowners and others were middle-class professionals. The latter were mainly lawyers, with a sprinkling of medical doctors.[80] Coptic ecclesiastics were not elected, although Muslim religious dignitaries sometimes were.

2. The Senate

The requirements for election or appointment to the Senate were more rigorous than those for election to the Chamber. Essentially, service was restricted to the well-to-do of at least forty years of age. Candidates who did not meet certain professional requirements were obliged to pay an annual land tax of £E150,[81] or show proof of an annual income of £E1,500.[82]

Three-fifths of the Senate were elected in three-stage elections and two-fifths appointed. This ratio was reversed in the Sidqi constitution of 1930 and the total number of seats decreased. Appointments were made by the government in power, with the consent of the King.[83] Terms were for ten years with replacement of half the seats every five years. Replacements were selected in 1940, 1941-2, 1946 and 1950. In addition, several governments cynically invalidated the appointments and elections of their predecessors and made new ones. The entire Senate was replaced in 1931 and 1936. Senators were also unseated in 1942, 1944 and 1950; those who were dislodged in 1942 were restored in 1944, and the 1942 candidates ousted.

Copts were well represented in the Senate. Until 1952, the percentage of seats they held was higher than their recorded proportion of the population. They were better represented, at least in numbers, in the Upper Chamber than in the Lower, as can be inferred from the chart below.

Year	Number of Copts	Number of Seats	Percentage of Coptic Seats
1924	11	122	9.1
1930	12[85]	130	9.3
1931	15	100	15.0
1936	14	132	10.6
1939	19	147	13.0
1942	16	147	10.9
1944	15[86]	147	10.2
1946	13	147	8.8
1950	13[87]	147	8.8
1952	12	172[88]	7.0

With two exceptions, no Coptic Senators were returned from the Delta.[89] Copts were elected from heavily Coptic constituencies in Cairo, Alexandria and Upper Egypt. More Copts were appointed to the

Senate than elected; 57.1 per cent of the total number of Coptic Senators were appointed. Appointments were used to ensure that Copts from all three sects had a voice. The government also used its power to appoint Senators to balance the number of elected Coptic Senators. For example, when five Copts were elected to the 1931 Senate, ten Copts were appointed to ensure adequate representation. Even more useful was the government's ability to use its appointment power to improve overall parliamentary representation. Opponents of minority representation had suggested in 1922 that any weakness in Chamber representation could be made up through Senate appointments.[90] When no Jew was elected to the 1924 Chamber, the government appointed a representative of that community to a seat in the Senate. In 1931, when Coptic representation in the Chamber fell to 2.6 per cent, the Sidqi Cabinet was able to placate Coptic fears, at least to an extent, by boosting Coptic representation in the Senate to fifteen per cent. When few Copts were elected to the 1950 Chamber and only three were later elected to the Senate, the Wafd government increased their total number by appointing Copts to Senate seats. Despite these appointments, Coptic representation still fell to its lowest point in the life of the Senate.

The Senate, for most of its life, had a Wafdist majority. Exceptions to this were the 1931-35 Senate and the 1946-50 Senate when non-Wafdists had a majority.[91] Unlike the Chamber, Coptic representation was not necessarily highest when the Wafd was in power. Coptic representation in Wafd-dominated Chambers generally was adequate and Senate seats were not needed to redress the balance. Coptic representation in the Senate reached peaks in 1931 and 1939, both years with non-Wafdist governments. After 1946 and in accordance with increasing communal tensions, Coptic representation declined. Comparing the first and last parliaments in 1924 and 1952, both houses indicate that the Wafd grew less interested in maintaining a high level of Coptic representation. Before the 1952 Senate election, _Misr_ complained that the Wafd had only seen fit to nominate one Copt;[92] subsequent to this criticism, the Wafd presented two more for election.

Although the appointment power was used to give all native ethnic groups and some sectional interests like the army a voice, seats were not formally or informally allocated to one or another. When the Syrian Senator Yusuf Saba died, a Muslim colleague suggested that Saba's seat be given to a Christian of Syrian extraction. His reasoning was not convincing, and Taha Husain was appointed to the seat.[93] Often when a Copt died or resigned, his seat was consigned to a Muslim. Just as often, when a Muslim resigned his seat early, it was offered to a Copt. Coptic senators came from the same backgrounds as their Muslim counterparts; large landowners, including several who owned more than a thousand *feddans*, were well represented, as were ex-cabinet ministers and high government officials. No Copt served as President of the Senate, but two, Nakhla al-Mutii, and Zaki Mikhail Bishara, were elected vice-presidents in 1932 and 1945 respectively. Copts were more frequently elected as Secretaries of the Senate.

The 1923 constitution permitted religious dignitaries to sit in the Senate, and consequently that body had representatives from both the Muslim ulama and the Coptic clergy. Two Coptic ecclesiastics, one Orthodox and the other Catholic, were appointed to the first Senate. Then in 1931, Sidqi, to the considerable displeasure of *Misr* and the Lay Council, appointed Patriarch Yuannis to the Senate.[94] *Misr* argued that the Patriarch's position and religious function required him to remain above the political fray;[95] but it really objected out of a fear that his appointment would increase his power. The Patriarch, perhaps due to this pressure, seems to have considered declining the appointment,[96] but ended by accepting it. Senate representation of Muslim ulama came to a temporary end and of Coptic clergy to a permanent end in 1936, when the Wafd refused to name representatives of either to the Senate. While no Coptic complaints seem to have been voiced at the time, Salama Musa proposed in 1950 that a Coptic Metropolitan be appointed to the Senate to be the official representative of the Coptic church.[97] The Wafd, again in power, did not heed his suggestion. However, the election to that last Senate of al-Minyawi Pasha, the lay Vice-President of the Majlis Milli, gave some satisfaction to the community.[98]

3. Local Councils

Coptic representation in some local bodies was adequate or more than adequate; in others, it was weak or non-existent. This generally, but not invariably, bore some relation to the number of Coptic inhabitants in an area. Even the predominantly Coptic population of Naqada, Qina did not always elect a Copt to their four-man town council, a failure which suggests that Muslims monopolised land, money and influence in the area. However, even a persistent failure to elect Copts to a given council probably had little effect on the community's welfare given the high degree of government centralisation. Little power was delegated and most important decisions were made in Cairo. Provincial and municipal councils had more prerogatives than town and village councils, as might be expected, but even the provincial councils had only executive powers. Town and village councils were transferred at one point from the Ministry of the Interior to the Ministry of Public Health, indicating the limited range of their interests. It is difficult to draw any correlation between the number of Copts elected to a council and the party affiliation of the government conducting the election.[99] Coptic representation does not seem to have been significantly better in Wafd-dominated councils. Often a Copt served on a council for a number of years or kept the seat within his family. For example, Jirjis Bey Abd al-Shahid eventually relinquished his seat on the Biba, Bani Suwaif town council to his son, Habib, who in turn passed it on to his brother Munir.

Copts generally were well represented on the Asyut and Jirja provincial councils; these were the only two which always included at least one Copt. Both provinces, of course, had large Coptic populations. Asyut officials in 1922 even unseated one of the four Muslims elected to their town council in order that one Copt should be represented.[100] Copts won election to provincial councils in other Upper Egyptian provinces, but with less frequency. Copts never served on the Aswan provincial council and seldom did so on the Bani Suwaif and al-Faiyum councils. More Copts managed to secure election to the Qina and al-Minya councils. The only Lower Egyptian provincial councils to include Copts were those of Bahaira, al-Gharbiyya and al-Minufiyya in 1939 and 1943. Their election may have been the result of Wafd-conducted provincial council elections.[101] Few town and village councils in the Delta included Copts, but more in Upper Egypt did so.[102] Copts often did secure election to municipal councils in both regions; these councils, however, were unique in including foreign representation as well.

4. The Limitations on Coptic Representation

Because Copts were elected to parliament to represent not only their constituents, a majority of whom usually were Muslim, but, in a more general sense, the entire country, it is not surprising to find that the level of formal representation on matters of concern to the Coptic community was low. This was particularly true of issues which also interested Muslims and was less so of those specific to the Coptic community, like the Lay Council reform of 1927. The latter, despite Palace concern, was not a matter of interest to Muslim voters or most Muslim members of Parliament; therefore, Coptic Senators and Deputies felt free to use this new forum to prosecute an old quarrel. Few Coptic members, however, would have had the courage or foolhardiness to contribute to the annual debate on al-Azhar's budget. The prudence of Coptic politicians on such points is well illustrated by Taha Husain's remark that al-Azhar was never as pampered as when Makram Ubaid was Finance Minister.[103]

The poor quality of representation can be illustrated by the issue of Christian religious instruction in state schools, a matter which is discussed in greater detail later. This was a subject close to the heart of the Coptic community because Islamic religious instruction formed part of the school curriculum. When the Chamber debated in 1933 the compulsory primary education bill, which provided for extensive Islamic religious studies, no Coptic Deputy suggested that Christian education also be provided. One Senator, Dr. Abd Allah Simaika, showed more courage, and at least raised the subject during the Senate debate on the bill.[104] In the Chamber, a motion to provide Christian education was made in the following session but found little Coptic or Muslim support. When a motion was made to increase the amount of Islamic education provided in state schools, no Copts demurred or spoke in favour of an equal amount of Christian education.[105] Often, when Coptic representatives did choose to speak out in defence of their community, they made their argument on technical or legal grounds and not on the actual merits or demerits of the case. For example, in the 1944 Chamber debate on a draft inheritance law and the 1946 Senate debate on personal status jurisdiction, Coptic representatives argued that both bills should be returned to committee on minor grounds; they said nothing directly against the provisions of either bill.[106]

Coptic senators may have been slightly more willing to represent the community than Coptic Deputies, as is indicated by Abd Allah Simaika's 1933 attempt in the Senate, and the 1926 proposal of Senator Suryal to change the Lay Council Charter. Some appointed senators may actually have seen themselves as communal representatives. It is certainly difficult to see the ecclesiastical senators as anything else, although many Copts would have argued that these man represented the clergy and not the community. Bishop Lukas' outspokenness on the subject of Majlis Millireform in 1926-27 is a case in point. Otherwise, the clerical senators seemed to keep a low profile and probably were busier with church than Senate duties.

Copts seem to have been conscious of this failure to defend their interests, if only because the Coptic press periodically mentioned it. In 1926, Misr took Murqus Hanna, deputy and cabinet minister, to task for not persuading the government to act on the matter of church reform and monastery endowments. However, the paper did go on to praise him for representing the general interests of his constituents.[107] In 1933, Murqus Simaika complained about Coptic deputies "who never open their mouths when bills of vital importance to the Coptic community...are discussed or when important grants out of public funds are voted in favour of Muslim institutions". He added that it was not only Coptic deputies who failed to show an interest in communal affairs, but those in the senate and cabinet as well.[108] Although Misr noted its pleasure in 1940 when Kamil Bey Ibrahim broke the "jealously-guarded silence" of his Christian colleagues to broach the subject of non-Muslim personal status courts, it expressed disappointment that he so quickly abandoned the topic. The paper asked Coptic senators, whom it claimed had said little since their election, to be more vigorous representatives of the community.[109]

Traditionally, the higher clergy had constituted the community's political élite, which was one which was almost entirely dependent on the good will of the government and ruling family. What this new political system did was to consolidate, if not actually establish, a new secular Coptic political élite, which sometimes looked to community, church or Palace for approval, but which could never entirely ignore the Muslim majority and shifting political and party alliances and strengths. This new situation was more confusing because it was more uncertain. The risk that a considerable portion of the community could choose to back the wrong horse must have seemed high.

Had the Copts been concentrated in one region

or had minority representation been instituted, then Egypt might have seen the rise of Coptic communal politicians. Coptic representatives would have been obliged to be more active in their defence of Coptic interests in parliament, but a more vigorous approach need not have contributed to the overall welfare of the community. The nationalist fear that proportional representation would divide the Egyptian people was not entirely far-fetched. An ethnic division of seats in Parliament would have set the Copts apart from the national community, and Coptic politicians, in competing with one another instead of with Muslim rivals, could have felt obliged to make increasingly extravagant and hopeless claims on behalf of their constituents. This could easily have led to a Muslim backlash against a community which had forgotten its place. Formal parliamentary representation, while not unimportant, was nothing compared to informal influence exercised in party and government circles, particularly when parliament was not a strong institution and was subject to summary dismissal.[110] This kind of influence Coptic politicians certainly had and it was sometimes used on behalf of their community. Any kind of proportional scheme would have allocated so few seats that their role would have been restricted to the less important formal one. There would have remained too, the possibility that percentage of the population could have become a criterion in other areas; for example, the civil service and state education. This would not have been in the interest of the Copts. Of course, with the great increase in the number of political groups competing in elections towards the end of the monarchy, proportional representation could have given the Copts more power than that provided by the same number of seats in a stable two-party system. Muslims, however, would have reacted negatively to any sign that a minority determined the balance of power.

5. Coptic Expectations and Demands

Muhammad Husain Haikal tells the story of a young Coptic lawyer who tried to persuade him of the virtues of minority representation in the wake of the 1924 election.[111] Haikal pointed out to him that under proportional representation, the Copts would have had fewer seats than they had just won.[112] The lawyer declared that he was willing to sacrifice those seats in return for a guarantee of future seats. He believed, with some prescience, that national solidarity would weaken, intercommunal tensions mount and the Copts end up unrepresented in parliament. While this situation did not specifically come to pass under the monarchy, the Copts, by the mid-1940s, felt that they no longer had an adequate number of representatives. Salama Musa complained repeatedly that the Abazas, a large and powerful Delta family, had more representatives in parliament than did the Copts.[113] This concern about the number of representatives was occasioned by a recognition that their constitutionally guaranteed religious freedom was not safe from the government or the mob.[114] Mounting hostility towards the Copts persuaded several Copts to call for the disestablishment of Islam as the state religion. At the same time, Copts and Misr began to call for the institutionalisation of proportional representation for minorities.[115] Misr was clearly concerned that the Muslim Brethren and others were working towards a theocratic state;[116] as the paper noted, religion had already been introduced into foreign and domestic policy.[117] With the prospect of a British withdrawal in the near future and the problem of an increasingly discredited and fragmented political system, the Copts perhaps saw minority representation as something which would safeguard the community. The irony is that they needed protection less from those who were willing to operate inside the bounds of the political system than from those who denied its legitimacy and wished to overthrow it.

NOTES

1. The Coptic Congress Held at Assiout, pp.6-12.
2. The four Copts were Tawfiq Dus, Qalini Fahmi, Ilyas Awad and Metropolitan Yuannis.
3. Mahadir al-Lajna Li-wad al-Mabadi al-Amma, thirteenth session, 7 May 1922 (Cairo, 1924).
4. Madabit Lajnat al-Mabadi al-Amma, thirteenth session, 7 May 1922.
5. Taqrir al-Lajna Li-Wad al-Mabadi al-Amma, Appendix I (Cairo, 1927).
6. This letter is included in Mahadir al-Lajna al-Amma Li-Wad al-Dustur (Cairo, 1927).
7. When Shaikh Bakhit, Mufti of Egypt, proposed naming Islam the religion of state, the president said that he had previously solicited opinions on this subject and that all members unanimously agreed on its inclusion in the constitution. Ibid., p.51 (seventeenth session, 19 May 1922).
8. Muhammad Khalil Subhi, Tarikh al-Hayat al-

Niyabiyya fi Misr, vol.5 (Matbaat Dar al-Kutub al-Misriyya, Cairo, 1939), p.489.

9. Musad Sadiq, a journalist, was only one of several Copts to note this contradiction in later years. See Misr, 15 February 1951, 1.

10. Al-Bishri, al-Katib 3, p.141. See also al-Watan, 23 September 1922, 2.

11. Colombe, who quotes this, does not mention the context. There is nothing similar to be found in Musa's Tarbiyyat Salama Musa. Marcel Colombe, "L'Islam dans la vie sociale et politique de l'Egypte contemporaine", Cahiers de l'Orient Contemporain XXI (1950), 19.

12. Misr, 15 February 1951, 1.

13. FO.371/53297, J2253/39/16; FO.371/3331, J2268/57/16; FO.371/53300, J2253/39/16; Misr, 4 April 1947, 1; Misr, 18 January 1952, 1.

14. He apparently drew up a petition, addressed to the Egyptian government, after receiving a number of petitions from individual Copts. His petition defended its demands by claiming that the Copts represented one-seventh (14.3 per cent) of the population and two-fifths of the tax payers. FO.141/1296, 506/3/48.

15. Misr, 5 October 1950, 1.

16. In Misr, June 1948, quoted in Zaghib Mikhail, Farriq Tasud!, p.311.

17. M. Tessler makes a similar point in "The identity of religious minorities in non-secular states - Jews in Tunisia and Morocco and Arabs in Israel", Comparative Studies in Society and History (20) (1978), 359-73.

18. The Copts were not slow to note this, particularly since they felt they paid a disproportionate share of the taxes. See Murqus Fahmi's speech at the Asyut Conference in 1911. The Coptic Conference Held at Assiout, pp.44-9; FO.141/1296, 506/3/48; Misr, 5 December 1946, 1.

19. FO.141/749, 20/26/33; Misr, 5 December 1946, 1.

20. Chamber Debates, second session, 23 July 1946.

21. Senate Debates, fourteenth session, 13 June 1939.

22. Budget of the Egyptian State, Cairo, 1923-27.

23. Russell Galt, The Effects of Centralization on Education in Modern Egypt (American University in Cairo Press, Cairo, 1936), p.19.

24. See Murqus Fahmi's speech, The Coptic Congress Held at Assiout, pp.44-9.

25. See Tessler's parallel comment about other minorities in _Comparative Studies in Society and History_ (20), 365.

26. _Al-Manara al-Misriyya_, 5 March 1951, quoted in _The Cry of Egypt's Copts_, pp.12-13.

27. The Residency noted that in May minority representation was _the_ burning issue. However, this issue in general did not have the emotional impact of the Sudan question. FO.371/7742, E5554/61/6.

28. Hanna first says that he objects to the idea of allowing the Copts a certain number of seats in elected bodies, but later he proposed a scheme which would, in operation, be the equivalent of this. _The Coptic Conference Held at Assiout_, pp.36-8.

29. The four were Qalini Fahmi Pasha, Murqus Simaika Bek, Sinut Hanna Bek, and Kamil Sidqi Bek. That no objections were voiced to these appointments may be an indication of the extent to which Kitchener was able to calm troubled communal waters. Severianus, "Les Coptes de l'Egypte Musulmane", _Etudes Méditerranéennes_ 6 (1959), 80.

30. Tariq al-Bishri, _al-Katib_ 119 (1971), 126.

31. Ibid., 127. Newspapers divided according to their political allegiance. Among those opposed to minority representation were _al-Afkar_, _al-Akhbar_, _Wadi al-Nil_, _al-Liwa_, _al-Basir_ and _Misr_. _Al-Watan_, _al-Istiqlal_, _Revue Egyptienne_ and _La Liberte_ supported it. _Al-Muqattam_ and _al-Ahram_, after publicising both sides, remained non-committal.

32. _Mahadir al-Lajna Li-Wad al-Mabadi al-Amma_, thirteenth session, 7 May 1922, Cairo, 1924.

33. Subcommittee Minutes, 11 May 1922.

34. The Constitution did not specify that the King had to be a Muslim. Article 30, however, stipulated that only a member of the family of Muhammad Ali could sit on the throne.

35. _Al-Watan_, 19 May 1922, PPF.

36. _Al-Ahram_, 15 May 1922, 1. See also, 26 May 1922, PPF.

37. _Al-Afkar_, 15 May 1922, PPF. _Wadi al-Nil_ made a similar comment, suggesting that his position became clear when it was realised that he was an Adlist and a friend of the English. _Wadi al-Nil_, 17 May 1922, PPF.

38. _Al-Akhbar_, 18 May 1922, 3.

39. Al-Bishri, _al-Katib_ 119 (1971), 117.

40. Kailani, _al-Adab al-Qibti_, p.168. Here he is merely echoing what many Wafdists believed.

The belief seems an illogical one unless Wafdists assumed that Egyptian minorities were inherently less loyal to Egypt.

41. Al-Bishri, _al-Katib_ 119 (1971), 117-8.
42. _Al-Istiqlal_, 22 June 1922, 1.
43. _Al-Ahram_, 11 May 1922, 1.
44. Al-Bishri, _al-Katib_ 119 (1971), 118.
45. Ibid., 119-20. Both these men were active in lecturing and organising support for their views.
46. Kailani, _al-Abad al-Qibti_, p.168.
47. _Al-Ahram_, 23 May 1922, 1. Doris Behrens Abouseif suggests that Taha Husain believed that proportional representation would give the Copts the means to create a state within a state. _Die Kopten in der Ägyptischen Gesellschaft von der Mitte 19 Jahrhundert bis 1923_ (Freiburg Im Breisnau, Klaus Schwartz Verlag, Freiburg, 1972), p.94.
48. _Al-Istiqlal_, 17 June 1922, 1.
49. The Vice-Presidents of the Copt Councils in Tanta, Banha and other towns also supported minority representation.
50. Al-Bishri, _al-Katib_ 119 (1971), 123.
51. FO.407/194, Enclosure in No.12, Situation Report, 20-30 June 1922.
52. _Al-Watan_, 8 March 1922, 1.
53. _Al-Watan_, 9 March 1922, 2.
54. _Al-Watan_, 17 May 1922, quoted in al-Bishri, _al-Katib_ 119 (1971), 122.
55. _Al-Watan_, 13 May 1922, PPF.
56. _Al-Ahram_, 27 May 1922, 4.
57. Al-Bishri, _al-Katib_ 119 (1971), 126
58. _Al-Nizam_, 8 October 1920, 2.
59. _Misr_, 14 May 1922, 3.
60. _Misr_, 17 May 1922, 1.
61. This statement was signed by what were probably the eight most important Wafdists then in Egypt. Their number included four Copts: George Khayyat, Murqus Hanna, Wasif Ghali and Wisa Wasif. Abd al-Rahman Fahmi also thought that minority representation would be divisive and would support the British claim to protect minorities. DW, Mahfaza Raqm 1, Makhtut 19, Memoirs of Abd al-Rahman Fahmi, 12 May 1922, p.1953.
62. _La Bourse Egyptienne_, 13 May 1922; quoted in al-Bishri, _al-Katib_ 119 (1971), 127-8.
63. Ibid., 128.
64. FO.407/193, E5709/61/16.
65. This meeting apparently was organised by Salama Mikhail, Jirjis Antun, Najib Iskandar and Talat Saat. FO.407/193, Enclosure in No.62,

Situation Report, 18-24 May 1922.

66. The Residency recorded attendance of 120 (ibid.), and al-Bishri the higher figure, _al-Katib_ 119 (1971), 129.

67. Ibid., 129.

68. DW, Abdin Palace Archives, Royal Diwan, al-Azhar Qisr 1.

69. _Mahadir al-Lajna al-Amma Li-Wad al-Dustur_, 27th session, 25 August 1922, Cairo, 1927.

70. Al-Bishri, _al-Katib_ 119 (1971), 129.

71. This election was indirect and Jacques Berque thinks that fifteen to twenty-five per cent of the major electors were Copts. Berque, _Imperialism and Revolution_, p.365.

72. Tariq al-Bishri has done similar computations (_al-Katib_ 121 (1971), 163), but has arrived at slightly different figures for some years. The above statistics are based on Muhammad Subhi's _Tarikh al-Hayat al-Niyabiyya fi Misr_, and were cross checked with _The Egyptian Directory_. Professors Abd al-Halim and Megalli, of the School of Oriental and African Studies and the Central London Polytechnic respectively, helped in distinguishing indeterminate names. Al-Bishri has more Copts represented in the following years: 1925 (fifteen Copts), 1926 (seventeen), 1929 (twenty-three), and 1942 (twenty-seven). Owing to deaths and resignations, the number of Copts probably did not remain consistent throughout a Chamber term. The difference between the author's count and al-Bishri's may be the result of taking that count at different points in the term.

73. The pressure of the administration was used against Wafdist candidates in this election. However, many Independents turned Wafdist when it came time to elect the Chamber's president.

74. The Wafd and the Liberal Constitutionalists boycotted this election.

75. Three Copts, one of whom was Mirrit Bey Ghali, ran as Independents, but as _Misr_ noted, it was very difficult for Independents to get elected. _Misr_, 26 November 1949, 1. Al-Kutla nominated seven Copts. See _al-Balagh_ for all nominations, 30 December, 31 December 1919, and 4 January 1950, 6. The Wafd's seven Coptic nominees plus Mirrit were the eight who won seats in the Chamber.

76. _Misr_, 7 July 1950, 1.

77. An Asyuti Muslim was elected instead and the British commented that, while this was supposed to have been a revolt against Wafdist autocratic methods by Upper Egyptian deputies, Wisa's religion was probably against him. FO.407/198, No.109,

Field-Marshal Viscount Allenby to Mr. MacDonald, 22 March 1924.

78. The 1928 election had its opponents. Both the Liberal _al-Kashkul_ and the National Party's _al-Akhbar_ wrote that the President of the Chamber should profess the religion of the state. FO.470/206, No.73 (Enclosure 7), Memorandum on the Egyptian Press, 22 March-4 April 1928.

79. Al-Bishri, _al-Katib_ 121 (1971), 165.

80. In the 1924 Chamber, proportionately more Coptic Wafdists had urban occupations than did Muslim Wafdists.

81. As the land tax was approximately £E1 per _feddan_, those who met this prerequisite owned 150 _feddans_. Cromer saw 50 _feddans_ as the dividing line between big and small landowners. Rauf Abbas Hamid accepts his distinction, although somewhat reluctantly, and applies it in his own work on landownership. See _al-Nizam al-Ijtimai fi Misr, 1837-1914_ (Cairo, 1973), pp.24-6, 189.

82. Abd al-Rahman al-Rafii, _Fi Aqab al-Thawra al-Misriyya_, vol.1 (Cairo, 1947), p.117.

83. This was always an issue when the Wafd was in power, since each claimed the right to appoint its own creatures; witness the quarrel over the appointment of Fakhri Abd al-Nur, al-Nahhas' second choice, to the Senate in 1937. The King refused to countenance it, and the matter was only settled when the ministry was dismissed. _Al-Dustur_, 8 March 1938, PPF; Muhammad Husain Haikal, _Mudhakkirat fi al-Siyasa al-Misriyya_, vol.II, pp.54-5.

84. There were other Christian senators who boosted Christian representation and who, although of Syrian origin, may or may not have married into the Coptic community. Two such men, who are not counted in the figures above, are Alfred Shamas, who was appointed in 1924 and drew a ballot to remain in 1930, and Yusuf Saba, who died in 1924.

85. Bishop Lukas, who is counted here, died in 1930. He was appointed in 1924, and in 1930 drew a ballot to remain in the Senate. Curiously, he was not replaced.

86. This excludes Senator Zakariya Mihran who could be either Copt or Muslim.

87. Of the thirty Senators unseated by the Wafd in 1950, four were Copts. Since four of the party's new appointees were also Copts, the Coptic percentage was maintained. _Al-Misri_, 18 June 1950, 1.

88. The opposition boycotted the August 1950 election which was designed to fill those new Senate seats created to compensate for the increase in population.

89. The two exceptions were Minya al-Qamh in al-Sharqiyya and Tukh in al-Qalyubiyya. Both districts had few Coptic inhabitants.

90. See al-Ahram, 26 May 1922, PPF.

91. In 1946 most Copts in the Senate were non-Wafdists.

92. Misr, 23 March 1951, 1.

93. Egyptian Gazette, 4 April 1924, 4.

94. FO.141/758, 92/15/31. There was a precedent for this. Patriarch Cyril had served in both the Legislative Council and the General Assembly in the 1890s.

95. Misr, 9 June 1931, 5; 14 June 1931, 1.

96. Ibid.

97. Misr, 5 January 1950, 1.

98. Curiously, Misr objected when al-Minyawi tried to run for election to the Chamber in 1949, and expressed the fear that this would give the Lay Council a political colouring. Due to communal pressure, al-Minyawi withdrew his candidature. He had been nominated by al-Kutla, as he had been in 1946 when he failed to secure a seat in the Senate. In 1951 Misr was pleased with his election. See Misr, 6 December 1949, 1.

99. Attempts to do so are complicated by the fact that, depending on the law then prevailing, only one-half of the members came up for election at any one time. In addition, the provincial council law was changed frequently. Among those provisions altered were the method of election, the term of office, the qualifications of candidates and the powers exercised.

100. The Coptic community voiced its dismay when it learnt that it had failed to return a Copt. To preserve civil harmony, one of the victors, a Wafdist, stepped down. Tawfiq Dus raised this example in the Constitutional Commission to support his demand for minority representation. Al-Watan, 27 February 1922, 3; FO.141/452, 14544/2/22.

101. Deeb suggests that the Wafd was stronger in the Delta and won proportionately more seats on Lower Egyptian than Upper Egyptian provincial councils. However, this does not help explain why Wafd-dominated Delta provincial councils in previous years contained no Copts. The Wafd would seem to have controlled provincial councils except for a time in the early 1930s and another in the late 1940s. See Marius Deeb, Party Politics in Egypt: the Wafd and its Rivals, 1919-39 (Ithaca Press, London, 1979), p.159.

102. Sometimes Copts were included in these

councils by virtue of their occupation; for example, the local sanitation inspector, who was sometimes a Copt, belonged by right.

103. Interview with Louis Awad, 29 February 1980. When Ubaid was Finance Minister in 1936, he apparently spent so much money on translating the Quran into other languages, building mosques and paying preachers, that a delegation of *ulama* came personally to thank him. This gave Ubaid the opportunity to reiterate that he was a Christian in religion and a Muslim in country.

104. *Misr*, 3 June 1933, 3.

105. *Chamber Debates*, thirty-third session, 7 March 1933. See also Alfred Yallouz, "Chronique legislative, 1932-33", *L'Egypte Contemporaine* 152 (1934), 800.

106. *Chamber Debates*, sixteenth session, 8 March 1944; *Senate Debates*, twenty-third session, 23 December 1946.

107. *Misr*, 27 September 1926, 1.

108. FO.141/755, 124/4/33.

109. *Misr*, 9 May 1940, 1.

110. For example, at least two laws affecting the Copts, the 1925 Majlis al-Hasbi law (See Chapter Six) and the 1936 personal status law (ditto), were decreed when parliament was not in session.

111. Haikal, *Mudhakkirat*, vol.1, pp.160-1.

112. Because of this, in 1930, when the Copts were well represented in parliament, *al-Siyasa* claimed that proportional representation was needed to protect the interests of the *majority* and not the minority. Al-Siyasa, 12 February 1930, quoted in al-Bishri, *al-Katib* 121 (1971), 155-6.

113. *Misr*, 20 April 1946, 1; 15 April 1946, 1.

114. *Misr*, March and April 1947, especially 4 April 1947, 1.

115. See *Misr*, 4 April 1947, 1. Curiously, in the next breath, this article demanded that government employment be equally open to all and not restricted to a community's proportion of the population. *Misr*, 11 January 1950, 1; 12 January 1950, 1; 18 January 1952, 1.

116. FO.371/53297, J2253/39/16; *Misr* 17 April 1948, 1.

117. *Misr* objected in part to Egyptian participation in an Islamic conference held in Pakistan. *Misr*, 11 January 1950, 1.

Chapter Five

THE COPTS AND PARTY POLITICS

A. THE WAFD

The Wafd party placed more Copts in visible positions of influence than did any other party, with the possible exception of Makram Ubaid's 1943 splinter group, al-Kutla. The party's concern to promote Coptic political participation derived partly from its self-image as the representative of the entire nation. The Wafd saw itself not as a party representing sectional interests, but as a movement whose wide-ranging support in all sectors of Egyptian society most fitted it to obtain genuine independence and exercise political power. In addition, the egalitarian and secular political beliefs of the party borrowed from Western thought, could be both demonstrated and reinforced by according a share of that power to minorities. On a practical level, many Coptic nationalists rose in party circles due to the 1918-23 arrests and exiles, which created a turnover in leadership. Their success in proving their loyalty, ability and courage gained them the respect of their Muslim comrades and attracted a popular following. This, in turn, drew still more Coptic supporters into the Wafdist fold.

In 1923, the Wafd, in preparing for a more orderly political life, appointed a new party Executive Committee of eight Muslims and six Copts. In order of seniority, the latter were Sinut Hanna, George Khayyat, Wasif Ghali, Wisa Wasif, Makram Ubaid and Murqus Hanna. A second group of eleven Muslims and three Copts, Salama Mikhail, Fakhri Abd al-Nur and Raghib Iskandar, was designated to join the first in plenary sessions.[1] Only Wisa Wasif, Murqus Hanna and Sinut stayed with the Wafd until their deaths in the 1930s. The three in the second group left the party in 1932 and later returned. Khayyat resigned at roughly the same time. Wasif Ghali, seemingly more interested in cultural than political affairs,[2] was inactive between 1932-6 and retired from party life in the late 1930s. The last of the nine, Makram, parted company with the Wafd in 1942. New Copts, however, were periodically appointed to the Executive Committee in an attempt to preserve the special character of the party.

The Wafd was perhaps the only party to devote much attention to local organisation. Local notables were useful campaigners; and, in heavily Coptic areas like Asyut and Qina, many Copts served on Wafdist provincial, district and constituency committees. Sinut Hanna, who made many a fund-raising tour in the party's early days,[3] was in charge of party organisation in Asyut. His colleague, Fakhri Abd al-Nur, held the same job in his home province of Jirja. Fakhri was also, for a time, responsible for organising Wafdist provincial tours.[4] Both were two of the most active Wafdist propagandists in the early period.[5]

The Wafd had support in all sectors of society. Several party members had influence in labour affairs. Raghib Iskandar was the only Coptic member of the Chamber's Labour Committee in 1924, and he ran as a workers' candidate in 1925. Along with Makram, who also professed a special interest in workers, he was defeated in this election; but this probably had more to do with government interference than with any inability in the proletariat to identify their interests with those of Makram and Raghib. Makram and the Copt, Aziz Mirhum, served as legal advisers to several unions; and the former, even after breaking with the Wafd, retained some influence with workers. Mirhum, in conjunction with a Muslim colleague, ran the Egyptian General Union of Workers' Syndicates, a federation of twelve unions with 4,800 members.[6] He was the most active Coptic labour leader in the 1930s and eventually became President of the Wafdist Council for the Union of Syndicates, founded in 1935, after ousting Abbas Halim.[7] Dr. Najib Iskandar, who represented a working-class district in the Chamber and who was arrested at one point for channelling funds to workers suspected of perpetrating anti-government bombings, also had some influence.[8]

Ubaid was very popular with students and youth, an increasingly important political force in the 1930s, and was intimately connected with the paramilitary youth organisation, the Blue Shirts.[9] Kamil Sidqi also had ties with this unruly group, which gave the King an excuse to dismiss the Wafd government in 1937.[10]

Wafdist Copts had even more influence among lawyers. A very large proportion of lawyers were Copts, so it is not surprising that the Copts played an important role in the Egyptian Bar Association, which was often controlled by the Wafd. Murqus Hanna, who was the first Copt to serve as this professional organisation's president, was elected five years in a row. Makram, Kamil Sidqi and a fourth Wafdist Copt, Kamil Yusuf Salib, also served as Bar Association presidents.[11]

Because Egypt's fate lay with those outside Egypt, propaganda missions abroad were an important political weapon. Those Wafdists who were assigned to work on European and American opinion included Wasif Ghali, Wisa Wasif, Makram, Sadiq Hinain and Louis Fanus. Their knowledge of Europe and perhaps even their Christianity was a help in dealing with Westerners. These men, particularly in the 1920s, made numerous trips to Europe to promote the Wafdist cause. Later, their religion was less of an advantage in dealing with the West because it made them suspect in Egyptian eyes.

To the British, many Wafdist Copts were "extremists", a term which denotes mainly the degree of intransigence displayed towards British rule. No doubt Coptic nationalists seemed more extreme in their political views than some of their Muslim colleagues because the British expected to have their support. The British division between "moderates" and "extremists" is retained here not for what it says about the views of Wafdist politicians, but for its usefulness in suggesting alliances within the party. Personal loyalties and enmities often had more to do with political position than devotion to a particular set of aims. Some of those the British labelled "extremist" in 1923 had materialised into "moderates" by 1932.

The British deplored the influence the early extremists, among them Sinut, Makram, the Iskandar brothers, Wisa Wasif, Murqus Hanna and Salama Mikhail,[12] had with Zaghlul. Sinut was devoted to the latter and was very influential in the party's early days; his zeal was such that the British described him as "unbalanced" rather than "extremist". Makram, whom one party luminary called the most influential of the younger Wafdists,[13] did not meet Zaghlul until 1921. He quickly became a protegé and was known publicly as "the faithful son of Sad"; this relationship was yet another symbol of

Muslim-Copt unity. Murqus Hanna seems to have been particularly powerful in the 1920s. He acquired a considerable reputation for anglophobia as Minister of Public Works in 1924; in consequence, Lord Lloyd, the British High Commissioner, was very unhappy with Hanna's appointment to the 1926 cabinet.[14]

There were Copts in the party who were credited with moderate views by the British. This designation was relative since in British eyes the true moderates were the Adlists and later the Liberal Constitutionalists. Two such Wafdists were Wasif Ghali and George Khayyat. Wasif's familiarity with Western culture may have done more to endear him to the British than his political views. Wasif had a powerful voice in the party and in 1924 successfully persuaded Zaghlul, over the advice of al-Nahhas and others, not to resign in his quarrel with the Palace over whose right it was to make Senate appointments.[15] In contrast with this, Khayyat had little influence in the party; his standing may have been critically injured by his brief defection in 1921.

In the first Wafd cabinet of 1924, Murqus Hanna and Wasif Ghali were given portfolios. Ghali's appointment to Foreign Affairs was perhaps obvious given his familiarity with Europe and the Palace.[16] His advice, according to al-Ahram's political editor, was generally taken by the Wafd on diplomatic affairs, but was not routinely sought on domestic matters.[17] Murqus' elevation offers some proof of his influence with Zaghlul. One contemporary opponent suggested that Murqus was then known only among lawyers,[18] but another source regarded him as "universally respected" and greatly liked by Muslims.[19] Sinut had seniority and should have had a portfolio, but his zeal probably damned him in both British and Palace eyes. Murqus was a more palatable candidate; he had earned the confidence of his party and appears to have been routinely consulted by Zaghlul.[20] His influence did not do the career of his new son-in-law, Makram Ubaid, any harm,[21] although the latter was not elevated to cabinet rank until 1928. In another important appointment, Sadiq Hinain was named Under-Secretary in the Ministry of Finance. Unfortunately accusations of favouritism hampered his usefulness to the party. In 1925, he was posted to the Egyptian Legation in Madrid as part of an effort to rid the administration of Wafdists, and this effecticely ended his political career.

The 1924 cabinet came to grief over the Sudan

and the assassination of the Sirdar. Makram was among those arrested on suspicion of complicity in the assassination. He was not directly implicated, but had delivered several incendiary speeches which had helped establish a climate for murder.[22] He was soon released and his influence, along with that of other party extremists, may have grown at the expense of more moderate Wafdists.[23] By 1927, the more radical party members were able to make Prime Minister Adli's position so untenable that he resigned. Zaghlul was not in good health and was perhaps losing control of his more unruly disciples. King Fuad, believing that the Wafd could successfully insist on the appointment of a Wafdist prime minister, idly mentioned Wasif Ghali as a candidate.[24] The previous year, the King had seen Murqus Hanna as the most acceptable Wafdist for the post on the grounds that a Copt would be more amenable to royal pleasure because he would be both more disliked and therefore more timid than a Muslim.[25] However, all Wafdists, whatever their differences, agreed that Zaghlul was the only candidate for prime minister. The British did not concur, and so Zaghlul was forced to accept the appointment of Tharwat.

Zaghlul's death in August 1927 threw the Wafd into a succession crisis which was aggravated by the absence of several Wafdists, including four Copts, from Egypt.[26] Sentimentalists in the party considered leaving Zaghlul's position vacant in memoriam or appointing Mme. Zaghlul as a figurehead with real power in the hands of al-Nahhas, Fath Allah Barakat and Wisa Wasif.[27] Both were fanciful solutions, and it is unlikely that al-Nahhas and Barakat would have comprised an amiable partnership. These two, the one as secretary-general of the party and the other as Zaghlul's nephew, were the main rivals for Zaghlul's mantle.

An election was held with surprising speed in September, and al-Nahhas was its victor. Haikal maliciously credited Copts with a special role in the election by pointing to the presence of Makram and Fakhri Abd al-Nur in a group which engineered the victory.[28] Sad, Fakhri's son, confirms his father's crucial role, contending that Fakhri switched his vote from Barakat to al-Nahhas and persuaded others to do likewise.[29] The British, who, unlike Sad but like Haikal, were hoping to discredit the Wafd, also suggested that the Copts played a role in the election.[30]

Fakhri may or may not have been able to carry

the votes of other Wafdists; there were certainly not enough Copts in the Wafd to elect al-Nahhas single-handed.[31] They may well have chosen to support al-Nahhas on his own merits. The latter was from an important Christian centre in the Delta and had been helped early in his career by a Christian notable; he was tolerant and unprejudiced. In addition Wafdist Copts may have known or suspected that Makram, as a very close friend of al-Nahhas, would be made party secretary-general.

Al-Nuqrashi, suspected of complicity in several political crimes, and Mme. Zaghlul probably had more to do with al-Nahhas' victory than either Fakhri or Makram. The former organised a demonstration in front of the polling place and earnestly reminded voters to cast their ballots for al-Nahhas. His words may have been innocent, but his past political record gave them a threatening ring,[32] which may well have unnerved voters. Mme. Zaghlul probably played a more important role. Al-Nahhas won her support by his readiness to allow her a say in party matters; a say that Barakat was unwilling to concede.

Both men had the advantage of rural backgrounds;[33] al-Nahhas, however, was much better educated, spoke a European language and had better moral credentials. Barakat had caused a scandal in 1924 when he had abused his position as Minister of Agriculture to get a considerable portion of his large landholdings worked without any personal cost.[34] He had also lost prestige when he referred the secretary-general of his ministry to the Council of Discipline and the man was unanimously acquitted of misdoing.[35] Since this man, who was influential enough to be appointed senator in 1941, was a Copt, the incident perhaps explained the reluctance of some Copts to back Barakat.

The royalist press played a mischievous and not insignificant role by advocating the election of Barakat. Not even the most respectable Wafdist could have survived branding as a Palace favourite. The Palace here seems to have hoped that al-Nahhas, as party head, would destroy the Wafd more quickly than Barakat.[36] Afaf Marsot suggests another reason for al-Nahhas' election: she feels he was nominated by the extremist faction because he was malleable and would do their bidding.[37] However, as the second most important party official after Zaghlul, he was an obvious candidate. It is true that he was close to a number of the more radical members of the Wafd, but the fact that he sought their advice does not mean that he was dominated by them.

It is equally true, however, that al-Nahhas was less well equipped than Zaghlul to balance those of moderate and radical views and bind all to him in personal loyalty. He was also perhaps less interested in doing this. None of the more moderate Wafdists who sat in the Tharwat cabinet had any influence in the new Wafd. In addition, Murqus Hanna was past his prime, as was Sinut.[38] Wasif Ghali remained influential, perhaps because he avoided factional squabbles. He replaced the moderate Hamid al-Basil as head of the Foreign Affairs Committee in the Chamber and he was also offered a portfolio in the 1928 Wafd cabinet.

Real power in the party became concentrated in the hands of al-Nahhas, Makram, Ahmad Mahir and al-Nuqrashi;[39] by 1930, the Residency was convinced of their predominance.[40] Other Wafdists who had backed al-Nahhas in the succession struggle improved their standing in the party; Fakhri Abd al-Nur,[41] Salama Mikhail and Raghib Iskandar were, like Mahir and al-Nuqrashi, added to the Executive in late 1927.

The moderates grew restive at their loss of influence. In 1928, they quarrelled with al-Nahhas over the enactment of a law ensuring freedom of assembly. They wished to drop the plan, fearing that British disapproval would result in a costly ultimatum. The British, in a fine piece of wishful thinking, predicted that the cabinet would be split on this issue and that a new one under Wasif Ghali, who sided with the moderates, would be formed. Fuad, however, had his heart set on a more tractable cabinet and therefore insisted to Lord Lloyd that Ghali was more of an extremist than Makram and was not a satisfactory candidate for prime minister.[42]

The al-Nahhas coterie became increasingly impatient with moderate thinking. At the end of 1931, when the exactions of the Sidqi regime forced the Wafd to consider Wafdist-Liberal collaboration, the moderate Barakat faction urged the acceptance of a Liberal plan for a coalition cabinet. This cabinet would conduct elections and its non-Wafdist Prime Minister would remain in office even in the event of a sweeping Wafdist victory. Their opponents found this plan naive; they would have little incentive to share power after their inevitable election victory.

Most members of the Executive, including some who had helped al-Nahhas triumph over Barakat, favoured collaboration with the Liberals. They included Fakhri Abd al-Nur, George Khayyat, Raghib Iskandar and Salama Mikhail. They may well have felt that co-operation with the moderate Liberals would strengthen their own position in a party whose leadership had grown less collective. Ranged against them was a group including al-Nahhas, Makram and Sinut.[43] Barakat had a majority on the Executive Committee, but since his opponents controlled the party treasury and the local Wafdist organisations, he was the one forced to make concessions. Working out the details of the compromise together, he and Makram abandoned the Liberal plan for a post-election cabinet and agreed that majority decisions would henceforth be respected by all members of the Executive Committee. Barakat's faction should have put their money on a better horse; only British insistence could have put a coalition cabinet into office and it soon became clear that the British were not going to co-operate. The moderates had offended al-Nahhas needlessly, and they must have realised that swallowing their pride was less traumatic than trying to survive in opposition to the Wafd and Sidqi.[44]

George Khayyat, who had been relatively inactive for years, resigned in early 1932 from the Executive. No doubt he disliked the moderate faction's loss of face, but he may have had a more cogent reason for breaking his long association with the party. He died in April and so may well have been too ill to attend to party matters. He was also rumoured to be in financial difficulties, and if he hoped for assistance from the Bank of Agricultural Credit, it was unwise to oppose Sidqi.[45] Khayyat was only the first to go; later in 1932, al-Nahhas, perhaps feeling the advantages of a more homogeneous Executive, expelled the moderate majority from the party. A quarrel between the moderate Najib al-Gharabli and Makram over a legal case they were jointly defending gave al-Nahhas the opportunity.

Makram, in the middle of his legal presentation, was obliged to absent himself from court for a few days. When he returned, the court refused to allow him to interrupt the lawyer then speaking in order to complete his case. In a fit of pique, he called upon his colleagues to withdraw from the defence with him. Al-Gharabli, believing such an action damaging to the accused, refused to withdraw and chastised Makram for his precipitous behaviour.[46] Al-Nahhas eventually sided with Makram, a decision that owed much to al-Gharabli's lack of tact as to Makram's greater persuasive talents, and al-Gharabli was expelled from the Wafd.[47] Al-Nahhas next excluded all the moderates, including Raghib Iskandar, Fakhri Abd al-Nur and Salama Mikhail. Najib Iskandar, who had too handsomely praised al-Gharabli's work for the defence, lost his place on the Cairo Central Committee.[48] Salama promptly published blistering attacks on Makram in al-Siyasa, calling him a viper and a shameless liar. Makram responded in a similar vein in Kawkab al-Sharq.[49]

Wasif Ghali, alarmed by events but maintaining a safe distance from the maelstrom, wrote to both sides in an attempt to repair the damage and to arrange a reconciliation.[50] One note of his survives; it condemns al-Nahhas' unilateral action as a "coup d'état".[51] The British expected Ghali to join the expelled,[52] but one cousin believed that Ghali disapproved equally of both sides in the dispute.[53] One contemporary scholar suggests that Ghali remained with the Wafd from a misguided sentimentality.[54] A more plausible explanation, and one which gives him credit for some intelligence, is that he realised how little hope the dissidents had of creating a viable political organisation. Ghali, obviously, was less than delighted with the outcome, and he announced that he was retiring from politics until such a time as the situation should clear. He did not attend party Executive meetings, and in 1935 he ceased to be a member of the Executive. He did, however, resume political activity with the formation of the United Front the following year and he accepted a portfolio in the 1936 cabinet.[55]

Eventually, several of the moderates drifted back to the Wafd. The Iskandar brothers, Salama Mikhail and Fakhri Abd al-Nur stood for election in 1936 and were not opposed by their old party. Najib Iskandar and Fakhri won election; the former again left the Wafd in 1937 and the latter, although never again a member of the Executive, remained a Wafdist until his death. Salama and Raghib lost the election. Salama ran again and lost in 1938; he was appointed to the Senate by a non-Wafdist government in 1939 and died a few months later. Raghib was compensated for his defeat when the Wafd appointed him to the Senate in 1937.

In the wake of the 1932 schism, twelve Wafdists were added to the Executive Committee. Kamil Sidqi, a lawyer, ex-senator and prominent member of the Bar, was the only Copt in this group. He was of little consequence in the party until Makram Ubaid's ignominious exit in 1942.[56] Due to expulsions and deaths, the Wafd Executive in the 1930s included far fewer Copts than it had in the 1920s. However, Makram's considerable influence and popularity[57] compensated in quality for any deficiency in quantity.

At least partly because of the reduction of the number of Copts at high levels in the party, Makram's influence began to stand out and by 1935 was causing problems. Al-Nahhas would hold no important meetings without Makram, and his calendar may have been increasingly controlled by the latter.[58] Whether Makram attempted to limit the access of certain Wafdists to al-Nahhas or not, it is clear that al-Nuqrashi and Ahmad Mahir came to resent al-Nahhas' reliance on Makram. As early as 1930, the Residency reported that Makram and al-Nuqrashi were on terms of armed neutrality while awaiting a future struggle for power.[59]

Makram's influence was not the only sore point. There were policy differences as well. One of these occurred in 1935 over the insistence of Mahir and al-Nuqrashi that the Wafd demand the immediate restitution of the 1923 constitution. Al-Nahhas and Makram, for once on the cautious side of the fence, thought this too risky but feared to appear irresolute.[60] Makram was further annoyed and blamed the unseen hands of Mahir and al-Nuqrashi when the party newspaper, <u>al-Jihad</u>, lost two of its best writers to the staff of the journal <u>Ruz al-Yusuf</u>. The latter's owner had made plans to publish a daily newspaper, and Makram feared that his two rivals would control it.[61] He accordingly convinced al-Nahhas that the new enterprise would harm <u>al-Jihad</u>, and al-Nahhas compliantly refused to sanction the paper. In retaliation, <u>Ruz al-Yusuf</u> began attacking the Wafdist-supported prime minister, Nasim Pasha. Both the journal and al-Nuqrashi appear to have been connected with scurrilous pamphlets attacking Makram and al-Nahhas.[62] The Wafd, pushed too far, renounced its link to <u>Ruz al-Yusuf</u>, and the journal avenged itself by mounting a vitriolic attack on Makram. In both articles and cartoons, the journal suggested that al-Nahhas listened only to Makram and Makram listened only to the English.[63]

The rivalry between al-Nuqrashi and Makram grew increasingly acrimonious and friction soon developed between the latter and al-Nuqrashi's friend, Ahmad Mahir. Al-Nahhas was no doubt cognisant of the problem and was reported, probably inaccurately, by the British, to be trying to free himself from Makram's "domination".[64] The British, of course, liked to suggest that Makram had some kind of malign hold over al-Nahhas.

Makram had certain advantages in this struggle. He had considerable influence with the Wafdist press.[65] He was even able to force Ahmad Mahir to relinquish his job as political editor of <u>Kawkab al-Sharq</u> in 1937 as a condition for joining the treaty negotiations. Mahir and al-Nuqrashi moved to get control of the party treasury and the local Wafdist committees, both of which were in Makram's competent hands, but Makram out-manoeuvred them.[66] That July, they lost control of the party's propaganda apparatus; and in 1937 Makram seduced the staff of the new Wafdist daily, al-Misri.[67] By 1937 the British Embassy believed that al-Nahhas took counsel only with Makram and it predicted, or perhaps merely hoped, that his reliance on a Copt would harm him in the long run.[68]

Makram and al-Nuqrashi finally quarrelled over a scheme to electrify the Aswan dam;[69] and this was the straw that persuaded al-Nahhas to drop al-Nuqrashi and three supporters from the cabinet in August 1937. At least two attempts at reconciliation failed,[70] and on 14 September 1937, al-Nuqrashi was ejected from the Wafd. Although it is difficult to determine when other Wafdists chose sides, it is known that the practical Wasif Ghali maintained strict neutrality all that summer.

In this way, the third major split in the party occurred. Several members left the Wafd; the only important Copt to do so was Najib Iskandar. To compensate for the loss, the Wafd added new members to its Executive, among them two wealthy Coptic landowners, Fahmi Wisa Bey and Bushra Hanna Bey. Aside from Makram, they were the only Copts on the Executive, and they could not hope to rival his influence. Bushra, as the late Sinut's brother, was greatly respected but was blind and past the prime of life. Fahmi, at least as far as the British were concerned, was a political nonentity.[71]

The characters of both men suggest that they were added because they would unquestioningly follow al-Nahhas' lead, would not upset Muslim opinion by seeking public exposure and would not threaten Makram's position, either nationally or within the party. There was, in fact, no one in the party at that point who was capable of leaping into the shoes of Mahir and al-Nuqrashi.

It has been suggested that Makram, believing

that al-Nahhas and the Wafd saw his political role as one of communal representation, sought to block the advance of other ambitious Wafdist Copts.[72] Certainly, Makram would not have put such an interpretation on his role in the party. He was always careful to present himself as an Egyptian, rather than a Christian, nationalist; and he must be credited with some success in persuading at least Wafdists, if not his political opponents, of that fact. He was in no position in the early days of the party to counteract the influence of men like Sinut, Wisa Wasif, Wasif Ghali and Murqus Hanna. The prestige and weight these Copts carried within and without the party proves that, at least in the 1920s, there was room for more than one Copt at the top. Most of these men had disappeared from the scene by the early 1930s and, even without a deliberate policy of obstruction on Makram's party, few Copts had the seniority or talent to rival his influence. The latter's main concern seems always to have been with Muslim and not Coptic competition; Muslim rivals were the most capable of weakening his position by playing on his religious background. It is true, however, that with the exception of Wasif Ghali, there were no additional Copts in the party who rose to prominence until after Makram's exit.

It was a favourite tactic of anti-Wafdists, both British and Egyptian, to claim that Makram dominated al-Nahhas,[73] and this is a claim accepted by some scholars.[74] The two men were very close: they were the same generation, they were both lawyers, they had shared exile and they held similar political views. To note a strong bond between the two is not the same thing as suggesting that one had achieved mastery over the other. The characters of the two men complemented one another and made for a powerful political combination. Rumours of al-Nahhas' weakness probably originated in his flashes of temper, which suggested instability, and unfortunate physical appearance.[75] It is likely that Makram's religion also had something to do with the rumour. Claiming that al-Nahhas, a Muslim was the slave of Makram, a Copt, was a far more telling blow than, for example, the later charge that al-Nahhas was dominated by the Muslim Fuad Siraj al-Din. It seems unlikely that al-Nahhas could have been held in such high regard and affection by Zaghlul and risen so high in the party had he been nothing more than the stooge and ninny his political opponents claimed. At least three times, he succeeded in persuading a fickle public that he was the real Wafd, while the other, dissenting Wafdists were only schismatics.

By degrees, others emerged to counter Makram's influence. Their work was not co-ordinated and, even as late as a few months before the final dénouement, Makram's power does not seem to have been substantially diminished. Al-Nahhas had begun to consult others in the party: Amin Uthman, Fuad Siraj al-Din, Najib al-Hilali and Sabri Abu Alam.[76] These men were of a younger generation and they were eager for political success. They were too new to leadership to rival Makram's power in the late 1930s, but, by the early 1940s, their position was more solid. Perhaps a greater threat to Makram came from al-Nahhas' wife. She may have been jealous of Makram's influence with her husband; Makram certainly suspected her of trying to counter it.

It has been argued by more than one individual that al-Nahhas consciously tried to balance power in the Wafd to prevent a future schism.[77] This is not an unreasonable analysis, and yet al-Nahhas did little to prevent major defections in 1932 and 1937; in fact, he seemed to encourage them in the interests of party peace and unity. Still, the Wafd in the 1940s was a weaker organisation than it had been in the first decade of constitutional life, and al-Nahhas may have realised that the party could not afford another schism. In addition, Makram was too crafty a politician to have made or responded to overtures from the Palace without cause,[78] particularly at a time when the Wafd had just returned to power. Only concern about his political future could have driven him into the arms of such an old and untrustworthy enemy.[79]

The only serious policy dispute between Makram and al-Nahhas on record before 1942 was one which surfaced in the previous year. The Wafd had, for some time, been waiting for the British to find an excuse to force the King to invite al-Nahhas to form a cabinet. The British were prepared to take such action in 1940 but were outsmarted by the Palace and hampered by al-Nahhas' contraction of cold feet. By the summer of 1941, al-Nahhas had grown restive; he asked Lampson to intervene but it was the latter's turn to be unco-operative. Al-Nahhas, in retaliation, flirted with the Palace and made a few sharp anti-British speeches just in case Lampson had overlooked the possibility of a Palace-Wafd alliance. Security reports suggest that al-Nahhas was actually considering such an alliance in the hope that the Palace would act more quickly than the

British in allowing the formation of a Wafd government. In contrast, Makram seems to have advocated keeping faith with the more reliable British. He feared that an anti-British campaign, at such a sensitive juncture, would only harm the Wafd.[80] On his own authority, Makram may even have ordered the Wafdist press to reduce the number of references they made to the King.[81] At one party meeting in October, al-Nahhas discussed his decision to tour the provinces making speeches against the government and the British. Ubaid opposed this idea of making violent speeches against the British. Wafdists attending the meeting were sufficiently divided on the issue that no decision was forthcoming, a failure which sent al-Nahhas from the meeting in a fury.[82] The quarrel between al-Nahhas and Ubaid lasted into the new year. In January, Makram was so angry that he refused to attend a holiday speech given by al-Nahhas at Zaghlul's tomb. Kamil Sidqi tried to mediate,[83] but few others were displeased to see the two men at odds.

The warrant for which Lampson had been waiting came with the resignation of the prime minister, an act which followed a crisis generated by the Palace over the government's break in relations with Vichy France; and a Wafdist government was imposed on the King.

Despite the fact that Makram's acquisition of the critical portfolio of finance, which now included the once separate portfolio of supplies, would seem to indicate a resolution of differences, two Wafdist contemporaries of Makram suggest that serious problems began their first day in office.[84] Amin Uthman, who had gained the confidence of al-Nahhas, almost immediately succeeded, with the latter's support, in blocking an attempt by Makram to fire Hassan Rifaat, under-secretary at the Ministry of the Interior. The Embassy suspected that Amin, who had turned down a portfolio for the possibly more useful post of Secretary-General of the Cabinet, was using Rifaat to increase his power in the party.[85] Less than two months later, Makram lost another round when he was unable to prevent the appointment of Amin as Auditor-General. This was an office Makram preferred to keep vacant because it undercut his own authority as Minister of Finance.

Differences between al-Nahhas and Makram soon became public knowledge. Al-Nahhas suspected Makram of intriguing with the Palace. The latter was known to be having direct contacts with Palace officials in March;[86] and, when Makram accepted an invitation to a Royal Audience, al-Nahhas was reported to be uneasy.[87] He was also annoyed since the King had shown great reluctance to receive him. Makram then infuriated al-Nahhas by publicly praising the King without seeking prior approval; in doing this, he gave sufficient scope to those party members eager to widen the rift.[88] He quarrelled with Mme. al-Nahhas, who was abusing her husband's position for private gain.[89] Playing an infuriatingly righteous politician, he also opposed the accepted practice of promoting Wafdist officials whose loyalty had earned them punishment under previous non-Wafdist governments.[90] Makram made both these issues, as petty as they were, the basis of his campaign against corruption in the party. His ad hominem attacks gave al-Nahhas so little room to arrange a face-saving compromise that it seems unlikely that Makram was still jockeying for position within the party. He probably had resolved upon leaving and hoped to take as many party members with him as possible. Al-Nahhas, on the other hand, could not have been eager to get rid of Makram; he knew only too well that the latter was as formidable an opponent as he was capable an ally.[91]

It is perhaps possible that al-Nahhas had come to see Ubaid not merely as a menace to party unity and harmony, but also as a threat to his own power in the party. Ubaid's disapproval of al-Nahhas' anti-British campaign was shared by other influential party members and a large part of the Wafdist Parliamentary Committee. The large number of defections from the Wafd to Makram between 1942 and 1944 suggests that Makram had considerable support among Wafdist deputies and senators. The fact that Makram was able to secure the Ministry of Finance, and to keep Supplies attached to it, in spite of the fact that he and al-Nahhas were at loggerheads a month earlier, indicates that Makram had considerable independent power in the party. Certainly, he had a strong base of support outside the party; he was, for example, particularly noted for his influence with workers and Wafdist youth. Perhaps Makram would not have been entirely crazy had he thought that, with the strong support of Wafdists in parliament, his great popularity among the public, and royal favour, he stood a chance of ousting al-Nahhas.

With the Palace behind him, Makram pushed the dispute to its logical conclusion. Like the Sadists before him, he could not hope for political survival alone; only an alliance with the Palace was likely to guarantee his political longevity. In May, al-Nahhas deprived Makram of the control of Supplies which the latter was using as a base from which to mount his campaign against corruption. Makram had already forfeited any support he had in the cabinet, and some influential Copts pressed him to be more conciliatory.[92]

Finally, on 26 May, the cabinet was reshuffled and Makram was left out. Kamil Sidqi Pasha, who had been Minister of Commerce, became Finance Minister and more visible to the public. Censorship was ordered to prohibit references to Makram as Secretary-General of the Wafd, although he nominally retained this position.[93] He was still, of course, a Deputy in the Chamber. Makram took advantage of an ensuing lull to muster support among Wafdists and members of parliament.[94]

Unfortunately for his political future, Makram had picked his time badly. Under martial law, the government was able to prevent any publicity unfavourable to it and the party.[95] It was difficult for Makram to attract attention, let alone popular support. His work in parliament was easier. There he had a legitimate and not unsympathetic forum in which to prosecute his case against al-Nahhas. Makram had had charge of the selection of most of the Wafdist deputies and senators.[96] Some of these men no doubt owed their political careers to Makram's patronage, and many Upper Egyptians, Muslim and Copt, were reputed to be well-wishers. Makram, in fact, persuaded the Senate to pass a resolution praising him for past services, although he failed in a similar attempt in the more heavily Wafdist Chamber. There seems to be little doubt that "the faithful son of Sad" hoped to establish his title to the name of Wafd by besmirching al-Nahhas' good name. In popularity, he was second to al-Nahhas, and even if the assessments made of their talents are only partly correct, he was a good deal more clever.

Makram, eager to carry on the war against concessions and favours, planned to make an interpellation in the Chamber on the subject of supplies, but strong pressure appears to have prevented him doing so. He also failed in an attempt to take his brother's place on the Chamber's Finance Committee, a position which would have enabled him to direct further attacks against the Wafd.[97] In June, there was a full-dress debate on supplies, during which al-Nahhas refrained from attacking Makram. He may have feared not only Makram's eloquent tongue, but the evidence that the latter had acquired against his wife and in-laws. Curiously, Makram did not use the opportunity to attack al-Nahhas;[98] the restraint of both men may sug est that attempts at reconciliation were being made.[99]

It has been suggested that Makram was seduced by the Palace with the promise that he could be prime minister if he succeeded in damaging the Wafd sufficiently.[100] The main interest of the Palace was probably less in acquiring a worthy ally than in weakening the Wafd by depriving it of the one man who was said to have the most influence over al-Nahhas. Al-Nahhas, adrift from his political moorings might quickly run into trouble coping with the troublesome currents of Egyptian political life. It is curious that such an astute politician as Makram would have not only believed a promise from such an unreliable source, but accepted that a King, who relied heavily on religious and anti-Coptic propaganda in the past, could appoint, with impugnity, a Coptic prime minister. There had been many prime ministers without even a trace of Makram's popularity, but they had all been Muslims. There had even been two Coptic prime ministers; but the greater amount of power exercised by the British at that time helped to make the appointments possible. Once the prime minister had represented the Khedive, and it was acceptable for a Christian to execute the orders of a Muslim superior. After 1923, the office became more powerful. The prime minister represented the will of the people and had independent authority; it was less acceptable for a Christian to exercise such direct power over Muslims. Even had the Palace retained a sterling reputation, it would have had trouble with the appointment of a Coptic prime minister. Perhaps Makram, in thinking it feasible, fell prey to the political ideas upon which his party and the Egyptian political system were based.

In attracting ten Copts, Makram succeeded in obtaining the support of only one-quarter of the total number in parliament, most of whom were Wafdists. Some members were probably reluctant to find themselves so soon in opposition, particularly after several years out of power. Those Copts who backed Makram may have done so out of some combination of familial, regional, personal, political and religious ties. Although Makram's supporters were disproportionately Christian, he attracted many Muslims as well. This fact alone suggests that the schism had nothing to do with religion.[103]

Given strict press censorship, an underground publication was the only way that Makram could be sure of reaching the public. With Palace collusion,[104] Makram had the Black Book, a catalogue of Wafdist corruption, illegally printed and distributed. The book insisted that the quarrel between al-Nahhas and Makram was due to the latter's refusal to tolerate corruption and not, as al-Nahhas had insisted, an attempt to trim Makram's power.[105] The censorship forbade any mention of the Black Book in the press; in any case, Ruz al-Yusuf was the only journal to take Makram's part openly.[106]

King Faruq and Makram hoped that the British would be unable to ignore the volume and seriousness of the charges and would allow the al-Nahhas cabinet to be dismissed.[107] However, Lampson, who had gone to so much trouble to put the Wafd in power, was unaccommodating. The charges in the Black Book were dealt with in parliament, but through an interpellation, which did not permit discussion, rather than a full-dress debate. Makram took three days to present his interpellation and stormed out of the Chamber when he was not allowed to continue. Al-Nahhas answered the charges and won a vote of confidence from the Chamber in May.[108] Two months later, Makram was deprived of his seat; his supporters in parliament shared his fate. The following year, Makram was arrested and only released in October 1944 when the Wafd government fell.

Some Copts feared that Makram's behaviour would cause a Wafdist backlash against the community. In 1943, Habib al-Masri publicly asked al-Nahhas not to confuse the views of a people with those of one individual.[109] Al-Masri need not have worried. The Wafd was eager to retain Coptic support. As early as July 1942, notice was sent to provincial Wafd committees that the problem was not a sectarian one; the party would keep its faith with the principles of Zaghlul and would not begin making distinctions on religious grounds.[110] Two Copts, Ibrahim Faraj Masiha and Kamil Sidqi, joined Fahmi Wisa on the Wafd's Executive Committee. Since Bushra Hanna, Fahmi's colleague, had died, this action put three Copts on the Executive and gave notice that the party was still a union of Muslims and Copts. In addition, Ibrahim Faraj, son of the man who had helped al-Nahhas get a professional start, was portrayed as a protégé of al-Nahhas. Al-Nahhas called on the Coptic Bishop in Makram's home town of Qina in January 1943 and later made a speech reaffirming Copt-Muslim solidarity.[111]

Al-Nahhas lost the good will of some Copts when Makram was defeated in a fixed election for the Presidency of the Bar Association. There were many Coptic lawyers and a majority of them, as well as of their Muslim colleagues, seem to have supported Makram.[112] The day of Makram's defeat, the Minister of the Interior made a conciliatory but hardly satisfactory speech about the patriotic unity of Muslims and Copts.[113] A few days later, in a speech celebrating the Islamic New Year, al-Nahhas spoke at great length about the need of religious tolerance and he reminded his audience of Muhammad's example.[114]

When the British demanded the replacement of the incompetent Kamil Sidqi as Finance Minister, al-Nahhas demurred. Sidqi was the only Copt in the cabinet, and al-Nahhas feared that some Copts, and maybe even Sidqi himself, would take offence and desert the Wafd. Not until May did al-Nahhas bow to British pressure and move Sidqi to the less consequential State Audit Department.

To compensate for the demotion of one Copt, Fahmi Wisa was made Minister of Civil Defence, a portfolio which had been abolished in 1942. Neither Fahmi nor Kamil exercised much influence in the party in the 1940s; their colleague, Ibrahim Faraj, seems to have played a more important role.[115]

From the mid-1940s, the Wafd showed a greater tendency towards fragmentation. Leftist members co-operated with Marxists and trade unionists to form in 1946 the Committee of Workers and Students. This body, which played a disruptive role and helped bring the Wafd to power in 1950, seems to have involved few Copts.[116] Some Copts were, however, associated with another organisation of the party's left wing, the Wafdist Vanguard (al-Talia al-Wadfiyya), and among them were Dr. Riyad Shams and Aziz Mirhum. Mirhum died in 1946 so he could not have had much of a role in the Vanguard. Louis Awad, another Copt, was a sympathiser.[117] As a poet and critic, he was particularly influential as someone around whom leftist students in the university could gather.

At the other end of the spectrum, the powerful Fuad Siraj al-Din was cultivating the Palace. He probably numbered at least one Copt, Stafan Basili, a relative newcomer to the Wafd, among his supporters. It is more difficult to tell where Ibrahim Faraj and Kamil Sidqi stood; their first loyalty was probably to al-Nahhas who was trying to hold the party together, but by 1950 was ailing.[118] The only important Copt to join the party in the post-Makram period was Jeffrey Najib Ghali who abandoned the Sadists in 1946 to become a member of the Wafd Executive.

There is no instrument so fine as to allow an accurate and easy assessment of shifts in support for the Wafd. In 1930, 1936 and 1942 more Coptic senators and deputies were elected than in 1924. The Wafd was either increasingly willing to back Coptic politicians, or Copts were increasingly willing to support the Wafd, which had proved itself to be the chief advocate of national unity. It seems clear that the 1932 and 1937 splits did not have much of an effect on the Copts in the Wafd. It is difficult to determine if there was an immediate and disproportionate decline of Coptic support after Makram's exit. There was, of course, a genuine and steady deterioration in the Wafd's reputation from 1942; the events of 4 February and the Black Book showed al-Nahhas and his cohorts to be flawed characters, and they badly tarnished al-Nahhas' personal aura of incorruptability. In addition, Makram's charge that al-Nahhas' wife was responsible for the split probably made al-Nahhas appear henpecked and slightly foolish. This growing disenchantment with the party which had most strongly backed Coptic participation in politics was bound to affect the community.

A more serious problem for the Copts was the Wafd's diminished commitment, statements of party leaders notwithstanding, to unity and equality. This was on symbolic and practical levels. The sundering of the al-Nahhas-Makram alliance destroyed a symbol of national unity as potent and meaningful as that of the 1919 crescent and cross flag. No new symbol, or partnership, emerged to take its place. There were fewer Copts in the party, and they had less influence as individuals and as a group after the split. In effect, the Coptic voice in the Wafd was neutralised; and, while the Wafd never formally abandoned its secular principles, Wafdist Copts were unable to counter their party's greater reliance on Muslim religious feeling in the late 1940s.

Possibly no party could have borne the burden of being the party of national unity after 1946. Even had the Wafd not split in 1942, it might have succumbed to the temptation to play with religious sentiment. There certainly was less pressure to resist this temptation after 1942. The Wafd expended so much of its energy on the pursuit of independence and power that it never had the time, nor perhaps the inclination, to devote to internal reform and to building solid political institutions. Only this latter focus could ultimately have secured the political integration of the Coptic community, as well as a stable political system which was responsive to the needs of ordinary Egyptians.

From the mid-1940s, a feeling grew that the Copts deserved the attacks made against them.[119] The Wafd, as the organisation most capable of calming sectarian hostility, did as little to combat the problem as did the Palace. In 1948, the French Embassy, in noting that no party defended the Copts, added that the Wafd appeared to have forsaken its supraconfessional stand for one of Arabism and "the Islamic idea".[120] Misr repeatedly complained in the early 1950s that the Wafd cabinet completely ignored the problem of religious fanaticism.[121] The paper made a clear distinction between the Wafd of the 1950s and the Wafd of Zaghlul; in reporting how few Copts had been nominated by the party in 1949, Misr commented savagely on this "new policy".[122] Many Copts felt that they had been abandoned along with the principles of Sad Zaghlul;[123] Misr criticised the Wafd for confusing religion and nation. Co-operation with and support for the Muslim Brethren did not improve the Wafd's image. Misr repeatedly returned to the days of Zaghlul as a paradigm for national unity and equality.[124] In 1952, the paper brought up the subject of the Black Book and accused al-Nahhas of disliking all Copts because he hated Makram.[125]

Misr was now quick to point out the disadvantage of relying on parties which continually acted to erode the political position of the community, in part by decreasing the number of its political representatives.[126] At the same, those same parties were eroding the political system on which Coptic participation and communal safety depended. The only solution was perhaps to withdraw from a political world in which the principles of Zaghlul seemed to be increasingly irrelevant.

B. THE LIBERAL CONSTITUTIONAL PARTY

This party, with less organisation and appeal than the Wafd, was, in the words of one wit, "a General Staff without an army".[127] The Liberals began with worthy convictions but were always rather half-hearted about expressing them in public;[128] they eventually seemed to grow half-hearted about the convictions as well.

The party grew out of the 1921 Adli-Zaghlul split; its founders backed the former and saw themselves as sensible moderates combating the alarming extremism of the Zaghlulists. Four Copts were elected to the party's Executive Committee at its founding in 1922: Ilyas Awad; Tawfiq Dus, who brought his two brothers into the party; Salib Sami, and Amin Khayyat, a relative of George. Abadir Hakim, a landowner, and Qalini Fahmi also joined the party at its inception but were never members of the Executive. The latter was a Liberal for only a very short time. Kamil Bulus, an umdah, landowner and former member of both the Wafd Central Committee and the Union Party, was elected to the Liberal Executive in 1926, perhaps as a replacement for Tawfiq Dus. By 1935, all these men had left the party. The only Copt to play an important role after this date was Shafiq Bey Sidum Ilyas, a former member of the Shab party, who was a senator and a member of the Liberal Parliamentary Committee from 1938-46. By the latter year, even he had defected to the Wafd.

Although the Copts had good reason for their lack of interest in the party, the main point illustrated by these defections is the weakness of party loyalty. Opportunism explains many shifts in party membership. It certainly accounts for the resignation of Tawfiq Dus in 1925. Dus, a minister in the Liberal-Unionist government of 1925, came increasingly under Palace influence and was unhappy when his party insisted he resign, along with other Liberal ministers, over the Shaikh Ali Abd al-Raziq affair.[129] This coalition had never been an easy one and, once before, Dus had managed to preserve it when the other Liberal ministers threatened to resign over the Unionist abuse of government machinery for party ends.[130] His arguments in September were less convincing than they had been the previous July; and he, with other Liberals, was obliged to resign from the cabinet.

Not long after this, Dus submitted a conditional resignation from the party.[131] His act was at least partly motivated by growing ties with the Palace. Given the Liberals' general lack of success at the polls, Dus may have felt that his political future could be better secured with royal backing. However, he seems to have maintained contacts with Liberals, perhaps out of a reluctance to burn his bridges too soon. Both he and Salib Sami were reported in 1926 to be opposing Liberal co-operation with the Wafd. Dus finally broke with the Liberals when a Wafd-Liberal coalition was established and Zaghlul adamantly refused to grant Dus a constituency for the upcoming Chamber election.[132] Dus ran as an Independent, but with Palace and government backing. He won but was almost immediately obliged to resign his seat due to flagrant election irregularities.

In a similar case, Salib Sami, a gifted lawyer, resigned from the party in 1933 because he wished to accept a portfolio in the Sidqi cabinet, which his party was opposing. Sami, who was rumoured to owe his career to Liberal leader Muhammad Mahmud's patronage, had been an important party member.[133]

Other Coptic notables drifted away from the party at different times and for different reasons. The Liberals' persistent use of anti-Coptic propaganda could not have encouraged old Coptic members to stay and new ones to join. In the wake of *al-Siyasa*'s 1929 assault on the Copts for their alleged opposition to the treaty, *Misr* asked how any Copts could consider themselves members of such an unscrupulous party.[134] At least one Copt agreed with *Misr*; Abadir Hakim resigned from the party in February 1930 because of *al-Siyasa*'s anti-Coptic bias. Predictably, *al-Siyasa* seems to have accused him of putting minority interests before national ones. Hakim may have been putting personal interests first as well; he went over to the then reigning Wafd.[135]

The Liberal Party began its political career with good and honourable intentions towards Egyptian minorities, as the number of Copts and even the one Jew who became party "Generals" indicates. However, few Christians hastened to fill out the ranks; Wafdist ideas and political behaviour were better known and more attractive. In addition, the Liberal press indulged in anti-Coptic statements as early as 1923. This may have caused many Copts to think twice, as did the punishing Liberal defeat at the polls in 1923. Very few Copts stood for election on the Liberal ticket in 1925, but perhaps the Liberals by then resented the fact that they had so little Coptic support. The 1923 defection of Qalini Fahmi and the 1925-26 loss of the Dus brothers meant that within the party there were fewer influential Copts who could argue against the tactic of linking the Copts with the Wafd in order to discredit the Wafd. Kamil Bulus Bey may have been the last Coptic member of the Executive. He still sat on the committee in 1931, but died shortly thereafter. By the mid-1930s, no Copts were represented on the Executive. In the 1938 and 1945 elections, not one victorious Liberal was a Copt. This does not mean that no Copts stood as Liberals,[136] but this is a likely conclusion since the coalitions winning the elections apportioned constituencies to reduce competition before the election. It may, of course, mean that no Coptic Liberal had a high enough standing within the party to demand a safe seat. In the 1950 election, however, there were no Coptic Liberal candidates. The party of liberalism and constitutionalism had become the party of Muslims.

C. THE PALACE

The Palace played such a critical and indeed even damaging role in the Egyptian party system that it merits inclusion here. The royal family, to begin with, had a certain problem of attitude; it was proud of its Turkish ancestry and disdainful of its Egyptian subjects. The inner circle of royal advisers were mainly Turkic in origin; few Christians worked in the Palace with the one exception of the European Administration, where Christian language skills were useful.[137]

There were, however, Coptic politicians who sought their political fortunes in conjunction with the Palace. Some clearly did so less out of a belief in the institution of monarchy than out of devotion to personal interests. While the Wafd and the Liberals can at least lay claim to holding certain principles, however poorly practised, it is difficult to find any principles to which the Palace and its allies were attached, beyond the advancement of their own power. Those Coptic politicians who sheltered under the wing of the Palace had little popular appeal, and few of them were involved in the nationalist movement in 1918-22. Their family circumstances varied: some were descended from great landowning families and others, who entered politics via a professional education, came from more modest backgrounds. Their involvement with the Palace may also have been indicative of a natural minority desire to be seen to be supporting and not opposing their government. While the Palace did not always have the upper hand in politics, it must have been seen by many Copts as the most permanent, identifiable and traditional manifestation of the Egyptian state. The Palace, although it used religion to attain its goals, was also happy to have Copts help pursue those same goals. Coptic support was, indeed, vital to helping the King maintain an image as the father of all his peoples.

In 1925, a number of Copts, mainly wealthy landowners like Amin Ghali, brother of the late prime minister Butrus; Bulus Hanna Pasha, an elected senator who probably had just resigned from the Wafd Parliamentary Committee;[138] Kamil Bulus Bey, who in the space of a few short years belonged to the Wafd, Ittihad and Liberal parties; and Sarufim Mina Ubaid, an ex-Wafdist, joined the Palace-sponsored al-Ittihad party. Ibrahim Ghali suggests that his father, Amin, and other landowners joined the party because they were in financial difficulties and they thought membership in a Palace-backed organisation would help. Amin and Bulus Hanna were members of the party Executive. Kamil Bey Bulus was a member of the Qina Committee, of which Bulus Hanna was President. Sarufim belonged to the Minya Markaz (District) Committee.[139] A few Coptic <u>umdahs</u> and merchants joined the party as well. Nakhla al-Mutii, whom the British respected, belonged to the party and was occasionally offered a cabinet post as well.

More Copts leapt on the bandwagon and joined a Palace-approved, if not sponsored, venture in 1930. This was Prime Minister Ismail Sidqi's misnamed al-Shab, or People's Party. Some who joined, like two members of the Wisa family, were landowners and relatively inactive politically; again, they probably joined because they hoped for financial benefit. Other members, like the three Dus brothers and Qalini Fahmi, were both more active and influential with the Palace. The lawyer, Salib Sami, joined al-Shab when he was offered a portfolio in the Sidqi cabinet.[140] At the local level, there were Copts on the provincial committees of the more heavily Christian provinces; for example, one-half of the members of the Asyut Committee were Copts.

The party outlived the Sidqi regime but after the prime minister's fall in 1933, it was scarcely a credible political force. Sidqi lost control of the party and eventually it was merged with al-Ittihad. At no point did al-Shab have any popular support. It was an artificial creation designed to brighten the democratic image of a basically repressive regime.

Tawfiq Dus and Qalini Fahmi were the two Copts who were probably the closest to the Palace. This relationship was in part derived from and sustained by the even tighter links Dus and Fahmi had forged with Patriarchs Cyril and Yuannis. Both men served as intermediaries between Patriarch and Palace. Qalini was the more influential with Cyril; by 1930, the latter's successor had come to prefer Dus.[141] This loss of position may have affected Qalini's usefulness to the Palace. Of course, his age and deteriorating mental ability probably made the Patriarch and Palace increasingly reluctant to rely on him.[142]

Dus had a more chequered career and was perhaps at his most powerful between 1925 and 1933. He was close to Sidqi and, during the latter's years as prime minister in the 1930s, he may also have been closer to the King than any other member of the cabinet.[143] He was also Sidqi's main support in the cabinet.[144] By 1933, however, the Palace was so embarrassed by charges of corruption against Dus and saw these as so threatening to an already weak government, that it pressed Sidqi to drop Dus from the cabinet.[145] Relations between Dus and Sidqi remained good despite this and, after the latter's eclipse, Dus refused to indulge in Palace-sponsored attacks on Sidqi but left these to his brother, Wahib.[146]

King Faruq's reliance on religious feeling and his pose as a devout monarch, probably made him more unwilling than Fuad to be seen working in close collaboration with certain Coptic politicians. He was, in any case, not terribly open to outside influence at the beginning of his reign due to the ascendancy of Ali Mahir and Shaikh al-Maraghi. Dus was _persona non grata_ for some time, but was sufficiently returned to favour in 1942 to be named to the Senate.[147] He may later have lost that favour with the Palace[148] because his appointment was cancelled in 1944.

Dus' brother, Wahib, was also close to the Palace but was without Tawfiq's influence. He was a great friend of Ali Mahir and was even persuaded by the latter to make contributions to Misr al-Fatat.[149] He was also to be found lecturing to the Young Men's Muslim Association.[150] These were connections which few Copts would have approved.

There were other Copts who were associated at times with the Palace. Unlike the Dus brothers, these tended, like Salib Sami,[151] Nakhla al-Mutii, and possibly Saba Habashi,[152] to be conscientious and respected functionaries who were useful as token Copts in Palace-dominated cabinets. They had no independent popularity or backing in the country and so can be presumed to have been obedient ministers. They threatened the power of no one.

D. THE SADIST PARTY

Only one important Copt, Najib Iskandar, left the Wafd with Mahir and al-Nuqrashi to form this party named after Sad Zaghlul. The British speculated that the reason more Copts did not abandon the Wafd was due to the shining example of Makram's influence, which had been so recently demonstrated and reaffirmed, in the party.[153] Iskandar may have joined because he finally realised that his 1932 defection had cost him any chance of achieving an important position in the Wafd. He was able to play an influential role in his new party and sat as Minister of Health in various cabinets which included Sadist participation. Another defector to the Sadists was Azir Jibran, Deputy for Baqur, Asyut.[154]

Copts were, in fact, well represented in the party. This may have had something to do with the Sadists' urban base, but it is still a little surprising given the party's predilection for anti-Coptic propaganda, as demonstrated particularly in the 1938 election campaign. Aziz Mishriqi, a young lawyer who was related to Najib Iskandar, joined the party, probably under Najib's influence, and was influential. He was considered for a portfolio in 1946 and finally became Vice-President of the Chamber.[155] Jeffrey Ghali, who was a personal friend of al-Nuqrashi, also belonged to the party and gave generously to its treasury. He resigned in 1946 over the draft Anglo-Egyptian treaty whose terms, he believed, demeaned Egypt. His second cousin suggests that he also felt that his political ambitions would be better served by the Wafd.[156]

It is interesting that most of those Copts who won election to the Chamber in 1938, stood as Sadists. The party improved its record in the 1945 and 1950 elections by nominating more Copts than in 1938. At least half those Copts represented urban constituencies. Had the party preached what it practised, it might have won the support of many more Copts; but this probably would not have been an advantage to a splinter group struggling to establish itself as a credible political force. As it was, in the post-1942 period, Copts may have played a greater role in Sadist inner councils than they did in the Wafd.

E. THE WAFDIST BLOC (AL-KUTLA AL-WAFDIYYA)

Soon after breaking with al-Nahhas, Makram founded his own political vehicle, the Wadfist Bloc. Its better known members seemed mainly to come from middle-class families in Upper Egypt; many were fairly young and none had strong links with the Wafd in the formative 1918-22 period. Most were relatively unknown, although some of al-Kutla's Copts were familiar to the community through their participation in various communal organisations. Unlike the other parties, al-Kutla was blessed with an absence of internal dissension, partly because of Makram's strength and partly because, as the American Ambassador pointed out, there were not enough members "to work up a good fight".[157]

Al-Kutla was not an overnight or even an eventual success. Until late 1944, the Wafd ministry was able to neutralise its activity. With both censorship and martial law in effect, there was little political freedom for those not backing the Wafd. The new party found it very difficult to place its rival claim to the Zaghlulist legacy in the public eye. Perhaps Makram miscalculated and saw his popularity as something that grew out of public perceptions of his talents and character rather than something that was due, at least in part, to his connection with Zaghlul, the Wafd and even al-Nahhas. His value as a symbol of Muslim tolerance perhaps required a Muslim at the top as a foil.

Particularly in the party's early years, Makram was the most ferociously anti-Wafdist of any politician.[158] That a party whose platform was largely restricted to complaints about Wafdist misdeeds could survive two-and-a-half years of Wafd government is something of a tribute to the talents of Makram.[159] Al-Kutla was only briefly a credible political force and that was due to the events of 1942-44 as well as to strong Palace backing. In the long run, however, the party's tie to the King only reflected discredit upon it.[160] A party newspaper was not published until 1944, and its collapse in 1949 signalled the virtual end of the party.

In an attempt to attract public attention, Makram adopted a more exaggerated anti-British stance than he had for some years.[161] The American Ambassador thought that Makram's views were more nationalist and anti-British than even those of the Wafd.[162] These views gave him something in common with the Muslim Brethren and he, like other politicians, courted them in particular and, to the extent he was able, the religious sentiment which made them popular in general. On more than one occasion, he addressed the subject of government maltreatment of al-Azhar and the Brethren; he mentioned in the Black Book, for example, that the Wafdist government had closed branch organisations of the Muslim Brethren.[163]

In the autumn of 1942, it was rumoured that Makram was meeting with Hassan al-Banna, the Brethren's Supreme Guide. Upon learning that al-Nahhas planned to ban Brethren meetings in Cairo in retaliation, al-Banna publicly denied that any meetings with Makram had taken place.[164] With the publication of the Black Book in 1943, the Wafd government, needing another ally, eased its pressure on the Brethren, and may have considered using the Brethren to intimidate Makram's Coptic supporters.[165] In later years, the Brethren would not need any encouragement to intimidate Copts. It is not clear that Makram's conciliatory attitude towards the Brethren was ever productive. When he tried to use the Brethren to ensure a good reception on a visit to Tanta in 1944, it backfired and he was loudly booed.[166] In 1947, Makram was again meeting with al-Banna. The following year, he was the only politician to condemn the dissolution of the Brethren organisation;[167] similarly, he was the only one to defy a government order and attend the funeral when al-Banna was assassinated.

However much Makram may have disliked the fact, his religion and the number of Copts in the party at its founding gave al-Kutla an immediate claim on the attention of the Coptic community. He did not attempt to fix that claim by representing communal interests both because he considered himself a national politician and because he realised that Muslim support was vital to his success. If anything Makram paid less attention to sectarian problems than many of his colleagues. He may, however, have worked both sides of the street and ordered Coptic party workers to explain to Copts that it was in their interest to back al-Kutla.[168] In 1944 it was rumoured that Coptic party workers were using communal and religious tensions to attract followers.[169]

The fall of the Wafd government in 1944 and the organisation of a coalition government, including four ministers from al-Kutla, gave the party its first real freedom to organise. In October, the party gained the support of ten deputies and senators who defected from the Wafd when they realised that their party was due for a long stretch in the political cold.[170]

In the summer of 1942, Makram had begun talks with the Liberals and Sadists; both, like him, were opposed to the Wafd and in some measure dependent on the Palace. They were not natural allies and only considerable pressure from the Palace forced their co-operation.[171] The personal antipathy between Makram and al-Nuqrashi would soon have destroyed the 1944 coalition government without this countervailing pressure. Some Copts feared that December that this enmity and Makram's troublesomeness would have unpleasant repercussions for the community.[172] Makram was not only being unnecessarily critical of the Wafd but he was creating many problems for his prime minister, Ahmad Mahir. Prince Muhammad Ali and Embassy personnel speculated that Makram and the Palace would, after thoroughly discrediting the Wafd, sabotage the present government and install a more subservient Palace ministry.[173] Perhaps Makram saw this as his chance to be prime minister.

The coalition quarrelled over the distribution of constituencies for the 1944 election. Makram wanted fewer seats left to open competition because he correctly calculated that, with Sadists as prime minister and Minister of the Interior, Sadists would win free constituencies. The Palace pressed Ahmad Mahir to agree to Makram's demand because it did not want the Sadists so strong that it reduced their dependency on the Palace. However, when Ahmad Mahir threatened to resign if he could not have his way, the Palace relented. Makram then threatened to resign unless the Sadist party disowned all Sadist candidates standing in constituencies earmarked for al-Kutla and stopped appointing Sadist village chiefs in al-Kutla constituencies. Mahir was tempted to let Makram resign, but his supporters dissuaded him because they were worried about Makram's considerable support among workers.[174] The Sadists were popular primarily in urban areas so it was important that the coalition not lose that support. While Makram was working out the details of a compromise, workers demonstrated in front of Abdin Palace and threatened a general strike if Makram resigned. King Faruq was moved to send Hassan Pasha Yusuf, a Palace adviser, to urge Makram to settle his differences with the prime minister.[175]

Makram was right to be concerned for al-Kutla did even less well in the elections than he expected. The party was allocated fifty-five safe seats by the coalition, but it presented a total of eighty-three candidates. Fourteen of these, or seventeen per cent, were Copts.[176] The party won only twenty seats, due to government interference on behalf of Sadist candidates and because many so-called "Independents" standing in al-Kutla constituencies were actually Sadists. There was talk of excluding al-Kutla from the cabinet and Makram tried to resign, but the Palace refused to allow it. Al-Nuqrashi became prime minister in February 1945 when Ahmad Mahir was assassinated; but his relations with Ubaid were no better, and they deteriorated throughout the year. At one point, the Palace patched things over but, by autumn Makram was complicating the Anglo-Egyptian treaty revision for al-Nuqrashi by insisting on formal negotiations rather than the useful prelude of informal talks. Makram seems to have feared being left out of informal discussions. When Raghib Hanna, a passive politician loyal to Makram,[177] died in November, Makram feared that al-Nuqrashi would give Hanna's portfolio to a Sadist. However, it turned out that Raghib, a Minister of State, was not replaced. This weakened Makram, without giving him too much cause to complain. Finally, in February 1946, Makram resigned on the grounds that al-Nuqrashi was not sharing information about the progress being made towards a revision of the treaty. He also outspokenly objected to the severe treatment the government had meted out to student demonstrators. This brought down the cabinet and Ismail Sidqi became prime minister.

Although Makram would never again occupy a cabinet position, he was invited to join Sidqi's team to negotiate a new treaty. Acting in character, he was reported to be the most intransigent and difficult member of the team.[178] Although the British remarked on his hostility, it was not really noteworthy; Makram was playing to an audience that had itself become increasingly anti-British. One rather concise description suggests that Makram's political tactice of the time involved "flattery of the Palace, resounding patriotic speeches, bitter attacks on the Wafd, appeals to the Coptic minority for support...and declarations of friendship towards the reactionary Muslim Brethren".[179] This is an odd combination, and must have seemed to to the public. While Makram continued to attack the Wafd, from the summer of 1946, his blows were aimed increasingly at the government and negotiations with the British.[180] He was very argumentative in the Chamber and was complaining indiscriminately.[181] In January 1947, he engaged in fisticuffs in the Chamber with a government deputy. By that autumn, he had turned on his former sponsor, the Palace. The latter was eager to obtain a treaty and had probably come to find Makram an obstacle in obtaining one.[182]

In 1946, perhaps sensing that he had antagonised many potential allies, Makram made a curious approach to the Wafd. Both parties were in opposition to the government and their newspapers, for a time, stopped attacking one another. It was rumoured that Fuad Siraj al-Din was trying to work out the details of a reconciliation.[183] This failed and Makram made another approach in 1947, when the post of party secretary-general fell vacant. Understandably, al-Nahhas was not willing to overlook the years of betrayal.[184] Makram again tried to improve his relations with the Wafd in 1949.[149] His brother, Hilmi, was a Wafdist and probably was used as a channel for communication. By this point, however, there was no incentive for the Wafd to collaborate with a party which commanded so little public support. Makram tried very hard to persuade al-Nahhas to boycott the elections because he feared that his party would do badly in them.[186] At the same time, he tried to come to an arrangement with the Liberals and Sadists but they wanted nothing to do with him.[187] He had earlier been invited to join the coalition cabinet of Sirri Pasha but his conditions were so extravagant that he was left out.[188] The best he could hope for was some sort of coalition government formed after the elections and he appears to have suggested to the British Embassy that they intervene to produce such a result.[189] How he intended to deal with the public reaction to such interference is not recorded. For someone who tried to build political support on the strength of his anti-British credentials, this was an astonishing *volte face*.

Makram soon gave up the idea of an election boycott and a rapprochement with either al-Nahhas or the British. He and al-Nahhas attacked one another freely during the election campaign. As the British Embassy noted, Marking was "fighting a losing battle and [had] made the fact all the more obvious by canvassing the support and collaboration of some of the more extreme elements of the dissolved Muslim Brethren..."[190] Al-Kuṭla failed to win any seats in the new Wafdist-dominated Chamber and this effectively finished Makram's career.

The reaction of the Coptic community to Makram was an ambivalent one. His father had converted to Protestantism, a religion Makram at least nominally shared until he returned to Orthodoxy in 1923. Many Orthodox resented those who fractured the unity of the Holy Church; they may also have disliked Makram's convenient conversion to Orthodoxy. Makram's lack of interest in the community and its welfare only reinforced the sense of estrangement. For example, Misr suggested that Makram's first name, William, which he never used, was somehow illustrative of his isolation from the community.[191] However, he was still a Christian and a Copt, only conversion to Islam could change this; and, as one who had overcome the handicap of religion to achieve great political success, he was an object of pride and a symbol of the new equality. He was both praised and criticised, paraded as a great patriot and branded as the betrayer of his community. Copts disliked his familiarity with and political use of Islam, not simply because it sounded hypocritical on the tongue of a non-Muslim, but because a Copt, of all Egyptians, ought to have had the sense to leave religion out of political debate. Misr criticised Makram for repeatedly referring to Christ as "Jesus, the son of Miriam", thereby implying a denial of Christ's divinity. The paper suggested that Makram would do well to seek instruction in Christianity and to alter his stock political phrase to "I am an Egyptian [instead of "a Muslim"] in country and a Christian in religion".[192]

From the mid-1940s, Makram became something of a liability and an embarrassment to the community. Even if he had shown an interest in lessening sectarian tensions, the weakness of al-Kutla would have given him little power to do so. His party's interest in the problem of Muslim hostility to Copts was limited to praising itself as an example of Copt-Muslim unity. As the party paper pointed out, al-Kutal's leader was a Copt and his followers mostly Muslims.[193] There were, of course, many Copts in his party. They may have believed, particularly in al-Kutla's early years, that the chances of the Copts obtaining more power via this party offset any damage Ubaid's tactics might do.

From 1937, there was always fear in the community that Makram's extravagant behaviour threatened them.[194] Misr blamed Ubaid in part for the bad pass to which the community had come by 1951. He had ignored, wrote the paper, his responsibility to the Copts and had never shown any concern with their affairs or problems. At a time when many were giving primacy to their religious beliefs, Makram was wearing a "patriotic cloak" over his.[195] To Misr, Makram seemed hardly to be a Copt.[196]

The Copts were not unaware that Makram had separated himself from them for political reasons. He was not the only Coptic politician to do this; he was simply the most successful. Without this separation, he would not have reached the position he did. Perhaps this is what many Copts came to resent the most: that one could not be devoutly Christian and show public concern for the community and be a noteworthy success in politics. To Muslims, Makram was a symbol of equality and unity, but he was also evidence that non-Muslims could rise above parochial concerns and make their first interests national ones. Despite Makram's clear evidence of this, his very success made him the object, as Misr realised, of more anti-Coptic propaganda than any other Christian politician. Makram seems to have retained some popularity with Egyptians, even though his political behaviour was very erratic in the late 1940s. Sectarian propaganda probably did have some effect on his party, but his own miscalculations and pervasive irascibility probably had more to do with the decline in his fortunes. It is interesting to speculate on the extent to which his political ideas and tactics merely reflected Egypt's political confusion and uncertainty of direction and to what extent it might have represented a loss of his political moorings after he left the Wafd. The dilemma of how to supplant, weaken or merely rival the Wafd while holding roughly the same political beliefs and being Christian must have seemed to him to be a serious one. He does seem to have made a mistake as to what was and was not possible for a Copt. Had he remained within the Wafdist fold, he might have withstood the political storm of the late 1940s and would surely have strengthened his old party.

F. SUMMARY

Copts, then, were represented and played a role in almost all political parties, the National Party excepted. Their choice of a party to support was individual and not communal. It was not at all unusual to find members of the same family backing different parties. While this is unlikely to have been a deliberate family policy, it did have the advantage of offering some protection from the vagaries of Egyptian politics. In 1942, for example, a Wafdist politician might have been able to protect his Sadist relative from excessive government revenge. In a more general sense, Coptic participation across the political board made it difficult to substantiate or even raise the spectre of communal disloyalty to the state since there were always some Copts supporting the government in power and having some kind of influence in it.

Until 1942 the Wafd was the champion of Coptic participation in the political arena. In 1923, the Copts formed almost forty-four per cent of the party's Executive Committee. In 1942, their percentage shrank to twelve. After 1942, al-Kutla and perhaps even the Sadists allowed the Copts more power than the Wafd. Both nominated more Copts to stand for parliament and entrusted more important portfolios to Copts than did the Wafd.

Coptic influence, however strong it might have been initially, was perhaps the weakest in the Liberal Constitutional party. This was in part due to the inherent weakness of a party that could not win free elections. Few minorities could afford the risk of betting on what appeared to be a sure loser. In addition, the party's reliance on religious and ethnic propaganda was discouraging. Copts seeking a political career could not be sure that such tactics did not have some bearing on the party's internal workings and that it did not reflect how party members felt about Copts. Of course, the Sadists also used ethnic propaganda, but their former connection with the Wafd probably offered some reassurance. Copts as well as Muslims split from the Wafd to form this party, and these ex-Wafdists Copts could have played an important role in persuading unaffiliated Copts that Sadist Muslims were not prejudiced and were willing to work with Copts.

Those Copts who allied themselves to the Palace and Palace-backed parties were making a traditional and safe choice. The Palace was always more supportive of the Patriarchate than other parties, it was a permanent and respected feature of the Egyptian political scene and, even in periods of Wafdists' ascendancy, it still exercised considerable power. The King had some responsibility, even if it was one that he did not always try to fulfil, to serve as an integrator and to show concern for the interests and well-being of all Egyptians.

Copts in Palace-dominated parties and cabinets had less chance of developing and exercising genuinely independent power than those in, for example, the Wafd. Unless they were tied to the Patriarchate, they did not have a basis of support outside the party, and this made them dependent on the whim of the Palace. This dependency had an effect, for example, on the career of Tawfiq Dus, who was in and out of royal favour more than once. In addition, there was probably less room for Copts to occupy an important place in Palace-dominated parties because of the small size and lack of broad appeal of those parties.

NOTES

1. The British were surprised at the omission of Sadiq Hinain, who probably played an important role in keeping the party going the first six months of 1923. He was frequently received by King Fuad who was then paying court to the Zaghlulists and who gave Hinain £E3,000 to help start the Wafdist paper al-Balagh. FO.371/8959, E1031/10/16.

2. FO.371/20916, 1989/815/16. Ghali spent most of the time that the Wafd was out of power in Europe.

3. Marius Deeb, "The Wafd and its Rivals: The Rise and Development of Political Parties in Egypt 1919-39", unpublished PhD thesis, University of Oxford 1971, p.120.

4. This was after Zaghlul's return from Paris. Interview with Sad Fakhri Abd al-Nur, 17 May 1979.

5. See Chapter Two; Egyptian Gazette, 6 July 1923, 4; FO.371/12361, J3215/8/16.

6. This federation was practically moribund by April 1931. FO.141/763, 506/1/31, 506/2A/31.

7. Deeb, Party Politics in Egypt: The Wafd and its Rivals, 1919-39, pp.264-5.

8. FO.371/15407, J3309/26/16.

9. The British and even al-Nahhas looked on Makram as "Director" of the Blue Shirts. In 1937 a Committee of Direction, formed of Kamil Sidqi and two others, was set up with the hope of strengthening al-Nahhas/Ubaid control of the organisation for the coming anticipated challenge from Mahir and al-Nuqrashi. FO.141/543, 19/18/36; FO.371/20124, J9095/2/16; FO.371/20098, J1048/2/16.

10. FO.141/543, 19/58/36.

11. Salib Sami was the only non-Wafdist Copt to play a prominent role. Don Reid, 'The National Bar Association and Egyptian Politics, 1912-14', The International Journal of African Historical Studies VII (1974), 608-46.

12. Salama was a close friend of Abd al-Rahman Fahmi, the head of the Wafdist secret terrorist apparatus. When the latter fell out with Zaghlul, Salama pleaded his case. Mustafa Amin, al-Kitab al-Mamnu: Asrar Thawrat 1919, vol.1 (Dar al-Maarif, Cairo, 1976), p.263.

13. Interview with Raghib Iskandar, Akhir Saa, 2 June 1976, 16.

14. Curiously Hanna's views were moderate enough to enable him to be considered for a portfolio in the 1922 Tharwat cabinet. In 1926, al-Ittihad, the Palace newspaper, suggested, possibly for reasons of its own, that Hanna sometimes sided with the moderate non-Wafdists. Quoted in the Egyptian Gazette, 27 July 1926, 4.

15. Wasif described the contemplated resignation as a 'revolt against the King'. Abd al-Khaliq Lashin, Sad Zaghlul wa Dawrahu fi al-Siyasa al-Misriyya (Maktabat Madbuli, Cairo, 1975), pp.363-5.

16. He had once worked in the Khedival household, an experience relevant to running a ministry over which the Palace had considerable control.

17. FO.407/199, No.2 (Enclosure 2), Field-Marshal Viscount Allenby to Mr. MacDonald, 18 July 1924.

18. Ahmad Shafiq asha, Hawliyyat Misr al-Siyasiyya, Vol.1 (1924) (Matbaat Shafiq Basha, Cairo, 1926), p.44.

19. FO.407/199, No.2 (Enclosure 2).

20. Ibid.

21. Zaghlul helped arrange Makram's 1923 marriage to Murqus' daughter, for which Makram had to convert to Orthodoxy.

22. FO.141/501, 13592/57/28.

23. Deeb, The Wafd and its Rivals, p.190.

24. FO.407/204, No.17, Lord Lloyd to Mr. Chamberlain, 21 April 1927.

25. FO.371/11584, J2218/25/16.

26. The four were Ghali, Sinut, Wisa Wasif and Salama Mikhail. The absentees do not seem to have returned to Egypt in time, but may have voted by proxy or cable. Ibrahim Amin Ghali believes that they were able to vote from Europe. Interview on 4 June 1980.

27. FO.407/205, No.21, Mr. Henderson to Sir

Austen Chamberlain, 24 September 1927.

28. Muhammad Husain Haikal, Mudhakkirat fi al-Siyasa al-Misriyya, p.279.

29. Sad suggests that his father betrayed Barakat only after receiving assurances that al-Nahhas was not prejudiced against Copts. The Residency, however, speculated that al-Nuqrashi had frightened Fakhri into voting for al-Nahhas. Interview with Sad Fakhi Abd al-Nur, 17 May 1979; FO.407/205, No.21, Henderson, 24 September 1927.

30. FO.371/12359, J2730/8/16. Leland Bowie accepts Haikal's interpretation that a group of Copts helped tip the balance in favour of al-Nahhas. Leland Bowie, 'The Copts, the Wafd and religious issues in Egyptian politics', Muslim World 67 (1977), 114.

31. Eight out of the twenty voters were Copts and four of these were in Europe.

32. FO.371/12359, J2730/8/16.

33. Deeb, The Wafd and its Rivals, p.173.

34. Interview with Ibrahim Amin Ghali, 4 June 1980.

35. FO.407/206, J615/4/16.

36. FO.371/12359, J2715/8/16.

37. Afaf Marsot, relying on Barakat's Memoirs, gives a very different picture of the election when she suggests that Mme. Zaghlul quarrelled with Barakat over some petty personal matter, and then was cajoled into supporting al-Nahhas by flattery. Marsot seems to find Barakat the better candidate; neither the British nor Fatima al-Yusuf share her attitude. The British thought his character unsavoury and his unpopularity deserved, but they were resigned to his usefulness as a moderating force in the Wafd. Fatima, in addition, suggested that many Wafdists feared his tyrannical nature. See Afaf Marsot, Egypt's Liberal Experiment 1922-36 (University of California Press, Los Angeles, 1977), 1928; Fatima al-Yusuf, Dhikrayat (Cairo, 1976), p.124.

38. Murqus was so inept as Minister of Foreign Affairs in 1926 that he was thought to be suffering from 'some form of mental collapse'. The British were not surprised when he was excluded from the 1928 cabinet. FO.407/213, J395/395/16.

39. Al-Nuqrashi seems to have been added to the party executive at the suggestion of Makram. FO.407/205, J2715/8/16.

40. The Residency saw Makram and al-Nuqrashi as the presiding evil geniuses, FO.407/210, Nos.10 and 22, Sir P. Loraine to Mr. A. Henderson, 4 and

19 January 1930.

41. Neither Henderson, Grafftey-Smith nor Keown-Boyd had a very high opinion of Fakhri. The latter had gained a reputation for his 'venal exploitation' of appointments. See, for example, FO.407/206, No.61 (enclosure), Notes on a visit to Sohag, 11-14 February 1928 by L.G. Grafftey-Smith; FO.141/770, 358/5/31.

42. FO.371/13117, J1378/4/16.

43. Wasif Ghali, perennially in Europe, was asked by both sides to return home to mediate. He seems to have stayed put, sensibly avoiding a job which would have earned him the resentment on one side or the other.

44. FO.371/16018, J451/14/16.

45. Ibid. Interview with Ibrahim Amin Ghali, 4 June 1980.

46. FO.141/744, 1167/1 and 2/33; FO.371/16109, J2552/14/16.

47. FO.407/216, No.22, R.I. Campbell to Sir J. Simon, 28 October 1932.

48. Ibid.

49. FO.407/216, No.39 (enclosure), Memorandum Respecting the Egyptian Press, 25 November to 1 December 1932.

50. Interview, lbrahim Amin Ghali, 19 March 1979.

51. CAS, File W/22. This note may be the draft of a letter, but it is undated and is not addressed to anyone.

52. FO.407/216, No.36, Sir P. Loraine to Sir J. Simon, 26 November 1932.

53. Interview with Ibrahim Amin Ghali, 4 June 1980.

54. Marsot, Egypt's Liberal Experiment, p.149.

55. FO.371/20916, J1989/815/16.

56. Curiously, Sidqi appears, for some unknown reason, to have been dropped from the Executive in the mid-1930s. He was reappointed to the Committee in 1942.

57. FO.371/15404, J1110/26/16.

58. Al-Yusuf, Dhikrayat, pp.131, 164.

59. FO.407/210, J317/3/16.

60. FO.371/19076, J5782/110/16. It is interesting to note that by 1935 the Residency is calling the al-Nahhas faction moderate and al-Nuqrashi's supporters left-wing.

61. Fatima al-Yusuf claims that Makram's fear was misplaced. Al-Yusuf, Dhikrayat, p.168.

62. One pamphlet called al-Nahhas a camel and Makram his driver. It also suggested that Makram

had persuaded al-Nahhas to frequent low dancing places. FO.371/19076, J5699/110/16. It should be noted that al-Nuqrashi was close to Abbas al-Aqqad, one of the two writers who left al-Jihad for Ruz al-Yusuf, and he pleaded on behalf of Abbas with al-Nahhas. Ruz' later attacks on Makram suggest that al-Nuqrashi maintained his link with the journal.

63. Ruz al-Yusuf, 14 October 1935, p.13, 32; 7 October 1935, 7.

64. This was in November 1936, FO.141/535, 1/183/36.

65. For example, when Makram suspected Ahmad Mahir of collaborating secretly with his brother, Prime Minister Ali Mahir in 1936, he was able to persuade Kawkab al-Sharq to treat both brothers hostilely. FO.371/20105, J3533/2/16.

66. This is from a Cairo Police Report. FO.371/20105, J3533/1/16.

67. His favours annoyed the previously loyal al-Jihad so much that the paper moved into opposition, even though only for a month. FO.371/22006, J2805/2/16.

68. FO.407/221, No.51, Mr. David Kelly to Mr. Eden, 28 October 1937.

69. Makram refused to submit the contract to competitive bidding. Haikal, Mudhakkirat, vol.2, p.35.

70. FO.371/20885, J3778/20/16.

71. FO.371/20886, J4060/20/16.

72. Abd al-Azim Ramadan, Tatawwur al-Haraka al-Wataniya fi Misr, vol.2 (Dar al-Katib al-Arabi, Cairo, 1960), p.259.

73. This allegation was particularly favoured by the Liberal press and Haikal repeats it in Mudhakkirat, vol.2, p.263.

74. Afaf Marsot (Egypt's Liberal Experiment, p.203), is one such scholar.

75. Al-Nahhas' eyes looked in different directions.

76. Muhammad al-Tabii, Misr min Qabl al-Thawra (Dar al-Maarif, Cairo, 1978), pp.240-1.

77. Salah al-Shahid, Dhikrayati fi Ahdayn (Dar al-Maarif, Cairo, 1976), p.40. Fuad Siraj al-Din is quoted as holding a similar opinion, which Ramadan accepts, in Ramadan, Tatawwur, vol.2 pp.272-3. Mustafa al-Feki also accepts this interpretation in his 'Makram Ubayd: A Coptic Leader in the Egyptian National Movement', unpublished PhD thesis, University of London, 1977, p.159.

78. Siraj al-Din believed that the Palace was

the initiator. Ramadan, Tatawwur, vol.2, p.265.

79. The Embassy periodically suggested that Ubaid was the one Wafdist most hated by the Palace. This information, however, was derived largely from Amin Uthman and Ali Mahir, so it can perhaps be regarded with suspicion. Lampson admitted at one point that Amin did not like Makram. FO.371/31572, J2564/38/16.

80. CCEH, F7/D7, Cards 757, 760, Security Reports (Palace) on Meetings of the Wafd, 8 October and 15 October 1971.

81. Two Security Reports confirm this. CCEH, F7/D7, Card 764, Security Reports (Cairo Police), 2 November 1941 and Card 765, Security Reports (Palace), 4 November 1941. However, a third report claims that at least al-Misri had received no orders about reducing the news it published about the King. Card 765, Security Reports (Cairo Police), 5 November 1941.

82. CCEH, F7/D7, Card 757, Security Report (Palace) on meeting of the Wafd, 8 October 1941.

83. CCEH, F7/D7, Cards 826/9, Public Security Reports, 21 January 1942.

84. Jalal al-Din al-Hamamsi, a supporter of Makram, and Fuad Siraj al-Din, an opponent, both think this. Ramada Tatawwur, vol.2, pp.266-7.

85. FO.371/31567, J649/38/16.

86. FO.371/31569,J1251/38/16 and J1319/38/16.

87. Salah al-Shahid wrongly claims that al-Nahhas did not know about the audience with the King until after it took place. He suggests that Makram as Minister, was fulfilling the wishes of the Palace without consulting al-Nahhas. Salah al-Shahid, Dhikrayati, pp.38, 41.

88. Al-Feki, "Makram Ubayd", p.162.

89. Apparently, Mme. al-Nahhas and Mme. Ubaid were not on good terms and this had some effect on their husbands' relationship. In addition, Amin Uthman was said to have some kind of friendly tie to Mme. al-Nahhas. FO.371/31570, J1619/38/16; FO.371/31572, J2564/38/16.

90. One of these officials was the Copt, Ibrahim Faraj Masiha.

91. The British commented that, after the exit of al-Nuqrashi, Makram was the only efficient organiser left in the party. FO.371/31571, J1885/38/16.

92. FO.371/31572, J2415/38/16, Kamil Sidqi was probably one of those Copts urging moderation.

93. CCEH, F7.D7, Cards 940-2, Security Reports, 30 May 1942.

94. CCEH, F7/D7, Cards 940-9, Security Rep-

orts 30 and 31 May 1942. Among those, including several journalists, reported to be helping Makram were Mustafa Amin, Muhammad al-Tabai, Qasim Judah, Jalal al-Din al-Hamamsi and Fikri Abaza.

95. In 1943, Makram's followers were still complaining about how difficult it was for them to publish or give speeches. Security Report 2250, 12 October 1943, quoted in Jamal Salim, al-Bulis al-Siyasi Yahkum Misr (Dar al-Qahira L-il-Thaqafa al-Arabiyya, Cairo, 1975), p.169.

96. FO.371/31572, J2564/38/16.

97. CCEH, F7/D7, Cards 943-9, Security Reports, 31 May 1942.

98. FO.371/32573, J2885/38/16.

99. CCEH, F7/D7, Cards 940-9, Security Reports, 30 and 31 May 1942.

100. Both Ramadan and al-Feki think that Makram genuinely thought that he could be prime minister. Ramadan, Tatawwur, vol.2, p.272; al-Feki, 'Makram Ubayd', p.163.

101. Raghib was his closest ally but was not, as is sometimes reported, his brother-in-law. Raghib was the brother of Bushra and Sinut Hanna. Makram married into a different Hanna family.

102. Ramadan lists seventeen names, as does al-Feki. Misr lists nineteen names, missing one of the names on al-Feki's list. The British records suggest that twenty-one were expelled with Makram and this probably included Raghib Hanna. The Copts were Charles Bushra Hanna, the nephew of Raghib; George Makram Ubaid, the brother of Makram; Mihana al-Qummus; Zaki and Najib Mikhail Bishara; Michel Rizq; Dr. Fahmi Suliman Sidhum; Alfred Qasis and Labib Gris. None were members of the Wafd Executive. See Ramadan, Tatawwur, vol.2, p.257; Misr, 13 July 1942, p.2; FO.371/31573, J3228/38/16. Haikal notes that, in general, the deputies who went over to Makram were young intellectuals and a few notables from Qina. Haikal, Mudhakkirat, vol.2, p.266.

103. It is possible, however, that the heavy use of ethnic propaganda in 1937-38 had an effect on a segment of the Wafd leadership. Some may have been concerned to reduce Makram's visibility not so much out of personal rivalry as a desire to leave the party less open to charges of Coptic domination.

104. Lampson speculated that the Palace, at a minimum encouraged Makram in the enterprise. Al-Hamamsi claims that Hassanain suggested the idea of a petition while Makram recommended its publication.

It would seem that the preliminaries were arranged by Ismail Sidqi and Murad Muhsin, head of the Royal Daira. Once the King agreed to the project, Hassanain seems to have taken charge of it. See Evans (ed.), The Killearn Diaries, 1934-46 (Sidgwick and Jackson, London, 1972), p.250; Jalal al-Din al-Hamamsi, Hiwar Wara al-Awar (al-Maktab al-Misri al-Hadith, Cairo, 1976), pp.31-6; FO.371/35525, J2855/2/16.

105. FO 371/35532, J1781/2/16.

106. FO.371/35533, J1951/2/16.

107. FO.371/35536, J2855/2/16.

108. FO.371/35536, J2855/2/16.

109. Misr, 9 September 1950, 1.

110. FO.371/31573, J3228/38/16.

111. At the same time, the Palace began competing for a share of this now uncertain Coptic support. Brotherhood and unity were praised, and even Shaikh al-Maraghi made friendly public references to the Copts. FO.371/41317, J1495/14/16. FO.371/35529, J665/2/16.

112. To secure the election of Makram's opponent, the Wafd government postponed the elections until the day after Christmas making it impossible for Coptic lawyers who had joined their families in the provinces for the holiday to return in time to vote. The following year the Wafd nominated Kamil Sidqi to run against Makram. Sidqi won by a considerable majority, but many Copts felt that this election had also been fixed. FO.371/46315, J151/14/16 and J223/14/16.

113. This was at a meeting he attended of the Coptic Benevolent Society. FO.371/41316, J223/14/16.

114. US Department of State Archives, No.883.404/116, Alexander Kirk to the Secretary of State, 31 December 1943.

115. Interview with Ibrahim Amin Ghali, 4 June 1980.

116. Louis Awad believes that few Copts generally were to be found in the party's left wing. Interview, 29 February 1980.

117. Ibid.

118. FO.371/80348, E1016/36/16.

119. Misr, 17 January 1951, 1.

120. French Embassy Archives, Box 144, File 21/2, Situation de la Communauté Copte en Egypte, 24 January 1948.

121. Misr, 23 October 1951, 1.

122. Misr, 26 November 1949, 1.

123. Misr did not only criticise the Wafd for

introducing Islam into secular matters, but this particular article clearly indicates a new perception of what the Wafd was and what it stood for. Misr, 11 January 1950, 1. See also, Misr, 9 September 1950, 1.

124. When al-Nahhas abrogated the treaty and appealed for unity between parties, Misr chided him for not also calling for unity between the ethnic groups. Misr, 12 November 1951, 1, and 10 October 1951, 1.

125. Misr, 28 March 1952, 1, and 1 April 1951, 1.

126. Misr, 26 November 1949, 1.

127. Cab.24/204, CP.181 (1929), Memorandum on Egypt.

128. FO.407/198, Enclosure in No.48, General Situation Report, 9-22 January 1924.

129. Abd al-Aziz Fahmi, the Liberal Minister of Justice, had been dismissed because he did not want to expel the Shaikh, who had Liberal connections, from the Judiciary when the latter published his controversial book on the Caliphate. Sidqi followed Fahmi out of the cabinet, and the party voted in favour of the resignation of the two remaining Liberal ministers. The British did not want the coalition to collapse, and Dus had actually been in touch with them over the matter. FO.407/201, No.33, Mr. Henderson to Mr. Austen Chamberlain, 12 September 1925; Haikal, Mudhakkirat, vol.1, pp.235-6, 241.

130. He persuaded his colleagues that the Liberals would lose the next election if they had to compete against the Wafd without government 'help'. FO.407/202, No.17, Lord Lloyd to Sir Austen Chamberlain, 9 April 1926.

131. The reason he gave was al-Siyasa's hostility to the Ittihadists. FO.407/201, No.35, Henderson to Chamberlain, 19 September 1925; Misr, 21 September 1925, 2; Haikal, Mudhakkirrat, vol.1, p.242.

132. FO.407/202, No.17, Lord Lloyd to Sir Austen Chamberlain, 9 April 1926.

133. One British official called him a 'directing element' in the party. FO.371/20916, J1989/815/16.

134. Misr, 13 September 1929, 1. This is discussed in Chapter Two.

135. See Hakim's articles in Misr, 10 March 1930, 1, and 20 February 1930, 4.

136. Curiously, al-Siyasa in these two years published a list of all the candidates without de-

noting Liberal candidates.

137. One Copt who did gain influence with King Faruq, particularly at the end of his reign, was the businessman, Ilyas Pasha Andrawus. A member of th boards of directors of several companies, he had an unsavoury reputation and was well placed to advise the Palace on its own unsavoury financial dealings. Ilyas' influence extended beyond business matters to other more critical areas. The King, for examples, used him as an intermediary with the British in 1952. Hassan Pasha Yusuf, head of the Royal Diwan just before the end of the monarchy, suggests that Ilyas interfered in practically all Palace concerns. Yusuf believes that Ilyas' reputation for corruption was richly deserved. Interview with Hassan Yusuf, 8 November 1978. Another Copt who had influence with the Palace was Adli Andrawus Bishara, the son of a wealthy landowner.

138. In early 1925, a number of members of the Wafd Parliamentary Committee resigned on the grounds that the Wafd was insufficiently loyal to the throne. Many then joined _al-Ittihad_. Ahmad Shafiq accused the British press and some English papers of trying to create a rift between the Wafd and the Palace. See his _Hawliyyat_, vol.2, pp.2-20.

139. See _al-Ittihad_, 29 January 1925, 4, and 4 October 1925, 5.

140. Sami remained a party member when he served in the cabinet of Sidqi's successor, Abd al-Fatah Yahya Pasha. Sami was reported to be the only minister who had the confidence of Yahya. FO.371/20916, 1989/815/16.

141. As the Residency noted in 1930, the Patriarch 'leans hard on Tawfiq Dus and pays well for his support'. FO.407/213, J395/395/16.

142. By 1929, the British reported that he no longer enjoyed great political influence. FO.141/686, 8609/55/29.

143. FO.407/213, J395/395/16.

144. FO.407/216, J3362/14/16.

145. In 1932, there were charges of corruption made against Sidqi and Dus. Partly because of the frequency of these charges, two other members of the cabinet were on such bad terms with both men that they were threatening to resign (FO.407/216, J3392/14/16; FO.141/650, 392/7/30). Sidqi suggested Dus for the US Legation, but given the likelihood of an unenthusiastic welcome by the Americans, Dus decided to remain a deputy (FO.371/20916, J1989/815/16). In any case, Dus' primary interest

seems to have been in making money; politics was just another means of acquisition.

146. In this way, Dus managed to satisfy royal pleasure without sacrificing Sidqi's friendship. FO.371/20916, J1989/815/16.

147. The prime minister, al-Nahhas, did not want to repeat his 1937 battle with the Palace over Senate appointments. He objected to some of the names proposed by the Palace, but settled on a compromise list which included Dus. FO.371/31571, J1926/38/16. FO.371/20916, 1939/815/16.

148. Interview with Hassan Pasha Yusuf, 8 November 1978.

149. WO.208/1560, Middle East Information Centre Summary, Report 431, 6 February 1941.

150. DW, HBM(QM), Security Report 4491, 20 November 1940.

151. His 1925 campaign experience was so shattering that he never ran for election again. He had a good reputation as a jurist although Mack in the Foreign Office did not think much of his ability. Salib Sami, Dhikrayyat Siyasiyya 1891-1952 (Cairo, 1952), pp.142-4; FO.371/17009, J1851/25/16.

152. The British may have used him as an intermediary with Ali Mahir in 1941. CCEH, F7/D7, Card 801, Public Security Report, 22 December 1941. Once a Sadist, he became, at some point, an 'Independent'. He served in the Sidqi cabinet in 1946 and was, during that time, appointed to the Senate. He resigned his portfolio in October 1946 because he did not want to be connected with the unsavoury Sidqi any more. FO.371/53313, J1478/39/16.

153. FO.371/20886, J3976/20/16. This report went on to suggest that the Copts of Asyut and Suhaj were particularly loyal to the Wafd.

154. Misr, 12 January 1938, 1. He was both cousin and brother-in-law to Tawfiq Dus.

155. See footnote 143.

156. Ibrahim Amin Ghali thinks that Jeffrey resigned because he wanted to be a cabinet minister. Interview on 4 June 1980.

157. US Department of State Archives, No.883.00, Ambassador Jefferson Caffery to the Secretary of State, 10 November 1949.

158. Haikal, Mudhakkirat, vol.2, p.276; FO.371/41328, J1731/31/16; FO.371/4137, J1694/14/16; Evans (ed.), The Killearn Diaries, 1934-46, p.255.

159. Lampson felt that Makram was 'too passionate and vindictive for wise leadership', and apparently many opposition elements felt Makram's vio-

lent tactics were not helping their cause. FO.371/35529, J812/2/16.

160. As Louis Awad commented, it was one thing to attack the Wafd but quite another to become a 'stooge' of the Palace. Interview on 19 February 1980.

161. This was evident as early as July 1942. FO.371/31573, J3301/28/16.

162. US Department of State Archives, No.883.00, Ambassador Jefferson Caffrey to the Secretary of State, 10 November 1949.

163. Al-Feki, 'Makram Ubayd', p.216. The Black Book was also careful to make mention of those Coptic officials who had unlawfully benefited from government largesse.

164. FO.141/838, 305/27/42.

165. FO.371/41329, J1880/31/16.

166. It is not clear who was doing the booing. FO.371/41335, J4164/31/16.

167. Akhir Saa wrote that al-Banna must think that Makram had become the last Muslim Brother. Quoted in Mitchell, The Society of Muslim Brothers, p.66.

168. CCEH, F7/D7, Cards 954-7, Security Report, 15 August 1942.

169. FO.371/41331, J3065/31/16.

170. This list included at least three Copts: Albert George Khayyat, Dr. Ramzi Jirjis and Dr. Iskandar Fahmi Jirjawi. The three were deputies.

171. One first fruit of their co-operation was an attack on al-Nahhas delivered in a joint letter to King Faruq that November. CCEH, F7/D7, Cards 954-7, Security Report, 18 August 1942.

172. FO.371/45916, J76/3/16.

173. FO.371/41335, J4013/31/16; J4052/31/16; J4154/31/16.

174. FO.371/41335, J4516/31/16.

175. Ibid.

176. Al-Kutla, 4 December 1944, 3.

177. He had been in poor health and virtual retirement from the time he joined the Mahir cabinet in October 1944. US Department of State Archives, No.883.002, Mr. Lyon to the Secretary of State, 28 November 1945.

178. For example, while Sidqi was willing to leave the matter of the Sudan until after the treaty had been signed, Makram insisted that it be settled in the treaty. FO.371/53312, J4138/39/16; FO.371/62993, J4516/3/16; FO.371/53313, J4161/39/16.

179. This summary was given at the conference

of communist parties of the British Empire in 1947. FO.371/62993, J4516/13/16.

180. Ibid.

181. FO.371/62990, J722/13/16.

182. FO.371/16302, J5178/79/16.

183. It seems unlikely that Siraj al-Din was behind the contacts. FO.371/53332, J5430/57/16.

184. FO.371/63020, J1952/79/16.

185. FO.371/74364, J5696/1015/16.

186. Ibid.

187. FO.371/73460, J5658/1015/16.

188. He demanded a second portfolio for his weak party and the abolition of martial law. FO.371/73465, J6035/1015/16.

189. FO.371/73464, J4279/1015/16.

190. FO.371/80347, E1016/1/16.

191. _Misr_, 23 April 1936, 1.

192. _Misr_, 15 April 1936, 1.

193. _Al-Kutla_, 20 December 1946, 2.

194. See FO.371/45930, J399/10/16, for an expression of just this fear before the 1945 election.

195. _Misr_, 27 August 1951, 1.

196. _Misr_, 7 April 1947, 3.

Chapter Six

THE COPTS AND THE STATE

The State hoped to see the Copts exchange their anachronistic communal identity for a modern, national one but was doubtful of both their ability and desire to do so. Consequently, it tried to bind the Copts more tightly to it at the same time that it hindered this work by protecting the Muslim hold on state institutions. Copts increasingly saw the state apparatus as biased against them; their access to it was restricted and its interference in their cultural and religious affairs was intolerable. By the late 1940s, the Copts could feel the state's chains tightening. There were more theoretical objections to equality than there had been in the 1920s; if anything, Egypt seemed to be moving farther and farther away from her ideal. Most Muslims probably did not care whether the state infringed upon or respected traditional millet autonomy; but they did care that the Copts in their practice of Christianity and their demands on the state remain relatively invisible. The state could offer the Copts protection and a degree of religious tolerance (although even this traditional obligation seemed to be questioned by the 1940s); anything more than this could and would be construed as catering to them.

A. THE ISSUE OF INEQUALITY

1. Economic Behaviour

The division between Copts and Muslims in this century was not complicated by a class division. Economic power was not in the hands of one community, while political power remained in the hands of the other; nor did the Muslims completely monopolise both. They assuredly held the balance of political power and their sheer numerical majority gave them vast economic resources on which to draw. Each community did complain about the economic behaviour of the other; however, grievances were based not on a serious inequity in the division of wealth but on a fundamental suspicion of those who were different. There was no sense in either community that they were completely shut out from all the economic goods life could afford; the Copts, however, were not entirely unjustified in thinking that they had a special problem of access to the goods the state could provide. Although Copts were sometimes inclined to attribute their lack of personal and communal material advancement to discrimination, they were, in this period, marginally better educated and marginally wealthier as a group than Muslims.[1] Education has always been a route of escape from minority status. This does not, however, imply that there were not many poor, illiterate Copts; about one-half of the Coptic population earned its living from agriculture,[2] and most of those were engaged in subsistence farming.

As far as can be determined, Copts and Muslims acquired land in much the same way in the nineteenth century. Influential and loyal Coptic officials were granted land by a grateful government or were given the first chance to buy choice state land, and wealthy merchants chose to invest their profits in land.[3] Most, but not all, of the big Coptic estates were in Upper Egypt; several exceeded one thousand _feddans_, including those of the Ghali, Dus, Khayyat, Wisa, Fanus, Abskharun, Hanna, Ubaid, Bishara and Jrais families.[4] By the end of the last century, the Copts were paying sixteen per cent of the taxes on agricultural land, although they were officially counted at around six per cent of the population.[5] Even allowing for the fact that they may have been undercounted, these figures suggest that they owned marginally more farm land than their proportion of the population would have suggested. Perhaps curiously and certainly fortunately, this does not seem to have roused Muslim ire. It was the large landowning families Muslim and Copt, which carried disproportionate weight in the political system; and their economic interests gave them a powerful incentive to co-operate against pressure from below and from the outside.

Unlike other, smaller minorities in Egypt, the Copts preferred to invest in farm land and real estate and not in the development of industry. The strong participation of foreign minorities in large-scale commercial and industrial ventures perhaps created problems for both Copts and Muslims. The only Copt on the Board of Bank Misr, an enterprise aimed at Egyptianising the economy, at its founding was Iskandar Masiha. Kamal Ibrahim eventually succeeded. Copts did serve on the Boards of Directors of Bank Misr subsidiaries and of other companies, but in 1952 only four per cent of all company directors were Copts.[6] Many of these men were wealthy landowners, and some were influential politicians. The list of Coptic directors was much longer by 1951; many Copts by then held more than two directorships although a 1947 law formally prohibited this. No doubt more Copts were nominated to directorships because of a second law requiring that one-third of the members of the board of any new company be Egyptian.

Muslims could and did sometimes hinder Coptic participation in various kinds of economic activity, a fact that helps explain the Coptic feeling of dependency on the civil service. The Coptic press periodically voiced complaints about discrimination in both state-owned and private companies;[7] and it does seem that, by the late 1940s, there was more government pressure on companies to hire Muslim Egyptians than Copts.[8] For example, in 1947 the Egyptian Labour Office denied a certificate of Egyptian nationality to a Copt who wished to work for an American firm in Alexandria.[9]

Curiously, there were few attempts at specifically communal commercial ventures. There was, however, in the late 1940s, when the Copts were meeting with increasing discrimination in both the public and private sectors, a push to establish specifically Coptic enterprises; a bank and other kinds of companies were among those suggested. In 1947, a Coptic bank, the Pharaonic Bank, was established. Salama Musa praised the venture,[10] and _Misr_ faithfully printed the names of all the subscribers in an effort to boost their number. Other newspapers condemned the bank as divisive; and Musa retorted that, in that case, so were the Muslim Brethren's economic projects which no one thought to criticise.[11] Unfortunately, the bank failed to sell enough shares and collapsed. Tawfiq Hinain, a Coptic journalist, speculated that the Copts had been afraid to buy shares in what would appear to Muslims to be a chauvinist venture.[12]

2. The Civil Service[13]

Government employment in this poor country with its relatively privileged bureaucracy was prized for its security and was the goal of many ill- and well-educated Egyptians. Fair access was considered critical by both Muslims and Copts, particularly as the bureaucracy grew and the number of posts held by the British declined.[14] In addition, the better-educated Copts had long occupied a greater proportion of bureaucratic posts than their percentage of the population justified. However, by the turn of the century, Muslims were becoming better-educated and were beginning to compete for these positions. Although the number of Coptic officials increased in this period, their share of the civil service declined. The 1937 census recorded a decline in the Coptic share of thirty-five per cent in twenty-seven years, to 9.1 per cent.[15] This was not a formal government policy but rather a tacit admission that a bureaucracy which was thought to be dominated by a minority would lose credibility.[16]

The Copts were unable to grasp the necessity of achieving an ethnic balance. They did not think that their percentage of the population should be a factor in making appointments,[17] but they did use percentages when the figures were in their favour. If fifty per cent of all Egyptian lawyers were Copts, they argued that fifty per cent of all judges should be Copts.[18] The British, who regarded the decline in the proportion of Coptic officials as fair, were unsympathetic.[19] Although they believed discrimination to exist and sometimes investigated Coptic allegations, they seem never to have intervened except perhaps occasionally on a strictly individual basis.[20]

The highest percentages of Copts between 1922 and 1952 were found in the Ministries of Communications and Public Works. Many Copts were employed by the Post Office and railway; there were also many Coptic engineers in the irrigation service of the Works Ministry. Coptic representation in the Finance Ministry was also good due to the Copts' traditional expertise in monetary matters.[21] It was probably in these three Ministries that the Copts had their best chances of promotion.

A fair number of Copts were employed by the Ministries of Justice, Public Health and the Interior, while relatively few worked for the Ministry of Agriculture. Even fewer were employed by the Ministries of Education, Defence, Social Affairs and Foreign Affairs. The latter was the preserve of the Palace and there seems to have been considerable pressure to keep the diplomatic corps Muslim and Turkic.[22] Those few Coptic diplomats who managed to overcome the Palace's prejudice were generally scions of old, prominent Coptic families, like the Wahbahs and Ghalis, who had considerable European experience. The Copts had good access to junior and intermediate positions; however, they complained repeatedly that all important civil service posts were reserved for Muslims.[23] There is some truth to this complaint. Not only were few Copts employed in some Ministeries and Departments that had considerable power over the Copts, like the police and the Ministries of Education and Social Affairs, but their access to positions of influence in other ministries was limited. Very rarely was a Copt made under-secretary; when Sadiq Hinain, a Wafdist Copt, was appointed to that post in the Ministry of Finance, the Liberal Constitutionalist journal al-Kashkul objected.[24] Few Copts reached the top posts in any ministry. Few directors of departments or sub-departments were Copts. This is almost as true of the postal service, where many Copts were employed, as it is of the Ministry of Education. There were perhaps more Copts in senior positions in the Ministry of Finance. Copts were appointed Financial Secretary to different ministries, and there were Copts at high levels in the State Legal Department (Contentieux d'Etat). In the Ministry of the Interior, there was never a Coptic governor or deputy governor of a province; nor, in this period, a Coptic district office (Mamur Markaz).[25] As one observer noted, the Muslim public might be induced to accept an iconclast as governor, but never a Copt.[26] There were some Coptic Umdas, appointed to head predominantly Coptic villages. Copts were represented in good numbers at lower levels in the provincial administration, particularly on the clerical and financial sides. Most of the provincial chief clerks were Copts; this was generally the most senior post they held in a province.

In other ministries, Copts were employed mainly in those departments concerned with accounting, record-keeping, the budget, purchasing and stocks, translation and, in some instances, personnel. It was in such departments that a Copt was most likely to be appointed director or assistant director. In addition, they often held technical positions; for example, those Copts employed by the Ministry of

Agriculture were mainly engineers. These were jobs which did not include much of a responsibility for making policy.

Copts charged that Muslims were favoured for the judiciary, but this claim has little merit. Often around ten per cent of those named judges of Courts of the First Instance and the lesser Summary Courts were Copts. Few Copts were appointed to the bench of the Appeals Court[27] and the superior Cour de Cassation.[28] Coptic complaints about the Parquet were more accurate. Very few Coptic lawyers were able to secure employment in this élite corps, from which judges were often drawn. In addition, few Copts seem to have worked at middle levels in the judicial administration.

The frequently voiced complaint that no Copt had ever served as director of a state school was, with one exception, correct. Ibrahim Takla headed a secondary school in Cairo in 1929-30.[29] The less exalted ranks of the Education Inspectorate did include Copts, whose numbers jumped from one in 1925 to nineteen in 1943 but without in any way improving the Coptic hold on the Inspectorate. Many Copts also taught in the University but only ten per cent held the title of professor and none were ever appointed to top administrative posts.[30] In the Ministry of Defence, there were some Copts in the personnel, budget and records offices, but few overall in the general administration. While there were some Coptic army officers,[31] their influence seems to have been slight.[32] This was as much due to the lack of a tradition of entering the army and making a career of it as to discrimination.

The number of senior posts open to Copts may have decreased over time. In 1932, the Financial Adviser, Hugh-Jones, reported that this was the case in the Ministries of Agriculture and Finance; in contrast with past practice, very few heads of sub-departments were Copts.[33] By 1951 the numbers of Coptic inspectors in the Ministry of Education and judges in Courts of the First Instance had declined. Misr complained on two occasions that there were too few Copts among recent appointments to the judiciary and the Parquet.[34] There were, in fact, more Copts in the Parquet in 1922 than in later years. In addition, there were fewer Copts in the provincial agricultural service and the post office by 1951-2; significantly more Copts were employed at higher levels in the latter in 1924. Muslims eventually broke into the ranks of the provincial chief clerks[35] and, at a lower level, they became tax collectors by gaining, under the Liberal Government of 1928-29, admittance to a tax collectors' school set up by the same Liberal government.[36] Both had been a Coptic preserve.

There seems to have been no appreciable difference, however, in the number of Copts employed by the railway, telegraph and telephone administration or by the Finance Ministry. Given the system of clientelism, Copts knew that the loss of one job to a Copt often entailed the loss of others to the community. Civil servants were expected to favour their co-religionists; accordingly, the Copts saw the long arm of fanaticism reaching into every Ministry. _Misr_ and _al-Manara al-Misriyya_ published many articles on this problem; if the frequency with which these articles appeared is any gauge, it was a problem which grew worse in the mid-1940s. The appointment of a Muslim as Director of the Coptic Museum in 1950 in defiance of the law was a blow which seemed to symbolise the mounting discrimination Copts felt they met with in all walks of Egyptian life.[37]

Misr was most likely to champion the cause of Coptic employment when a non-Wafdist government was in power.[38] However, one serious campaign was mounted by the paper in 1928 when a Wafd-Liberal coalition government under Tharwat was in power. _Misr_ published articles in almost every issue criticising particularly the Ministry of Finance, which had transferred several officials in an economy move. The campaign seemed designed to embarrass the cabinet, already in some difficulty over the treaty. As _al-Kashif_ remarked, it was an inopportune moment to raise a matter which could affect Britain's willingness to relinquish the third Reserved Point.[39] _Misr_ was Wafdist in sympathy and it ceased its complaints when al-Nahhas became prime minister in March. It might seem that _Misr_ was preparing the way for a purely Wafdist government; however, the Wafdist press strenuously attacked _Misr_'s charges as lies. There is no indication that the Wafd was trying to break up the coalition by devious means.[40] Wasif Ghali expressed surprise at _Misr_'s behaviour and reaffirmed that there was no difference between Muslims and Copts in national affairs.[41] The answer may lie in the fact that the Wafd, with its own press, had ceased to subsidise _Misr_. Accordingly, _Misr_ was in financial difficulties, which served to spur sensationalism. Hugh-Jones noted that the paper, normally of 'insignificant circulation', sold very well during its campaign.[42] In addition, Tawfiq Hinain, sometime editor of Misr and perennial advocate of Coptic rights, led the campaign. Another possible explanation was the desire to secure, through pressure, the newly-vacant Directorship of Direct Taxes for a Copt.[43] The Residency reported that Tawfiq Dus was said to be behind Misr's campaign;[44] this fits with another report that the Palace was intriguing for the fall of the Tharwat cabinet.[45] However, Misr never exhibited any affection for Tawfiq Dus, and it is unlikely that it would have been amenable to his suggestions, unless they were accompanied by some kind of financial incentive. Still yet another and more convincing explanation can be sought in the fact that the government had been ordered to make a civil service-wide review and to take action to reduce the excessive and unnecessary numbers of government officials. Misr may have feared that a failure to act in the matter of the Department of Direct Taxes would lead to serious incursions into Coptic preserves in other ministries.

There were areas for legitimate complaint, but Misr's facts in this case seem twisted. The paper alleged that an unreasonable number of those dismissed in the Department of Direct Taxes were Copts.[46] If the British Financial Adviser and the Egyptian Minister of Finance are to be believed, officials were only transferred and not dismissed, and more Muslims were transferred than Copts.[47] Selection of these officials to be transferred was entrusted to a committee headed by Holden, a member of the Financial Adviser's staff.[48] Holden believed both that there was some discrimination against the Copts in promotions and that neither the minister nor the under-secretary liked Copts. Hugh-Jones noted that neither official was likely to victimise Copts in any significant way unless the political situation suddenly called for it.[49] As Copts held most of the positions in this department, there was no reason, as al-Balagh pointed out, that a majority of those transferred should not have been Copts.[50] Al-Balagh asked if the Copts were going to declare themselves oppressed every time the government was obliged to transfer or discipline a Coptic employee;[51] such was the Copts' sensitivity that sometimes the complaints were out of proportion to the misdeeds. Kawkab al-Sharq suggested that British officials had encouraged their Coptic colleagues in an attempt to provoke fanaticism and provide an excuse for intervention.[52] Sinut Hanna and Makram Ubaid also publicly denied Misr's charges and the latter, in an al-Ahram interview, condemned Misr's communal approach.[53] Misr responded by attacking the Wafd in February.[54]

At other times, Misr presented evidence of discrimination in virtually every ministry. In 1926 it published several articles recounting the sad fate of Dr. Kamil Hanna, an employee of the Ministry of Public Health, who committed suicide when he failed to obtain an expected promotion.[55] Several articles complaining of demotions, unjust transfers, the promotions of Muslims over the heads of Copts and a general reluctance to appoint Copts appeared in the summer of 1935.[56] Misr mourned the days of Sad Zaghlul, when, claimed the paper, no distinction was made between Copts and Muslims;[57] and, when the Wafd came back into power in 1936, the paper promised a return to equality.[58] In 1939, Misr complained about discrimination in the Ministries of Justice and Agriculture,[59] and in 1946 in the Ministry of Education.[60] In the latter year, Misr was convinced that the heads of certain government departments had issued instructions not to hire any non-Muslims.[61] The Wafd itself was capable of using this weapon to rally the Coptic faithful; in 1941 it was the source of a rumour which suggested that the King had ordered all ministers and senior officials not to appoint any Copts to government posts.[62]

Although Misr generally refrained from attacking Wafd governments, it made clear its dissatisfaction with the 1950 Wafd cabinet. The paper published several articles, as did al-Manara al-Misriyya, on discrimination in various government departments.[63]

Non-Wafdists reversed the charges of discrimination and used them to prove the Wafd's partiality to Copts. Muslims were equally ready to suspect the Copts of an ambition to monopolise the civil service,[64] so the non-Wafdist press had an audience for its allegations. The Liberal Constitutionalist papers were particularly vigilant. As early as 1923, al-Kashkul pointed out that Coptic judges were biased in favour of their co-religionists.[65] During the 1930 Wafd ministry, al-Siyasa published several articles which suggested that the Wafd was conspiring to advance the interests of the Copts. First al-Siyasa, reporting that the Wafd was considering making Makram Ubaid Minister to London, protested, insisting that there were already enough Coptic diplomats.[66] A few days later, the paper complained that three Egyptian ambassadors were Copts, in clear contravention of the interests of the Muslim majority.[67] Another article alleged that all the important officials of the Wafd ministry had dismissed were Muslims and that more than one-half of the ministry's promotions and appointments were Copts.[68] For this, Haikal was called before the Public Prosecutor's office and he was later able to report, probably with some effect, that the Prosecutor was a Copt.[69] Misr answered the allegations and printed the names of prominent Coptic officials who had been sacked.[70] It also published several articles defending tax collectors, whose honour al-Siyasa had besmirched.[71] When Sadiq Hinain, former Wafdist under-secretary in the Ministry of Finance, was again attacked by al-Siyasa for favouring Copts, Misr observed that the Copts sometimes hated to see a co-religionist successful for fear that criticism would follow his appointment.[72] In 1935, al-Shab reproached the Wafdist, Kamil Sidqi, for stirring up trouble when no Copts were included in a list of judicial appointments.[73]

Just before the 1936 election, the British reported that Misr al-Fatat planned, as part of its campaign, to accuse Makram of using his influence to obtain government appointments for Copts.[74] The opposition then criticised the 1936 Wafd government for appointing and promoting too many Copts and it decried Coptic influence, which was slight, in the Ministry of Education.75

Similar accusations followed in 1937 and during the 1938 election campaign. As Hamilton, the Assistant Oriental Secretary, noted, the opposition was prepared to inflame passions against the Copts for party purposes.[76] In November the government felt obliged to issue a statement denying al-Balagh's report that favouritism had been shown towards Copts in recent appointments.77 Al-Kashkul suggested that Copts formed seventy-three per cent of the student body of the College of Medicine, ninety-three per cent of the Railway, Telegraph and Telephone Administration, seventy per cent of the Ministry of the Interior, and eighty per cent of the Post Office, and that the Copts earned £E8 million out of £E12 million allocated for salaries in the top civil service grades.[78] The journal also accused Coptic professors of favouring Coptic students.[79]

Complaints by both Copts and Muslims were not always timed for political effect. Copts generally were concerned to preserve or increase the share of the bureaucracy they had held in the nineteenth century. Muslims complaints usually were characterised by a strong feeling that the Copts had risen above themselves; that it was the minority which was obliged to made adjustments to satisfy the majority and not vice versa. Often articles in the non-Wafdist press had a threatening tone.[80] Shaikh al-Maraghi, complaining about Coptic influence in the Ministry of the Interior, suggested that religious fanaticism could play a valid part in reducing that influence.[81] Such charges and counter-charges lead to the question of whether some cabinets did discriminate against or favour Copts. It is a question which is difficult to answer with any accuracy given the expansion of the bureaucracy, changes in civil service legislation, periodic ministerial reorganisations and the ineffectiveness of those rules governing the civil service.[82] One authority believes that the first Wafd ministry appointed many Copts to important positions in the civil service.[83] Another contemporary scholar suggests that the 1928 and 1938 Muhammad Mahmud cabinets deliberately reduced the number of Coptic officials and that each return of the Wafd to power brought compensation for the Copts.[84] The British in both 1928 and 1938 did record strong Christian feelings of victimisation,[85] and they confirmed that there was considerable discrimination against Copts in the late 1920s and early 1930s.[86] Mahmud and some of his cabinet members had anti-Coptic reputations,[87] so it is possible that their report is true. It should, however, be noted that the British were sometimes as susceptible to political rumours as the Egyptian press. In addition, it is perhaps worth noting that Mahmud was reputed to be responsible for advancing Salib Sami's career and for persuading the Wafd to add George Khayyat to the party's Executive Committee.[88]

Taking the suggestion about the Wafd first and examining the 1922 and 1924 lists of Ministry of Finance employees, it cannot be said that the Wafd brought significantly more Copts into the ministry. This would seem to be true of other ministries as well. Most Copts appearing on the 1924-5 Egyptian Directory lists were also on the 1922 list, and they were not in substantially different positions.

In general, there do not seem to have been

significantly more Copts employed at senior and middle levels in Wafdist ministries than in non-Wafdist ones. A surprising number of Coptic employees were left to work in peace regardless of who was in power.[89] It is possible that it was at lower levels that the Mahmud cabinets dismissed most Copts, but it seems unlikely that the ubiquitous teamen would be a matter of much attention. It does not appear from government pension lists that either Mahmud cabinet placed an unusual number of Copts on pension; but, of course, those dismissed might not have been entitled to a pension.[90] However, it may be safe to conclude that those officials fired by any ministry had unsatisfactory political ties and since Coptic support for the Wafd was strong, many of those dismissed by non-Wafdist cabinets were Copts.[91] It may also be correct to say that most of those dismissed belonged to the upper levels of the provincial administration and the ministries. Since few Copts penetrated this rarified atmosphere, they may not have suffered disproportionately. Finally, and perhaps most importantly, it should be pointed out that most cabinets were in office for too short a time to be able to alter radically the way the bureaucracy behaved.

a. Coptic cabinet ministers. It was traditional even for cabinets in the period before independence to include one Copt. This was both expected and accepted. For example, when Lampson insisted in 1943 that Kamil Sidqi be removed as Minister of Finance, another Copt was immediately made Minister of Civil Defence to maintain Coptic representation. Only the Wafd broke with this custom, and then it did so by appointing two Copts. Haikal recalls in his *Memoirs* that there was considerable surprise when the Wafd named Murqus Hanna and Wasif Ghali to its first cabinet in 1924. Haikal praises himself for not exploiting the fact, although he did note the departure from tradition in *al-Siyasa*.[92] *Al-Siyasa*'s Liberal colleague, *al-Kashkul*, was not as restrained. It featured a conversation, purportedly overheard at the Coptic Ramses Club, between prominent Wafdist Copts. In it, these Copts quarrelled over cabinet posts, and how many they could justifiably demand. Finally they agreed that the Copts should be rewarded with three portfolios, two under-secretaryships and at least one ambassadorship.[93] Later *al-Kashkul* reported that there were to have been three Copts in the cabinet but that opposition was so strong that the proposal was dropped.[94] In 1929, al-Siyasa retroactively criticised the appointment of two Coptic cabinet ministers in 1924 as part of a general anti-Wafd campaign.[95] In 1928, the Watanist al-Akhbar wrote that there were so many Copts in the Wafd cabinet that the government might as well name Christians as Shaikh al-Azhar and Mufti of Egypt.[96] Criticism was also levelled at the 1930 Wafd cabinet,[97] and in 1937 al-Kashkul incorrectly suggested that the party was planning to add a third Copt to the cabinet.[98]

After Makram left the Wafd in 1942, the Wafd named only one Copt to its cabinets, and, once Kamil Sidqi was demoted at British insistence, to only uninfluential ministries. This does not necessarily suggest that Makram was responsible for the earlier policy; the schism simply left fewer Copts entitled to cabinet rank in the party. In addition, the symbolic value of having Copts in the cabinet had declined and in the 1940s would have earned the Wafd little praise from any quarter. Most non-Wafdist cabinets conformed to the older custom and included only one Copt and one portfolio. There were two Copts in the Ahmad Mahir and al-Nuqrashi cabinets of 1944 and 1946; both were coalition governments including the heavily Coptic al-Kutla party. There were only three other exceptions.

The November 1934 Nasim cabinet had one Copt holding two portfolios. The 1946 Sidqi cabinet gave Saba Habashi responsibility for two ministries, Trade and Industry, and Supplies. Supplies, however, ceased to be a separate portfolio in March and was reattached to Trade and Industry. Then, in 1952, Najib al-Hilali included two Copts with three portfolios in his cabinet. The portfolios were Trade and Industry, Supplies, and Public Works.

The Ministries of the Interior, Justice, Education and Endowments were never entrusted to a Copt.[99] From the April 1919 Rushdi cabinet until the July 1952 Ali Mahir cabinet, the portfolio most frequently held by a Copt was Finance, an obvious choice given the number of Copts employed in the ministry. From the 1924 Zaghlul cabinet until Ubaid's split in 1942, the Wafd alone appointed Copts Finance Minister; Ubaid was the only Copt to serve as Finance Minister in non-Wafdist Cabinets after this. Agriculture and Foreign Affairs were the two ministries most often entrusted to Copts after Finance. Foreign Affairs was an unimportant portfolio before 1936 and, even after that, the ministry was hampered by excessive Palace interference and the tendency of the British to ignore it. The post did require a man who was familiar with Europe, and this partly explains why Copts were often appointed. The Wafd again was more willing to appoint a Copt to Foreign Affairs than other parties, while all Coptic Ministers of Agriculture, a post of very little power, served in non-Wafdist cabinets. Trade and Industry, a ministry created in the 1930s, often had a Coptic minister, again usually in non-Wafdist cabinets; this ministry seems to have had a good number of Coptic employees. The Ministry of Communications was held by a Copt in five cabinets; other portfolios held by Copts included Health (Dr. Najib Iskandar only), Village and Local Affairs (Ibrahim Faraj), Supplies,[100] Civil Defence and War (Fahmi Wisa). Salib Sami, who had served as Royal Adviser to the ministry, was, to his considerable surprise, appointed Minister of War in the 1933 Yahya cabinet. Sami claims that he was uneasy with the appointment because he felt that an officer should be minister, but it is more likely that he was concerned about the effect his religion would have on the high command.[101] A decade later, the repercussions Sami probably expected in 1933 occurred when Prime Minister Husain Sirri tried to move Sami from Foreign Affairs to the Ministry of Defence. Senior army officers objected, and Sami was transferred back to Foreign Affairs.[102]

Although the number of portfolios expanded from ten in 1925 to sixteen in 1951, Coptic representation did not increase.[103] Obviously the appointment of two Copts to some cabinets was an innovation to which some Egyptians were unable to reconcile themselves in more than two decades. By the late 1940s, increasing resentment of any visible Coptic role in politics may have made it impossible for any willing party to appoint two Copts to the cabinet. In addition, from February 1946, those Copts who were appointed were relegated to uninfluential ministries. The accusations of political opponents notwithstanding, Coptic cabinet ministers did not populate their ministries with Copts.[104] Occasionally, they did employ a Copt as personal secretary, but this was surely an excusable indulgence.

Some Copts, as well as Muslims, viewed Coptic cabinet ministers as communal representatives or as men who were well placed to ensure that Coptic rights were respected. This was less a reflection of reality than a forlorn hope, and some Copts became increasingly angry in the 1940s that these representatives did so little for the community.[105]

b. <u>Religious instruction in state schools</u>. The problem of religious instruction in government schools was one new to the twentieth century; before this, education was largely private. Copts educated their own children and taught them what they liked. Religious education only became a point of contention, for Muslims as well as Copts, when parents began to desire a modern education for their children and as the state came increasingly to provide that education. There were many private and church-affiliated Christian schools, but they could not educate all Coptic children.[106] The state had resources the community could never hope to match. Many parents could not afford a private education, and even some of those who could wanted their children to have the government school certificates which admitted their holders for many years to the civil service.[107] Education was one way to produce uniformity in the citizenry, and this uniformity was more likely to threaten the cultural integrity of the minority than the majority.

The state dictated what Coptic children would be taught, first in state-owned schools and later in private Christian schools. In the former, Islamic religious instruction formed a larger part of the curriculum, particularly for the younger, more impressionable children. Not only were the Copts upset at the exposure of their children to lectures on Islam, but they were angry at the state's failure to use public revenue to provide equal Christian religious instruction. They believed that this failure had direct bearing on the health and vitality of the community, and they feared their children growing up with too little knowledge of their own religion and too much temptation to convert to Islam. Ultimately, Christian protests were aimed at protecting the community's autonomy and resolving inequities in the division of public money.

In this half-century of debate, no one in the Coptic community except the socialist Salama Musa[108] criticised the principal of offering religious instruction in state schools and urged the complete secularisation of education. Copts did argue for the use of secular materials in Arabic teaching, but mainly they were interested in seeing that their children were instructed in Christianity. Few Muslims proposed the secularisation of public education; even Lutfi al-Sayyid[109] and Taha Husain[110] thought it was in the Egyptian interest for the state to provide a firm grounding in Islam. In fact, many Muslims clamoured for more and more Islamic education as this period progressed.

The principle of providing Christian education in state schools was established early on when Khedive Ismail, in endowing land for the expansion of elementary education, stipulated that Christian instruction for Christian students be included in the curriculum.[111] In 1907, in response to Coptic demands, the ministry decided that Christianity could be taught in those state schools which had fifteen Coptic students enrolled, on the condition that the Church pay the teachers.[112] In some heavily Coptic areas, there were exclusively Coptic <u>kuttabs</u>, providing the most basic kind of education, and these were run by Provincial Councils.[113] Other Copts attending government <u>kuttabs</u> were not so lucky; approximately four out of six hours day were devoted to Islamic religious subjects.[114] When Christian instruction was offered, it was often taught by an ill-trained Coptic teacher or an equally ill-prepared priest. It annoyed the Copts that the government allocated funds for the training of Muslim religious teachers but would not do so for Christians, but this problem seemed secondary.[115] A more fundamental problem was that the Provincial Councils seemed to make so little effort to provide Christian instruction. Copts felt that this was distinctly unfair given that, in certain areas, they paid a high proportion of the tax which supported council education.[116] Some of the more radical Copts of Asyut demanded a rebate of the school taxes Copts paid so that they could organise their own education.[117] Copts in Jirja and elsewhere felt likewise.[118] In the late 1920s, some Copts were still complaining that their council failed to meet its responsibility to teach religion to Christian students.[119] Given that one-third of the children in government schools in 1927 were Copts, the numbers of Copts and the feasibility of providing them with Christian instruction was not the real problem.[120] The problem was, as Eldon Gorst noted in 1907, that there was considerable Muslim opposition to Christian education in schools.[121] In 1911, delegates at the Heliopolis Conference voted to oppose the teaching of Christianity in government schools.[122] A more important concern to many Muslims was the government's failure to provide adequate training in Islam.

In 1923, the Ministry of Education expressed a desire to expand Islamic instruction in state schools.[123] The *ulama* repeatedly demanded that a larger share of the curriculum be devoted to Islam, and, by the 1930s, religion was a large part of the set programme in all government schools. At the highest level of pre-university training, twenty per cent of class time was devoted to Arabic and Islam.[124]

In 1921, the Ministry of Education agreed to provide Christian education in those primary schools enrolling ten Christian students.[125] Complaints in the communal press suggest that this decision, like the one in 1907, was executed piecemeal, if at all. In 1925, Ibrahim Takla, the highest ranking Copt in the Ministry of Education, was put in charge of a committee developing a programme of Christian education for primary and secondary schools. His writ did not include developing a programme for the more widely attended elementary schools.[126]

In 1927, a memorandum was submitted by the Coptic Orthodox, Coptic Catholic and Protestant churches to the Minister of Education, asking that the compulsory education bill, then in preparation, provide Christian instruction in all schools with ten Christian pupils. It appealed to the constitutional guarantee of equality and reminded the government that the Copts too paid taxes.[127]

In 1931, the Minister of Education, in announcing plans for compulsory elementary education legislation, stated that religious education would be mandatory for Muslims. It would not be provided for Christian students, but they could make their own arrangements for instruction to be given during the periods Islam was taught. *Misr* accused the then prime minister, Sidqi, of so resenting Coptic opposition to his regime that he was trying to weaken the community's morals by denying its children religious instruction.[128]

In 1933, the bill came before Parliament. Those who criticised its provisions wished to see the curriculum include more Islamic religious instruction.[129] When the Coptic Senator Abd Allah Simaika bravely asked that Christian education be provided, the Minister of Education objected, claiming that it was impossible for a state with a constitutionally established religion to teach a second religion in its schools. This, of course, overlooked the fact that some government schools already offered Christian instruction and that there was a precedent for doing so. Coptic senators planned to raise the issue again, but, in compliance with a royal request, did not.[130] Curiously, the Majlis al-Milli and the Patriarch kept a closely guarded silence; that of the latter was almost certainly due to a fear of royal displeasure.

The law, when finally passed, did exempt non-Muslims from Islamic instruction,[131] which was designed to consume one-third of classroom hours. Even if Christian children absented themselves from school during those hours, they would still have been exposed to Islam in their Arabic lessons. In practice, however, social pressure apparently made it difficult for Christian parents to withdraw their children from Islamic instruction.[132]

The Residency concluded that the law was discriminatory.[133] Campbell, the Acting High Commissioner, spoke to the Minister of Education who agreed to allow Copts, chosen by the community, to teach religion in elementary schools. Furthermore, he promised that the ministry would pay their salary. The Copts, not trusting the word of the minister, asked for a formal Directive. Campbell, who felt that the King and not the cabinet was the real problem, none the less asked the acting prime minister about a Ministerial Decree.[134] Shafiq Pasha, who had already discussed the matter with a delegation of Coptic notables, reiterated the government's promise to provide Christian instruction. He felt that there would be too much Muslim opposition to a Ministerial Decree, just as there would have been had he tried to include it in the compulsory education bill.[135] He promised, however, to issue a circular to all ministry offices calling for the implementation of Christian education in elementary schools.

The Foreign Office was disappointed with his proposal and so were the Copts.[136] Abd Allah Simaika wished to move to amend the bill in the Senate but he failed to get the ten signatures required to begin the process.[137] The Patriarch still refused to enter the controversy, but the Lay Council was at least preparing to present its views in a petition.[138] In the autumn, the ministry sent out a circular asking about the number of Christian students enrolled. The ministry intended to make a decision after it obtained the responses, and the British decided to wait for that decision.

Unfortunately, the anti-missionary campaign

that summer and the Caliphal ambitions of the King made it difficult for the government to take concrete action.[139] The first led to demands for a more thorough Islamic education in state schools.[140] The following year, some Muslim Deputies insisted during the debate on the Ministry of Education's budget that the programme of religious instruction was inadequate.[141] No Coptic Deputy spoke up, but Misr, in making clear its dissatisfaction, commented that parliamentary representatives were supposed to represent the whole nation and not only its Muslim component.[142] The Copts kept up their pressure and, with strong Residency support which was given at Foreign Office insistence, they made some progress in 1935. They obtained an exemption for non-Muslim primary students from Qur'an memorization.[143] The Minister of Education, al-Hilali, was willing to fund Christian education at the elementary level but not in school buildings. He was even willing to defray the cost of renting sites, should some churches, the logical places for such instruction, be too far from schools. Coptic opinion divided on this offer: some insisted that the government must supply both premises and teachers, and others were willing to accept government funds and organise the instruction themselves. The former group may have been anxious to keep religious instruction out of the hands of the ill-educated clergy; otherwise, they ran the risk of increasing the latter's power. The second, more pragmatic group saw the advantage of the community, rather than the government, having control of religious instruction. The Patriarch was not blind to this; al-Hilali claimed to have obtained his assent. Murqus Simaika, however, noted that the Patriarch was so timid and fearful of offending the King that the community could count on him for little help in its battles with the government. The Majlis al-Milli was less amenable to the scheme than the Patriarch and the Residency was drawn into mediating between the government and the Copts, a task it never enjoyed.[144] Christian instruction this time seems to have been sacrificed on the altar of the Copts' inability to agree among themselves and their reluctance to compromise with the government.

The tide was, in any case, running the other way; suddenly the Copts found that they were spending more time arguing for an exemption from Islamic instruction than they were for the institution of Christian instruction. In 1936, a Qur'anic examination was made mandatory for all students in the first two years of secondary school. The Patriarch, under some pressure from his flock, finally requested an exemption for Coptic students; and the Wafd, in power in 1937, agreed. It was a decision the party may well have regretted because it raised an unexpected degree of opposition.[145] Azharis, others of similar religious ilk and the Wafd's political opponents objected to the exemption; one petition, from the Central Committee of Young Muslim Societies, is typical:

> The Arabic Language is the official language of the state and the Qur'an is the noblest expression of this language. It is truly astonishing that a group of the sons of the nation is to be deprived from tasting the literature of the official language of the country...Unity of teaching is the foundation of the unity of the nation. We cannot have one set of students taught one thing and another set something else.[146]

That same month, a group of law students advocated the introduction of compulsory religious instruction at the University.[147] Al-Azhar was jubilant, and Shaikh al-Maraghi expressed his approval to senior university officials.[148] The Wafdist al-Misri also backed the idea, but then changed its mind. Muhammad al-Ashmawi, Under-Secretary at the Ministry of Education, told the press that students came to the University so well instructed in Islam that further teaching was unnecessary.[149] Such comments disrupted classes at al-Azhar and sent student delegations to call on university deans.

A few months later, this pressure pushed the Wafd into showing some support for Islamic religious instruction. It developed a list of recommendations which were supported by the Muslim Brethren and included the following: (1) setting a religious examination for students in the final two years of secondary school; (2) building a mosque in every school and appointing one of the teachers to lead prayers; (3) requiring a sermon every day before the noon prayer, and (4) establishing a religious library in every school.[150]

As the Wafd learnt, religious education could be a potent political weapon. In September 1937, the opposition press reported that the government was developing a programme of Christian religious instruction for state primary and secondary schools.[151] The Wafd was obliged to deny the report,[152] and also felt compelled to counter the following year's attack on Makram and al-Nahhas for opposing Islamic religious instruction in schools.[153]

The pressure for more and more elaborate programmes of Islamic religious instruction was maintained throughout the 1940s. Azharis,[154] the Muslim Brethren and the Young Men's Muslim Association[155] were particularly troublesome on this issue. It became increasingly difficult for an incumbent government to reject such demands, let alone meet those of the Copts. The ministry eventually acquired extensive supervisory powers, including approval of curricula and texts, over foreign and private schools; and it obliged them to teach their Muslim students about Islam.[156] Coptic schools accepted Muslim students, and it was not always easy for them to comply with the new regulations.

From 1946 the Copts were particularly vehement about the need for Christian religious education, an unsurprising response to the increased degree of Muslim pressure. The Coptic Lay Council was particularly vigorous in this debate, as were _Misr_ and _al-Manara al-Misriyya_. _Misr_ sometimes asked that a proportion of the education budget equal to the Coptic percentage of the population be devoted to Christian education and, at other times, only asked the government to help the Copts build their own schools. From 1949, the Copts used Law No.10 (1949), which guaranteed equal education for all Egyptians regardless of creed, to support their demand for religious instruction. In 1949, the ministry considered making Christianity an examination subject for Christian students,[157] and both the Lay Council and the Patriarch pushed hard for it. A committee of Coptic educators was appointed to develop a programme, and the Patriarch was asked to submit a report with his ideas. The matter went no further because the cabinet then fell.

The Copts hoped that the new Wafd cabinet would implement the programme. In February 1951, the Patriarch sent the minister a note of inquiry, but not until the end of the year did the Minister of Education announce that Christian students would be taught the principles of their religions.[158] The fall of the monarchy seven months later prevented the plan's implementation in the next school year; but, if it had not, something else surely would have.

No easy generalisations can be made about which government schools offered Christian instruction.

It was not available in elementary schools but seems sometimes to have been taught in primary and secondary schools. It was an unsystematic arrangement which was made less acceptable by the fact that the ease in obtaining exemptions for Christian children from Islamic classes probably varied; much depended on local school and ministry authorities. It was difficult for any ministry, Wafdist or otherwise, to respond positively to Coptic demands for equality in the provision of religious education. Although the Wafd was accused by its opponents of being 'soft' on the issue of Christian instruction, with the one exception of the Wafd promise to implement Christian instruction in 1951, the Copts came closest to their goal in 1935 and 1949, both years of non-Wafd government. Even cabinet approval of Christian exemptions from lessons or examinations which were overtly Islamic was problematic. Part of the difficulty was that the Muslims who were inclined to be the most vocal on the issue of Islamic religious instruction were probably also the ones who were the least inclined to grant Copts true equality. The state could hardly fulfil its obligation to Islam by propagating Christianity, even among Christians.

B. THE ISSUE OF STATE CONTROL

The state, in this period, showed an increasing ability to affect the lives of its citizens. Its power over Muslims and Copts grew and it extended its authority into those areas where clerical competence had prevailed. Muslims found the state's tightening grasp less disturbing than did Copts, for they had always had a closer relationship with the state. The Copts reacted strongly when the government attempted to encroach on their traditional autonomy; some who supported integration in the political sphere fought the government in this other area. Paradoxically, they wanted both political equality and special safeguards. The road to integration was, at best, a long and dangerous one; and it was not unwise of them to want some protection along the way. As long as the constitution and Islam imposed certain duties on the state, many Copts believed that the community had a right to protect its religion and culture. Should they relinquish that autonomy, they had no guarantee that the government would establish an appropriate secular alternative for both Muslims and Copts. The Copts were particularly sensitive on two subjects, personal status jurisdiction and government restrictions on their freedom of worship. If they were to survive as a community in a Muslim-dominated state, it was vital to protect their autonomy in the first and their freedom from restrictions in the second.

1. Personal Status Jurisdiction

Non-Muslims traditionally followed the prescriptions of their own religion and were bound by Islamic law in only a few cases.[159] There were separate personal status courts for the fourteen non-Muslim religious communities in Egypt. Some, including those of the three Coptic sects, were formally recognised by the government; others were unrecognised but tolerated. This system of multiple jurisdictions was antiquated, inefficient and lacking in uniformity.[160] The government had no control over millet court verdicts but was theoretically responsible for the execution of those verdicts in those communities it had recognised. As the government sometimes declined to accept this responsibility,[161] the communal courts ultimately were dependent on whatever religious sanctions the church could impose on a fractious litigant. A further complication, in the Church's eyes, was that non-Muslims were not bound by their court's decision but could always take their case to a Sharia court.[162] There were other serious problems. The appointment of judges was arbitrary, and they were sometimes unqualified. No court protected against conflicts of interest, and the Coptic Orthodox community was one of the few whose courts followed a rule of procedure. The government, in the hope of abolishing inconsistencies within and between the millets, wanted one rule of procedure for all the millets; it also wished to establish a uniform scale of fees. Both would also have made government oversight easier.

Between 1918 and 1956, when the millet courts were abolished, the government made repeated attempts to reform this system. Every attempt, however sensible, and however limited, was fought by the Coptic community on the grounds that reform 'represented the thin end of a wedge' directed at the abolition of the Majlis Millis and their control over communal revenues.[163] Personal status jurisdiction was one of the few issues able to spark some measure of agreement among the Majlis al-Milli, the clergy and the Coptic press and, by the 1940s, it had even brought together the normally hostile Christian communities. There were some Christians, however, who wanted reform; they realised the judicial system's corruption and inefficiency and were willing to see an increase in government power over the community because they had abandoned hope that the community would reform itself. When Senator Alfred Shammas tabled a motion to make non-Muslim marriage a civil contract, it was to overcome evils in the millet system.[164] Salama Musa also advocated civil marriage.[165] He believed that the government would be less arbitrary in its judicial behaviour than the communal courts, although on what grounds is not clear. Some Copts supported personal status reforms because they wished to see a decrease in the Lay Council's power and, in some cases possibly, a corresponding increase in their own. Qalini Fahmi, for example, suggested to the Palace in 1926 that personal status matters be taken over by the government, a plan he was still advocating in the 1940s. He described the lay councils as small governments whose existence was not in line with the spirit of the constitution.[166]

The British followed the government's attempts at reform closely and their help was often solicited by minorities. The Foreign Office was more likely to disapprove of draft legislation than the Residency; this may have been due to their sensitivity to the influence of the Anglican church in parliament. At one stage, however, the Foreign Office inexplicably reversed its stand and openly pushed for reform.

The first encroachment on the millet courts was made in the nineteenth century with the establishment of the Court of Wards (Majlis al-Hasbi). The court was designed to administer the property of minors and the incompetent for those who chose to have it do so. This was not a religious function, and the Majlis was not really a religious court. However, there was no civil code and so the court applied Sharia law whenever possible. Many Copts, including members of the Lay Council, did not approve of the Court of Wards or a 1925 law obliging them to use the Court. They were not comforted by the fact that the latter law stipulated that a member of the appropriate millet join the bench in non-Muslim cases in place of the usual Sharia Judge.[167] The Lay Council regarded the Hasbi courts as Islamic courts and believed that if certain family questions were secular, they should be under the jurisdiction of the Native Courts. _Misr_ and _al-Watan_ also opposed the 1925 law.[168] A few Copts, feeling that the measure provided more protection to wards than did the chaotic organisation of Majlis al-Milli courts, approved it. The British did not find the 1925 law threatening to Coptic interests, although three years earlier M.S. Amos advocated British intervention to prevent a similar reform if the minorities opposed it.[169] The Hasbi Court was again strengthened by royal decree in 1929. Copts were still objecting to these laws in 1951 because these courts ruled according to Sharia law.[170]

Numerous committees discussed the reform of the entire court system but, as Ali Mahir noted in 1936, their discussions bore little fruit.[171] One committee, meeting in 1920-1, conceded that the state was unable to legislate a personal status code for all Egyptians and must find another solution to the contradictions. Accordingly, this committee outlined rules of competence to determine jurisdiction. The committee wanted to create a special court to which cases involving a conflict of competence or verdict could be referred.[172] However, the draft law was shelved, as was a similar project drawn up in 1923.[173]

The confusion in judicial prerogatives resulted in many complaints from non-Muslims, and the Senate Finance Committee in 1927 asked the Minister of Justice to study the matter.[174] The ministry, in turn, asked non-Muslims to present their ideas on the unification of millet jurisdiction. The latter responded that, due to variations in canon law, it would be impossible to draft one code which would satisfy all communities; many mentioned the difference in divorce laws as problematic. Some also insisted that only their clergy could alter canon law. Both _Misr_ and _al-Watan_ opposed new legislation.[175]

In 1931 the Minister of Justice, Ali Mahir, revived the 1923 plan.[176] The Copts were annoyed that he chose to take a sounding of minority opinion in the summer when few communal leaders were available. _Misr_ and _al-Watan_ voiced their opposition and their resentment that neither the Patriarch nor the Lay Council had acted with speed or firmness.[177] The Majlis finally published in November a brochure claiming communal privilege in all matters of personal status.[178]

Because of this opposition, the cabinet in December appointed a special advisory committee, including non-Muslims, to help the ministry.[179] The Ministry hoped to attach a Christian personal status court to each native Court of the First Instance. Its bench would be drawn partly from the Native Courts and would include two lay members who shared the religion of the disputants. A similar Appeals

Court would be established. The ministry here was trying to regularise the application of the law and not produce a new civil code. If the parties were Orthodox and belonged to a community with a recognised code of law, they would be justiciable under Coptic Orthodox law, and, if Catholic, under Catholic canon law. If the disputants were of different sects, then lex contractus or the canon law which validated the marriage would apply, except when one party had converted to Islam.[180] This latter point met an important Coptic demand. Christians desiring a divorce frequently converted to a different Christian sect so that they could take their case to an Islamic court.

Many in the Residency, including the High Commissioner, thought that the proposals, in laicising non-Muslim jurisdiction only, were unfair.[181] There was no provision for clerical representation on the bench and, theoretically, Muslims could be appointed judges. A more serious problem was that the reform entailed considerable loss of power to the Lay Councils and probably foreshadowed their eventual demise. Booth, the Judicial Adviser, did see some good in the reform and felt that Christian religious sensibilities, given the narrower scope of issues considered religious in Christianity would be less offended by the project than Muslim feeling in a similar instance.[182]

Booth's reasoning was not shared by Egyptian Christians. Some, along with the Protestant Majlis al-Milli, insisted that the old system functioned perfectly well and did not require reform. One delegation of Copts told a member of Booth's staff that matters reserved for the Sharia courts must also be set aside for the communal courts.[183] Those Copts on the government committee showed themselves no more amenable to the reform. They admitted the necessity of uniform procedure and the desirability of depositing with the ministry the code of laws of each community, but they refused to agree to more radical changes.[184] Obviously, their loss of power vis-à-vis the government disturbed the Copts more than long-time abuses in the system.

The ministry took these strong feelings into account and drafted concessionary legislation. Communal courts were not to be amalgamated or reduced in number, but their competence was to be restricted and they were to be brought into a closer relationship with the Ministry of Justice.[185] Judges were to be approved by the ministry, and their verdicts pronounced in the name of the King. Although a compromise, this still increased government power at the expense of the communal courts. The Copts objected to this scheme, and even Smart feared that it opened the door to the kind of government conduct witnessed in the 1928 Patriarchal election.[186] Both he and the Foreign Office concluded that as long as there were special courts for Muslims, there must be parallel courts for non-Muslims.[187]

In discussing the appropriate British response, Sir Charles Dilke and Sir Maurice Peterson in the Foreign Office believed that intervention could be justified by the third Reserved Point because, as Dilke noted, 'the liberties of the Copts were being infringed and...the constitution which we had supposed ensured sufficient protection was being broken...'[188] Peterson instructed an unhappy Loraine to object if the government persisted with the legislation. Loraine agreed with Booth that the government's desire to supervise millet courts was not unreasonable, although he saw Smart's point that the government could approve judges with strong Patriarchal sympathies, thereby strengthening the hand of the clerical party.[189] Booth approved the legislation because both inheritance and cases involving disputants of different religions would go to the Native Courts. Although this was not quite what the Copts wanted, it was a concession which involved some loss of power to the Sharia courts.[190]

Nothing happened until the next year when the Foreign Office, suddenly and inexplicably, instructed the Residency to see that the reform was not buried forever in the Ministry of Justice.[191] Arthur Yencken, the Acting High Commissioner, noted his opinion that, due to Coptic opposition, it was enough for the British to acquiesce to the legislation without actively promoting it.[192] Peterson agreed to a temporary postponement only. Despite obvious procrastination, little pressure was applied to the government before it fell in November.[193]

Ali Mahir returned to the reform when he became Prime Minister in 1936. A new draft was prepared and the Council of Ministers approved it in May. Some changes were made to satisfy the British, but these did not in any way placate the minorities. Still, having settled British, if not Coptic objections, the government declared the project law. Ali Mahir, in fact enacted a considerable number of laws by royal decree during his short interim ministry. The succeeding Wafdist cabinet declared these enactments the proper business of Parliament and abrogated most of them, including the personal status law. The British did not protest, either because they had lost interest in the reform or because, following the strict letter of the 1936 treaty, it was none of their affair.

In 1944, the government was once again considering reform. Rumour and speculation ran riot. The Copts were already alarmed due to the enactment of a law formally obliging non-Muslims to follow Islamic inheritance laws. When the bill came up for debate in the Chamber, three Coptic deputies argued for its postponement until the planned personal status law could be drafted. Their tactic failed and the law passed, seemingly without Coptic opposition to the substance of the bill.[194]

With regard to its personal status legislation, this government made a greater effort to consult minority opinion than had Ali Mahir in 1936. The Minister of Justice, Sabri Abu Alam, received many representations from communal leaders and met with Fahmi Wisa, Minister of Civil Defence, and Kamil Sidqi, an ex-minister.[195] As a result of these meetings, minor changes were made in the government's draft. Minorities still insisted on <u>lex contractus</u>; but the government, handicapped by a parliament with which Ali Mahir had not had to deal, was not amenable on this point.[196] In mid-September, Abu Alam met with the press to explain that the government's intention was to abolish discrepancies in jurisdiction and procedure and not alter canon law.[197] This was of little comfort to the Patriarch, who withdrew in October to a monastery in the eastern desert partly because of his distress that this law might actually be enacted. He was persuaded by Copts close to the government to announce that his real reason for retiring to a monastery was to experience a change of air.[198] Even without this explanation, the government would probably have had to back down on its proposed legislation had not the dismissal of the cabinet made the issue a dead letter.

Both the Patriarch and the Orthodox Majlis al-Milli made their objections known to the succeeding cabinet whose Minister of Justice, Hafiz Ramadan, soon announced the formation of yet another committee to study the subject. In June 1945, another draft law organising non-Muslim religious courts was ready for submission to Parliament. A month later, the heads of some of the minority communities complained to the Presidents of the Chamber and the Senate that their views had not been solicited. They also presented a counter-draft law to the government. Neither the Coptic nor Greek Orthodox Patriarchs associated themselves ith this intercommunal venture. Makram immediately announced that the government intended to redraft the law, which closely resembled that of the previous Wafd government.[199]

A year later a new draft was almost ready. The Committee of Liaison, founded to represent the various Christian sects and to defend religious liberty, met to co-ordinate non-Muslim opposition to the new draft.[200] Saba Habashi, who was in close touch with this committee, met with the Ministers of Social and Foreign Affairs during the summer and emphasised the importance of including <u>lex contractus</u>. The Liaison Committee, however, decided that draft legislation would be unacceptable whatever modifications were made in it. The Palace was besieged with petitions claiming that the reform violated the essence of the Christian religion.[201] The Senate, without any real discussion, voted to send the bill back to Committee.[202]

The millets wanted the bill withdrawn altogether and, to this purpose, showed a 'unity of view and action' never before achieved.[203] In January, the prime minister, in a rare meeting with the Coptic Patriarch, discussed millet demands. The Greek Orthodox and Greek Catholic Patriarchs and the Grand Rabbi of Alexandria registered formal complaints. In Cairo, a protest meeting was held and the government's action characterised as a <u>coup d'état</u>.[204] A minor victory was achieved when a delegation meeting with the King's secretary was told to prepare a report which could serve as the basis of new draft legislation.

The British Embassy, whose help was sought by the Greek Orthodox Patriarch, declined to intervene. Characteristic of British irritation was the opinion of one official who noted that reform had been discussed for sixteen years and that a new development was always 'just around the corner'.[205] Although the embassy continued to follow events, it did not confide any opinion, private or official, to the Egyptian government after the 1936 treaty. It was not a matter which impinged on critical British interests.

In June a deputation called on the prime minister and the President of the Senate to present a counter-draft. The Senate Judiciary Committee issued its plan, which French Embassy officials described as making substantial concessions, at the end of the month. One such gain was the awarding of competence in cases in which one party had converted to Islam to the Native Courts. In addition, this draft, unlike its predecessor in 1932, prohibited Muslims from sitting on the bench of the non-Muslim appeals courts, and it also provided for clerical representation.[206] None the less, opposition was so strong that the government was forced to withdraw the bill from Parliament. Elections and a new Wafd cabinet which sensibly avoided this troublesome issue brought the saga to an end.

In conclusion, the Copts, with some British backing as well as hindrance, were able to block any major reform in non-Muslim personal status jurisdiction. The government, at least in this one area, became increasingly willing to make concessions to communal desiderata; while the Copts, paradoxically, became increasingly resistant to any changes.

No doubt many politicians would have liked to create an entirely secular court system, under complete government control, but the system of multiple jurisdictions they inherited, partly Islamic and partly Western in inspiration, must have seemed frustratingly impervious to change. The attempt to reform non-Muslim personal status jurisdiction was not simply a matter of a well-meaning Muslim government trying to improve a chaotic and sometimes corrupt court system, but nor was it entirely an attempt by the government to gain power at the expense of its religious minorities. The government was also interested in reforming Muslim family law and its administration.[207] Recognising the likelihood of an unfavourable public reaction, its attempts to do so were less energetic and radical than attempts to reform non-Muslim courts. Government reformers perhaps felt that it was more feasible, given the weakness of the millets and the fact that their religions did not specify such a detailed family law, to begin a general legal reform with their courts. They were wrong and eventually discovered that the changes they could effect in this area were hardly more far-reaching than those they could make in the Islamic legal system. The government was sometimes lax in consulting minority opinion[208] and was not entirely unwilling to impose reform by fiat. That it met with such stiff opposition was as much due to the minorities' unwillingness to lose more power over their communal affairs to a government whose secularism was suspect as it was to a desire to hold fast to religion. Most Copts, even some of those interested in internal reform, preferred to endure the abuses of the old system rather than relinquish communal control. No doubt they were also aware that a government-imposed reform would not necessarily guarantee efficiency or honesty, but it is also true that there was no genuinely strong movement within the community to correct abuses in the community's juridical systems, perhaps owing to a fear of adding fuel to the government's fire.

Non-Wafdist governments, which so often manipulated Muslim religious sentiment for political gain, were much more willing to reform non-Muslim personal status jurisdiction than the Wafd. Non-Wafdist parties had, or felt themselves to have, little significant Coptic support; the political risks entailed in reform were not that great. For the Wafd, however, the political risks were considerable, and the social benefits to be derived from any such reform could not offset them. The only serious attempt made by a Wafd government to deal with the problem was in 1944, after Makram Ubaid and several other Copts left the party. This attempt is curious because the Wafd was then eager to retain some of its traditional support. There were, however, few Copts in the party to argue against personal status reforms.

2. Government Limitations on the Freedom of Belief

Traditionally, churches could be built only with the permission of the government; the government, however, was often loth to grant this permission. The restrictions were manifold: churches could not be built near a mosque or in a Muslim area if the inhabitants objected, nor could they be built if the government decided that an adequate number of churches already existed in the area. Although permits fell within the purview of the Ministry of the Interior, if the church was too near a public building, a bank of the Nile or an irrigation canal, the appropriate ministry had first to approve the proposed construction. One Coptic society in Kafr al-Shaikh, after waiting four years for permission to build a church on land the state had sold it *for that purpose*, was told by the government that there were too few Copts in the area to justify a new church. It was said also that the planned church was too close to Kafr al-Shaikh town and would somehow threaten public security.[209] This example does not seem atypical; sometimes Copts waited as long as ten years only to be denied a permit.[210] What often seems to have happened was that no sooner was a site chosen and a permit requested than a mosque was built nearby in order to defeat the petition.[211] In 1949, a Ministry of Social Affairs directive seems to have made permission even more difficult to acquire,[212] and in 1951, Misr expressed dismay because, at a time when many mosques were being built in heavily Coptic Shubra, it was so difficult to build churches in such quarters. It was also difficult to obtain permits to repair existing churches.[213]

The Copts correctly construed the difficulty in building churches as an illegal restriction on the constitutional guarantee of freedom of worship. Misr frequently complained about the problem.[214] In 1950, Ibrahim Luqa wrote an open letter to the Minister of the Interior asking him to ease restrictions, and the following year the Patriarch wrote to the prime minister and asked him to abolish them.[215]

Minor problems which bothered Copts were the functional ban on ringing church bells and the conscription of Coptic theological students in the 1950s. A more serious inequity was the impossibility of broadcasting Coptic religious programmes and services on state radio when much of the airtime was taken up with Islamic religious broadcasts. Originally, the Copts were refused permission to broadcast on the grounds that they would do so in Coptic, and foreign languages were not allowed. Copts frequently asked for this prohibition to be lifted, but were unsuccessful.[216] Only once during Coptic Christmas in 1951 were the Copts permitted to broadcast a religious service.[217]

C. ONE RESPONSE TO PRESSURE: CONVERSION

The state's attitude towards the Copts was replete with contradictions. While acknowledging the state's publicly proclaimed desire to promote equality, it would, at the same time, be easy to interpret the pressures put on the Copts and the difficulties placed in their way as a state responsibility to encourage conversion to Islam, or at least as proof to a sometimes sceptical Muslim populace that the state was upholding Islam by encouraging conversion. In centuries past, the jizya tax may have provided a powerful incentive for state tolerance. Its abolition left the state not only without this useful addition to its revenues, but also without a symbol of its stern attitude towards non-Muslims who had been exposed to the teachings of Islam and yet had declined to accept the religion's truth. Into this attitude can perhaps also be read an interest in producing citizens as alike one another as possible, so that all Egyptians might be assumed to support, in relatively reliable fashion, the ideals of the state and to be predictable in their behaviour.

Given the disadvantages of being Christian in this society, surprisingly few Copts seem to have converted; most estimates range from a few hundred to less than a thousand per year. These estimates may not, however, have accurately reflected the number of rural conversions; isolated villagers may have been subject to a coercion that urban Copts either did not encounter or could more easily resist.[218] Judging from the number of articles published in Misr and al-Manara al-Misriya, concern about the conversion rate became more acute in the mid-1940s. Salama Musa, commenting on the case of a young Copt who had joined the Muslim Brethren, accused the Brethren of mounting a campaign to convert Copts.[219] The French Embassy reported that Brethren zealots were abducting young Christian girls, marrying hem and then forcing them to convert to Islam.[220]

The Islamic religious establishment seems to have overlooked such abuses. It was required to ensure that the conversion was sincere, but this was an empty formality; Copts were not turned away.[221] Copts, in fact, converted for a variety of practical reasons; among them to find work, escape discrimination and obtain divorce.[222] No stigma was attached to being an ex-Christian. Some newspapers printed articles about converts who had been hired by the government, and Muslim societies published figures showing the sums spent to help new converts.[223] Sometimes a convert later wished to return to the Christian fold, but the law on apostacy forbade this.[224] Copts could not and did not demand that conversion to Islam be prohibited, but they did want to make it more difficult.

D. SUMMARY

The constitution established an ideal of equality which the Copts looked to meet in practice, but which was impossible to realise. The country lacked an apparatus which could effectively enforce identical access to public and private sector employment, equivalent powers for the religious courts and an equal opportunity to build houses of worship for both communities. While equality was an important goal for the Copts, and was for many years regarded as an achievable one, it was eventually superseded by a concern to prevent the slippage of members across the communal border into the perpetually attractive land of an increasingly aggressive Islam. The growing number of communal complaints heard in the 1940s may reflect discouragement with the possibilities of obtaining genuine equality and a new anxiety about the preservation of the community.

The communal press was the most vocal defender of Coptic interests. Coptic politicians and the clergy were often faulted in that press and by their constituents for their lack of vigour in posting guards at the communal border. They did little, for example, to combat discrimination in employment. This was, however, a fuzzy area in which individual cases were difficult to substantiate. The Coptic press was sometimes able to embarrass official Coptic representatives into taking stronger stands. More vocal positions were adopted in the 1940s on the subject of religious education, but then this became a critical issue with the community's future, its children, being threatened by increasing exposure to Islamic education. Another area of growing concern was the building of churches. Complaints grew louder in the 1940s, perhaps because more churches were needed to serve an increased population. The government would have found it difficult to issue a larger number of permits in the face of so much Islamic religious pressure.

The issue of reforming personal status jurisdiction drew by far the most strenuous of protests, although Coptic politicians were less than vigorous on this subject. The Majlis al-Milli and the clergy, on the other hand, had vested interests as well as a desire to protect communal and familial bonds. Their success in this, the most traditional and hallowed preserve of the Copts, was striking. The Patriarch did generally become more active in his flock's defence in the late 1940s. His stronger stance may have been less the result of conviction than a response to pressures generated by his community and other millets. He remained, as might be expected, more likely to be assertive on religious rather than civil issues.

The Copts came to believe in the 1940s that the government was treating them more harshly. It is true that the government, in attempting to increase its own power, was trespassing on Coptic territory. While there was suspicion, there was no seemingly deliberate policy that the community had to be watched, regulated and increasingly controlled. Many government decisions represented *ad hoc* reactions to various pressures in its increasingly chaotic environment.

NOTES

1. In 1917, 12.3 per cent of Muslim Egyptians and 30.7 per cent of Copts were literate. See also Gorst's Report on the Affairs of Egypt, 1911 (Accounts and Papers, C111), Cd.5633.

2. Gabriel Baer, *Population and Society in the Arab East* (Oxford University Press, London, 1964), p.97.

3. Rauf Abbas Hamid, *al-Nizam al-Ijtimai fi Misr, 1837-1914* (Dar al-Fikr al-Hadith, Cairo, 1973), pp.96-100. Gabriel Baer, *A History of Land Ownership in Modern Egypt, 1800-1950* (Oxford University Press, London, 1962), pp.63-137. Baer notes that the Copts did not stand out as an important group of landowners until the 1880s, but this emergence seems to have had nothing to do with the British Occupation. It is possible, however, that the Copts believed that the British presence would protect their investment in land and so were more willing to purchase property. Cromer's establishment of credit in the 1890s did make it easier to buy big estates.

4. CCEH, Abdin Palace Archives, Biographical Card Index; Ali Barakat, *Tatawwur al-Malakiyya al-Ziraiyya fi Misr*, appendix 6 (Dar al-Thaqafa al-Jadida, Cairo, 1977); Hamid, *al-Nizam al-Ijtimai*, pp.96-100.

5. Charles Issawi, *Egypt: An Economic and Social Analysis* (Oxford University Press, Oxford, 1947), p.34. Another source contradicts this and suggests that the Copts paid 16 per cent of all property taxes. See 'al-Aqbat fi al-Duwal al-Islamiyya', *al-Hilal 19* (1910-11), pp.104-5.

6. Charles Issawi, *Egypt in Revolution: An Economic Analysis* (Oxford University Press, London, 1963), p.90. Tawfiq Dus, who was a member of the boards of directors of ten companies, and Sadiq Wahbah of eleven in 1941, were the most active in this sphere. Others appointed to various boards included Wahib Dus, Nakhla al-Mutii,

Charles Bushra Hanna, Raghib Hanna, Sadiq Hinain, Kamil Sidqi, Wasif Simaika and Shukri and Fahmi Wisa. See, The Stock Exchange Yearbook of Egypt (Cairo, 1941).

7. See the complaints about discrimination in Abbud's companies and particularly in the sugar company in Naj Hamadi. Misr, 10 December 1947, 1, and 23 December 1949, 4.

8. FO.371/63029, J1974/152/16.

9. FO.371/63029, J2860/152/16.

10. Misr, 10 November 1947, 1.

11. Ibid.

12. Misr, 6 December 1947, 1.

13. Information on the civil service is derived largely from The Egyptian Directory, an annual publication which listed Ministry officials of senior and middle grades. However, by the 1950s, the Directory included fewer middle-level positions. In addition, pension lists and individual files deposited in the Dar al-Mahfuzat were used. The pension index is only in moderately good order, and occasionally an individual died or retired before or after the year he actually appears in it. One problem in working with lists of names must be noted: it is not always possible to distinguish between Muslim and Coptic names and between Coptic names and those of Syrian origin.

14. The cadres increased from 15,000 in 1915 to 42,000 in 1940, but in 1930 there were about 190,000 non-cadre employees. Marius Deeb, 'The Wafd and its Rivals', unpublished DPhil thesis, Oxford University, 1971, pp.442, 445.

15. Baer, Population and Society, p.97.

16. Cynthia Enloe, 'Ethnicity, Bureaucracy and State-building in Africa and Latin America', Ethnic and Racial Studies 1 (1978), p.340.

17. Tawfiq Dus argued this at the Asyut Conference on the curious grounds that it might enable the Copts to obtain posts for which they were unqualified. The Coptic Congress Held at Assiout on March 6, 7 and 8, 1911, pp.22-3.

18. Misr, 16 November 1951, 1.

19. FO.407/215, no.52, Sir P. Loraine to Sir J. Simon, 21 May 1932; FO.407/221, Part 122, Enclosure in No.5, An Appreciation of the Situation of the Copts by Mr. Hamilton, 1937.

20. FO.371/16118, J1475/194/16.

21. The British noted in 1928 that eighty-seven per cent of the officials in the Direct Taxes Department were Copts. The percentage is not nearly this high in the Egyptian Directory, so pre-

sumably they occupied predominantly junior posts. FO.407/206, Enclosure in No.32, Complaint by Coptic Officials, February 1928. A list of routine transfers in the Department in August 1937 included no Muslim names. Found in the pension file of Aziz Habashi in Dar al-Mahfuzat, No.368/3/3656/44073.

22. The Wafdist Copt, Ibrahim Faraj Masiha, claims that such pressure was put on him when he was Minister of Foreign Affairs in the last Wafdist cabinet. Interview, 13 June 1979.

23. See _Misr_, 21 June 1935, 1, and 15 January 1938, 1; Zaghib Mikhail, _Farriq Tasud_!, pp.11-12, 40.

24. _Al-Kashkul_, March 1924, 14.

25. One 1911 report recorded that there were a few Coptic District Officers. FO.371/111, 31390/4079/16.

26. Ibid.

27. In 1925, three out of thirty-four judges were Copts but, by 1950, only two out of about fifty judges were.

28. There were no Coptic '_conseillers_' in 1939 and only one in 1943 and 1951.

29. _Misr_ recalled in 1946 that objections had been voiced to his appointment. _Misr_, 12 December 1946, 1.

30. In addition, periodic complaints were voiced about discrimination against Coptic students. _Misr_ was disturbed in 1929 when _al-Siyasa_ suggested that only a certain percentage of Coptic students be allowed to pass the exams. _Misr_, 16 September 1929, 3.

31. R.H. Dekmejian suggests that seven per cent of the officer corps was Christian in the late 1940s. _Egypt Under Nasser_ (Oxford University Press, London, 1972), p.21. However, more officers seem to have been in the Medical Corps than any other branch of the service.

32. FO.407/221, part 122, Enclosure in No.5, An Appreciation of the Situation of the Copts by Mr. Hamilton, 1937. He also noted that those who did have influence were gradually being sidetracked. Only one Copt, Miralai Farid Abd Allah, conspired with the Free Officers.

33. It is not clear whether he is comparing 1932 with the 1920s or some earlier time. FO.371/16118, J1475/194/16.

34. The paper also alleged that the Minister of Justice's predecessor had announced that Coptic appointments to the Parquet and the bench must be kept in line with their proportion of the popula-

tion. Misr, 6 November 1951, 6, and 16 November 1951, 1. However, more Copts sat on the bench of Summary Courts in 1951 than in 1949.

35. FO.371/16118, J1475/194/16.

36. Just before the 1936 election, Misr al-Fatat made a point of contention of Makram's closure of the school, claiming that he did so on behalf of the Copts. This was the second time Makram had closed the school so perhaps the notion was not far fetched. FO.141/543, 19/44/36. Al-Bishri notes that the Wafd did have considerable support among Coptic tax collectors and was not happy with Liberal tampering. Al-Bishri, al-Muslimun w-al-Aqbat(GEBO, Cairo 1980), p.265-7.

37. This contravened Law No.14 (1933) which specified that only a Copt who had the approval of the Patriarch could be Director.

38. Several such articles were published in 1935, 1938 and 1946.

39. Al-Kashif, 21 January 1928,4, and 28 January 1928, 4.

40. See FO.407/206, for December 1927 and January-February 1928.

41. Al-Ahram, 30 January 1928, 5; FO.407/206, J519/18/16.

42. FO.141/685, 8424/65/28.

43. Ibid.

44. FO.407/206, Enclosure in No.32, Complaint by Coptic Officials, February 1928.

45. FO.371/13117, J846/4/16.

46. Ninety-four Copts and thirteen Muslims, Misr, 23 January and 2 February 1928, p.1. Al-Bishri writes that eighty-seven Copts (ten per cent of the department's Copts) and twenty Muslims (fourteen per cent of all Muslim employees) were cut. He adds that the committee making the decision took care to cut Copts and Muslims from each civil service grade. Al-Bishri, al-Muslimun w-al-Aqbat, p.255.

47. FO.407/206, Enclosure in No.32, Complaint by Coptic Officials, February 1928; No.32, Lord Lloyd to Sir Austen Chamberlain, 23 February 1928.

48. FO.141/685, 8424/65/28.

49. Ibid.

50. Al-Balagh, 29 January 1928, PPF.

51. Ibid., 30 January 1928, PPF. See also Chamber Debates, twenty-fifth session, 31 January 1928; Misr, 17 January 1928, 2.

52. FO.407/206, J683/18/16.

53. Al-Ahram, 6 February 1928, 6; al-Balagh, 7 February 1928, 1, and 13 February 1928, 1.

54. *Misr*, 24 February 1928, 1, and 28 February 1928, 1. *Misr* could conceivably have wanted to destroy the treaty, but this was also the goal of Wafd extremists, like Makram Ubaid, who criticised *Misr's* campaign. Tawfiq Hinain, in one *Misr* article, alleged that the Wafd had tricked the Copts into believing that it supported equality, and he warned the Copts to examine carefully a party's attitude towards the Copts before rushing to its support. Al-Bishri, *al-Muslimun w-al-Aqbat*, p.263.

55. The paper did, however, present at least two dissenting opinions. *Misr*, 25 October 1926, 2; 27 October 1926, 1; 3 November 1926, 1; 29 November 1926, 1; 17 December 1926, 1. *La Bourse Egyptienne*, 23 October 1926, 3.

56. All officials, however, were subject to arbitrary treatment by their ministries. See *Misr*, 17 June 1935, 3; 19 July 1935, 1; 26 July 1935, 1; 1 August 1935, 1.

57. *Misr*, 19 July 1935, 1. Wafd ministries, claimed *Misr* in another article, worked to realise equality. *Misr*, 29 June 1935, 1.

58. *Misr*, 27 May 1936, 1.

59. *Misr*, 4 March 1939, 5, and 14 March 1939, 5. *Al-Kashkul* took up the subject of Coptic complaints on 10 March and suggested that Copts believed that the Palace had blessed this policy of discrimination. *Al-Kashkul*, 10 March 1939, pp.3-5.

60. However, the paper was pleased when the new Minister of Education announced that there was no reason that Copts could not be headmasters. *Misr*, 12 December 1946, 1.

61. *Misr*, 14 May 1946, 2.

62. *CCEH*, F7/D7, Card 805, Security Reports: Report on Religious Discord, December 1941.

63. *Misr*, 1 November 1950, 1; 6 December 1950, 1; 3 September 1951, 1; 6 November 1951, 6; *al-Manara al-Misriyya*, 12 June 1950, 1-2.

64. *Al-Minbar* claimed that the Copts' principal object in life was to amass wealth, obtain high ranks and fill government offices. Quoted in the *Egyptian Mail*, 4 November 1920, 2. See also allegations of Coptic trickery, in *al-Kashkul*, 20 May 1923.

65. *Al-Kashkul*, 31 August 1923, 4.

66. *Al-Siyasa*, 9 February 1930, PPF. There is no confirmation in the Public Record Office archives that the Wafd considered this. Ubaid was entitled to a portfolio and might not have wanted to risk losing his influence by remaining outside

the country when the Wafd was in power.

67. Misr asked what was Islamic about the work of representing Egypt in Switzerland or Washington. Misr, 13 February 1930, 1.

68. Al-Siyasa, 9 February 1930, PPF.

69. Ibid., 20 April 1930, 5.

70. Misr, 10 February 1930, 1.

71. Misr alleged that tax collectors had been subjected to an unreasonable number of transfers in the previous government. Misr, 12 March 1930, 5.

72. Ibid., 5.

73. Makram was reported to be trying to get his brother-in-law appointed judge. Al-Shab, 5 March 1935, 4, and 7 March 1935, 4.

74. FO.141/543. 19/44/36.

75. Misr, 19 October 1936, 1.

76. FO.407/221, part 122, Enclosure in No.5, An Appreciation of the Situation of the Copts by Mr. Hamilton, 1937.

77. Henry Ayrout, 'Egypt: Interférences de la politique et de la religion', En Terre d'Islam 13 (1938), 194.

78. Al-Kashkul 25 February 1938, 1-2. This was repeated, with minor alternations in the percentages, on 20 March 1939, 3-5.

79. Al-Kashkul, 25 February 1938, 4.

80. See al-Kashkul, 10 March 1939, 3-5.

81. FO.407/221, No.27, D.V. Kelly to Mr. Eden, 2 September 1937.

82. There was no central agency whose task it was to regulate the civil service. Nazih Ayubi, Bureaucracy and Politics in Contemporary Egypt (London, Ithaca Press, 1980), p.302.

83. Although he notes that it is impossible to prove that the cabinet issues a set of instructions to this effect. Interview, Dr. Zahir Riyad, 1 June 1979.

84. He noted that this was especially true of Finance and Communications, but he presents no evidence to support what is probably hearsay, Pierre Rondot, 'L'Evolution historique des Coptes d'Egypte', Cahiers de l'Orient Contemporain 22 (1950), 140. Al-Bishri also thinks that the 1928-9 Mahmud government sacked many Coptic employees. Al-Bishri, al-Muslimun w-al-Aqbat, p.264.

85. FO.371/21948, J4332/6/16. FO.407/206, No.61 (Enclosure 3), Note on a Visit to Asyut, February 1928 by L. Grafftey-Smith.

86. FO.407/208, No.27 (Enclosure 1), Note on a Visit to Mansura, February 1929. FO.407/217, Part 115, No.126, Sir M. Lampson to Sir J. Simon,

13 June 1934. FO.371/16118, J1485/194/16; J1719/194/16.

87. FO.141/489, 71/5/32.

88. FO.407/127, No.10, Mr. R.I. Campbell to Sir John Simon, 15 July 1933; FO.371/20916, J1989/815/16; Lashin, Sad Zaghlul, p.163, quoting from Zaghlul's diary.

89. This is not true of judicial positions which had a high turnover, probably because so many politicians were lawyers.

90. The government in power often declined to put an opponent it had fired on pension. This was part of the punishment for opposition, and it gave rise to much litigation. Depending on the results of such litigation, this practice could explain the appearance of some individuals on the pension lists after they had left the bureaucracy.

91. On the general subject of dismissals, see Haikal, Mudhakkirat fi al-Siyasa al-Misriyya, vol.II, pp.93-4; Abd al-Rahman al-Rafii, Fi Aqab al-Thawra al-Misriyya (Maktabat al-Nahda al-Misriyya, Cairo, 1951), vol.3, pp.69, 118; and Ramadan, Tatawwur, p.47.

92. See al-Siyasa, 30 January 1924; Haikal, Mudhakkirat, I, p.180.

93. To cast further suspicion on Coptic allegiances, the dialogue is half in Egyptian colloquial and half in French. Al-Kashkul, 18 January 1924, 7-9, 12.

94. Al-Kashkul, 1 February 1924, 3.

95. Al-Siyasa, 17 September 1929, PPF.

96. FO.407/206, No.73 (Enclosure 7), Memorandum on the Egyptian Press, 22 March-4 April 1928.

97. Al-Siyasa, 20 April 1930, 5.

98. Quoted by Jacques Berque, in Egypt: Imperialism and Revolution, p.505.

99. In 1910 when Butrus Ghali was made prime minister, it was decided that although it was then customary for a prime minister to be his own Minister of the Interior, he could not do so. Part of the reason for this was that al-Azhar was under the jurisdiction of the Interior. Butrus Ghali retained Foreign Affairs instead; interview with Ibrahim Amin Ghali, 19 March 1979.

100. Supply was at times a separate portfolio and at others attached to another ministry, but it was only in wartime that it was important.

101. Salib Sami, Dhikrayat Siyasi, pp.206-8. King Fuad told Sami that he personally desired his appointment, and Sami appears to have suspected that this was a manoeuvre designed to increase royal con-

trol over the army because of the intrinsically precarious position of any Coptic minister. See also, Abd al-Azim Ramadan, al-Jaish al-Misri fi al-Siyasa 1882-1936 (Dar al-Katib al-Arabi, Cairo, 1977), p.312.

102. This doomed the cabinet reshuffle to failure and left an impression of instability. Sami soon ran into trouble with the King when he broke off relations with the Vichy government without royal consent. Faruq's behaviour over this issue resulted in the incident of 4 February 1942. FO.371/31566, J334/38/16.

103. This did not escape Coptic notice. See Misr, 6 July 1950, 1.

104. For example, some Muslim employees in the Ministry of Agriculture accused their minister, Nakhla al-Mutii, of discrimination, and this was repeated in the press. Al-Ahram, 2 August 1919, al-Siyasa, 17 September 1929, PPF; al-Kashkul, 4 September 1946; and al-Siyasa, 19 September 1929, quoted in Pierre Condot in 'L'Evolution historique des Coptes d'Egyptes', p.139.

105. Misr occasionally took a Coptic minister to task when it felt that he was not fulfilling this function. In 1949 it criticised the minister for failing to protect Coptic employees in the civil service, and in 1950 for failing to deal with the increase in violence against the Copts. In the aftermath of the Suez church burning in January 1952, many Copts called for their minister to resign to express communal despair. See Misr, 21 December 1949, 3, and 9 October 1950, 1. In 1951, when reviewing Makram's career, Misr noted that Makram as Finance Minister had always supported al-Azhar and the ministry of Awqaf in budget matters. The newspaper went on to complain that the Copts had always had to take their problems to other ministers because Makram was of no help. Misr, 27 August 1951, 1.

106. In 1927, the Copts had 403 schools, including Evangelical institutions, with a student body of 40,089. Misr, 29 June 1927, 1.

107. FO.371/1111, 5672/5672/16.

108. See Misr, 15 March 1937, 1.

109. Mounah Khouri, Poetry and the Making of Modern Egypt (E.J. Brill, Leiden, 1977), p.189.

110. He thought that Coptic children should be taught their own religion in state schools. The Future of Culture in Egypt, translated by Sidney Glazer (American Council of Learned Societies, Washington, D.C., 1954), p.140.

111. FO.141/675, 45/7/37.

112. The Copts wanted the government to pay the teacher. Misr, 22 November 1949, 3.

113. In 1911, for example, the Asyut Provincial Council administered seventy-nine kuttabs, nine of which were reserved for Copts.

114. Kyriakos Mikhail, Copts and Muslims under British Control (Kennikat Press, Port Washington, New York, 1971, originally published in 1911), pp.46, 53, 79.

115. Interview with Mirrit Ghali, 4 December 1978.

116. FO.371/1111, 5672/5672/16.

117. FO.371/111, 10869/5672/16.

118. In 1911, a concerted protest by the Copts led Sir William Bull on 24 February to ask the Secretary of State for Foreign Affairs in the House of Commons whether discrimination in the kuttab system had received the government's attention. Ibid.

119. Particularly in Qina. Misr, 16 February 1928, 1, and 23 February 1928, 1.

120. These figures excluded kuttabs and madaris, religious schools connected to mosques; 58,557 Copts and 102,435 Muslims. The statistics are those of the Ministry of Education. Misr, 29 June 1929, 1.

121. Gorst's Report on the Affairs of Egypt, 1907 (Accounts and Papers, C), Cd.3452.

122. Mikhail, Copts and Muslims, p.35.

123. Al-Watan applauded the idea but asked that Christianity be taught to Christian students, 15 November 1923, 1.

124. Until 1935, students in the fourth year of secondary school were exempt from religious classes. James Jankowski, Egypt's Young Rebels (Hoover Institution, Stanford, 1975), p.2.

125. Kuttabs were eventually absorbed by elementary schools, which provided basic literacy training. Primary schools were attended by students who planned a longer, more expensive education. Secondary schools were open only to the graduates of primary schools.

126. Misr, 1 October 1925, 1.

127. FO.371/ 7302, J1941/1647/16.

128. Misr, 17 December 1931, 1.

129. Alfred Yallouz, 'Chronique législatif, 1921-3', in L'Egypte Contemporaine 146-7 (1934), pp.126-8. FO.371/17302, J1647/1647/16.

130. FO.371/17302, J1647/1647/16.

131. Chamber Debates, 58th Session, 22 May 1933.

132. A. Morrison, 'Christian Minorities in

Egypt', December 1945, unpublished paper, Middle East Centre Library, University of Oxford.

133. FO.371/17 0 , J1647/1647/16.

134. The Foreign Office told Campbell that he could discuss the matter with the King if the cabinet ministers proved unhelpful.

135. FO.371/17302, J1727/1647/16.

136. FO.371/17302, J1941/1647/16.

137. There were more than ten Coptic senators at this time.

138. The Majlis' petition asked for six periods per week of Christian instruction in those schools with at least fifteen Christian students enrolled. _Misr_, 2 April 1946, 2.

139. FO.371/17976, J2067/7/16.

140. _Al-Siyasa_, 26 June 1933, 1. In 1930, the Young Men's Muslim Association reprimanded the Minister of Education for paying too little attention to religious instruction. G. Kampffmyer, 'Egypt and Western Asia', in H.A.R. Gibb (ed.), _Whither Islam_? (Victor Gollancz, London, 1932), pp.130-7, 149.

141. _Egyptian Gazette_, 15 March 1934, 5.

142. _Misr_, 13 March 1934, 1.

143. It is not clear that this was enforced. FO.141/675, 45/2 and 3/37.

144. FO.371/19082, J515/153/16; J1548/153/16; J3022/153/16.

145. _Al-Balagh_, 8 March 1937, PPF; _al-Jihad_, 5 February 1937, PPF.

146. _Al-Balagh_, 8 March 1937, PPF; _al-Jihad_, 5 February 1937, PPF.

147. _Al-Misri_, 7 March 1937, PPF.

148. _Al-Ahram_, 8 March 1937, PPF.

149. _Al-Misri_, 12 March 1937, PPF. _Misr_ noted that the government was negotiating the abolition of the Capitulations and wanted to appear egalitarian. _Misr_, 15 March 1937, 1.

150. _Al-Misri_, 18 July and 12 August 1937, PPF. At this time pressure was also being put on parents sending their children to missionary schools. In some places, Coptic parents were fined for sending their children to missionary schools instead of state schools. FO.371/20914, J3162/369/16; J2477/369/16; J2253/369/16; FO.141/675, 45/5 and 6/37/

151. _Al-Balagh_, 25 September 1937, PPF.

152. _Al-Misri_, 26 September 1937, PPF.

153. _Al-Kashkul_, 11 February 1938, 34-5.

154. FO.371/31569, J1226/38/16; _Egyptian Gazette_, 25 February 1947, 3.

155. DW, HBM (QM): Security Reports, 1938; Misr, 15 April 1940, 1.

156. La Bourse Egyptienne, 23 September 1943. In 1947, the Ministry of Education was rumoured to be bringing suit against an evangelical school in Port Said for failing to provide its Muslim students with Islamic instruction. FO.371/63029, J3339/152/16. In 1948, the ministry demanded that private schools teach the same subjects with the same materials as government schools. Copts complained that some of the materials used in state schools were anti-Christian. Georgie Hyde, Education in Modern Egypt (Routledge and Kegan Paul, London, 1978), p.168; Mikhail, Farriq Tasud!, pp.16, 23 and 24; and Misr, 15 April 1948, 1.

157. Misr, 2 July 1949, 1.

158. Misr, 1 December 1951, 3.

159. Such cases involved Muslims, members of different millets, inheritance, or a non-Muslim's appeal to a Muslim court in the hope of obtaining a favourable verdict. Inheritance traditionally followed Islamic law, applied by the millet courts, unless the heirs privately agreed to a different division of the property. See al-Khulasa al-Qanuniyya fi al-Ahwal al-Shakhsiyya Li-Kanisa al-Aqbat al-Urthudhuksiyya (Matbaat al-Tawfiq, Cairo, 1923), p.327.

160. FO.371/17976, J2067/7/16.

161. Kosroff Zohrab, 'Etude sur les privilèges de Patriarcats', L'Egypte Contemporaine 112 (1929), p.155.

162. Misr, 21 June 1934, 1.

163. FO.371/16118, J1719/194/16.

164. In his plan, the Sharia courts, with a non-Muslim added to the bench, would have jurisdiction over the validity of marriage. Senate Debates, 23 August 1926; Egyptian Gazette, 28 August 1926, 4.

165. Misr, 22 January 1938, 1.

166. CCEH, Abdin Palace Index, Index on the Copts, No.4039.

167. Ahmad Muhammad Hassan Bey and Isador Feldman, Majmua al-Qawanin - l-Lawaih, II (Taba Misr, Cairo, 1926), p.1088. Decree Law of 13 October 1925.

168. Al-Watan, 15 July 1925, 2; 11 August 1925, 1.

169. FO.141/451, 14544/1/22.

170. Misr, 30 March 1951, 1.

171. Mahmud Azmi, al-Ayyam al-Mia (Maktabat al-Nahda al-Misriyya, Cairo, 1939), p.51.

172. DW, Abdin Palace Archives, Tawaif wa Jamiyat Diniyya 2, Report dated 1 May 1921.

173. Egyptian Gazette, 2 March 1923, 6. Both Committees had a Coptic representative.

174. Senate Debates, forty-eighth session, 6 June 1927.

175. Misr, 25 February 1928, 3. See also FO.407/206, J519/18/16 (January).

176. Ali Mahir had a special interest in the badly organised Majlis al-Hasbi, having been its director of administration until 1918.

177. Misr, 14 October 1931, 6.

178. FO.141/755, 124/9/33.

179. FO.141/566, 78/20/34.

180. FO.141/488, 94/1/32.

181. See FO.141/488 file.

182. FO.141/488, 94/2/32.

183. FO.141/488, 94/12/32.

184. FO.141/488, 94/8/32.

185. FO.141/488, 94/9/32.

186. FO.141/488, 94/8/32.

187. FO.141/488, 94/11/32.

188. FO.371/16117, J1263/171/16.

189. FO.407/215, No.67, Sir P. Loraine to Sir J. Simon, 10 June 1932. For a copy of the draft law, see FO.141/488, 94/9/32.

190. It elicited sharp protests from Muslims. FO.371/16118, J1719/194/16.

191. FO.141/566, 78/2/34.

192. FO.141/566, 78/1/34.

193. FO.141/566. 78/10/34.

194. Chamber Debates, sixteenth session, 8 March 1944.

195. Egyptian Gazette, 6 September 1944, 3.

196. Egyptian Gazette, 8 September 1944, 3.

197. FO.371/41318, J3444/14/16.

198. FO.371/41319. J3638/14/16.

199. FO.371/45931, J2425/10/16.

200. FO.141/1159, 73/41/46.

201. One petition was from Ibrahim Luqa. DW, Abdin Palace Archives, Tawaif Diniyya 1, No.29, Petition to the head of the Royal Diwan.

202. This was done with the help of Senators Tawfiq and Wahib Dus. Senate Debates, twenty-third session, 23 December 1946.

203. French Embassy Archives, Box 144, File 31/2, letter from Ambassador Gilbert Arvengas to the Minister of Foreign Affairs, Georges Bidault, No.248, 21 February 1948.

204. FO.371/63029, J1074/152/16.

205. FO.141/1159, 73/24/47.

206. In addition it legitimised the view of those non-Muslims who saw marriage as a religious bond by stipulating that marriages must first be sanctioned by the appropriate religious authority and then registered with the government, French Embassy Archives, Box 144, File 31/2, 'Coptic Catholics', No.1447.

207. In 1926-27, proposals for the revision of Islamic personal status jurisdiction and the abolition of private endowments were presented to the Chamber. FO.407/205, No.18, Mr. Henderson to Sir Austen Chamberlain, 8 September 1927.

208. Non-Muslims were sometimes asked to give an opinion only after a draft had been prepared.

209. Mikhail, _Farriq Tassud!_, pp.83-4, 87.

210. In 1952, Copts in Suhaj had waited seven years for a permit. _Misr_, 29 December 1951, 1.

211. _Misr_, 5 August 1950, 1; Y. Masriya, 'A Christian Minority: the Copts in Egypt', in W. Beenhoven (ed.), _Case Studies in Human Rights and Fundamental Freedoms_ VI (Martinus Nijhoff, The Hague, 1976), p.79.

212. This decision applied to churches built with money collected from the public, and its intent seems to have been to protect the donors. _Misr_, 28 June 1949, 3.

213. _Misr_, 10 January 1950, 3.

214. See _Misr_, 15 May 1936, 1, and 4 August 1951, 1.

215. _Misr_, 10 January 1950, 3; 18 January 1951, 1951, 1; 28 March 1951, 1.

216. See _Misr_, 17 March 1938, 1; French Embassy Archives, Box 144, File 31/2, 'Coptic Catholics', No.661, M. Gilbert Arvengas to M. Georges Bidault, 29 April 1948; Mikhail, _Farriq Tasud!_, p.310.

217. See _Misr_, 2 January 1951, 1, and 15 January 1951, 1.

218. One Copt wrote to _Misr_ that he had been forced to convert. _Misr_, 23 June 1951, 1.

219. _Misr_, 18 April 1946, 1.

220. French Embassy Archives, Box 144, File 31/2, Situation de la Communauté Copte en Egypt, 24 January 1948.

221. _Misr_, 17 May 1947, 3.

222. For examples of court cases, see Mikhail, _Farriq Tasud!_, pp.150-64.

223. Rev. Qummus Sergius, 'Why Copts become Moslems', _The Moslem World_ 26 (1936), 377.

224. _Misr_, 15 February 1951, 1.

Chapter Seven

ETHNICITY AND RELIGION IN THE STRUGGLE FOR POWER

A. THE RELIGIOUS IDIOM AND PARTY POLITICS

The use of religious issues, prejudices and sentiments became a feature of political discourse in this period. There were those who felt that this was only right and proper, that Islam required political decisions to accord with its dictates. Others were uncomfortable with this stance but still made political use of religion because their opponents did it and they knew it was an easy way to reach the masses. Still others, secularists of a more principled type, saw this as discreditable conduct. Many politicians resided, however, uncomfortably, in the middle category. Even when party interests were opposed to some Islam-inspired goal like the re-establishment of the Caliphate, party loyalists rarely dared to declare their disapproval for fear that their obedience to Islam would be questioned. Islamic affairs were discussed with lively interest by the party, and sometimes even the Coptic, press and attendance at Friday services and other displays of piety helped keep a party's devotion to Islam before the public eye. Certain Coptic politicians even made a point of sometimes attending mosque services, although few were able to make such profitable use of Islam as Makram.

All parties, then, used religion to strengthen their support and explain their aims, actions and policies. An integral part of this strategy sometimes was to make a public issue of the role that the Copts played in politics. Some parties claimed to see conspiracies at every hand. They also, by questioning the amount of power some Muslim politicians placed in the hands of their Coptic colleagues, were able to question those politicians' dedication to Islam and responsiveness to their constituents. This tactic was used mainly against the Wafd by the Liberals, the Sadists and the Palace and its affiliates. The Liberals were among the worst offenders; their journal, al-Kashkul, was perhaps the most consistently anti-Coptic of any published in Egypt. The record of al-Siyasa was not uch better. A later offender, and one with the dubious merit of sincerity, was the Muslim Brethren organisation. Hassan al-Banna, the Supreme Guide, believed that Coptic participation in politics should be strictly limited; Muhammad Husain Haikal, however scurrilous his newspaper al-Siyasa, believed at least theoretically in the right of the Copts, as Egyptian citizens, to play a political role. The problem for the Liberals, who were perhaps the first to use ethnic propaganda in this period, was that the Wafd's credentials were such that they had few means of undermining that reputation and enhancing their own. The role the Copts played in the Wafd had not only been commented on during the revolution, but had actually been praised; the Liberals tried to make it into an object of criticism.

Partly because personalities took precedence over policies, politicians were frequently criticised for adhering to the wrong religion or being insufficiently attentive to the right one. Even the mere use of names, which generally marked the holder as Copt or Muslim, could serve as a political weapon. Two Wafdist Copts went so far as to alter their names, an hypocrisy which displeased many of their co-religionists. Early in his political career, Makram Ubaid dropped his first name, William. William was a double misfortune; not only was it the only part of his name that labelled him a Christian but it had foreign and Protestant connections which were capable of arousing even Coptic distaste. The anti-Wafdist press was able to capitalise on this by almost unfailingly referring to Makram as 'William' or 'William Makram'. Years later, Ibrahim Faraj Masiha dropped his last name, which means 'Christ'. The Wafdist press, which called Makram 'Makram Ubaid', now referred to Masiha as 'Ibrahim Faraj'. Muslims unacquainted with Wafdist personalities could have been excused for thinking both Muslim.

Copts active in parties other than the Wafd were not above suspicion. In December 1933, two Ministry of Justice officials were overheard deploring the Coptic role in the Shab and al-Ittihad parties. The two men were convinced that the Coptic members of both met secretly to vote on party matters and then persuaded their Muslim colleagues to adopt their view.[1] This was a suspicion that was most frequently voiced about the Copts in the Wafd. The Wafd was the only party to defend Coptic political participation and to go on promoting a Coptic role in defiance of its opponents. It almost never, as a party policy, used divisive tactics, although there is some evidence to suggest that it could not resist an occasional ethnic jab at Makram's al-Kutla. In general, however, the Wafd did not use ethnic appeals because it was so vulnerable to them itself.

Until 1927, the charge most frequently brought against the Wafd was that it was a Coptic clique. Once Makram became Secretary-General, that clique gained a leader; both the party and al-Nahhas were portrayed as puppets in the hands of a sly, evil genius.[2] Both accusations at least implied that there was a Coptic conspiracy to rule Egypt.[3] At times, the charges were most explicit and ugly. In the 1930s, the Copts sometimes were likened to the Jews as described by Nazi propaganda.[4] They were also accused of working for a national home in Egypt as were the Jews in Palestine.[5]

Such charges, as absurd as they were, cast aspersion upon and ultimately undermined the right of the Copts to participate in politics. They suggested that the Copts in politics could only act as Copts; they would always think, work and vote as Copts and could not, therefore, represent the general interest. These charges perpetuated the traditional view of non-Muslims, which was one which could never mesh with Western political thought. The Liberals, the Sadists and the Palace never publicly came to grips with the kind of place they envisioned for the Copts; such an explicit formulation was left to tradition and some of the more religiously oriented groups like the Muslim Brethren.

The Wafd, to its credit, never allowed its accusers the dignity of trying to prove that the Copts did not dominate party councils. Unless circumstantial evidence, i.e., the obvious decline of Copts in the Wafd, is taken as proof, there are few signs that the Wafd consciously tried to reduce Coptic visibility, except in the matter of names, in order to render the party less vulnerable to these charges. Generally, the Wafd countered by accusing its opponents of trying to divide the nation. This was an accusation which was taken more seriously in the 1920s when the ideals of the revolution were still fresh, than in the 1930s. By the end of the latter decade, those ideals had grown somewhat stale and the Wafd's response was not adequate to the charge. Perhaps realising this, the Wafd defended national unity and the Coptic role in politics less in the 1940s than it had in the previous two decades. Its defence of secularism decreased with its reliance on religion, but it had always stressed, as one reply, that Wafdists were good Muslims and patriots. It also tried to cast doubt on its opponents' charges of favouring Copts by discrediting the religiosity of those opponents.

Two contemporary scholars, possibly acting on the suggestion of Ahmad Shafiq Pasha, accept 1928-9 as the point at which the Liberals began to attack the Wafd for excessive reliance on Copts.[6] One carries this argument further and suggests that the Liberals tended to reside 'above the political fray' until 1929 and that the Wafd was the first 'to play on Islamic loyalties for political gain'.[7] He sees Wafdist attacks on the Liberals' 'atheism' as provoking Liberal anti-Coptic propaganda in retaliation.[8] This judgment may be excessively generous to the Liberals. The Wafd probably made no more than the cursory appeals to religious feeling that were _de rigeur_ until 1925 when the book of Ali Abd al-Raziq, an _alim_ with Liberal connections, gave the party ample ammunition. In the eyes of many Egyptians, the Wafd was correct to call the Liberals atheists and Wafdists seemed to relinquish few opportunities to do so.[9] This charge, of course, was only one of many aimed at the Liberals, but it may have been the most damaging one. Even in 1930, when the Wafd was arguing with the Liberals over the design of Zaghlul's tomb, the party press attacked the Liberals, who were promoting an Islamic style, as hypocrites in zealots' clothing. One article noted that they were among those who were least interested in religion and had the least respect for its people.[10] No doubt the Liberals were rendered more desperate in their search to counter this charge and therefore began to use anti-Coptic propaganda more heavily. However, the purity of the party was compromised somewhat earlier since it first began to appeal to sectarian sentiment in 1923 and not in 1928-9.

It is true that the Wafdist accusation of atheism was damaging to the political system in that it hampered the development of a secular state, but anti-Coptic propaganda must be counted at least equally harmful. The Liberals manufactured it throughout this era and, although they did rely on communal sentiment more from 1929, the difference was one of quantity and not type. Liberal and later Ittihadist and Sadist propaganda made the need for the Wafdists to pose as good Muslims more acute and only refuelled the religious rivalry.

What is perhaps most remarkable is that the British believed many of the things said about the Copts in the Wafd. Just as they were convinced that the Copts supported the nationalist movement out of fear, so they were persuaded that the Copts were the most influential members of the Wafd and that al-Nahhas was clay in the hands of Makram. The Residency used this belief to discredit the Wafd in the eyes of the Foreign Office. In 1923, for example, the Residency described Zaghlul as being under the influence of 'the Coptic and extremist wing'.[11] Six years later, H.M. Anthony disparaged al-Nahhas by claiming that 'his sole active supporters (...those who pay and not those who shout) are the Copts. I need not tell you what that means in a Muslim country'.[12]

B. RELIGIOUS APPEALS AND THE PALACE

The two reigning monarchs of this period, Fuad and Faruq, had both a traditional and a constitutional responsibility to protect the religion of the state. Both kings bolstered their political power and popularity by relying on their religious authority and their support in al-Azhar. With regional ambitions as well as local imperatives, the Palace made a great show of its piety and frequently appealed to religious sentiment. Its pursuit of the Caliphate is only one example. While the Palace never allowed its name to be directly tied to anti-Coptic propaganda, it did permit its partisans to produce it in the pursuit of their mutual interest. The 1938 election campaign, discussed later, provides the clearest example of this.

As the most serious rival to its power, the Wafd was the party most feared and hated by the Palace. One way the latter attempted to discredit the Wafd was by accusing it of disloyalty to the throne. Because the Wafd was also said to be dominated by Copts, Coptic loyalty to the throne was placed under suspicion. It was, however, not simply this connection with the Wafd that damned the

Copts in Palace eyes; the Palace appears to have felt that the Copts, more than any other Egyptians, were natural anti-monarchists and republicans.[13] The Coptic press frequently felt obliged to proclaim its allegiance as well as its gratitude to the House of Muhammad Ali.[14]

The Wafd probably was not unduly damaged by accusations of disloyalty until Faruq succeeded his father in 1936. In the few years following this, the Palace was able to draw a clear parallel between the devout Muslim monarch and the secular, irreligious and Coptic-dominated Wafd party. Palace manipulation of Islamic sentiment focused at this time on two issues: (1) Faruq's stated desire for a religious rather than a secular coronation ceremony, and (2) his wish to receive religious instruction from Shaikh Mustafa al-Maraghi. With a Wafd government in power, it was only natural that the Wafd in general and Makram in particular would be accused of prohibiting both. It was also proposed that the Wafd had sought British backing for these actions against Islam.

The coronation issue was energetically discussed by the press in 1937 and was returned to during the 1938 election campaign. The constitution demanded only that the King swear an oath before Parliament. The Wafd, on both constitutional and tactical grounds, refused to contemplate the religious service advocated by the Palace. It feared that such a ceremony would suggest that royal power emanated not from the people but from Islam and would accordingly increase Palace power at Wafdist expense. The Wafdist press, therefore, described the proposed flamboyant ceremony as almost idolatrous and a violation of the simplicity inherent in Islam.[15] One Deputy, speaking on behalf of the Palace, claimed in the Chamber that a religious ceremony would uphold Egypt's dignity as an Islamic state, and he asked Prime Minister al-Nahhas if he was aware of the danger run by excluding the ulama from the coronation. The latter replied that the King's assumption of his constitutional powers was a national matter and that all Egyptians, Muslim and non-Muslim, had a right to participate in the ceremony.[16]

Shaikh al-Maraghi, perhaps guiding the Palace by playing on its fears and prejudices, insisted rather curiously that public antagonism to Coptic influence was behind the controversy over the religious ceremony. He added that Egyptians wished to re-emphasise, through the ceremony, that the government of Egypt was an Islamic one,[17] and he held up the spectre of a Coptic takeover which would produce a new Christian aristocracy before which Muslims would be forced to kneel.[18] Copts clearly were unnerved by the charge that they had a hand in this religious issue;[19] Misr dared not even mention it. The Patriarch sent a note to the King deploring rumours which questioned Coptic loyalty to the throne.[20] The King reassured the Patriarch, in writing and later in person, that he was aware of their fealty.[21] At the same time, Najib Iskandar, now a Palace ally, condemned the Patriarch's note for implying that the Copts were separate from the rest of the nation.[22] Latif Nakhla, a Coptic notable and probable Palace loyalist, voiced a similar objection.[23] The same fracas occurred over the religious tutorials with al-Maraghi; the King was far more interested in using the Wafd's refusal against the party than he was in studying Islam with the Shaikh.

Not only did the Palace, through its manipulation of religious sentiment, encourage sectarian tensions, but it also failed to try to improve relations between the two communities when they began to sour. Faruq, whose reputation had suffered by the late 1940s, was probably unwilling to appear overly conciliatory towards the Copts; but it is just as likely that he was simply not interested in their problems. Faruq probably became even less well disposed to the community in 1950 when his sister, Fathiyya, elopes with Riyad Ghali, a Coptic diplomat. Islamic law forbade such marriages and the Coptic church was not enthusiastic about any mixed marriages, let alone this one. The royal *mésalliance* caused a considerable stir. Riyad Ghali was condemned by the press; and the government, to forestall violence, put guards on churches the first Sunday after the event was publicised.[24] In an action Misr reported, the Coptic Patriarch apologised to the King for the groom's behaviour. As the paper pointed out, the Coptic community was not collectively responsible for the actions of one of its members.[25]

C. ELECTIONS

No better examples of the use of anti-Coptic propaganda exist than election campaigns. In some campaigns ethnic propaganda was widespread and the result of a party decision to exploit religious feeling. In others, it was either not a general strategy or it was simply less apparent. In all elections, however, individual Muslim candidates used sectarian tactics against Coptic opponents. It was a temptation to which even Wafdist candidates sometimes succumbed. Given the advantages that might have accrued to a Muslim running against a Copt in a predominantly Muslim district, it is interesting that Muslims were not routinely nominated to run against Copts. Certainly it was the pattern in the more heavily Coptic constituencies to run Copts against Copts.

Little benefit would be derived from a discussion of every campaign because the propaganda differed less in kind than in quantity. Nor is there any kind of steady increase in the amount of propaganda dispensed. Ethnic appeals, for example, were more heavily used in 1923 than in 1942. However, the general increase in communal tensions from the mid-1940s meant that the population was more receptive to sectarian and Islamic propaganda and that it had a more telling effect then than in earlier years. The 1923 and 1938 Chamber elections will be the ones focused on here; in addition, an interesting by-election in 1943 will be examined. Favourite themes in these and other campaigns were that the Copts were unscrupulous, that they had joined the nationalist movement to advance communal interests, that they had too great a hold on various Egyptian institutions, and that the Wafd was the means by which they sought to rule.

The 1923 campaign saw the first significant use of anti-Coptic propaganda since before the war. The Liberal Constitutionalists manufactured it for use against the Wafd; as Tariq al-Bishri has noted, their journal <u>al-Kashkul</u> consistently implied that the election was a struggle between Copts and Muslims, Wafdists and Liberals.[26]

The Liberals, gearing up for the campaign, first objected to the number of Copts appointed to Wafdist election committees.[27] Copts were, in fact, well represented on these committees but hardly dominated them. The Liberal press blamed Copts for posing as the greatest patriots in Egypt, for supporting the British presence and for monopolising the civil service.[28] It also reminded voters of the names of those Coptic candidates who had attended the 1911 Coptic Congress.[29] Markam was accused of having backed the 1919-20 Milner plan in return for the promise of a provincial governership,[30] while Wisa Wasif and Wasif Ghali were said to have taken control of the Wafd.[31]

Fakhri Abd al-Nur was worried by the anti-Coptic statements of his opponent and expressed a fear that Jirja Muslims were not ready to elect a non-Muslim representative.[32]

The Wafd did not let these charges pass unremarked; al-Balagh, Misr and individual Wafdists all responded. Makram, speaking in Shubra, declared that the unity of Copts and Muslims was inviolable.[33] Zaghlul, upon his return from exile, criticised attempts to divide the Egyptians and he celebrated the holy unity between cross and crescent.[34] In a special visit to the Patriarch, Zaghlul again emphasised the need for unity.[35] When the Wafd won the election, its egalitarian attitude seemed vindicated. Unfortunately, the mauling received by the Liberals probably only increased their willingness to rely on discreditable tactics.

In 1938, it was the Wafd's turn to be thrashed when it failed to secure a neutral ministry to conduct the elections and all the administrative means at the government's disposal were used against Wafdist candidates.[36] Even setting aside blatant corruption, the innovative scheduling of the election in Upper Egypt, where the prime minister had considerable influence, first inevitably affected later voting in the Delta. Government candidates won by inconceivable majorities; one even obtained a vote of over one hundred per cent.

One French newspaper concluded that the election was a personality contest between al-Nahhas and the King.[37] It would have been more accurate to describe it as a match between Makram representing Coptic participation in politics and King Faruq symbolising the pious Muslim ruler. Makram was the main target. Both he and al-Nahhas were attacked for their hostility to the popular King.[38] Religious and ethnic appeals played a large part in the government's campaign and anti-Coptic circulars were distributed. Misr al-Fatat, the Liberals and the Sadists were all allied with the Palace, and al-Azhar was active on behalf of Palace candidates.

Young Egypt's leader, Ahmad Husain, was released from prison in January 1938 to enable him to promote the Palace cause. In a favourite refrain, he accused al-Nahhas and Makram of worshipping the British,[39] and suggested that Makram had solicited British help to prevent Faruq's religious tutorials with al-Maraghi.[40] Articles in the organisation's newspaper, claimed that ninety per cent of al-Nahhas' supporters were Copts, and that these Copts would back Makram no matter what his crimes.[41] In addition to discouraging Muslim supporters of the Wafd, Young Egypt may have been trying, as Salama Musa charged, to frighten the party's Coptic followers.[42] In a country where election procedures were routinely abused, this was a useful tactic.

The Sadist and Liberal press attacked Makram and his puppet al-Nahhas on every issue. The Sadists accused the latter of being 'enchanted with the idea of sacred leadership imagined by Makram Ubaid Pasha'.[43] Sadist speeches emphasised the Wafd's insensitivity to Muslim religious feeling. The religious coronation ceremony and al-Maraghi's tutorials were returned to time and again.[44] Both Sadists and Liberals complained that Makram, in his capacity as Finance Minister, had literally short-changed al-Azhar.[45] The Copts' lust for power, although well known, required endless comment. Al-Kashkul noted that too many Copts (30 out of 230) had been nominated by the Wafd for Chamber seats, when a more reasonable number would have been three.[46]

Al-Kashkul remarked that Makram and al-Nahhas were hostile to Islam and added that trusting them to protect religion was like throwing a lamb to the wolves.[47] Al-Nahhas was criticised for shamming piety and Makram for hypocrisy in quoting from the Qur'an.[48] The Wafd ministry, according to al-Kashkul, had been a Coptic ministry serving Copts; twisting Makram's slogan, the journal wrote that both al-Nahhas and 'Willam Pasha' were Muslims in religion and Copts in country.[49] The journal somehow managed to reconcile the fact that Makram was leading a Coptic clique with its new charge that he, as a Protestant, was not a genuine member of the Coptic community.[50]

The Wafdist press responded vigorously to this propaganda, but Misr, as the one remaining Coptic daily, bore the brunt of the work. Salama Musa reminded readers who were unlikely to need reminding that the Copts, feeling their interests to be identical with those of their Muslim compatriots, had rejected British and League guarantees for their safety.[51] He condemned al-Siyasa for writing about the Copts as though they were the Untouchables of India.[52]

Musa defended Makram but his real interest was in protecting the community. Makram was able to look after himself. In speeches and interviews he condemned the Ministry for encouraging religious fanaticism.[53] He noted that this had long been a tactic used against the Wafd, and he asserted that he had been so worried by it in 1937 that he had almost resigned from the cabinet.54 Throughout the campaign, al-Nahhas praised Makram and reaffirmed the brotherhood of Copts and Muslims.

Azhari activity in the campaign is one sign of both the politicisation of Egyptian students by the late 1930s and the increased use made of religion in politics. Azhari students travelled the country promoting the idea that a vote for al-Nahhas was a vote against Islam.[56] They booed Wafdist candidates, were ill-behaved and caused particular trouble in cities where there were religious institutes.

Ulama also became involved in the campaign, and sermons in mosques were used to stir up religious feeling. Shaikh Muhammad Ali, of Cairo's al-Rifai mosque, expounded at one Sadist meeting on the close ties between Islam and politics. He blamed al-Nahhas for sundering this tie and announced that Muslims would not allow their religion to be undermined by a Christian enemy like Makram.[57] Shaikh al-Maraghi also used his more lavish talents on the government's behalf; his manipulation of sectarian and religious feeling upset first the Copts and then the British. Like his allies, he used Islam's supposed place in the political arena as grounds for attacking the Copts. His Friday sermons became diatribes against the Copts, Christian missionaries and secularism,[58] as well as a means of guaranteeing his own power by advancing that of Islam. He attacked Makram and, in one radio broadcast slandered the Copts as 'foxes'.[59] He appears to have recommended publicly that Muslims make political choices according to a religious criterion.[60] He declared in one interview that no Muslim who knew anything about Islam could claim to be apolitical, and he added that he wished to see Islam rule Egyptian life because the country's population was mainly Muslim and because the official religion of state was Islam: 'Islam is not like other religions which make a distinction between religion and politics and, in fact, consider them as separate matters and entirely different from one another'.[61] In a February broadcast, he criticised those missionaries who told their Muslims disciples that if they wanted to be heroes of civilisation and pioneers of reform they had to announce that their religion was not good for civilisation.[62] This attack on Epyptian secularists was part of his general defence of Islam from the attacks of others. In one interview, he claimed that Islam was as relevant to the present as to the past.[63] He noted, rather forbiddingly, that non-Muslims should be happy to see a strengthened Islam because it was only the fear of Judgment Day that kept Muslims from slaughtering non-Muslims.[64] In an earlier interview, he insisted that Muslims had always lived on good terms with Christians and Jews and had never persecuted them. He pointed to the strong and adequate guarantees Islam offered non-Muslims; guarantees which consisted of forbidding Muslims 'to attack the life, honour and worldly goods of Christians and Jews'.[65] The welfare of Islam neatly coincided with the Shaikh's own interests and ambitions; it is not clear to what extent he believed his public statements. Even as late as 1937, the British were describing him as holding 'enlightened views'.[66]

Even if the Shaikh and his audience believed implicitly in his ideas, there were many candidates who held a more jaundiced view and encouraged religious feeling as one of the more effective weapons at hand. Hassan Rifaat, who as Under-Secretary at the Interior helped fix the elections, told the British that the government was justified in using the religious issue to win.[67] Prince Muhammad Ali shared, at least in part, this pragmatic view of religion. Lampson recorded that the Prince was open about 'the part played during the elections by the religious element and made no bones about it that he and his family had spurred on the Azharis throughout the country to link up religion with the case against al-Nahhas'.[68] Shaikh al-Maraghi excused his own activity to Lampson in May when he pointed out that all parties used religion and, even if they did not, the Copts had grown arrogant and needed to be reminded of their place.[69] This was a conviction that was shared by the Brethren some ten years later.

However concerned Lampson may have been with anti-Coptic propaganda, he made no move to do anything about it until March. In the wake of a conversation his Oriental Secretary had with a very worried S.A. Morrison of the Egypt Inter-Mission Council,[70] Lampson talked to the prime minister on 8 March. Lampson expressed his dislike of the government's anti-Christian strategy and noted that Shaikh al-Maraghi's behaviour was particularly offensive. Mahmud was conciliatory. He could, in fact, point to the number of statements extolling unity and brotherhood which he had made during the campaign but, as prime minister, he was bound by more constraints than his followers. Mahmud admitted that the propaganda was designed for electoral ends only, as though the fact that the government had a practical aim and did not actually believe its statements made its tactic somehow more acceptable. Mahmud added that he had already called a halt to the Shaikh's activities and that all similar propaganda would cease.[71] Two days later, al-Maraghi insisted to Smart that his aim had not been to increase anti-Coptic feeling. He pointed out that, at the end of his sermon on Coptic 'foxes', he had reminded his audience of their duty to respect the People of the Book,[72] a palliative that must have appeared inadequate to the Copts.

While the government may have decreased its manufacture of religious propaganda after Lampson's conversation with Mahmud, it by no means stopped it.[73] The Wafd continued to be accused of working against Islam, and Makram's objections to the religious tutorials were still retailed. It would have been particularly difficult to prevent individual candidates from appealing to sectarian sentiment in their constituencies. With the election only three weeks away, however, ethnic propaganda had probably already done all the damage it was going to do.

The British intervention was too late and too little. When reassured that the campaign would halt with the election, they were satisfied. Prince Muhammad Ali correctly gauged Lampson's real interest when he told him that al-Maraghi's declarations were anti-Coptic and not anti-missionary.[74] Al-Maraghi had spoken against missionaries and anti-missionary tracts were in circulation,[75] and the British feared a recurrence pf earlier anti-missionary campaigns. Lampson told Shaikh al-Maraghi after the election that he had raised the issue of campaign tactics only because of Britain's indirect interest in the welfare of Egypt and direct interest in the well-being of foreign Christian communities.[76] The Foreign Office seems to have feared that anti-Christian propaganda would spread to the Sudan or lead to an outburst of feeling against the British policy in Palestine,[77] but felt that the propaganda was an 'act of folly which we must regret but cannot in post-treaty conditions prevent'.[78] What this particular official meant was that British strategic interests were not seriously threatened by the government's policy on this issue.

Understandably, the Coptic community was more concerned with the government's methods than the British. Some apparently blamed Makram for giving the government a stick with which to beat the whole community.[79] Murad Wahbah, son of the ex-prime minister Yusuf Wahbah, even resigned his post as Minister of Agriculture because he so disliked his colleagues' anti-Coptic campaign. Unfortunately, he then sacrificed his principles to ambition by accepting a portfolio in the post-election cabinet. Other non-Wafdist candidates such as Najib Iskandar and Tawfiq Dus showed no concern with the government's methods. The latter even had the gall to blame Makram for causing problems between Muslims and Copts.[80] The Wafd was so troubled that its Parliamentary Committee commented, in a petition to the King, that the use of religious issues in the campaign was undermining the spirit of national unity.[81]

The same day that Lampson mentioned his concern to the prime minister, the latter learnt of the anxiety of the Copts from a delegation consisting of the Patriarch and several notables. Mahmud reassured them that the government was doing all within its power to discourage factional strife.[82] The Patriarch's visit, however, may actually have been made at the behest of the Palace and not the community. Such visits were not common, and this one certainly gave the government an opportunity to placate the community which was perhaps even further soothed by the government's timely contribution of £E30,000 towards the Coptic quota for repairs to the Church of the Holy Sepulchre. The Patriarch did, at one point, become directly involved in the campaign. Aziz Mishriqi, standing against Makram in Shubra, paid a call on the Patriarch and the latter returned his visit. Ahmad Mahir, speaking on Mishriqi's behalf, referred to these visits, and so alarmed the Patriarch that the latter issued a statement deploring the use of his name in party politics.[83] Of course, by then, the damage was done.

There was some violence, including attacks on churches, but probably little more occurred than was usual in campaigns. In one typical incident, the Wafdist Coptic candidate, Louis Fanus, was beaten up on the steps of the Asyut courthouse in full view of placid authorities.[84] In general, however, Coptic candidates do not seem to have met with any more violence than Muslim candidates.

After Makram and his followers left the Wafd, the party was relieved of many Copts whose influence could be attacked. Ethnic propaganda was never again so systematically used by the government, Palace or political parties. However, the increase in communal tensions inevitably weakened the position of Coptic politicians and made campaigning difficult.

As *Misr* noted, ethnic appeals were something all Coptic candidates had to face.[85] As fewer and fewer Copts stood for election, the spectre of Coptic conspiracies could not so easily be raised. In the declining years of the monarchy, al-Kutla, with its many Copts, probably occasioned more ethnic comments than any other political party; but not nearly the number it would have faced had it been more of a threat. Its weakness offered it considerable protection.

Not even the Wafd was able to resist an occasional ethnic jab at al-Kutla; only the fact that the latter had inherited so many of the Wafd's Copts allowed the Wafd to use a weapon so long available only to its opponents. On at least one occasion the Wafd accused al-Kutla of sparking communal hostilities.[86] In a more serious incident, partisans of the Muslim Wafdist candidate in the 1943 Jirja by-election mounted an anti-Coptic campaign against the chief contender, Maurice Fakhri Abd al-Nur, who hoped to inherit his late father's seat.[87] Christians were victimised during the campaign and churches were attacked both before and after the election. The election was, of course, fixed; Maurice lost despite the backing of his powerful family and his descent from a great Wafdist and revolutionary figure. His constituency was also one-third Copt.

One way in which Copts tried to circumvent the problem of their religion was to campaign in the company of a Muslim Shaikh.[88] When Fakhri al-Nur was troubled by anti-Coptic propaganda in the 1923 campaign, Zaghlul sent the peerless revolutionary orator, Shaikh al-Qayati, to Jirja to help Fakhri. The Shaikh made the rounds of town mosques claiming that Fakhri was a better Muslim than those Muslims who helped the British by opposing Zaghlul.[89] Fakhri, like so many other Wafdists, went on to win this first Chamber election. Makram, who relied heavily on his knowledge of Islam in campaigns, was the only Copt whose knowledge of the Qur'an and the Hadith was adequate enough to risk quotation; but it was not unheard of for other Coptic politicians to help celebrate Muslim holidays.[90] Sometimes Copts were criticized for exhibiting excessive familiarity with the Prophet Muhammad. When Makram compared al-Nahhas to the Prophet in a speech in September 1929, the opposition press, with some justice, raised a furore.[91] *Al-Siyasa* demanded to know why the Christian Makram did not compare his friend to Christ. The paper added that Makram was only duping the Egyptians by quoting from the texts of a religion in which he did not believe. At the same time, Fakhri Abd al-Nur was accused of poking fun at Muslim beliefs by praying in mosques alongside Muslims.[92]

At times, Copts were faced not only with the implicit shortcoming of not being Muslim, but the more direct one that they were not good Christians. The latter charge was probably meant to deflect Coptic support from a given candidate and was usually aimed at Makram who was particularly vulnerable on this score. None the less, other Coptic politicians were similarly criticised. In 1925, for example, al-Siyasa insisted that Murqus Hanna only went to church to use the pulpit as a political platform.[93]

Copts competing in largely Coptic constituencies against other Copts were less troubled by ethnic propaganda. Except for one election in which Murqus Sergius was standing, appeals were not made to specifically Coptic interests. In 1949, Ibrahim Faraj Masiha, Aziz Mishriqi and Sergius were all competing to represent the same Shubra constituency in the Chamber. Sergius emphasised his long championship of Coptic rights and church reform.[94] He had the added advantage of then being the Patriarch's Wakil or Deputy. He accused Ibrahim Faraj of trying to pass as a Muslim by omitting the Masiha from his name.[95] Those cautious members of the community who found Makram's behaviour worrisome were probably doubly alarmed by Sergius' candidacy. Although the pages of Misr had for some years been filled with complaints about the inequities in Egyptian society, the paper expressed the fear that Sergius' election would give the Chamber a religious colour.[96] What Misr neglected to mention was its fear that the election of the Patriarch's deputy would strengthen the hand of the clergy. The Patriarch, probably under some government pressure, finally forced Sergius to withdraw from the race.[97] Sergius could not, at this point, have helped calm troubled communal waters. Ibrahim Faraj, the victor, felt compelled to promise constituents that he would work to achieve greater equality,[98] a promise that would never have been made had not the issue been raised by Sergius.

It is very difficult to gauge the effect that ethnic and religious propaganda had on voting due to election boycotts and irregularities. It seems to have had little or no effect in 1923-4; the popularity of the Wafd was able to ensure the election of many of its Coptic candidates. Perhaps the ethnic issue influenced or confused voters in later elections. One peasant, only dimly following the candidates' claims and counter-claims, believed that the 1936 election was meant to determine whether the Egyptians wanted to be Copts or Muslims.[99] The Wafd had nominated in his district a Copt lawyer to stand against a local Muslim notable who was trying to take advantage of his religion. Ethnic propaganda may have been employed to more telling effect against al-Kutla than the Wafd, but then al-Kutla was both more obviously Coptic and weaker than the Wafd. When used in campaigns, such propaganda inevitably resulted in minor incidents of violence against Copts. Churches were stoned, priests abused, Copts beaten up and occasionally anti-Coptic demonstrations sparked.[100] Its most serious effect may ultimately have been to make parties reluctant to nominate candidates whose position would be tenuous and Copts reluctant to stand in an election that might put their person, property and community at risk. In addition, by the late 1940s, the political use of Islam by the regular parties had backfired; the public recognised it as hypocrisy and was disinclined to credit either parties or Palace with a serious concern for Islam, or indeed anything other than their own power.

D. COMMUNAL VIOLENCE AND THE ROLE OF THE MUSLIM BRETHREN

Lawlessness was endemic in the Egyptian countryside; the greater the economic pressures, the more visible its manifestations. Muslims as well as Copts were its victims, and it was not always possible to separate ordinary criminal behaviour from violence inspired solely by religious feeling. It was particularly difficult to distinguish cause when the attacks were on individual Copts. <u>Misr</u> was always tempted to ascribe motive to the Copts' Christianity.[101] However, a murder, robbery or beating might just as well have been the result of a grudge or plain mischance. The perpetrator might not have known or cared about his victim's religion. It is, however, possible to say that a quarrel between a Muslim and a Copt or their respective families was likely to be articulated, at least eventually in communal terms.[102] An additional problem for the Coptic minority was that public Christian rituals often roused Muslim ire; Christian processions were attacked and sometimes mocked.[103] Funerals and wedding were set upon, prayer meetings broken up, and priests, so visible in their distinctive garb, abused and beaten.[104] Habit was an important element in this violence. Communal problems were not necessarily the result of political rhetoric; and press incitement probably played a small role in the countryside, if a larger one in the cities. The press was, however, a potent source of rumour, and it exacerbated those problems which it did not actually create. For example, the anti-missionary campaign waged by the government's opponents in 1932-3 was greatly abetted by press incitement. It had unpleasant repercussions for some Coptic individuals and for a time caused grave concern in the community, among the missionaries, and in the Residency.

The ever-alert Coptic press reported relatively little communal violence in the 1920s. *Misr* could perhaps be suspected of turning a wilfully blind eye in its nationalist zeal, but other components of the Coptic press would not have been so tolerant. If violence occurred that could have been interpreted in a communal light, it would have been reported. There was probably more communal violence in the 1930s and still more in the 1940s, when press reports became more frequent and angry. These were both stressful decades; it is not surprising that sectarian violence increased along with the crime rate.

Ethnic problems seem to have occurred more often in places with a goodly number of Copts, but neither a majority nor so few as to render the community almost invisible. Because many Copts lived in urban areas, anti-Coptic outbursts occurred in Alexandria, Cairo, Suez, Tahta, Luxor, Samalut, Suhaj and Zaqaziq. Eruptions were more likely in Upper Egypt than in the Delta; they occurred in almost every province of Upper Egypt except Aswan, a province with few Copts. The government was probably unable and may have been unwilling to protect Copts because the latter claimed repeatedly that the authorities looked the other way when they were victimised.[105] There was some truth in this. Government officials understandably were not eager to be seen taking vigorous steps against activities which many Muslims interpreted as in the best interests of their religion. It would, in any case, have been difficult to prevent sporadic incidents of violence against Copts, and the government may even have seen the Copts as a convenient safety valve for releasing the frustrations of the mob.

From 1946 the Copts focused on the Muslim

Brethren and related religious groups like the Shabab Muhammad and the Young Men's Muslim Association as the greatest threat to both their safety and the concept of national unity. There were frequent reports in that year of the 'aggressive attitude' Brethren in the provinces had taken towards the Copts. Given the tendency to place all postwar outrages on the Brethren, it is probably too easy to lay the responsibility for all anti-Coptic incidents at their door. However, their religious and political beliefs, as well as their zeal in promoting them, played an important role in exacerbating tensions. _Misr_ and _al-Manara al-Misriyya_ described the Brethren as fanatics and worried that Brethren incitement would lead Muslims to despise Egyptians as well as foreign Christians. _Misr_ saw Brethren activity as aimed at the creation of an Islamic state and abhorred their encouragement of anti-Coptic feeling.[106] The Brethren used both mosques and leaflets to spread their anti-Coptic message.[107] So worried were the Copts by al-Banna's ambitions and so often did they hear themselves compared to the Jews in Europe, that they feared that they would meet a similar fate.[108]

The Brethren were not blessed with innovative ideas on the place of religious minorities in a Muslim society. They adhered to earlier and more traditional arrangements and beliefs; these confined non-Muslims to an inferior position, and one which the Copts thought that they had left far behind.[109] Al-Banna repeatedly denied that the Brethren were hostile to minorities; Islam did not tolerate fanaticism.[110] He quoted Qur'anic verses enjoining Muslims to treat non-Muslims well and to tolerate the practice of minority religions.[111] He claimed that Islam taught Muslims to revere Christ and his divine mission.[112] Al-Banna, however, was very critical of the Christian religious establishment.[113]

Even Murqus Sergius conceded that the problem was not with Islam but with those adherents who twisted its teachings.[114] One reason for the Brethren's hostility, despite the tolerance recommended by their religion, was a belief that the Copts had acquired far more power than they had a right to have. All authority exercised by non-Muslims over Muslims was offensive and against the God-given order. In a Brethren demonstration in Shubra, one speaker called on businesses to fire all their Coptic employees;[115] apparently some Brethren believed that only Muslims had a right to employment. The Shabab Muhammad shared a similar view: they announced that they would boycott objects and services provided by Copts. They claimed that they would allow non-Muslims freedom of worship only if they paid the old jizya tax.[116]

The Wafd came in for particular criticism; the Brethren thought the party was too attentive to the needs of non-Muslims,[117] and allowed the Copts to play too great a role in its councils. One Brethren ideologue, Muhammad al-Ghazzali, wrote that the Wafd had allocated 150 out of 214 constituencies to Coptic candidates in the 1923 election, an exaggeration so gross that sensible people would have dismissed it out of hand had they not been hearing similar charges for years.[118] The Brethren attacked the Wafd for displaying hostility towards Islam and blamed the party's enmity on 'William Makram, the Egyptian Englishman and Muslim Christian'.[119] Ten years later, al-Banna was reproving al-Nahhas for his love of Christians, an attachment which many Copts had come to doubt.

In 1946, Misr published a series of articles attacking the Brethren by Salama Musa. For some weeks, the Brethren let them go unanswered and finally al-Banna published an open letter, which was addressed to the Patriarch, objecting to Misr's campaign.[120] Even if Yusab had been a strong Patriarch, Musa's articles would have worried him; they were useless as information since both the Copts and the government were aware of the problems the community faced. Musa's purpose was probably to strengthen the community's resolve to do something and to press the government by embarrassing it. The only problem with this was that the articles were most likely to anger the Brethren who would direct that anger against individual Copts. The Metropolitan of al-Sharqiyya province, Anba Aghabiyus, had been working to ease sectarian tensions; Musa's articles only complicated his task.[121] The Patriarch, unable to reach Musa, threatened to cancel Misr's annual subsidy of £E1,400 if he continued to publish inflamatory articles. Since the paper's owners relied heavily on the subsidy, Musa was obliged to resign as editor.[122]

During 1946, there were attacks on Christian churches in Cairo.[123] In March 1947, tensions in Zaqaziq flared when an angry mob burned a Coptic church. Communal relations there had been strained for at least two years, partly due to Brethren activity.[124] It is not clear, however, that the Brethren were directly responsible for inciting the mob on that March day. Al-Banna, in a letter to the Patriarch, denied Brethren involvement and said that he had sent a letter to branch organisation reminding them of their obligation to dhimmis.[125] He, the Patriarch and the Majlis Milli all exchanged letters emphasising the importance of national unity.[125] The government, whose officials had taken no action to stop the mob, sent an apology to the local bishop; and the provincial governor organised a festival of unity, to which an estimated 10,000 people came.[127] According to the British, the government was partly responsible for the incident because it was still employing ethnic propaganda, through elements like the Brethren, against the Wafd.[128] In fact, only a month after the fire a Palace official announced that the government would support the efforts of the Muslim Brethren.[129]

Both the Copts and the British, the former perhaps with alarm and the latter with irony, noticed that the arson occurred at the same time as the British evacuation of the Delta.[130] Some Copts were beginning to doubt the wisdom of British withdrawal. The only official British reaction was a letter to the prime minister, expressing concern about the riot and for the safety of British lives and property in the area.[131] The Brethren blamed the fire on the long-suffering British, and their newspaper Ikhwan al-Muslimin accused the British of trying to divide the Egyptians. When Murqus Sergius held a meeting to discuss the arson, he was accused of collaborating with the British.[132] Both Akhbar al-Yawm and Ruz al-Yusuf speculated that the British provoked the incident to demonstrate that the Egyptians were incapable of governing themselves.[133]

Various cabinets courted the Brethren in the hope of directing their prodigious zeal against political opponents. In early 1944, for example, the Wafd was reported to be playing up to the Brethren, in part by paying them a subvention, in the hope that they could count the Brethren as allies when their cabinet fell.[134] In postwar Egypt, most political groups recognised the value of and competed for Brethren support. Both al-Manara al-Misriyya and Misr were angered by the government's failure to control the Brethren. In October 1948, Murqus Sergius drew up a petition, calling for the dissolution of the Brethren and all organisations which mixed religion and politics and were detrimental to equality, and then circulated it among Coptic notables.[135] In the wake of a number of political assassinations and the discovery of the Brethren's secret paramilitary apparatus, the government finally acted by dissolving the society in December 1948. The Copts were relieved,[136] but the Brethren continued to operate underground and were implicated in the sacking of a Coptic church in 1949.[137] They were also involved in a number of minor incidents, like removing crosses from the tops of churches.[138]

The Brethren were not hampered in their activities for long. The Wafd returned to power, partly through Brethren assistance, in 1950 and felt weak enough to need continued Brethren support. Despite the fact that its relations with the Brethren were not always easy, the latter were allowed to operate relatively freely. The Copts were somewhat disenchanted with the Wafd party by this point; and, although Misr did claim to be pleased with the formation of a Wafd cabinet, it was unhappy with the party's conciliatory attitude towards the Brethren.[139] Certainly the paper had good reason to be concerned. During the campaign, the Wafdist press had praised the principles of the Brethren, defended them from various criminal charges and called the persecution of previous governments unjustified.[140] Misr again insisted that any society which wanted to divide the Egyptian people by establishing a religious dictatorship be banned.[141] The paper continued to attack the Brethren,[142] and, by the autumn of 1951, was publishing daily comppaints about incidents of religious fanaticism. There were anti-Coptic demonstrations in Cairo, with marchers shouting 'Christianity is finished in Egypt', 'One faith in Egypt - Islam', and 'Today the English, tomorrow the Christians'.[143] One activity of the Cairene Brethren at this time was to visit heavily Coptic quarters and paint crosses on the houses.[144]

To the Copts, the government's December 1952 decision to restore the property of the Brethren was a sign that the Wafd had finally renounced its commitment to national unity. The sacking of a Suez church less than a month later underlined the fact that the Wafd would put its own interests ahead of the safety of those people who had for so many years seen the party as their best hope.

On 4 January 1952, a Coptic church, school and Benevolent Society building were destroyed and three Copts murdered by a mob in Suez. The government did nothing to stop the mob but probably had little control in an area that had become a theatre for guerrilla war against British troops. There was much fighting and little co-ordination. The mob, deciding that religion dictated political allegiance, murdered the three Copts on the assumption that they must be British spies. Some blamed the British for the incident,[145] but it was also rumoured that the Brethren were responsible.[146] There were certainly many Brethren fighting in the area. The Patriarch, probably under considerable political pressure, exonerated the Brethren publicly.[147] Makram Ubaid, always ready to befriend the Brethren, visited Hassan al-Hadaibi, the Supreme Guide; and the two of them, along with other Brethren officials, chatted about the inviolability of national unity. Makram then invited al-Hadaibi to visit the Patriarch and the two men did so on 18 January.[148]

Coptic communities all over Egypt responded quickly. Telegrams of grief and protest were sent to the government and the Palace. Copts demanded that the government act promptly.[149] The Patriarch and the Majlis Milli announced that Christmas would be a time of mourning and not celebration. The government tried to dissuade the church from making this very public gesture, but failed. Ibrahim Faraj, the only Copt in the cabinet, carried the government's apologies to the Patriarch. Al-Nahhas both telephoned the Patriarch and paid a personal visit to express his grief and announced a grant of £E5,000 to rebuild the church.[150] The Lay Council rejected the compensation and demanded an investigation in its place; as Misr commented, the money could not replace lives. The paper blamed the government for failing in its duty to protect all Egyptian citizens.[151] The government finally agreed to conduct an investigation.[152]

The Copts were understandably annoyed that the government made no official announcement about the incident. Cairene Copts demonstrated outside the Patriarchate and one group shouted that although the burning of the church was a great crime, silence was an even greater crime.[153] This was a comment on what was believed to be the inadequate response of both the Patriarch and the government. Al-Nahhas followed Faraj's footsteps and made two visits to the Patriarchate in a further attempt to placate angry Copts, and finally made a statement deploring the incident.[154] Messages of brotherhood were broadcast on the radio, and the Palace sent two of its people to the Patriarch to express King Faruq's grief. To many Copts, however, these fine words meant little.[155] Copts particularly questioned the behaviour of Ibrahim Faraj; the editor of Misr condemned Faraj for failing to take steps to clear the atmosphere which had produced the incident.[156] Many Copts wanted Faraj to resign.[157]

The contemporary Egyptian historian, Muhammad Anis, believes that the incident was so well handled by the government that it did not lead to the threatened withdrawal of the Copts from the nationalist movement.[158] His conclusion seems unduly optimistic. The Copts did not think that the government's response was satisfactory; they would have preferred to see the Wafd take more of a stand on communal violence before it culminated in the Suez riot. They had unsuccessfully begged the government for some time to keep a tighter rein on the Brethren. In many ways, Suez was the *coup de grâce*, the blow that destroyed any remaining confidence in the goals of the nationalist movement and in the ability of Copts and Muslims to co-exist in peace. As *Misr's* articles continued to prove, the Copts were not conciliated by the government's actions. Without a commitment to equality, the nationalist movement could not retain the loyalty of a minority no longer certain of its place in a shifting society.

E. ANOTHER COPTIC RESPONSE TO PRESSURE

As noted in Chapter Two, the government's increasing attempts to control Coptic voluntary associations indicated some kind of concern that these societies were being used as platforms from which to defend Coptic interests and challenge the government. It was not, of course, only the Copts about whom the government was concerned. Political activities peripheral to the established system had multiplied and were increasingly threatening the state's stability. There were, however, surprisingly few attempts to form Coptic communal political organisations and only one example, although an important one, of a group with political goals growing out of a religious association. This reluctance to so visibly defend Coptic interests by forming associations specifically devoted to the attainment of minority political interests is related to a minority belief that calling attention to one's community in what would be viewed as a belligerent and provocative fashion, would not only not protect the community, but would cruelly expose it to Muslim ire. Some Copts, however, clearly believed that the only defence was a vigorous one; otherwise, the Copts would be increasingly taken advantage of by their compatriots and the government.

In 1949, Ramsis Jabrawi, a lawyer, labour leader and Misr correspondent,[159] founded a Coptic party, the National Democratic Party, in reaction to troubled communal relations. The party criticised restrictions on the freedom of worship and demanded that they be lifted.[160] It also complained about discrimination and inadequate parliamentary representation; one call was for the establishment of proportional representation. Despite Misr's support, the party soon floundered. Copts perhaps failed to join it from a fear that it would aggravate an already bad situation.

The most important Coptic political organisation was the Coptic Nation (al-Umma al-Qibtiyya). Active between September 1952 and 1954, the group's roots lay in the violence and discrimination of the 1940s and 1950s. Sometimes called the Coptic Brethren, it modelled itself on the Muslim Brethren in its mix of politics and religion and its desire to purify the Coptic religion. Both societies manipulated traditional religious symbols in their quest for power. The Coptic Nation was the only organisation that Copts determined to alleviate the community's grievances could join.[161]

Founded by a young lawyer, Ibrahim Fahmi Hilal, the group had many young professional members, including Ramsis Jibrawi. Hilal and his friends had talked about the need for a Coptic political organisation since secondary school, but the catalyst was added only with the burning of a Coptic church in Suez in January 1952.[162] The party claimed to be a social or religious organisation and not a political one, but its activist bent ensured its rapid growth among the disenchanted young.[163]

Al-Umma identified the Muslim Brethren as the chief threat to the Copts and, like the Brethren, illegally collected arms and trained members in their use.[164] Because the Brethren asked for an Islamic state, al-Umma demanded a Coptic one. Hilal now claims that this was only propaganda and that the group's real goal was the separation of religion and state.[165] Nevertheless, the demand may have been a serious one at the time. The party had a flag and a motto that declared that God was their king, Egypt their country, the Gospels their law and the Cross their badge.[166] They published pamphlets and a newspaper and asked the government to give the Copts their own radio station. They complained that the census undercounted Copts, and they demanded a constitutional amendment naming the Copts a 'nation' (umma).

Members worked to strengthen religions feeling. Cultural differences in Egypt were no longer so acute so the society took old, devalued symbols, like the Coptic language, and tried to reinvest them with meaning.[167] Members assumed a puritanical outlook, studied and spoke Coptic, wore special clothes and adhered strictly to Biblical injunctions.

The group also supported church reform and opposed the Orthodox religious establishment. Much of its emphasis was on cleaning the church's Augean stables because it saw internal corruption and disunity as responsible for the community's external weakness. One solution advocated by the Society was the deposition of Patriarch Yusab,[168] and it is curious that members focused on this rather than fighting the government as a way of settling their grievances. The Patriarch asked for and received a government order dissolving the Society in 1954.[169] The Society went underground and made an unsuccessful attempt to kidnap the Patriarch and later to assassinate him. Leading members of the Society, including Hilal and Jibrawi, were tried, convicted and sentenced to several years in prison.

F. SUMMARY

Ethnic propaganda should not be considered in isolation from the more purely religious propaganda because it was a natural outgrowth and, for some, the constant companion of the use of religion in politics. Increasing concern with the public role of religion made a reliance on sectarian appeals more profitable and eventually drove many Copts out of the political arena. The formation of the Society of the Coptic Nation in 1952 indicates how disaffected many young Copts had become.

Those legitimate political parties who leant most heavily on ethnicity and religion tended to be tied, at least at times, to the Palace. Their tactics were as indicative of their weakness as was the alliance. As Grafftey-Smith observed, 'Islam in danger' was a popular card for non-Wafdists to play.[170] The Wafd, perhaps somewhat more honourable in its greater strength, represented 'as near as possible...a lay tendency in Egyptian administration and politics'.[171] Both Campbell and Smart agreed that the Wafd had always raised less of a furore over religious questions than had Palace elements and the 'agnostic Liberals'.[172]

For many years, the Copts expected that whenever the Wafd came to power, the state's attitude towards them would change for the better. The anti-Wafdist press also promoted this view, but its aim was to prove that the Wafd acted to limit Muslim access to the institutions of an Islamic state and that it showed insufficient sensitivity to the religious feelings of the majority. The Wafd made very little use of the ethnic weapon; but as its strength and support faded, it did turn increasingly to religion and finally ended by pandering to groups like the Muslim Brethren. Its inability to stand fast on its secular principles undermined everything for which it had originally fought. The most severe censure, however, must be reserved for those others, principled or otherwise, whose activities not only weakened the new political system, but sometimes made mockery of the old one by placing Coptic lives, property and the right to worship in jeopardy.

NOTES

1. FO.141/744, 1167/2/33.

2. There is evidence to suggest that criticism of the role Makram played in the Wafd dates to 1923. See _al-Kashkul_, 31 August 1923, 4.

3. _Al-Kashkul_, 20 September 1929, 5.

4. FO.141/744, 1167/2/33.

5. _Al-Siyasa_, 9 September 1929, PPF.

6. Leland Bowie, 'The Copts, the Wafd and religious issues in Egyptian politics', _The Muslim World_ 67 (1977), 123; Charles Smith, 'The Crisis of Orientation: The Shift of Egyptian intellectuals to Islamic subjects in the 1930s', _International Journal of Middle Eastern Studies_ 4 (1973), 399. Ahmad Shafiq believed that national unity was not threatened until 1929, and that after that date the Egyptians became two peoples, Copts and Muslims. See his _Hawliyat Misr al-Siyasa_, vol.6, pp.1253-4.

7. Bowie, 'The Copts, the Wafd and religious issues in Egyptian politics', 120-1.

8. _Ibid._, 106.

9. In the 1926 election, for example, Haikal's Wafdist opponent accused him of atheism and of working to destroy Islam. The Wafdist _al-Balagh_ also accused the Liberals of atheism, in

spite of the formal collaboration of the two parties. Charles Smith, 'Muhammad Husayn Haykal: An Intellectual and Political Biography', unpublished PhD thesis, University of Michigan 1968, pp.221-3.

10. Al-Balagh, 6 February 1930, 1.

11. FO.407/197, No.97 (Enclosure), Situation Report, 19 September-2 October 1923; FO.371/20883, J1411/20/16; FO.371/20884, J3105/20/16; Lampson/Killearn Diaries, 10 March 1937, pp.48-9; 30 May 1936, p.144.

12. FO.371/13843, J1744/5/16.

13. FO.141/722, 616/50/36; FO.141/644; 158/149/37. This is curious given Palace tied with the Patriarch, but may reflect the Patriarch's loss of power over a large segment of his flock.

14. Several such articles appeared in the summer of 1937. See Misr, 27 July 1937, 1.

15. Al-Misri, 26 June 1937, PPF.

16. The Deputy was Abd al-Raziq Wahbah al-Qadi. Chamber Debates, second session, 21 July 1937.

17. FO.141/481, 158/49/37.

18. FO.371/20914, J3809/369/16.

19. Two of the Regents, Sabri and Izzat Pashas, did not think that the Copts were behind the objections since al-Nuqrashi and Ahmad Mahir were also known to oppose the religious ceremony. FO.141/644, 158/49/37.

20. CCEH, Abdin Palace Files on the Copts, F2/D2, card 641, letter dated 1 December 1937.

21. The Patriarch, in a rather fulsome response, compared the King to King Solomon. Al- Muqattam, 24 January 1938, PPF.

22. Al-Ahram, 30 December 1937, PPF.

23. Al-Ahram, 20 December 1937, PPF.

24. Zaghib Mikhail, Farriq Tasud!, pp.122-6.

25. Misr, 16 May 1950, 1. The romance ended unhappily when Ghali murdered his estranged wife and then shot himself in 1976. Herald Tribune, 13 December 1976, 5.

26. Tariq al-Bishri, 'Misr al-Haditha Bain Ahmad w-al-Masih', Al-Katib, 121 (1971), 146; al-Kashkul, 24 August 1923, 3.

27. Ibid.

28. Al-Kashkul, 17 August 1923, 19, and 24 August 1923, 3; al-Bishri, al-Katib, 145.

29. Ibid.

30. See al-Kashkul, 31 August 1923, 4.

31. Al-Kashkul, 6 July 1923, 4.

32. Fakhri and Ahmad Mustafa Abu Rahab frequently ran against one another and the latter,

according to Sad Fakhri Abd al-Nur, always raised the ethnic issue. Interview with Sad Fakhri Abd al-Nur, 17 May 1979.

33. Ahmad Qasim Judah (ed.), al-Makramiyyat (Cairo, n.d.), pp.163-4.

34. Egyptian Gazette, 21 September 1923, 3.

35. Al-Bishri, al-Katib, 148.

36. Grafftey-Smith described the process succinctly in 1931: 'The Mudir instructs the Mamur Markaz, the Mamur Markaz instructs the umda and possibly sends out a couple of camel corps to each village to assist and there goes the electorate, trooping to the polls'. FO.471/15404, J1110/26/16.

37. Journal des Debats, 20 April 1938, PPF.

38. One such circular was entitled 'al-Kharijan ala al-Malik' ('Outsiders/Rebels Against the King) PHS, American Mission in Egypt Archives.

39. Egyptian Gazette, 25 January 1938, 5.

40. Misr, 24 March 1938, 2. This theme was explored in at least one election handbill. Al-Nahhas was said to have objected to the religious tutorials in order to please Makram. See handbill entitled 'Makram', PHS, American Mission in Egypt Archives.

41. Misr al-Fatat, 31 January 1938, 11.

42. Misr, 3 February 1938, 1.

43. Egyptian Gazette, 6 January 1938, 5.

44. Al-Balagh, 20 March 1938, PPF.

45. Makram was so worried by this criticism that he lodged complaints with the Parquet against al-Balagh and al-Siyasa. Al-Balagh, 16 January 1938, PPF.

46. Al-Kashkul, 25 February 1938, 4, 6.

47. Al-Kashkul, 11 February 1938, 34-5.

48. Ibid.

49. Al-Kashkul, 25 February 1938, 4.

50. Ibid., 1-2.

51. Misr, 6 January 1938, 3, and 3 February 1938, 1.

52. Misr, 15 January 1938, 1.

53. Al-Misri, 8 March 1938, PPF; al-Ahram, 9 March 1938, 9.

54. He said that al-Nahhas had dissuaded him. Al-Wafd al-Misri, 10 March 1938, PPF.

55. Al-Ahram, 18 January 1938; al-Manara al-Misriyya, 11 March 1938, quoted in Samir Bahr, 'al-Aqbat fi al-Hayat al-Siyasiyya fi Misr', p.703.

56. FO.371/21947, J1211/6/16.

57. La Réforme, 29 March 1938, PPF.

58. Misr, 15 February 1938, 1.

59. FO.371/21945, J893/6/16.

60. US Department of State Archives, No.883.00, General Conditions/73, Political Summary, March 1938.

61. US Department of State Archives, No.383.1163/46.

62. US Department of State Archives, No.383.1163/45, Despatch dated 21 February 1938.

63. *Misr*, 7 March 1938. 1.

64. US Department of State Archives, No.383/1163/47, quoting *La Bourse Egyptienne*, 19 March 1938.

65. US Department of State Archives, No.383.1163/46, quoting the *Egyptian Mail*, 5 March 1938.

66. FO.371/21947, J1097/6/16. See also R. Campbell's view in FO.371/19068, J411/110/16. Al-Maraghi's reappointment as Rector of al-Azhar was owing, in good part, to British pressure. FO.371/19069, J615/110/16; J1671/110/16.

67. FO.371/21947, J1097/6/16.

68. Lampson's unpublished Diaries, 3 April 1938, p.60.

69. FO.371/21947, J2086/6/16.

70. FO.371/21946, J1079/6/16.

71. FO.371/21946, J1079/6/16. After speaking to the prime minister, Lampson took up the same matter with the Minister of Foreign Affairs. FO.371/21946, J1153/6/16.

72. FO.371/21946, J1079/6/16.

73. Leland Bowie suggests that after several weeks the Liberals halted their campaign against the Copts because they feared that events might get out of hand. This generous interpretation sees forced. Bowie, 'The Copts, the Wafd and religious issues in Egyptian politics', 125.

74. Kedourie, *The Chatham House Version*, p.200.

75. US Department of State Archives, No.383.1163/45, 21 February 1938.

76. FO.371/21947, J2086/6/16. One article in *al-Kashkul* had resurrected all the false reports about missionary activity which had surfaced in 1933. FO.371/21946, J1079/6/16.

77. Ibid.

78. FO.371/21946, J1211/1/16.

79. FO.371/21945, J859/6/16.

80. *Egyptian Gazette*, 19 March 1938, 7-8.

81. Translated copies of this petition were sent to England for distribution to the British people. FO.371/21946, J1100/6/16.

82. *Al-Ahram*, 9 March 1938, 9.

83. Misr, 24 March 1938, 3.

84. The long-suffering Fanus took only twenty-two votes to his rival's 13,000 in a district which had sent him to parliament in previous elections. Egyptian Gazette, 12 March 1938, 7-8.

85. Misr, 26 March 1946, 1.

86. Al-Balagh, 20 March 1946, 2; Misr, 23 March 1946, 1.

87. FO.371/35529, J880/2/16; FO.371/35530, J1321/2/16; FO.371/35531, J1626/2/16.

88. Both Ibrahim Faraj and Mirrit Ghali said they did this. Interview with Ibrahim Faraj, 13 June 1979; interview with Mirrit Ghali, 8 May 1979.

89. Interview with Sad Fakhri Abd al-Nur, 17 May 1979.

90. Fakhri Abd al-Nur celebrated the holy month of Ramadan by having the Qur'an recited in his house in the evenings during the 1929 election campaign. Tariq al-Bishri, al-Katib, 152.

91. Al-Akhbar, 10 September 1929, PPF.

92. The Wafdist al-Balagh only accused al-Siyasa of trying to divide the nation. Al-Siyasa, 9 September 1929; al-Balagh, 9 September 1929, PPF.

93. See al-Watan's vigorous protest of this on 4 February 1925, 1. Sometimes, however, the Coptic press did indicate some disappointment with the religiosity of a particular Coptic politician.

94. See the entire issue of al-Manara al-Misriyya, 4 January 1950. This is curious since he was now supporting the Patriarch's insistence on clerical privilege in the matter of the monastic endowments.

95. Al-Manara al-Misriyya, 30 November 1949, 4.

96. Misr, 5 January 1950, 1.

97. Misr, 11 January 1950, 1.

98. Ibid.

99. FO.141/757, 491/10/36.

100. In 1945, for example, there were anti-Coptic demonstrations in Suhaj, Asyut and Alexandria. FO.371/45918, J777/3/16.

101. Misr, 8 July 1937, 5.

102. Urban Egyptians were more likely than the peasantry, who did not trust government institutions, to settle such disputes in court.

103. Following the 1930 election of the Copt Yaqub Bibawi to the town council of Samalut in Bani Suwaif, a mock funeral procession paraded around the town and shouted threats at the houses of those Copts and Muslims who had voted for Bibawi. La Bourse Egyptienne, 1 May 1930, 4. Sixteen years later, during a Senate race, loudspeakers in the

mosques of Samalut would inform voters that Bibawi was the candidate of the Coptic party and stones would be thrown at a local church.

104. For examples of unpleasant incidents, see Misr, 18 May 1934, 2, 2 October 1945, 2, and 1 December 1951, 1; al-Manara al-Misriyya, 5 October 1949, 1.

105. See Misr, 4 December 1930, 2, 17 May 1934, 1, 8 July 1937, 5, 2 October 1945, 4, and 11 May 1946, 3; al-Manara al-Misriyya, 4 February 1935, 7.

106. Misr, 9 May 1946, 1.

107. In May 1946, for three days before the Prophet's birthday, the Shabab Muhammad abused the Copts from a Luxor mosque. Predictably, this sparked ugly anti-Coptic incidents. Misr, 11 May 1946, 3, 18 April 1947, 1, and 19 April 1947, 1.

108. Al-Manara al-Misriyya, 24 April 1947, 1-4; Misr, 18 April 1946, 1, and 5 April 1948, 1.

109. Misr sometimes portrayed al-Banna as a throwback to an earlier age. Misr, 18 April 1946, 1, 1 May 1946, 1, and 5 April 1948, 1.

110. Al-Musawwar, 22 March 1946, 5.

111. Charles Wendel (ed.), Five Tracts of Hasan al-Banna, pp.119-21.

112. Egyptian Gazette, 27 December 1946, 3.

113. For al-Banna, true Christianity was not to be found in the Vatican or amidst 'the luxury of the Patriarches'. DW HBM (QM), Security Report 4515, 21 November 1940.

114. French Embassy Archives, Cairo, Box 144, File 31/2, Revue des Periodiques Arabes, 31 December 1947, quoting al-Manara al-Misriyya, 27 December 1947.

115. Mikhail, Farriq Tasud!, p.111, quoting Misr, 3 May 1947.

116. It is not unreasonable to assume, as did Misr, that the Brethren supported this as well. Misr, 26 April 1946, 1, and 1 May 1946, 1.

117. Al-Nadhir, Year I, No.12 (26 Jamad Thanin 1357: mid-summer or autumn 1938), 3-7.

118. Muhammad al-Ghazzali, Our Beginning in Wisdom, p.100.

119. Al-Nadhir, Year I, No.11 (12 Jamad Thanin 1357: 1938), 4-6.

120. Misr, 13 May 1946, 1.

121. It is not clear whether the Metropolitan was working on his own or at the behest of the Patriarch. DW Abdin Palace Archives, Tawaif Diniyya 1, Mamorandum 15, 8 December 1946.

122. Ibid. These were not, however, the last articles which Musa contributed on the subject of

the Brethren. Musa was arrested in both 1946 and 1947 as a communist, but the government's action probably had more to do with Musa's rabble-rousing among the Copts.

123. Misr, 1 April 1947, 1.

124. Ibid., 1, 4.

125. FO.371/63020, J1743/79/16.

126. FO.371/63020, J1952/79/16.

127. FO.371/63020, J1630/79/16.

128. Ibid.

129. Mikhail, Farriq Tasud!, p.114, quoting Misr, 27 April 1947.

130. FO.371/63020, J1630/79/16.

131. FO.371/62991. J2406/13/16.

132. Al-Manara al-Misriyya, 31 May 1947, 1-3.

133. FO.371/63020, J1743/79/16; FO.371/63029, J2411/13/16.

134. FO.371/41316, J223/14/16 and J906/14/16.

135. Sergius wrote the petition after receiving letters of concern from Copts. FO.141/1296, 506/3/48.

136. Misr, 10 December 1948, 1.

137. In Giza. FO.371/73466, J919/1015/16.

138. FO.141/1333, 38/58/49G.

139. Misr, 4 March 1950, 3.

140. FO.371/80348, E1016/42/50; FO.371/80351, E1018/1/16.

141. Misr, 1 November 1950, 1.

142. See Misr, 2 June 1950, 1, and 5 May 1951, 1.

143. See The Times, press clippings on Egypt, 13 November 1951. Even the Vatican was concerned.

144. Interview with Zahir Riyad, Chairman, African Studies Department, Coptic Higher Research Institute, 1 June 1979.

145. Suez notables issued a pamphlet calling for inter-communal co-operation and warning against plots to divide Copts and Muslims. See Misr, 8 January 1952, 2. Muhammad Anis seems to accept this interpretation when he suggests that it was confirmed that one of the riot's instigators worked in a British military camp, but it is difficult to extrapolate any firm meaning from this. See Anis, Hariq al-Qahira 26 January 1952 (Beirut 1972), pp.23-5.

146. Misr, 18 January 1952, 2.

147. Not only was the Patriarch visited by Ibrahim Faraj and al-Nahhas, but Makram Ubaid also paid a call.

148. Misr, 18 January 1952, 1. Al-Hubaidi had actually been trying to make the organisation a respectable one. He was a man of a different cast

of character from al-Banna, and had sat, at one time, on the bench of the Cour de Cassation. By early 1952, he had begun to lose control of the Brethren. See FO.371/96870, J1018/1/16; FO.371/96874, J1018/104/16 and J1018/117/16.

149. DW Abdin Palace Archives, Tawaif Diniyya 1.

150. Misr, 8 January 1952, 1.

151. Ibid., and 11 January 1952, 1.

152. The Copts also wanted it proved that the three Copts who were murdered were not British spies.

153. Misr, 14 January 1952, 1, and 15 January 1952, 2.

154. Misr, 11 January 1952, 1, and 17 January 1952, 2.

155. Misr, 18 January 1952, 1.

156. Misr, 11 January 1952, 1.

157. Anis, Hariq al-Qahira, pp.23-4.

158. Ibid., pp.22-5, 45-7.

159. He was adviser to several unions in the early 1950s and was the second vice-president of Abbas Halim's Egyptian Labour Party. FO.141/763, 506/33/31; 506/2A/31, and 506/2/31.

160. Misr, 11 June 1949, 1.

161. Interview with Zahir Riyad, Chairman, African Studies Department, Coptic Higher Research Institute, 1 June 1979.

162. Interview with Ibrahim Fahmi Hilal, 22 May 1979.

163. Hilal claimed that the society, within one year, had a membership of 92,000. Ibid.

164. The 1964 government order banning the party claimed that it had created a paramilitary organisation. Bahr, 'al-Aqbat fi al-Hayat al-Siyasiyya fi Misr', p.354.

165. Interview with Ibrahim Fahmi Hilal, 22 May 1979.

166. Bahr, 'al-Aqbat fi al-Hayat al-Siyasiyya fi Misr', p.354.

167. See Abner Cohen on this subject in Two-Dimensional Man (Routledge and Kegan Paul, London, 1974), p.103.

168. French Embassy Archives, Box 144, File 31/2, letter to the Ambassador from S. Fishawi, a member of the society, August 1954.

169. Bahr, 'al-Aqbat fi al-Hayat al-Siyasiyya fi Misr', p.359.

170. FO.141/702, 225/8/32.

171. FO.371/20914, J3809/369/16.

172. FO.141/752, 353/59/33; FO.141/749, 20/31/33.

CONCLUSION

Religion is for God alone and the Homeland for ALL ITS PEOPLE[1]

This formulation, which expresses the conviction that there was a fundamental separation between religion and state, seems to have been coined by Tawfiq Dus in 1911. It was the only statement to come out of the Coptic Congress in Asyut that was not only accepted by many Muslims, but was raised by them to the level of political cant. It became a favourite slogan of nationalists and politicians.[2] Although cheapened by frequent repetition and increasingly irrelevant with time, it neatly summarised the main political hope of the best-educated and most vocal segment of the Coptic community; a segment which wanted to institute a state free from religious bias and a religion free from state interference and, at the same time, gain its own freedom from ecclesiastical control.

With the creation of a new political system came new opportunities to realise that hope. It was to this end, an escape from the uncertainty of marginality, that the Copts' advocacy of democratic government, secularism, civil equality and integration in its widest sense were aimed. Many worked to develop a new collective identity with new ways of interacting for Muslims and Copts. Throughout the 1920s, their enthusiasm for this political and social experiment was matched by that of many Egyptian Muslims who seemed willing to make concessions of power in order to achieve true unity.

This experiment was advanced by a number of secondary factors. Political energies were largely consumed by the struggle against the British who assisted the development of unity by providing an enemy against whom Copts and Muslims could join forces. In addition, relatively few groups were competing for political power; and the main one, the Wafd, helped ensure that Coptic participation in politics was not only tolerated but applauded. It was, if course, an advantage that the new political ideas were from outside Egypt and were not associated with either ethnic group, although eventually Western political forms were discredited in the minds of some by their association with foreign Christian power. However, early and fairly widespread adherence to these ideas and forms permitted the emergence of a Coptic élite with political aspirations. In the traditional structure, of course, Coptic notables had found their opportunities for advancement and power restricted to the civil service and the ecclesiastical and economic sectors; and, as noted previously, the first and last did not always allow unlimited advancement.

At a time when the British were slowly and reluctantly relinquishing power to the Egyptians, some Copts thought it folly to cling to the older ways whose safety appeared both illusory and unnecessary when the new arrangements offered a heady, if uncertain, reward for victory. It was clear that Muslims were going to outlast the British, and that a partnership with the former held the promise of a security far greater than that provided by the latter, whose first priority had never been Coptic well-being.

Not all Copts subscribed to this new venture or supported it without reservation. Some, and particularly those in the church, were reluctant to risk their special governing arrangements and culture on what they saw as the far from certain success of this experiment in political and social integration. They wished instead to protect a system they knew and understood, one which had worked reasonably well in the past and which had, perhaps more important, given them power. True integration would have completely upset the balance of power in the Coptic community, and there were some who had already found the struggle with laymen in the Majlis Milli trying enough. In addition, these Copts were suspicious, not necessarily of the intentions of Muslims offering equality, but of the durability of the Muslims' support and of their ability to deliver genuine equality.

As many of these Copts suspected, Egypt was not a tabula rasa, and centuries of a particular political tradition could not be so easily erased. There was little agreement on what was an appropriate role for religion in this society, and religion inevitably worked its way into the new arrangements. One scholar has pointed out how difficult it was for

Muslims, who had long seen themselves as the natural political community, to accept Western political and social concepts which dictated sharing power with people they had scorned and ruled for centuries. For Christians, of course, the borrowing was easier. They had little to lose and much to gain, or so many thought. No matter what effect this new system had on the church, it still held out the promise of more individual power and greater equality.[3]

Over the course of this period, Egyptians were drawn into a closer relationship with their state. The number of government institutions with which Egyptians had to deal and the number of statutes which regulated their lives increased. This may be particularly true of the Copts over whom the government had always had less control. Mahmud Azmi, for example once remarked on Ali Mahir's interest in reducing communal privileges so that the government would one day have equal power over all its citizens.[4] Mahir's 1936 non-Muslim personal status law would have increased, to no little extent, government control in this most sensitive of areas. Given the clear direction of this new association with the state, it was perhaps not unwise to aim for a formal say in running that state. Even had the millet not been weakened from within by reformers seeking to eliminate corruption and waste and by secularists eager to be free of its restrictions, it would eventually have been destroyed from without by a state hungry for more power.

The Egyptian state's attitude towards the Copts manifested itself in three somewhat contradictory practices.[5] It aided the maintenance of Muslim supremacy by countenancing private and practising public discrimination. At the same time, it adhered to a political ideology which declared all men equal and which tried to replace a communal identity with a national one. It also offered, in a practice long sanctioned by tradition, the status of the majority to those who assimilated. While few Copts followed the path of ultimate assimilation and converted to Islam, a number of politicians managed to some extent to divest themselves of much of their ethnic identity. In 1922, the state did contemplate a fourth method of dealing with minorities, _viz_., the formal incorporation of communal loyalties into the political system; however, the rejection of proportional representation in parliament by the Constitutional Commission ruled out this approach. This was not, however, the last time that some Copts would express a preference for this method which would have guaranteed their separate political existence but would not, at least initially, have granted them appreciably more power. By 1946, with political activity increasingly fragmented, minority representation made more sense. Even Salama Musa who had scoffed at the idea in 1922, became an advocate. In a much divided parliament, even a small number of closely aligned delegates could have considerable influence.

During much of the 1920s, hopes invested in the new political arrangements seemed to bear some fruit, and many Copts were reasonably satisfied with the progress made towards equality. The state of the economy had some bearing on this progress. There seemed to be more for everyone, so Muslims could afford to be generous to the Copts. Later, when there seemed to be less, Muslims were more inclined to interpret any improvement in the Copts' situation as an unacceptable loss to them. The increasingly desperate economic situation from the 1930s and the government's unwillingness to help the poor had a deleterious effect on intercommunal relations by increasing social tensions generally. Coptic hopes began to evaporate. The failure of Egypt's democratic institutions to work as planned and the increasing role played by Islam in political mobilisation caused great unease in Coptic circles. Copts came to realise that the price of political acceptance was assimilation, the sacrifice of their ways for those of the majority.

Coptic support for the nationalist movement was useful. It brought more activists into the struggle and proved Muslim tolerance to sceptical outsiders. It was never, however, either essential to the success of the movement or vital to governing the country. As the British relinquished more and more power, the need for the Copts was less and less. Once the Anglo-Egyptian treaty was signed in 1936 and an agreement to end the Capitulations obtained in 1937, there was less of a need to accommodate non-Muslim minorities in order to appear democratic, tolerant and deserving of genuine independence in Western eyes. Factored into many concessions to minorities prior to this time had been a strong desire to seem modern. Much of the public and greatly celebrated fellowship between Copts and Muslims during the 1919 revolution was, while by no means forced, the result of a need to make a strong point to Europe about the equality of all Egyptians. Later, Rushdi explained his wish to guarantee minorities equal rights in the 1923 constitution by saying that this would deprive the British of grounds for maintaining the third Reserved Point. Constitutional Commission members debated whether or not proportional representation would prevent British intervention on behalf of minorities. Then, in 1932-3, the Egyptian government showed great concern to limit the successes of the anti-missionary movement lest it damage Egypt's chances of obtaining a favourable treaty and ending the Capitulations. This is not, of course, to suggest that there was no desire or will among the Muslim population to accord an equal place in Egyptian society and politics to the Copts, but there was also a recognition that it was essential to project a picture of Egypt as a state ready to assume modern political responsibilities and to banish forever the image of a medieval Muslim polity.

From the 1940s, there were not only fewer restraints on how the Egyptians preferred to conduct their politics, but the West had also come to seem a somewhat discredited model which was less and less deserving of emulation. The usefulness of those Westernised Copts, who could so eloquently present Egyptian views to the European powers was diminished. These marks of Westernisation, such as Makram's first name, Ghali's French poetry and the Wisas' Protestantism, became increasingly suspect.

As it became clear that the new government was not able to carry out the promises made in the constitution, some Copts, like those whose voice _Misr_ was, first pointed out defects in the hope of remedying them and later became more and more prepared to promote the special interests of their group. This was perhaps less a matter of protecting their cultural integrity than of preserving that quantum of power that had previously been held by them. They had been willing to make sacrifices in some areas in order to achieve what were perceived of as greater gains in others. Once the latter turned out to be mainly illusory, they felt compelled to fight for all the old protections. Perhaps one of the reasons the reformers were still fighting so hard for control of the church at the end of the monarchy was that they saw it as a vehicle for fighting oppression and protecting the community. If they could only reform the institution, then they could make it serve the whole range of present-day needs from running schools to lobbying with the government. The clergy, in general, vitiated this plan not only by their near-sightedness and stubbornness, but by their quiescent loyalty to the monarchy. The activities of the Liaison Committee and the church's behaviour over the Suez murders and church sacking in 1952 are some of the first signs of a break in that quiescence.

The 1938 election campaign was one turning point. It forced upon many Copts the realisation that they could not act in politics without risk to themselves, their party and their community. Some perhaps saw that both Palace and government were following the practice of medieval rulers who allowed the mob to vent its frustrations upon a vulnerable and disliked minority as a means of defusing resentments having little to do with minority behaviour and much generally to do with that of the government. A more serious turning point came with the general loosening of political restrictions at the end of the war. Intolerence of the Coptic right to participate in politics became widespread among Muslims. As Misr dismally concluded in the late 1940s, there was no equality in Egypt, nor was there ever likely tp be any.

The extent to which Coptic communal demands snowballed in this decade is curious, but may merely reflect the wide-ranging complaints levelled at minority behaviour by Muslims. Complaints about the prohibition on ringing church bells and the refusal to admit Copts to the Arabic Language Academy were routinely coupled with grimmer accounts of communal violence and often received the same weight. These grievances seemingly compounded one another and added up to a whole that may have seemed far greater than the sum of the parts. Discrimination no doubt was more of a problem in the Egypt of 1947 than the Egypt of 1927, but the more vigorous and belligerent discussion of the problem by both sides certainly added to that problem and increased tensions. The persistence with which the Copts continued to voice unattainable goals is indicative of both a degree of communal hysteria and a certain obliviousness to reality. Some Copts seemingly failed to realise how powerless the community was; others perhaps hoped that the advertisement of their grievances would spark European intervention or British determination to remain in Egypt.

No doubt part of the Copts' belligerence was due to a keenly felt sense of betrayal; while discrimination had been an accepted and legitimate part of the traditional system, it was a clear moral and legal wrong in democratic Egypt. There was a larger gap between the ideal and the real, and this perhaps unsettled them. They understood their position under the millet system; in democratic Egypt, they could not be sure where they stood. The Constitution, which was supposed to define the parameters of political activity, had almost ceased to be a meaningful document. Certainly, changes had occurred, but there was still no consensus on where non-Muslims fitted into this society. Individual Copts could no longer predict what kinds of behaviour were in bounds and what kinds were out, what would earn Muslim approval and what would draw fire. The anxiety caused by the uncertainty of their position must have been more trying, at least in some ways, than the old system, whose limits they had understood.

By this time, Muslims were inclined to see a malign Coptic hand in everything. The Copts were thought to be conspiring to monopolise the civil service, take over the government and help the British and the missionaries, in their nefarious designs. Muslims did not, however, develop any coherent and well-thought-out conspiracy theories. Not a single individual, nor any group or movement, in Egypt, sought to build political power on an anti-Coptic foundation alone. In some cases, the use of sectarian propaganda was almost offhand; in all cases, it was a supplement and not the main diet. This propaganda was never very systematic or sophisticated. It most often echoed traditional sentiments about the place of the Copts and expressed the feeling, sometimes in print and sometimes in violence, that as a people the Copts had risen above their proper station. This is a key point; as Shaikh al-Maraghi acutely observed, the problem was as much social as it was political or religious.[6] A reversal of the natural order had occurred, and this demanded an adjustment in the relative positions of the two peoples. As early as 1923, al-Kashkul complained that it was not proper for the Copts to attack Muslim notables.[7] What the journal meant was that a people who were suspect by their very nature were not in a position to cast aspersions on the loyalty, competence and sincerity of Muslims, the people in whose interest the state had traditionally been organised.

Curiously, given Samala Musa's advanced and sometimes eccentric views, his career provides a kind of paradigm for the community. Like so many of his co-religionists, he voiced little discontent with the British role in Egypt before the First World War. However, his European experience gave him a strong interest in new intellectual and political trends; and he spent a few months, sandwiched in between periods spent in France in 1910-1, writing for al-Liwa, then under the moderate Uthman Sabri. His interest in nationalism does not seem to have flowered at this time, but he became, after the war, a committed nationalist and secularist and was, for some time, an ardent supporter of the Wafd. These commitments also paralleled those of many Copts. As the father of Egyptian socialism, he was not interested in church or communal affairs; like many Coptic politicians, he leant towards a wider national or even international perspective. In spite of this, he had retreated, by the mid-1940s, into communalism. For him too, the turning point may have been the 1938 election. He was at that time writing editorials for Misr, and carried the heavy burden of trying to counter anti-Coptic propaganda. Through 1937, he still showed a strong secularist bent. He insisted, in that year, for example, that the amount of religious instruction provided in government schools was entirely adequate. Musa was always a forceful advocate, whether of nationalism or Coptic rights, but his influence on the Coptic community was greatest between 1945 and 1952 when he was promoting Coptic interests in the pages of Misr. His communalism was less disliked than his earlier social and political radicalism, but some in the community saw his new views as dangerously provocative. They felt that the risks involved in repeated confrontation with Muslims on a wide range of issues were too great for so weak a community. However, the despair that lay beneath those views was shared. Like other Copts, Musa came to realise that the experiment had failed and that the Copts, as a community, required special protection. The clergy, much compromised by inaction and quiet submission, could not be relied upon and no longer seemed to have the power, although they did appear to awake to the danger in their midst towards the end of the period. Musa, as one remedy, called for proportional representation in parliament and the abolition of Islam as the religion of state. His chances of instituting the one were about as great as his opportunities of disestablishing the other. He also demanded that Muslim religious groups be controlled by the government and their political activities prohibited.[8] He, who had once promoted secular institutions, insisted on the provision of Christian religious instruction in government schools and air time for Christian religious broadcasts. If the Copts could not be genuinely equal, then they would have to work towards a position that would grant them safety through separation.

A small segment of the Coptic community did become, along with Salama Musa, politicised in the fact of this increasing Muslim hostility. However, with the sole exception of Murqus Sergius who, like Salama Musa, belongs to a special category, not one Coptic politician became a communal politician. The policies and thinking of most Coptic politicians so mirrored that of their Muslim counterparts that their presence at all levels in the government may have done little to ensure Coptic interests a hearing, let alone acceptance.[9] The behaviour of Ibrahim Faraj in the case of the Suez church-sacking is evidence of how little such politicians could do for the community. Some Coptic politicians had the good fortune to die before political activity became fraught with difficulties, and they were not replaced. Others gave up politics. Those who remained active until the bitter end may have worked behind the scenes to ease sectarian tensions, but they did not defend Coptic rights publicly. By 1952, they could not have done so without opting out of the political system and without risking their personal safety. They had been co-opted into the ruling élite and their community had to manage as best it could without their talents. At least in the early period, these politicians had helped to serve as an integrating force; but, by the 1940s, there were fewer Coptic politicians who could serve as a buffer for the community, and the influence of those who were active was diminished. As the church was no longer the middleman in government-communal affairs and had been discredited within the community, a serious gap in representing the community's interests to the government ultimately resulted. As early as 1939, Misr stated baldly that the Copts were thinking of abandoning Egyptian patriotism because they had failed to build any kind of national consensus with the Muslims, in the paper's view, Coptic access to public life was and was likely to remain limited.[10] The community had begun to feel that political action was ineffective, if not dangerous, and it withdrew the precarious safety of its ethnic boundaries. Elie Kedourie's conclusion about the position of the Jews in the Iraqi state has its parallel here: in terms of their civil responsibilities, the Copts were Egyptians first and Christians second; when it came to apportioning rights, their Christianity suddenly became paramount and assigned them to an inferior place.[11]

Although co-operation among Muslim and Coptic élite facilitated political unity, a portion of the Muslim élite was partly responsible for exaggerating ethnic divisions and manipulating them for political gain. However large a share of the responsibility they bear for destroying the political hopes of the Copts, they were still less frightening than those who were unwilling to work within the constitutional limits. It was, after all, the constitution which established the Copts' legal equality and their right to participate in politics. The Copts, because of their numbers and geographic situation, were confined to operating within the bounds of the institutional framework. It was not that they opposed the rules, although they disliked the constitutional article naming Islam the religion of state, but that they objected to the fact that the rules had not been followed and that there was so little consensus regarding their legitimacy. Many had believed, for a very long time, that the rules offered the community its very best hope. The only Coptic group to act outside the law was the Society of the Coptic Nation, whose purpose was to create a radically different society in part by increasing the distance between Muslims and Copts. Other groups, like the Muslim Brethren, Misr al-Fatat, and the Shabab Muhammad also wished to create a different kind of society, constructed on a basis other than the constitution, but they could act more easily outside the law.

The political appeals of such groups were often based on Islam. This perhaps forced the state and the regular parties into more extreme positions on religion than they might otherwise have taken. Muslims running against other Muslims would beg the voters to elect them as the candidates with the greatest desire to protect and glority Islam. Each group hoped to be seen as the one, true defender of the faith; in this endeavour, Coptic support could only be an embarrassment. Complaints about discrimination disconcerted the government but did not move it into action. On the one hand, it was failing to provide what it was legally obliged to provide; on the other, its very failure could be commended as Muslim zeal.

Muslims clearly relied on their religious identity to assist them in political organisation. Religious and ethnic differences were manipulated by individuals, organisations and the state to advance interests that had little to do with ethnicity or religion. Perhaps because it promised at best little pay-off and at worst to exacerbate problems, the Copts, by and large, did not use their ethnic identity to organise in the political arena. As the need for communal defence grew, they began to use community organisations that were essentially non-political as platforms from which to make political claims and defend minority interests. It was only towards the end of this period that the Copts turned to their ethnicity to organise for political gain. The Society of the Coptic Nation is, of course, the most noteworthy example of this phenomenon. The Liaison Committee is perhaps an equally interesting development: various minorities, normally hostile to one another, combining forces to promote their joint interests.

The attempt to achieve equality was not a total fiasco, and it would be wrong to stress the Copts' relative failure to become part of the political community in the 1940s at the expense of their success in doing so during the revolution and its aftermath. The middle class perhaps benefited the most from the limited integration which was all that was achieved. The real situation of the Coptic peasantry probably remained largely unimproved although they too may have profited from the peaceful relations that the nationalist movement for a time bestowed. The rich, as always, were exempt from most problems. The new system gave them more power, but their money and European tastes gave them the option of leaving any time difficulties arose. These men, however, no matter how concerned they were in the late 1940s, did not choose to emigrate, perhaps because their economic power seemed secure.

It was, of course, the Copts' success, however modest it might have appeared to them, that caused a backlash in the last part of the monarchy. Until almost the end, the Copts were generally adequately represented, at least numerically, in politics; and opposition to their participation, although seemingly widespread, was not unanimous. Statements of brotherly love had become a standard part of political theory. There was some acceptance of the idea that religion ought not to be a factor in politics, the bureaucracy or any sector of civil life. What discrimination there was was usually unofficial and informal; the constitutional article naming Islam the religion of state mandated no specific discriminatory practices to be carried out by the government. The Copts succeeded in making some kind of place for themselves, even if it was not quite the place for which they had hoped. The notion of equality had its adherents, and at least held a potential for some future ascendancy.

Perhaps the most persistent, if not always fully conscious, debate among Copts concerned how best they could protect their community. Traditionalists argued for the time-favoured belief in silent invisibility. Even opponents of this nothing-ventured, nothing-gained-but-nothing-lost-either timidity had to concede that it was a policy that had helped preserve the community through the centuries and had allowed its people to live in relative peace. If permanent subservience was the cost of this invisibility and hence this peace, then many Copts were willing to pay it. The belief that the Copts were calling too much attention to themselves and, in doing so, risked rousing Muslim ire, was one which was heard frequently in this era. Copts worried that Copts in the Wafd were too many and too visible, that Makram's behaviour was too provocative and his power too great, that Salama Musa and Murqus Sergius were too belligerent in their defence of their community, and that the attitude of the Coptic press was too extreme.[12] From this perspective, no Copt had the right to follow his conscience, lest his co-religionists be punished for its dictates. This view became at times even more extreme and assumed that no Copt could or should possess a consciousness separate from that of his people. The periodic criticisms of Coptis politicians who had not met communal desiderata occasionally expressed a sense that these men had fallen from grace and become lost to their community.

By contrast, there were many who believed that it was, at least by the late 1940s, too late and too humiliating to overlook difficulties in the hope that the trouble would go away. They had believed in the possibility of equality and fought hard for it, and had come to see most of their hopes disappointed. To acquiese willingly again to a marginality which relegated the Copts to perpetual, if tolerable, vulnerability seemed no way to serve the community. So instead of working with Muslims to obtain equality, a door that now seemed permanently shut, they began to press Muslims and the Muslim state for the granting of protections both old and new. They wanted to retain their communal courts and their right to adjudicate family disputes, but they also demanded complete freedom to build churches and broadcast sermons. Men like Musa and Sergius fought aggressively for solutions to age-old discriminatory practices that feelings of brotherhood and unity had in no way obliterated. Some Copts clearly had been changed by the political ideas and events of the period: while others gave up and withdrew to the precarious safety of communal boundaries, they assumed a new spirit of activism that no amount of trouble seemed able to diminish. They were determined not to allow Muslims to establish their place ever again.

After more than thirty years, the Copts had still not been able to persuade Muslims that they were loyal to Egypt. An aura of being a fifth column clung to them despite their hard work, sacrifice and energetically expressed Anglophobia. Their difference in religion was assumed to be synonymous with a difference in interests, interests which, if pursued unhindered, could harm the Egyptian state and her Muslim majority. For example, one of the Copts murdered in Suez was assumed by many to be a British spy. The sole evidence to this was that he was a Christian. Makram's position, although hardly as pitiable as the fate of the three Suez Copts, was at times unenviable. Accused over and over again of preventing, in his desire to preserve the British presence, the achievement of a treaty, he was immediately charged with acceding to every single British demand in 1936 in his haste to attain said treaty. Whatever action he took, some kind of communal cast could be put on it.

The Copts, of course, had never been completely without power. Egypt, due to its homogeneity, had experienced less ethnic strife than many other parts of the Middle East. Violence was muted and sporadic; whatever the hatreds, they had rarely exploded in massacre and pillage. Copts had always had at least limited access to positions of authority in Egyptian society. New opportunities had been opened to them in the twentieth century, and what many middle-class and perhaps even upper-class Copts probably resented most was what they saw as the gradual restriction or withdrawal of those opportunities in the 1940s. Men who possessed the talent for politics or diplomacy were consigned to a career in business. Others who entered the professions with ambitions for judgeships or professorships of medicine found themselves stuck on the middle rungs of the career ladder. Many worked hard to obtain a good education only to be denied the rewards which were earned so easily by Muslim colleagues. Untimately, the Assistant Oriental Secretary's 1937 conclusion was perhaps pessimistic but not wrong: as long as the Copts were content to remain underdogs and not aspire to power, Islam would prove tolerant.[13]

Despite the clear benefits of majority status and growing Coptic beliefs that they could only win second place and that their lives and property were at risk, few Copts opted out of this system by emigration or conversion. This says something about the strength of Coptic ties to family, community and religion and the effectiveness of the informal sanctions that could be brought to bear on the wayward. Communal bonds grew stronger and more relevant as the pressure on the Copts increased. Secularism had failed, and in its place, kinship, communal networks and the church became increasingly important to those trying to escape the effects of discrimination. This was not surprising given the degree of external pressure. Their "Copticness", relevant to relatively few public situations in the 1920s, had become pertinent to every conceivable situation in the 1940s. In the latter decade, the aim of many Copts, Misr and al-Umma al-Qibtiyya alike, was to convince the Copts to act not as individuals pursuing disparate goals, but as a group defending common interests. In part, the Copts used their surprising freedom to form communal societies with differing aims to organise their defence. While there were occasional Muslim objections to the Coptic exercise of this prerogative, there was no serious attempt to limit it. Some communal organisations, such as the Society of the Coptic Nation, tried to strengthen faith as a means of strengthening both the will to resist and the possibilities for collective action. Members of al-Umma al-Qibtiyya perhaps hoped that in increasing the distance between Copts and Muslims by emphasising their differences rather than their similarities, they might ultimately be able to reduce the number of clashes. Attempts such as these were finally defeated by the fall of the monarchy and the institution of a new regime which was less tolerant of all kinds of peripheral activity. The Copts no longer had to fear a gradually worsening communal situation with its concomitant of violence, but equality remained as distant a notion as ever.

NOTES

1. 'Al-Din l-Allah w-al-Watan l-il-Jami.'

2. The first part of the equation appeared in an Arab nationalist manifesto published in Cairo during World War I. It is quoted in Sylvia Haim's Arab Nationalism: An Anthology, pp.83-8. Al-Nahhas quoted it as late as 1951 when its bearing on reality was slight. Misr, 17 January 1951, 1. See also Misr, 3 March 1934, 1, for an early editorial comment on the slogan's meaninglessness.

3. Robert Haddad, Syrian Christians in Muslim Society, p.88.

4. Mahmud Azmi, al-Ayyam al-Mia (Maktabat al-Nahda al-Misriyya, Cairo, 1939), p.49.

5. See an interesting article by Milton Esman on state policies towards minorities, 'The Management of Communal Conflict', Public Policy 21 (1973), 49-78.

6. FO.371/20914, J3809/369/16.

7. Al-Bishri, al-Katib III, 146.

8. See his mocking suggestion that the Copts form organisations like those of the Muslim Brethren and Shabab Muhammad in Misr, 10 May 1946, 1.

9. See a discussion on the phenomenon with relation to other minorities in Cynthia Enloe, Ethnic Soldiers: State Security in Divided Societies (Harmondsworth, Middlesex, Penguin, 1980), p.226.

10. Misr, 3 March 1939, 1.

11. Kedourie, The Chatham House Version. p.306.

12. Senator Jirjis Antun was one who expressed concern about Misr's tone. Misr, 28 May 1947, 1.

13. FO.407/221, part 122, No.5 (Enclosure), An Appreciation of the Situation of the Copts under the new regime in Egypt by Mr. Hamilton, 1937.

BIBLIOGRAPHY

UNPUBLISHED SOURCES : European and American

Archives

1. Church Missionary Society Archives, CMS, London. Record relating to CMS activities in Egypt
2. French Embassy Archives, Cairo, Egypt. Box 144 relating to the Copts
3. Presbyterian Historical Society, Philadelphia, Pennsylvania. American Mission in Egypt Records
4. Public Record Office, Kew. Foreign Office Archives on Egypt of the following series:
   FO.407 (Confidential print)
   FO.141 (Embassy and Consular Archives)
   FO.371 (General Correspondence)
5. National Archives, Washington, D.C. US Department of State Records on Egypt

Theses, Papers and Diaries

1. Baer, Gabriel, 'Basic Factors affecting Cohesion and Change in Modern Egyptian Society', unpublished paper delivered at the Center for Middle Eastern Studies, Harvard University, 1970
2. Deeb, Marius, 'The Wafd and its Rivals: The Rise and Development of Political Parties in Egypt, 1919-1939', unpublished DPhil thesis, Oxford University, 1971
3. Al-Feki, Mustafa, 'Makram Ubayd: A Coptic Leader in the Egyptian National Movement', unpublished PhD thesis, University of London, 1977
4. Ibrahim, Ibrahim, 'The Egyptian Intellectuals between Tradition and Modernity: A Study of Some Important Trends in Egyptian Thought, 1922-1952, unpublished DPhil thesis, University of Oxford, 1967

5. Kazziha, Walid, 'The Evolution of the Egyptian Political Elite', unpublished PhD thesis, University of London, 1970
6. The Lampson/Killearn Diaries, Middle East Centre, St. Antony's College, University of Oxford
7. Rugh, Andrea, 'Religious Community and Social Control in a Lower-Class Area of Cairo', unpublished PhD thesis, American University, 1978
8. Seikaly, Samir, 'The Copts under British Rule, 1882-1914', unpublished PhD thesis, University of London, 1967
9. Smith, Charles, 'Muhammad Husayn Haykal: An Intellectual and Political Biography', unpublished PhD thesis, University of Michigan, 1968

UNPUBLISHED SOURCES : Egyptian

Archives

1. Coptic Archaeological Society, al-Abbasiyya, Cairo
2. Dar al-Kutub, Centre for Contemporary Egyptian History, Cairo. Abdin Palace Archives, including: Palace Press files (Arabic and European languages); biographical card index (probably compiled by the Palace in the 1920s): index cards summarising some of the Palace files which were not available to researchers 1977-79
3. Dar al-Mahfuzat, Cairo, Pension Records
4. Dar al-Wathaiq, Cairo, Government archives

Theses and Memoirs

1. Abd al-Nur, Fakhri, 'Mudhakkirati', unpublished typescript in the possession of Sad Fakhri Abd al-Nur, 1942
2. Bahr, Samira, 'Al-Aqbat fi al-Hayat al-Siyasiyya fi Misr', unpublished PhD thesis, Cairo University, 1977
3. Fahmi, Abd al-Rahman, 'Mudhakkirat', unpublished diaries held in Dar al-Wathaiq Mahfuzat Raqm 1
4. Hinain, Sadiq, 'Mudhakkirat', unpublished typescript held in the Coptic Archaeological Society, S/1, 1959

PUBLISHED SOURCES : European Languages

Abduh, Muhammad. (1966) <u>The Theology of Unity</u> (Risalat al-Tawhid), trans. by Ishaq Musaad and Kenneth Cragg, George Allen and Unwin, London

Adams, Charles. (1963) Islam and Modernism in Egypt, Oxford University Press, London

Agwami, M.S. (1969) Communism in the Arab East Asia Publishing House, London

Alexander, Rev. J.R. (1930) A Sketch of the Story of the Evangelical Church, Whitehead Morris, Alexandria

Amin, Ahmad. (1978) My Life, trans. by Issa Boullata, E.J. Brill, Leiden

Arnold, Thomas. (1965) The Caliphate, Routledge and Kegan Paul, London

Ayub, Nazih. (1980) Bureaucracy and Politics, Ithaca Press, London

Baer, Gabriel. (1962) A History of Landownership in Modern Egypt, 1800-1950, Oxford University Press, London

———. (1964) Population and Society, Routledge and Kegan Paul, London

———. (1969) Studies in the Social History of Modern Egypt, University of Chicago Press, Chicago

Barth, Frederik. (1970) 'Introduction' in Frederik Barth (ed.) Ethnic Groups and Boundaries, Allen and Unwin, London

Behrens-Abouseif, Doris. (1972) Die Kopten in der Ägyptischen Gesellschaft von der Mitte 19 Jahrhunderts bis 1923, Klaus Schwarz, Freiburg Im Breisgau

Bell, Wendell and Freeman, Walter (eds.). (1974) Ethnicity and National Building, Sage Publications, Beverly Hills

Berque, Jacques. (1972) Egypt: Imperialism and Revolution, trans. by Jean Stewart, Faber and Faber, London

Betts, Robert. (1975) Christians in the Arab East, Lycabettus Press, Athens

Binder, Leonard. (1964) 'Ideological Foundations of Egyptian-Arab Nationalism' in David Apter (ed.), Ideology and Discontent, Free Press of Glencoe, New York

———. (1964) The Ideological Revolution in the Middle East, John Wiley and Son, New York

Blackman, Winifred. (1927) The Fellahin of Upper Egypt, George G. Harrap, London

Bowring, Sir John. (1840) Report on Egypt and Candia, W. Clowes and Son, London

The Census of Egypt (1917), Vol.2. (1921), Government Press, Cairo

Cleveland, William. (1971) The Making of an Arab Nationalist: Ottomanism and Arabism in the Life of Sati al-Husri, Princeton Studies on

the Near East, Princeton
Cohen, Abner. (1974) Two-Dimensional Man, Routledge and Kegan Paul, London
Colombe, M. (1951) L'Evolution de l'Egypte 1924-1950, C.P. Maisonneuve, Paris
The Coptic Congress Held at Assiout on March 6, 7 and 8, 1911. (Translation of proceedings.) No place, no publisher, no date
Coulson, N.J. (1964) A History of Islamic Law University Press, Edinburgh
Cromer, Lord. (1908) Modern Egypt (two volumes). Macmillan, London
The Cry of Egypt's Copts. (1951) Phoenicia Press, New York
Cunningham, Alfred. (1912) Today in Egypt, Hurst and Blackett, London
Davison, Roderic. (1963) Reform in the Ottoman Empire, 1856-1876, Princeton University Press, Princeton
Dawn, Ernest. (1973) From Ottomanism to Arabism, University of Illinois Press, Urbana.
Deeb, Marius. (1979) Party Politics in Egypt: the Wafd and its Rivals, 1919-1939, Ithaca Press, London
Dekmejian, R.H. (1972) Egypt under Nasir. University of London Press, London
Ebeid, W. Makram. (1921) Complete Independence v. the Milner Scheme (or the Zaghlul-Adli Issue), The Caledonian Press, London
Egypt, Ministry of Finance. (1952) Annuaire Statistique 1947-48 and 1948-49, Imprimerie Nationale, Cairo
———. (1921-1936) Budget of the Egyptian State, annual Government publication, Cairo
Enloe, Cynthia. (1973) Ethnic Conflict and Political Development, Little Brown, Boston, Mass.
———. (1980) Ethnic Soldiers: State Security in a Divided Society, Penguin Books, Harmondsworth
Fischer, Max (ed.). (1921-52) The Egyptian Directory (annual publication), Imprimeri Lencioni, Cairo
Galt, Russell. (1936) The Effects of Centralization on Education in Modern Egypt, American University in Cairo Press, Cairo
Gendzier, Irene. (1966) The Practical Visions of Yaqub Sannu (Harvard Middle Eastern Monographs IV), Center for Middle Eastern Studies, Cambridge, Mass.
Ghali, Ibrahim Amin. (1969) L'Egypte Nationaliste et Libérale, Martinus Nijhoff, The Hague

Ghali, Mirrit. (1953) The Policy of Tomorrow, trans. by Ismail al-Faruqi, American Council of Learned Societies, Washington, D.C., originally published in Arabic 1938
al-Ghazzali, Muhammad. (1953) Our Beginning in Wisdom, trans. by Ismail al-Faruqi, American Council of Learned Societies, Washington, D.C., originally published in Arabic 1951
Giamerardini, P. Gabreile. (1958) I Primi Copti Cattolici, Edizionia del Centro Francescano di Studi Orientali Christiani, Cairo
Gibb, H.A.R., and Bowen, Harold. (1957) Islamic Society and the West (two volumes), Oxford University Press, London
Gibb, H.A.R. (ed.). (1932) Whither Islam?, Victor Gollancz, London
Grafftey-Smith, Lawrence. (1970) Bright Levant, John Murray, London
Haddad, Robert. (1970) Syrian Christians in Muslim Society, Princeton University Press, Princeton
Haim, Sylvia. (1962) Arab Nationalism: An Anthology, University of California Press, Berkeley
Harik, Ilya. (1977) 'The Ethnic Revolution and Political Integration in the Middle East', in Saad Ibrahim and Nicholas Hopkins (eds.), Arab Society in Transition, American University in Cairo Press, Cairo
———. (1977) 'Mobilization Policy and Political Change in Rural Egypt', also in Ibrahim and Hopkins
Harris, Murray. (1925) Egypt under the Egyptians, Chapman and Hall, London
Hartmann, Martin. (1899) The Arabic Press of Egypt, Luzac and Co., London
Heikal, Mohamed. (1978) Sphinx and Commissar: The Rise and Fall of Soviet Influence in the Arab World, Collins, London
Heyworth-Dunne, J. (1968) An Introduction to the History of Education in Modern Egypt, Frank Cass, London
———. (1950) Religious and Political Trends in Modern Egypt, no publisher, Washington, D.C.
al-Hilali, Neguib. (1943) Report on Educational Reform in Egypt, Bulaq Press, Cairo
Hodgson, Marshall. (1974) The Venture of Islam: The Gunpowder Empires and Modern Times, vol.3, University of Chicago Press, Chicago
Hourani, Albert. (1947) Minorities in the Arab World, no publisher, London

Hourani, Albert. (1961) A Vision of History: Near Eastern and Other Essays, Khayats, Beirut

———. (1962) Arabic Thought in the Liberal Age, 1798-1939, Oxford University Press, London

Husain, Taha. (1954) The Future of Culture in Egypt, trans. by Sidney Glazer, American Council of Learned Societies, Washington, D.C.

Hussein, Mahmud. (1973) Class Conflict in Egypt, 1945-1970, Monthly Review Press, New York

Hyde, Georgie. (1978) Education in Modern Egypt, Routledge and Kegan Paul, London

Indicateur Egyptien. (1892, 1895) Imprimerie Générale, Alexandria

Issawi, Charles. (1947) Egypt: An Economic and Social Analysis, Oxford University Press, London

———. (1954) Egypt at Mid-Century: An Economic Survey, Oxford University Press, London

———. (1963) Egypt in Revolution: An Economic Survey, Oxford University Press, London

Jankowski, James P. (1979) Egypt's Young Rebels Hoover Institute Press, Stanford, California

Jones, Kenneth. (1976) Arya Dharm: Hindu Consciousness in the Nineteenth-century Punjab University of California Press, Berkeley

Joseph, John. (1961) The Nestorians and their Muslim Neighbors: A Study of Western Influence on their Relations, Princeton University Press, Princeton

Elie, Kedourie. (1966) Afghani and Abduh, Frank Cass, London

———. (1970) The Chatham House Version and Other Middle Eastern Studies, Frank Cass, London

———. (1976) 'Religion and Secular Nationalism in the Arab World', in A.L. Udovitch (ed.) The Middle East: Oil Conflict and Hope, Lexington Books, Lexington, Mass.

Kedourie, Elie and Haim, Sylvia (eds.). (1980) Modern Egypt: Studies in Politics and Society Frank Cass, London

Kelly, Sir David. (1952) The Ruling Few, Hollis and Carter, London

Kerr, Malcolm. (1966) Islamic Reform: The Political and Legal Theories of Muhammad Abduh and Rashid Rida, University of California Press, Berkeley

Khalid, Khalid Muhammad. (1953) From Here we Start, trans. by Ismail al-Faruqi, American Council of Learned Societies, Washington, D.C., originally published in Arabic 1950

Khouri, Mounah. (1971) Poetry and the Making of Modern Egypt, E.J. Brill, Leiden

Kilpatrick, Hilary. (1974) The Modern Egyptian Novel, Ithaca Press, London

The Koran Interpreted. A Translation by A.J. Arberry, Part 1. (1973) Macmillan, New York

Kotb, Sayed. (1970) Social Justice in Islam, trans. by John Hardie, Octagon Books, New York, originally published in Arabic 1945

Landau, Jacob. (1953) Parliaments and Parties in Egypt, Israel Oriental Society, Tel Aviv

Lane, Edward. (1908) Manners and Customs of the Modern Egyptians, Everyman's Library, London, originally published 1836

Laqueur, Walter. (1956) Communism and Nationalism in the Middle East, Frederick Praeger, New York

LaRoui, Abdallah. (1976) The Crisis of the Arab Intellectual: Traditionalism or Historicism, University of California Press, Berkeley

Leeder, S.H. (1973) Modern Sons of the Pharaohs, Arno Press, New York, first published 1918

Marlowe, John. (1965) Anglo-Egyptian Relations, 1800-1956, Frank Cass, London

———. (1970) Cromer in Egypt, Elek Books, London

Marsot, Afaf Lutfi al-Sayyid. (1977) Egypt's Liberal Experiment, 1922-1936, University of California Press, Los Angeles

Masriya, Y. (1976) 'A Christian Minority: The Copts in Egypt', in W. Veenhoven (ed.), Case Studies on Human Rights and Fundamental Freedoms, vol.4, Martinus Nijhoff, The Hague.

Mehta, Asoka and Parwardhad, Achyut. (1942) The Communal Triangle in India, Kitabistan, Allahabad

Meinardus, Otto. (1970) Christian Egypt: Faith and Life, American University in Cairo Press, Cairo

———. (1977) Christian Egypt: Ancient and Modern, American University in Cairo Press, Cairo

Mellini, Peter. (1977) Sir Eldon Gorst: The Overshadowed Proconsul, Hoover Institution Press, Stanford, California

Mikhail, Kyriakos. (1971) Copts and Muslims under British Control, Kennikat Press, Port Washington, New York, originally published 1911

Mitchell, Richard. (1969) The Society of Muslim Brothers, Oxford University Press, London

Musa, Salama. (1961) The Education of Salama Musa, trans. by L.O. Schuman, E.J. Brill,

Leiden, originally published in Arabic 1950
Perleman, Moshe (ed. and trans.). (1975) Shaykh Damanhuri on the Churches of Cairo, University of California Press, Berkeley
James P. Piscatori (ed.). (1983) Islam in the Political Process, Cambridge University Press, Cambridge
Quraishi, Zaheer Masood. (1967) Liberal Nationalism in Egypt: Rise and Fall of the Wafd Party The Jamal Printing Press, Delhi
Reid, Donald. (1975) The Odyssey of Farah Antun, Bibliotheca Islamica, Minneapolis
Rosenthal, E.I.J. (1958) Political Thought in Medieval Islam, Cambridge University Press, Cambridge
———. (1965) Islam in the Modern Nation State, Cambridge University Press, Cambridge
Safran, Nadav. (1961) Egypt in Search of Political Community, Harvard University Press, Cambridge, Mass.
Said, Edward. (1978) Orientalism, Pantheon Books, New York
Sanjian, Avedis. (1961) The Armenian Communities in Syria under Ottoman Dominion, Harvard University Press, Cambridge, Mass.
al-Sayyid, Afaf Lutfi. (1968) Egypt and Cromer: A Study in Anglo-Egyptian Relations, John Murray, London
Schacht, Joseph. (1964) An Introduction to Islamic Law, The Clarendon Press, Oxford
The Stock Exchange Yearbook of Egypt 1941, compiled by Clement Levy, no publisher, Cairo
Storrs, Ronald. (1945) Orientations, Nicholson and Watson, London
Tritton, A.S. (1930) The Caliphs and their Non-Muslim Subjects, Oxford University Press, London
Van den Berghe, Pierre. (1970) Race and Ethnicity: Essays in Comparative Sociology, Basic Books, New York
Vatikiotis, P.J. (1969) The Modern History of Egypt, Weidenfeld, London
———. (1978) Nasser and his Generation, Croom Helm, London
———. (1980) The History of Egypt from Muhammad Ali to Sadat (second edition), Weidenfeld, London, and Johns Hopkins University Press, Baltimore
Wakin, Edward. (1963) A Lonely Minority: The Modern Story of Egypt's Copts, William Morrow, New York

Wendell, Charles. (1972) The Evolution of the Egyptian National Image: From its Origins to Ahmad Lutfi al-Sayyid, University of California Press, Berkeley

Wendell, Charles (ed. and trans.). (1978) Five Tracts of Hassan al-Banna (1906-49), University of California Press, Berkeley

Whately, M.L. (1873) Among the Huts in Egypt, Seeley, Jackson and Halliday, London

PUBLISHED SOURCES : Arabic Language

Abd al-Hamid, Husni. (1935) al-Zaim fi al-Said Matbaat al-Nahda, Cairo

Abd al-Hamid, Muhammad. (1949) Fuad al-Awwal, Matbaat Lajnat al-Talif w-al-Tarjama w-al-Nashr, Cairo

Abd al-Raziq, Ali. (1972) al-Islam wa Usul al-Hukm, al-Muassasa al-Arabiyya l-il-Dirasat al-Nashr, Beirut, first published 1925

Abd al-Said, Kamil Mikhail. (1956) al-Aqbat, Abna al-Faraina, Matbaat al-Najah, Cairo

Abu al-Fatah, Mahmud. (n.d.) Maa al-Wafd al-Misri, no publisher, no place

Afifi, Hafiz. (1938) Ala Hamish al-Siyasa, Matbaat Dar al-Kutub, Cairo

Alluba, Muhammad Ali. (1942) Mabadi fi al-Siyasa al-Misriyya, Matbaat Dar al-Kutub al-Misriyya, Cairo

Amin, Mustafa. (1976) al-Kutab al-Mamnu: Asrar Thawrat 1919, vols. 1 and 2, Dar al-Maarif, Cairo

Anis, Muhammad. (1963) Dirasat fi Wathaiq Thawrat 1919, vol.1, Maktabat al-Anglu al-Misriyya, Cairo

———. (1972) Hariq al-Qahira 26 Yanayir 1952 al-Muassasa al-Arabiyya l-il-Dirasat w-al-Nashr, Beirut

al-Aqqad, Abbas Muhammad. (1936) Sad Zaghlul, Sira wa Tahiyya, al-Matbaat al-Hijaziyya, Cairo

Awad, Jirjis Filuthawus. (1920) Biwaraq al-Islah: Tariq al-Islah al-Manshud, Parts 6 and 7, al-Matbaat al-Misriyya, Cairo

Awad, Luwis. (1947) Blutuland, Matbaat al-Karnak, Cairo

Azmi, Mahmud. (1939) al-Ayyam al-Mia: Ahd Wizara Ali Mahir Basha, Maktabat al-Nahda al-Misriyya, Cairo

Barakat, Ali. (1977) Tatawwur al-Malakiyya al-Ziraiyya fi Misr, Dar al-Thaqafaal-Jadida, Cairo al-Bishri, Tariq. (1972) al-Haraka al-Siyasiyya fi Misr, 1945-52, al-Hayat al-Misriyya al-Ammal l-il-Kitab, Cairo.

———. (1980) al-Muslimun w-al-Aqbat fi Itar al-Jamaa al-Wataniyya, GEBO, Cairo

Darwazah, Muhammad Izzat. (1957) al-Wahda al-Arabiyya, al-Maktaba al-Tijari l-il-Tabaa, Cairo

al-Dasatir al-Misriyya. 1805-1971. (1977) al-Tanzim w-al-Mikrufilm, Cairo

Fahmi, Qalini. (1943-44) Mudhakkirat, vols.1 and 2, Matbaat Misr, Cairo

Ghannam, Mahmud Suliman. (1969) Adwa ala Ahdath Thawrat Sanat 1919, no publisher, Cairo

Haikal, Muhammad Husain. (1951, 1953) Mudhakkirat fi al-Siyasa al-Misriyya, vols. 1 and 2, Maktabat al-Nahda al-Misriyya, Cairo

———. (1965) Thawrat al-Abad, Maktabat al-Nahda al-Misriyya, Cairo, first published 1933

al-Hakim, Tawfiq. (1973) Awdat al-Ruh, Maktabat al-Adab wa Matbaatuha, Cairo

al-Hamamsi, Jalal al-Din. (1976) Hiwar Wara al-Aswar, al-Maktab al-Misri al-Hadith, Cairo

Hamid, Rauf Abbas. (1973) al-Nizam al-Ijtimai fi Misr, 1837-1914, Dar al-Fikr al-Hadith, Cairo

Hamza, Abd al-Qadir. (1922) Adhkuru Sad wa Suhbat al-Mutaqalin, privately printed, Cairo

Hamza, Abd al-Latif. (1967) Qissat al-Sihafa al-Arabiyya fi Misr, Matbaat al-Maarif, Baghdad

Hanna, Milad. (1980) Nam Aqbat Lakin Misriyyun Maktabat Madbuli, Cairo

Hassan Bey, Ahmad Muhammad, and Feldman, Isador. (1926) Majmuat al-Qaqanin w-al-Lawaih, vols.1 and 2, Taba Misr, Cairo

Husain, Taha. (1938) Mustaqbil al-Thaqafa fi Misr Dar al-Maarif, Cairo

al-Husri, Sati. (1965) al-Uruba Awwalan, no publisher, Beirut

Jirjis, Hilmi. (1956) al-Aqbat, no publisher, Cairo.

Judah, Ahmad Qasim. (n.d.) al-Makramiyyat, no publisher, Cairo

al-Jundi, Anwar. (1962) al-Sihafa al-Siyasiyya, Matbaat al-Risala, Cairo

Kailani, Muhammad Sayyid. (1962) al-Adab al-Qibti Qadiman wa Hadithan, Dar al-Qawmiyya al-Arabiyya, Cairo

Kamil, Murad. (n.d.) Hadarat Misr fi al-Asr al-Qibti, no publisher, Cairo

al-Khulasa al-Qanuniyya fi al-Ahwal al-Shakhsiyya Li-Kanisat al-Aqbat al-Urthudhuksiyya. (1923)

Matbaat al-Tawfiq, Cairo

Lashin, Lashin Abd al-Khaliq. (1975) Sad Zaghlul wa Dawruhu fi al-Siyasa al-Misriyya, Maktabat Madbuli, Cairo

Mahadir al-Lajna al-Amma Li-Wad al-Dustur. (1927) Bulaq Press, Cairo

Mahadir al-Lajna Li-Wad al-Mabadi al-Amma. (1924) Bulaq Press, Cairo

al-Majlis al-Milli al-Amm. (1938) Qanun al-Ahwal al-Shakhsiyya L-il-Aqbat al-Urthudhuksiyiin, no publisher, Cairo

Majmuat Khutab wa Ahadith wa Bayanat Hadrat Sahib al-Mualli Rais al-Wafd al-Misri. (n.d.) Matbaat Matr b-il-Marur bi-Misr, Cairo.

Mikhail, Zaghib. (n.d.) Farriq Tasud! al-Wahda al-Watanniya w-al-Akhlaq al-Qawmiyya, no publisher, no place

Musa, Salam . (1927) al-Yawm w-al-Ghad, al-Matbaat al-Asriyya, Cairo

———. (1945) al-Balagha al-Asriyya w-al-Lugha al-Arabiyya, al-Matbaat al-Asriyya, Cairo

Mutamar Misri. (1911) Majmuat Amal al-Mutamar al-Misri al-Awwal, no publisher, Heliopolis

al-Rafii, Abd al-Rahman. (1946) Thawrat Sanat 1919: Min Tarikh Misr al-Qawmi, Maktabat al-Nahda al-Misriyya, Cairo

———. (1947-51) Fi Aqab al-Thawra al-Misriyya, three volumes, Maktabat al-Nahda al-Misriyya, Cairo

———. (1948) Muhammad Farid, Ramz al-Ikhlas w-al-Tadhiya, Maktabat al-Nahda al-Misriyya, Cairo

Ramadan, Abd al-Azim. (1968) Tatawwur al-Harakat al-Wataniyya fi Misr, 1937-48, two volumes, Dar al-Katib al-Arabi, Cairo

———. (1979) al-Sira bain al-Wafd w-al-Arsh, 1939-46, Muassasa al-Arabiyya lil-Dirasat w-al-Nashr, Cairo

Riyad, Zahir. (1979) al-Masihiyun w-al-Qawmiyya al-Misriyya fi al-Asr al-Hadith, Dar al-Thaqafa, Cairo

Rizq, Yunan Labib. (1970) al-Hayat al-Hizbiyya fi Misr, 1882-1914, al-Ahram, Cairo

———. (1975) Tarikh al-Wizarat al-Misriyya 1878-1952, al-Ahram, Cairo

Sad, Ahmad Sadiq. (1976) Safahat Min al-Yasar al-Misri, 1945-46, Maktabat Madbuli, Cairo

al-Said, Rifat. (1977) al-Sihafa al-Yasariyya fi Misr, 1925-48, Maktabat Madbuli, Cairo

Salim, Jamal. (1975) al-Bulis al-Siyasi Yahkum Misr, Dar al-Qahira l-il-Thawafa al-Arabiyya, Cairo

Sami, Salib. (1942) Wisaya Ghair al-Muslim, Matabaat al-Maarif, Cairo
———. (1952) Dhikrayyat Siyasiyya, no publisher, Cairo
Sayigh, Anis. (1959) al-Fikra al-Arabiyya fi Misr, Matbaat Haikal al-Gharib, Beirut
Shafiq, Ahmad. (1926-29) Hawliyyat Misr al-Siyasiyya, vols.1-3,(1924-26), Matbaat Shafiq Basha, Cairo
Shahid, Salah. (1976) Dhikrayati fi Ahdain, Dar al-Maarif, Cairo
Sidqi, Ismail. (1950) Mudhakkirati, Dar al-Hilal, Cairo
Subhi, Muhammad Khalil. (1947-48) Tarikh al-Hayat al-Niyabiyya fi Misr, VI, Appendix I, Matbaat Dar al-Kutub al-Misriyya, Cairo
al-Tabii, Muhammad. (1978) Misr ma qabl al-Thawra: Asrar al-Sasa w-al-Siyasa, Dar al-Maarif, Cairo
Tadrus, Ramzi. (1910-11) al-Aqbat fi al-Qarn al-Ishrin, four volumes, Jaridat Misr, Cairo
Tajir, Jak. (1951) al-Aqbat w-al-Muslimun Mundhu al-Fath al-Arabi ila Am 1922, no publisher, Cairo
Tarabain, Ahmad. (1957) al-Wahda al-Arabiyya bain 1916-1945, Mahad al-Darasat al-Arabiyya al-aliyy, Cairo
Thawrat 1919 (n.d.) Muassasat al-Ahram, Markaz al-Wathaiq w-al-Buhuth al-Tarikhiyya Li-Misr al-Muasira, Cairo
al-Yusuf, Fatima. (1976) Dhikrayat, Ruz al-Yusuf, Cairo
al-Zawahiri, Fakhr al-Din. (1945) al-Siyasa w-al-Azhar, Tabaat al-Itimad, Cairo

PERIODICALS : European Languages
Anderson, J.N.D., 'Recent developments in Sharia Law', Muslim World 40 (1950), 244-56; 41 (1951), 34-48, 113-26, 186-98, 271-88; 42 (1952), 33-47, 124-40, 257-76
———. (1954) 'The Sharia and civil law', The Islamic Quarterly 1, 29-46
Ayrout, Henri Habib. (1938) 'Egypte: Interférences de la politique et de la religion', En Terre d'Islam 13, 192-8
———. (1965) 'Regards sur le Christianisme en Egypte hier et aujord'hui', Proche-Orient Chrétien XV, pp.3-42
Belin, M., 'Fetoua relatif a la condition des Zimmis', Journal Asiatique (4eme serie) XVIII (1851), 417-516; XIX (1852), 97-140

Birch, Anthony. (1978) 'Minority nationalist movements and theories of political integration', World Politics 30, 325-44

Bowie, Leland. (1977) 'The Copts, the Wafd and religious issues in Egyptian politics', The Muslim World 67, 106-26

CENAM Staff. (1972-73) 'The Coptic-Muslim conflict in Egypt: modernization of society and religious renovation', CENAM Reports: Tensions in Middle Eastern Society, 31-54

Chejne, Anwar. (1957) Egyptian attitudes to pan-Arabism', Middle East Journal XI, 253-68

————. (1960) 'The use of history by modern Arab writers', Middle East Journal XIV, 382-96

————. (1965) 'Arabic: its significance and place in Arab Muslim society', Middle East Journal, XIX, 447-68

Colombe, Marcel. (1950) 'L'Islam dans la vie sociale et politique de l'Egypte contemporaine', Cahiers de l'Orient Contemporain XXI, 1-26

Coury, Ralph. (1982) 'Who "invented" Egyptian Arab nationalism?', Part I, International Journal of Middle East Studies 14, 249-81

Deeb, Marius. (1979) 'Labour and politics in Egypt, 1919-1939', International Journal of Middle Eastern Studies 10, 187-203

Enloe, Cynthia. (1978) 'Ethnicity, bureaucracy and state-building in Africa and Latin America', Ethnic and Racial Studies 1, 336-51

Esman, Milton. (1973) 'The management of communal conflict', Public Policy 21, 49-78

'Ethnic conflict in the world today', Annals of the American Academy of Political and Social Science 433 (1973)

Ghali, Mirrit Butros. (1978) 'Essay: The Egyptian national consciousness', Middle East Journal 32, 59-77

Glazer, Nathan. (1975) 'The universalisation of ethnicity', Encounter 44, 8-17

Gottheil, Richard. (1921) 'An answer to the Dhimmis: Translation of a manuscript by Ghazi Ibn al-Wasiti in Cairo', Journal of the American Oriental Society XLI, 383-457

Gray, J.W.D. (1962) 'Arab nationalism: Abdin against the Wafd', The Middle East Forum 38, 17-20, 48

Harik, Ilya. (1972) 'Political integration in the Middle East', International Journal of Middle Eastern Studies 3, 302-23

Heyworth-Dunne, J. (1940) 'Education in Egypt and the Copts', Bulletin de la Société d'Archéologie Copte VI, 91-108

Hourani, Albert. (1955) 'The Anglo-Egyptian agreement: Some causes and its implications', Middle East Journal IX, 239-55

Jankowski, J.P. (1970) 'The Egyptian Blue Shirts and the Egyptian Wafd, 1935-1938', Middle Eastern Studies 6, 77-95

Jeffrey, Arthur. (1925) 'A collection of anti-Christian books and pamphlets found in actual use among the Mohammadans of Cairo', Moslem World 15, 26-34

Kamil, Murad. (1957-57) 'La dernière phase des relations historiques entre l'Eglise Copte d'Egypte et celle d'Ethiopie', Bulletin de la Société d'Archéologie Copte XIV, 1-22

Oriente Moderno 7 (1937), 'Nomina d'una commissione', 51-2

Perleman, M. (1950) 'The Egyptian elections', Middle Eastern Affairs I, 46-8

Pennington, J.D. (1982) 'The Copts in modern Egypt', Middle Eastern Affairs 18, 158-79

Riad, Zahir. (1975) 'Religious policy of Ethiopia during the Italian Occupation (1936-1941) and its results', Bulletin of the Institute of Coptic Studies, 31-48

Reid, Donald. (1977) 'Educational career choices of Egyptian students, 1882-1922', International Journal of Middle Eastern Studies 8, 349-78

Rondot, Pierre. (1950) 'L'evolution historique des Coptes d'Egypte', Cahiers de l'Orient Contemporain 22, 129-42

Seikaly, Samir. (1977) 'Prime Minister and assassin: Butrus Ghali and Wardani', Middle Eastern Studies 13, 112-23

Sergius, Rev. Qummus. (1936) 'Why Copts become Moslems', The Moslem World 26, 372-9

Severianus. (1959) 'Les Coptes de l'Egypte Musulmane', Etudes Mediterranéennes 6, 70-87

Smith, Charles. (1973) 'The "crisis of orientation", the shift of Egyptian intellectuals to Islamic subjects in the 1930s', International Journal of Middle Eastern Studies 4, 382-410

Szaszy, Etienne de. (1939) 'Le Statut Personnel des non-Musulmans en Egypte et sa réforme', L'Egypte Contemporaine 184, 297-375

Tessler, M. (1978) 'The identity of religious minorities in non-secular states – Jews in Tunisia and Morocco and Arabs in Israel',

Comparative Studies in Society and History _20_, 359-73

de Vries, Father. (1942) 'Islam and Christianity in contemporary Egypt', _La Civilta Cattolica_ _93_, 8-15

Wilkie, Mary. (1977) 'Colonials, marginals and immigrants: contributions to a theory of ethnic stratification', _Comparative Studies in Society and History_ _19_, 67-95.

Yallouz, Alfred. (1934) 'Chronique legislative 1932-1933', _L'Egypte Contemporaine_ _146_-_147_, 105-65

————. (1934) 'Chronique legislative 1933-1934', _L'Egypte Contemporaine_ _152_, 761-809

Zohrab, Kosroff. (1929) 'Etude sur les privilèges des Patriarcats', _L'Egypte Contemporaine_ _112_, 113-60

PERIODICALS : Egyptian

The Press

The Coptic newspapers, _Misr_ and _al-Watan_, while not covered in entirety, were read for much of the period. The following newspapers and journals were consulted for their coverage of specific issues and events:

al-Afkar, _al-Ahali_, _al-Ahram_, _al-Akhbar_, _Akhir Saa_, _Avenir_, _al-Balagh_, _al-Balagh al-Usbuiyya_, _al-Basir_, _al-Dustur_, _Egyptian Gazette_, _Egyptian Mail_, _al-Hilal_, _al-Ikhwan al Muslimin_, _al-Istiqlal_, _al-Ittihad_, _al-Jihad_, _al-Kashif_, _al-Kashkul_, _al-Kutla_, _al-Lawa_, _al-Majalla al-Jadida_, _Majallat al-Azhar_, _al-Manar_, _al-Manara al-Misriyya_, _al-Minbar_, _al-Misa_, _Misr al-Fatat_, _al-Misri_, _al-Muqattam_, _al-Musawwar_, _al-Nadhir_, _al-Nizam_, _Nur al-Islam_, _al-Risala_, _Ruz al-Yusuf_, _al-Shab_, _al-Shubra_, _al-Siyasa_, _al-Siyasa al-Usbuiyya_, _al-Thaghr_, _al-Urwa al-Wuthqa_, _al-Wafd Misri_, _Wadi al-Nil_, _al-Yaqza_

Special references:

Abd al-Nur, Fakhri. (1969) 'Mudhakkirati', _al-Musawwar_, 21 March, 32-7

Abukif, Ahmad. (1969), 'Sergius khatib thawrat 1919', _al-Musawwar_, 7 March, 34

al-Bishri, Tariq. (1970) 'Misr al-Haditha bain Ahmad w-al-Masih', _al-Katib_ _107_, 9-26, _109_, 98-127, _111_, 113-31, _115_, 11-41

————. (1971) 'Misr al-Haditha bain Ahmad w-al-Masih', _al-Katib_ _119_, 106-32, _121_, 139-69 al-Bishri, Tariq and al-Sayyid, Rifat (eds.). (1971) 'Wathaiq Dustur 1923', _al-Talia_ _7/7_, 142-60; _7/8_, 155-60; _7/9_, 177-92

———. (1971) 'Wathaiq Dustur 1923', _al-Talia_ _7/9_, 177-92

Iskandar, Raghib. (1976) 'al-Shadid al-Wahid al-Hayy', _Akhir Saa_, 2 June, 15-18

Kamla, Rashad. (1977) 'Awwal Risalat Dukturah an Dawr al-Aqbat fi Hayat Misr al-Siyasiyya', _Sabah al-Khayr_, 20 September, 6-11

Munis, H. (1973) 'Dawr al-Aqbat fi Thawrat 1919', _Akhir Saa_ _I_, 9th May, 9-11; _II_, 16 May, 20-3: _III_, 23 May, 15-18; _IV_, 30 May, 11-13

Musa, Salama. (1931) 'Tahqiq al-Qawmiyya al-Misriyya', _al-Majalla al-Jadida_ 11, 789-90

INTERVIEWS

Sad Fakhri Abd al-Nur, 17 May 1979

Father Anawati, 23 April 1979

Louis Awad, 26 April 1978, 11 May 1978, and 29 February 1980

Husni Georgi, 10 February 1979

Ibrahim Amin Ghali, 4 December 1978, 19 March 1979 and 4 June 1980

Mirrit Ghali, 14 November 1977, 31 January 1978, autumn and winter of 1978-79; lecture at the Institut d'Egypte, 7 November 1977

Bishop Gregorious, 27 October 1977

Ibrahim Fahmi Hilal, 22 May 1979

Kamal al-Malakh, Assistant Chief Editor of _al-Ahram_, 9 November 1978

Ibrahim Faraj Masiha, 13 June 1979

Iris Habib al-Masri, 7 December 1977, 25 October 1979, and August 1979.

Dr. Zahir Riyad, Chairman, African Studies Department, Coptic Institute of Higher Studies, 1 June 1979

Esther Fahmi Wisa, 16 March 1978

Hassan Pasha Yusuf, 8 November 1978

INDEX

Abd al-Nur, Fakhri 11, 13, 64-5, 80, 140, 158, 161-2, 165-9, 198-9, 264, 270-1
Abd al-Riziq, Ali 101, 117-18, 182, 204, 259
al-Afghani, Jamal al-Din 90, 116
Ali, Muhammad 8, 9, 261
Anglo-Egyptian Treaty (1936) 39, 73, 75, 79, 236-7, 293, 302
al-Aqqad, Abbas Mahmud 45, 80-1, 100, 200
Arab League 99, 104-5, 223, 225-6, 228
Arabic, pan-Arabism 104-10, 113, 117, 121, 181
Awad, Ilyas 13, 153, 182
Awad, Louis 99, 107, 137, 179, 203
al-Azhar 18, 62, 83, 91, 109, 118, 130, 132, 140, 150, 189, 221, 228-9, 249, 260, 264, 266
Azmi, Mahmud 44, 94, 136-7, 140, 292

al-Banna, Hassan 100, 109, 117, 207, 257, 275-6
Barakat, Fath Allah, 165-8, 198
Black Book 178, 180, 189, 202-3, 207
Blue Shirts, 162-3, 196
British 9-16, 18-19, 23-4, 28, 30-4, 36, 39-40, 44-7, 50, 52-6, 58-89, 93, 95, 107, 112-15, 121, 123, 125, 129, 134-9, 142, 155-7, 163-8, 170-9, 187-8, 190-2, 196, 198-9, 201-2, 204-6, 212, 215-16, 219-22, 226-7, 232-8, 252, 260-1, 163-70, 276, 278, 291, 294-6, 302

Caliphate, 91-2, 106, 117-18, 204, 227, 256, 260
Chamber of Deputies 27, 30, 51, 54, 132-3, 135, 142-7, 150-1, 162, 167, 176-8, 190, 192-3, 227, 236, 261, 263-72, 275
Churches (building and repair) 4, 20, 239-42, 225, 302
Civil Service 4, 10-11, 13-15, 49, 59, 76, 80, 102, 148, 152, 207, 211-20, 242, 244-50, 296

INDEX

Clergy 3, 6-7, 27-32, 44, 46, 48, 50, 53, 61, 62, 74, 145, 148, 151, 227, 230-1, 233-5, 237, 242, 271-3, 291, 295, 297
Conference, Asyut (Coptic) (1911) 13-14, 23, 51, 133, 154, 244, 163, 290
Conference, Heliopolis (1911) 14-15, 94, 131, 224
Constitution (1923) 2, 73-5, 84, 128-42, 148, 153, 155, 170, 235, 241-2, 261, 294, 296, 299-301
Constitution (1930) 146
Constitutional Commission (1922) 128-42, 159, 292, 294
Conversion to Islam 93, 133, 237-8, 240-1, 292
Coptic Catholics 6-8, 21, 138, 148, 225, 231, 234
Coptic Protestants 6-9, 12, 22, 72, 138, 193, 225, 231, 234, 257, 265, 294
Cromer, Earl 6, 58, 66, 80, 135, 243
Cyril, Patriarch 13, 30-1, 50, 62, 135-40, 157, 186, 264

Democratic Party 136
Dus, Tawfiq 13, 23, 31, 34, 40-1, 53, 63, 134-6, 140-2, 153, 159, 182-3, 185-6, 196, 204-6, 216, 243-4, 254, 269, 290

Egyptian Bar Association 163, 169, 179, 197, 203
Elections for Parliament 17, 75, 109, 118, 140-7, 149, 152, 157-9, 162, 169, 180, 183-4, 187, 190-3, 208, 218, 238, 263-72, 286-7
Ethiopia 31, 52, 55, 77, 108

Fahmi, Abd al-Rahman 63, 67-9, 83, 156, 197
Fahmi, Qalini 13, 31, 53, 55, 84, 141, 153, 155, 182-3, 185-6, 232
Fanus, Akhnukh 10, 60, 70, 126, 133
Fanus, Louis 163, 269
Faruq, king of Egypt 92, 106, 158, 163, 173-8, 186, 188, 190, 203, 205, 207, 217, 250, 252, 260-2, 264, 269, 278

INDEX

Fuad, sultan then king of Egypt 31-4, 51-2, 68, 70, 72, 85, 92, 140-2, 165, 167, 182-3, 186, 196, 226-7, 249-50, 260-1

Ghali, Butrus 12, 23, 60, 66-7, 185, 249
Ghali, Wasif 13, 60, 63-5, 73, 80-1, 103, 105-6, 156, 161-4, 167, 169-70, 172, 197, 199, 215, 220, 263, 294
Gorst, Sir Eldon 11-13, 15, 66-7, 83, 224

Hadith 3, 19-20, 105, 118, 270
Haikal, Muhammad Husain 93-4, 97, 99, 101, 152-3, 165, 198, 200, 218, 220, 257
al-Hakim, Tawfiq 94, 98
Hanna, Bushra 13, 23, 171, 178
Hanna, Murqus 10, 13, 22, 63-5, 83, 126, 133, 151, 156, 161, 163-5, 167, 172, 197-8, 220, 271
Hanna, Sinut 10, 13, 23, 44, 60, 63-5, 80-2, 155, 161-4, 167-8, 172, 197, 217
Hilal, Ibrahim Fahmi 280-1
Hinain, Sadiq 65, 82, 112, 164, 196, 213, 218, 244
Husain, Ahmad 101, 113, 264
Husain, Taha 93-4, 97, 101-3, 137-8, 148, 150, 156, 224
al-Husri, Sati 101, 104-5

Iskandar, Dr. Najib 81, 156, 162-3, 169-70, 187, 222, 262, 269
Iskandar, Raghib 64, 81-2, 139-40, 161-3, 167, 168-9
Islam 1, 2, 11, 14, 17-18, 58, 64, 78, 89-96, 98-101, 103, 116-17, 130-3, 138, 140, 143, 150, 153, 181, 193, 204, 223-6, 228-30, 240, 253, 256-8, 261-8, 271-2, 277, 280-4, 298-301, 303
pan-Islam 10, 11, 60, 91-3, 104, 107
al-Ittihad Party 51, 144, 182, 185, 204-5, 257-60

Jews 3, 51, 63, 106, 109, 110-11, 113, 141, 144, 147, 183, 237, 258, 267, 299
Jibrawi, Ramses 280-1
Jizya 9, 91, 240, 275
Kamil, Mustafa 10, 114

INDEX

Khayyat, George 13, 60, 63-5, 80, 82, 156, 161-3, 168, 219
al-Kutla al-Wafdiyya 94, 143, 157, 159, 161, 188-95, 221, 258, 272

Lampson, Sir Miles 75, 173-4, 178, 202, 206, 267-8
Landownership 9, 49, 63-4, 148, 158, 184-5, 210-1, 243
Legislative Assembly (1913-4) 15, 60, 130, 133-4, 141
Lex Contractus 234, 236-7
Liaison Committee 7, 237, 295, 300
Liberal Constitutionalist Party 44, 76-8, 90, 94, 98, 101, 106, 118, 144, 158, 164, 167-8, 181-5, 190, 192, 200, 204, 213-14, 217, 220, 246, 257-9, 263-5, 282
Lloyd, Lord 164, 167
Loraine, Sir Percy 33-4, 40, 77, 235
Lukas, Bishop 29-30, 151, 158
Luqa, Ibrahim, 41-2, 50, 53, 56, 240

Mahir, Ahmad 45, 167, 170-1, 187, 190-1, 196, 200, 208, 221, 269
Mahir, Ali 186, 200-1, 206, 221, 233, 235-6, 254
Mahmud, Muhammad 44-5, 60, 73, 78-9, 80, 82, 88, 183, 219-20, 248, 267-9
Majlis al-Hasbi 51, 159-60, 232-3, 254
Majlis al-Milli 28, 30, 32-42, 44, 50-2, 54, 138, 148, 150-1, 226-7, 229, 231-4, 236, 242, 252, 286, 278, 291
Makarios, Bishop of Asyut, then Patriarch 13, 30, 34-7, 41-2, 47, 50-, 53, 56, 236-7
al-Manara al-Misriyya 43, 47, 56, 86, 215, 217, 229, 241, 274, 276
al-Maraghi, Shaikh Muhammad Mustafa 114, 186, 203, 219. 228, 261-2, 264-8, 296
Marxism, 110-13, 179
Masiha, Ibrahim Faraj 51, 121, 178-9, 201, 222, 245, 257, 271, 278-9, 298
Mediterraneanism 97, 102-4
Mikhail, Salama 72, 82, 136, 139-40, 156, 161, 167-9, 197

INDEX

Milner Mission, 46, 63, 68, 263
al-Minyawi Pasha 37-8, 148, 159
Mirhum, Aziz 82, 136-7, 162, 179
Misr al-Fatat (Young Egypt) 91, 108, 186, 218, 246, 264-5, 299
Misr 11, 21, 29-30, 34-5, 37, 43-7, 50, 52, 54, 55, 61, 63, 68, 74, 78, 93, 98, 101, 108-9, 114, 118, 131-2, 138-9, 144, 147-8, 151, 153, 181, 183, 188, 194, 214-18, 225, 227, 229, 231-3, 240-1, 247-8, 250-3, 262, 264-5, 270-3, 275-80, 294-98, 303
Missionaries 7-8, 23, 26, 58, 66, 71, 73, 75, 86, 226-9, 252, 267, 273, 294
Monasteries 28-9, 40, 51
Muslim Brethren (Ikhwan al-Muslimin) 2, 45, 47, 90-2, 100-1, 108, 113, 117-19, 124-5, 181, 189, 191, 193, 208, 211, 229, 241, 257-8, 267, 274-80, 282, 299, 304
Musa, Salama 11, 22, 37, 45, 49, 55, 61, 92-3, 98-9, 102-3, 107, 109-11, 117, 119, 122, 131-2, 137, 148, 153, 211, 223, 232, 241, 265, 275, 293, 296-8, 301
al-Mutii, Nakhla 32, 148, 185-6, 243, 250

al-Nahhas, Mustafa 74, 78, 101, 106, 158, 164-81, 188, 192, 196, 198-201, 206-7, 229, 258-61, 264-6, 270, 275, 278
National Party, 10-11, 14, 133, 140, 158, 194
National Democratic Party 280
al-Nuqrashi, Mahmud Fahmi 107, 166-7, 170-1, 187, 190-1, 198-201, 221

Palace 13, 27, 28, 32-3, 39, 41, 48, 50, 53, 118, 131, 135, 150-1, 164, 166, 173-5, 177-9, 181, 188, 190-1, 195-7, 200-6, 216, 222-3, 237, 247, 258, 260-2, 264, 269, 278, 281-2, 295
Palestine 105-9, 113, 124, 268
Personal status jurisdiction 7-9, 29, 34, 40, 54, 85, 150-1, 160,

INDEX

231-9, 241, 253-5, 292, 302
Pharaonism 95-102, 103, 108, 114, 121, 126
Proportional representation (Parliament) 133-42, 152-3, 156, 160, 80, 292-3, 297
Provincial and local councils 51, 148-9, 156, 224, 251, 286

<u>Qur'an</u> 3, 19, 105, 118, 160, 227-8, 270, 274

Religious instruction in schools 13, 74, 85, 132-3, 150, 223-30, 242, 250-3, 297-8
Reserved Points 71-3, 128, 235, 294
Revolution (1919) 16, 46-7, 60-2, 65, 71, 114-5, 128-9, 131, 134, 144, 293, 300
Rida, Muhammad Rashis 90, 100, 117
Rushdi, Husain 129, 221, 294

Sadist Party 94, 175, 187, 190-2, 195, 206, 260, 264-5
Said, Muhammad 44, 68-9, 80, 84
Said, Wadi 35-7, 53
Salama, Yuhanna 31
Sami, Salib 182-3, 185-6, 205-6, 219, 222, 249-50
al-Sayyid, Ahmad Lufti 14, 94-6, 99, 107, 119, 224
Secularism 17-18, 65, 89, 93-6, 104, 112-13, 133, 139-40, 161, 180, 223-4, 238, 256, 259-61, 290, 297-8, 303
Senate 29-30, 51, 55, 76, 106, 132, 142, 146-8, 150-2, 158, 166, 169, 176, 185-6, 190, 206, 225-6, 232-3, 236-7, 252
Sergius, Murqus 41-2, 47, 50, 54, 56, 62, 68, 74, 80, 86, 109, 132, 271, 276, 298, 301-2
Shab Party (People's) 182, 185, 218, 257-8
Shabab Muhammad (Young Men of Muhammad) 91, 108, 117, 124, 275, 299, 304
Sharia (Islamic law) 91, 231-5, 238, 253, 262
Sidqi, Ismail 33-4, 39, 45, 52-3, 75, 82, 113, 118, 143, 147-8, 167-8, 183, 185-6, 191, 203-6, 208, 221, 225
Sidqi, Kamil 144, 155,